W9-BYB-477

A Traveled First Lady

A Traveled First Lady

WRITINGS OF LOUISA CATHERINE ADAMS

Edited by Margaret A. Hogan and C. James Taylor

Foreword by Laura Bush

The Belknap Press of Harvard University Press

CAMBRIDGE, MASSACHUSETTS

LONDON, ENGLAND

2014

Copyright © 2014 by the Massachusetts Historical Society
All rights reserved
Printed in the United States of America

Designed by Dean Bornstein

An excerpt from Henry Adams, *The Education of Henry Adams:
A Centennial Version,* ed. Edward Chalfant and Conrad Edick Wright
(Boston: Massachusetts Historical Society, 2007), pp. 13–15, appears
in the Epilogue, courtesy of the Massachusetts Historical Society.

Library of Congress Cataloging-in-Publication Data
Adams, Louisa Catherine, 1775–1852.
A traveled first lady : writings of Louisa Catherine Adams / edited by
Margaret A. Hogan and C. James Taylor ; foreword by Laura Bush.
pages   cm
Includes bibliographical references and index.
ISBN 978-0-674-04801-0 (alk. paper)
1. Adams, Louisa Catherine, 1775–1852.   2. Presidents' spouses—
United States—Biography.   3. Adams, John Quincy, 1767–1848.
I. Hogan, Margaret A.   II. Taylor, C. James, 1945–   III. Title.
E377.2.A34   2014
973.5'5092—dc23
[B]   2013031131

For our mothers:

KATHERINE ANN HOGAN

DOROTHY ISABEL TAYLOR

One of the greatest taxes I have to pay is that of concealing that I am a travelled Lady.

—Louisa Catherine Adams, 9 February 1821

Contents

Foreword by Laura Bush   xi

Introduction   xv

Note to the Reader   xxiii

1.	"All Was Joy and Peace and Love": Youth	1
2.	"An Object of General Attention": Prussia	34
3.	"Had I Steped into Noah's Ark": United States	86
4.	"The Savage Had Been Expected": Russia	144
5.	"The Memory of One, Who Was": St. Petersburg to Paris	187
6.	"The Wife of a Man of Superior Talents": Washington, D.C., 1819–1820	216
7.	"I Am a Very Good Diplomate": Washington, D.C., 1821–1824	265
8.	"This Apparent Fate": Retirement	326
	Epilogue: Henry Adams on Louisa	362

Chronology   367

Acknowledgments   375

Index   377

Illustrations follow page 166.

Foreword

LAURA BUSH

To live in the White House is to live with our nation's past. The president's family makes a home in the midst of history—not just public history, but private history as well. Almost every day for eight years, I passed the West Sitting Hall, where Ike and Mamie Eisenhower liked to have their dinner on TV trays, side by side, each watching his or her own television. Mamie preferred *I Love Lucy,* Ike liked Westerns. Both watched the brief nightly news. I often paused at the solarium, where Lynda and Luci Johnson entertained their teenage friends and my own daughters, Barbara and Jenna, liked to host their college friends. I would walk into the room where Willie Lincoln died in February 1862 after a two-week battle with a typhoid-like illness. More than the portraits on the walls, more than the well-preserved furniture, to live in the White House is to live with the knowledge of the lives that have passed through this home before you.

Once, returning from a state visit to England, I discovered that the painters and plasterers who were repairing the upstairs Cross Hall had found perfectly preserved bookshelves, which had been hidden for decades by a "false" wall. Also uncovered were delicately carved shells in niches above two doors along the hallway. None of the current staff or curators knew that these architectural details existed. They were simply waiting to be rediscovered, one by one. So it is with some of our past first ladies; they too are waiting to be rediscovered. Time has dimmed the stories of their lives, yet they have much to contribute to our understanding of American history. Louisa Catherine Adams, wife of President John Quincy Adams, is one of these first ladies, and we are fortunate that many of her letters and other writings have been preserved, so that today we may come to know this interesting woman.

Louisa and I share the special distinction of being both the wife of one U.S. president and the daughter-in-law of another. Remarkably, Louisa did not set foot on American soil until 1801, when she was twenty-six years old.

While her father was an American, her mother was British, and Louisa and her siblings were born in either England or France. After years navigating the courts of Europe, she found herself in Quincy, Massachusetts, a small, rather provincial town that was a bumpy carriage ride away from Boston. From the time she arrived, she was expected to manage a country household and support her lawyer-trained husband.

Louisa quickly discovered that she had married into a family of strong-minded souls. Where she was quiet and demure, raised to listen rather than speak, her in-laws were used to free-flowing political debates and strong-minded women. Her ever-practical mother-in-law considered Louisa a "fine lady," a phrase that Abigail Adams may not have meant as a compliment. Even Louisa's religion set her apart. She was an Anglican amid staunch Congregationalists and Unitarians.

But in the United States, Louisa found her own strengths. She learned the ways of Massachusetts just as she had learned the ways of Europe, and when John Quincy chose politics, she devoted her energies to raising their children and to supporting her husband's work. When John Quincy was appointed U.S. minister to Russia, it was Louisa who charmed nobles and diplomats in St. Petersburg, even winning the favor of the tsar and helping to dispel the image of Americans as rustic clods with no manners or style. She proved her mettle, traveling with her young son from Russia to France in the wake of Napoleon's bloody drive across the continent. She vividly recounts her journey in the depth of winter, as she met with broken wheels and battlefield destruction, dishonest servants and boisterous soldiers, yet she never faltered, finally reuniting with John Quincy in Paris.

When John Quincy took up the post of secretary of state under President James Monroe, Louisa became the preeminent hostess in Washington. With no staff to help—just her own family members and a few household servants—she hosted an enormous ball for Andrew Jackson, her husband's political rival, and welcomed nearly a thousand people to her home. Looking back from the twenty-first century, her party was worthy of any modern White House event, with a few exceptions. In her day, oil lamps were the norm in Washington, and Louisa was, in her own words, "anointed" by one during that ball; she had to slip away to change her oil-drenched dress. That she could laugh about such a mishap, and that she can make us laugh nearly two hundred years hence, testifies to her abilities as a writer.

Indeed, Louisa's writings give many tantalizing glimpses into her life and her private thoughts. The town of Quincy was a "Noah's Ark" of eccentric personalities and strange customs. A diplomat's wife leads a "killing life" of endless rounds of balls and dinners and meetings and travel. Within the U.S. government, it is a "plausable [*sic*] solicitude of deep interest in concerns to which you must feel totally indifferent" that will lead you up the first "steps on the ladder of promotion." Her diaries paint a vibrant picture of the political and social world of a time long past, yet one that read today seems remarkably familiar.

Louisa Adams and I lived in the same house, walked the same halls, and shared the unique perspective that every first lady has in American society. It is a pleasure to see one of my historical predecessors receive her due recognition and for her at last to tell her own story in her own words.

Introduction

When Congress adjourned on 18 May 1852 for Louisa Catherine Adams's funeral, it accorded her an extraordinary honor never before offered to a first lady. While more than twenty-three years had passed since Louisa had last entertained at the White House, she had remained a prominent figure in Washington society well into the 1840s. Still, time erodes memory. Once-significant public figures fade into oblivion, and only the most remarkable or notorious names remain recognizable to the general public. Such is the case with most first ladies. A few have reputations in their own right that have survived the generations—Abigail, Eleanor, and Jackie do not need their husbands' surnames to identify them—but that is the exception, not the rule.

Louisa Catherine Adams, America's only foreign-born first lady, despite her prominence a century and a half ago, does not have this name recognition today. At best she is "the other Mrs. Adams." Obvious and glaring evidence of her historical anonymity is found in the titles of Andrew Oliver's two volumes of Adams portraits. *Portraits of John and Abigail Adams* was published in 1967; three years later, *Portraits of John Quincy Adams and His Wife* appeared. While it is unthinkable to identify Abigail as merely John Adams's wife, the disappearance of Louisa's name by the mid-twentieth century, as evidenced in the title of that work, demonstrates the fleeting fame enjoyed by most first ladies. Fortunately, however, Louisa left her own writings to help modern readers learn of her extraordinary life. She may not be the best-known Mrs. Adams, and likely never will be, but she proved herself an excellent match for her President Adams.

Born in London in 1775, Louisa was the second of nine children of Joshua and Catherine Nuth Johnson. Joshua, originally a partner in an Annapolis mercantile firm, moved to London for business in the 1770s and lived there for over twenty-five years, save five wartime years spent in Nantes, France. He eventually served as U.S. consul in London from 1790 to 1797. Louisa lived an idyllic life with her successful and prominent parents until she left to marry John Quincy Adams in July 1797. The couple had met two full years before and had been engaged for more than a year. Louisa's joy at being a newlywed was damped, if not crushed, by her father's financial collapse at virtually the same time. Years later, recalling her emotions upon taking up life with her husband, she makes it clear that she was shocked and humiliated by her father's fall. A recurring theme in her writing is her need to exonerate her loving, honorable, and patriotic father, who she believed had been treated unjustly. That his failure, followed by a hasty departure for the United States, occurred at the beginning of her marriage, and just as her husband's father was being elevated to the highest office in the United States, no doubt exacerbated her dismay. Furthermore, Joshua had promised her a substantial dowry; instead, the only thing John Quincy received from his father-in-law was the demands of disgruntled creditors in London. As a result, Louisa saw herself as damaged goods—believing that other people thought she had been foisted off on John Quincy.

Three months married and only twenty-two years old, Louisa sailed with her husband to his new diplomatic post in Berlin. For more than fifty years, from this time until John Quincy's death in 1848, Louisa remained a public figure, spending time in Berlin, Boston, Washington, St. Petersburg, and London as required by her husband's positions: American minister to Prussia (1797–1801), to Russia (1809–1814), and to Great Britain (1815–1817); a member of the Massachusetts legislature (1802–1803), U.S. Senate (1803–1808), and U.S. House of Representatives (1831–1848); secretary of state (1817–1825); and U.S. president (1825–1829). Fairly early in their marriage, Louisa realized that, when necessary, all domestic tranquility would be sacrificed to national duty. By 1820 she could "safely declare before heaven, I have seen too much of publick life not to value it for what it is worth— I think however I know my husbands character, and with the conviction that his habits and tastes are fixed beyond the possibility of change, I fear that he could not live long out of an active sphere of publick life and that it is absolutely essential to his existence." The great question that recurred until the end of her life was whether the many sacrifices that she and her children had made for her husband's career were worth it.

Louisa's health, never robust, suffered from the peripatetic lifestyle necessitated by John Quincy's public service. She frequently alludes in her diaries to depression-like symptoms and other unspecified ailments as well as numerous pregnancies, many of which terminated in miscarriages. During these physical and psychological crises, John Quincy showed himself to be a kind and sensitive husband. The usual view of him as cold, severe, and distant is belied by his devotion to Louisa, especially during her troubled times. In fact, one of the most interesting revelations in her writings is John Quincy's humanity.

When Louisa married John Quincy, she also entered into the whole Adams family of Quincy, Massachusetts. Pampered as a child and youth, residing in relative ease in London, she was ill prepared for life with her new spouse and later his family. She recognized that she did not possess the experience to manage a household and thus was often dependent on servants—usually selected and directed by her husband. Her domestic short-comings became especially glaring when compared to the abilities of her take-charge mother-in-law, Abigail Adams. Louisa was utterly unprepared for what she found upon arrival at the Adams home in Quincy in late 1801. Many years later she recalled, "Quincy! What shall I say of my impressions of Quincy! Had I steped into Noah's Ark I do-not think I could have been more utterly astonished." The food, the religious practices, and the large intergenerational Adams family with their numerous friends and relatives centered around her in-laws, Abigail and John, made for a difficult adjustment. Foreign-born Louisa never became fully integrated into the Adams family. In January 1829, shortly before vacating the White House, she confided to her son Charles Francis that she did not wish to return to the Quincy home, "there to become a boarder in the family"—certainly a strange attitude considering that her husband owned the property. And, as her historian grandson Henry recalled, she even late in life remained an "exotic . . . hardly more Bostonian than she had been fifty years before, on her wedding-day, in the shadow of the Tower of London."

Louisa struggled with her relationship with her mother-in-law, often left feeling oppressed by Abigail's apparently domineering ways. When Louisa and John Quincy were preparing to travel to Russia in 1809, it was Abigail and John Quincy who planned for the care and education of the couple's two elder sons, George Washington Adams and John Adams 2d—without consulting Louisa. As a consequence she did not see her children for six years. Much later, Louisa recalled that she had misjudged Abigail's intentions and that they had reconciled their differences upon her return from

Europe in 1817. No occasion ever arose for the need of reconciliation with her father-in-law, John. She held the same unswerving admiration for him that she did for her own father. "From the hour that I entered into his family," she wrote, he "never said an unkind word to me; but ever to the hour of his death, treated me with the utmost tenderness, and distinction the most flattering."

In her time, Louisa rose to become one of the most famous and accomplished of American political and diplomatic wives. Her life story, as revealed in her diary and reminiscences, includes all the stuff of a romance novel. Her early education in England and France prepared her in music, dance, and the arts. As a young woman, she was schooled, as the wife of an American diplomat, in the most rigorous etiquette at the imperial courts of Berlin and St. Petersburg. Despite early fears and anxieties, she moved gracefully among the aristocracy and royalty of Europe. A friend of Empress Louise and other members of the Prussian imperial family, Louisa later was a regular visitor at the Russian court, where she danced with Tsar Alexander I. Her diaries describe the elaborate costumes she wore for her formal presentations at court and the numerous parties, plays, and operas she attended. With her husband the social equal of many of the great diplomats of the age, she saw her life as "too much like a fairy tale." She had become a "travelled Lady."

She rapidly developed the social skills in which her otherwise-abled husband was congenitally challenged. Louisa's charming presence proved to be the perfect counterpoint to her brilliant but dour New England spouse. By the time John Quincy had been appointed secretary of state in 1817 and they took up residence in Washington, Louisa had no peer among the capital's social elite. Ironically, however, Louisa's cosmopolitan outlook was not always seen in a positive light in the provincial world of Washington, D.C. As she herself wrote, "One of the greatest taxes I have to pay is that of concealing that I am a travelled Lady." Some Americans, especially John Quincy's political opponents, deemed her a foreigner and one who had likely been corrupted in the courts of Europe. Furthermore, despite her unparalleled experience, charm, and grace, she had throughout her life difficulty surmounting her insecurities and anxieties. Her intimate writings form a memoir that soars with pride in her family's accomplishments, only to be undermined by self-doubts and the certainty that John Quincy should have chosen a different mate.

Louisa's writing is emotional, critical, witty, and, in the Adams tradition, always frank. Her descriptions of people in every station, from servants to members of the imperial courts, are sharply drawn. Despite claims of ignorance of public affairs—the proper role for women her husband had taught her—her private thoughts as recorded in her memoirs demonstrate clear and well-formed opinions. Her depictions of the major political personalities of the era reveal her belief in the importance of character over policy. Policy could change when politically convenient, but character remained fixed. Her assessment of Thomas Jefferson demonstrates this particular interest in character. She recalled that "his countenance indicated strongly the hypocrisy of his nature and all about him his smile and his actions indicated a sort of tricky cunning, the sure attendant of a sophisticated mind devoid of a strong basis of substantial principle." She was equally annoyed that he was also too inconsiderate to keep the White House warmed to an acceptable temperature for his state dinners, reporting that the guests "were under the necessity of keeping our teeth close shut, lest their chattering should proclaim that, 'our sufferins was intolerable.' while the gallant President drew his Chair close into the centre of the hearth, and seemed impatiently to await our exit."

Louisa was not above gossip and repeated humorous and sometimes vaguely prurient stories, especially concerning the aristocracy and royalty of Europe. She seemed to take a certain amount of malicious pleasure recounting the foibles of court life, such as the story of one woman in Berlin who ate her way through seventeen dishes in a single meal and died subsequently of indigestion, or that of two poor country girls experiencing their first taste of city life—drinking too much punch and dancing too heartily, to the point that one threw up all over Queen Louise's lovely ball gown. Despite dismissing and ridiculing the superstitions and superstitious she had encountered in Europe, she leaves hints of the accuracy of fortune-tellers in predicting events in her life.

Louisa's strongly held views on religion are stated throughout her writings. Having been raised as an Episcopalian, she had some Roman Catholic education as a girl in France, experienced much of the Russian Orthodox ritual and met many members of its clergy while at St. Petersburg, and agreed to have her sons raised in her husband's Unitarian faith. While she made this concession to John Quincy, she personally remained critical of

Unitarianism, which she described as a "Sect enveloped in a cloud of Mist." She composed many of the diary entries in her later years in the form of prayers, seeking divine guidance and understanding. Nothing would shake her faith in the divinity of Jesus, and she was buried, at her own explicit request, with an Episcopal funeral service.

———————

Louisa's writings in this book are culled from her diaries and other autobiographical writings, arranged chronologically by the time periods they describe, rather than when the pieces were actually written, for two major sections come from memoirs produced long after the events that they describe. Louisa first set down her memories of life from childhood to her move to Berlin in "Record of a Life," which she composed in 1825. She subsequently continued the story up to her infant daughter's death in September 1812 in "Adventures of a Nobody," written in 1840. In the former, she clearly states her purpose, explaining that "some day or other my Children may be amused with it." But she also claimed, "I have no pretensions to be a writer." Louisa never intended this or any of the other entries to be published—perhaps with one exception.

A third autobiographical piece, "Narrative of a Journey from Russia to France" (1836), recounts her dangerous but exciting six-week dash from St. Petersburg across Europe in early 1815 to rejoin her husband in Paris after his diplomatic mission to help settle the peace ending the War of 1812. At the conclusion of the essay, she states that what should have been a relatively simple undertaking was "rendered peculiarly interesting" by "extraordinary circumstances," not the least of which was the return of Napoleon Bonaparte from Elba to again disrupt the European scene during his "Hundred Days." Her ability to complete the trek with a small child and servants of uncertain loyalty was a lesson, she believed, that may "at some future day serve to recal the memory of one, *who was*—and show that many undertakings which appear very difficult and arduous to my Sex, are by no means so trying as imagination forever depicts them."

Louisa's earliest diary, initiated in October 1812, a month after her daughter's death, was undertaken "with a view to write my thoughts and if possible to avoid dwelling on the secret and bitter reproaches of my heart for my conduct as it regarded my lost adored Child." Here especially, and again when she resumed keeping a diary toward the later stages of her life, writing served as therapy—more for her own well-being than to inform anyone else. Throughout her reminiscences, her failure to care for her children when they were young, either by her own fault or the interference of others, haunted Louisa.

Some of her diary-like writings, especially between 1819 and 1824, served dual purposes. Most Louisa composed in Washington. Full of news about the family, with added grist from the capital's social and political mills, these entries were copied and sent as long journal letters to family members in other parts of the country. Perhaps her favorite correspondent during these years was her father-in-law. Louisa kept the former president up to date on all the news, especially as it related to his son. At other times her brother, Thomas Baker Johnson, her son Charles Francis, and her husband received the letters. Regardless of the recipient, these diary entries were addressed to others and reflect Louisa's self-consciousness. As with her memoirs, Louisa wrote for a variety of audiences, not just for herself.

There are, sadly, significant chronological blanks in the narrative. Whether Louisa failed to write or nothing survives, there are two particularly glaring omissions. The period from early 1815 until early 1819, which included all of John Quincy's service as U.S. minister to Great Britain and his first year and a half as secretary of state, go unrecorded here. Even more troublesome is the omission of the White House years, 1825 to 1829. It is difficult to imagine she did not have much to say during John Quincy's presidency, but, unfortunately, no diaries from the period have been found. Louisa's keen observations and sharp assessment of the people and events from these years are sorely missed.

Apart from skipping periods altogether, Louisa is sometimes rather loose with her facts. As she herself notes in her "Narrative of a Journey," "Research is not in my way— Indolence wars with exertion, and is too often victorious; and as I know nothing of style, or composition, those who may read this memento mori, must endeavour to extract light from the chaos which lies before them; and I wish them joy of the trouble." Datelines are guesses, names are misremembered, and even her route from St. Petersburg to Paris takes liberties with geographical realities. Readers should remember that, with Louisa's diaries, the precision of the details matters less than the broader truths behind her tales.

Even without a complete—or completely accurate—narrative, however, Louisa's writings are well worth the reading. Telling the story of her own life, juxtaposed with rich descriptions of European court life, Washington political maneuvers, and continuing family drama, Louisa has left us her own best introduction. We hope the excerpts presented here will begin to return her to the place she held in 1852 when Congress adjourned to honor her: as one of the preeminent women of the nineteenth century.

Note to the Reader

The editors have created this volume to introduce readers to Louisa's writings—against her own wishes, admittedly—so that her distinctive voice and wry observations on the world might be appreciated more broadly. Those interested in a fully annotated, scholarly edition of her complete memoirs and diaries should consult the two-volume *Diary and Autobiographical Writings of Louisa Catherine Adams* (Cambridge, Mass.: Belknap Press of Harvard University Press, 2013).

The texts presented here have been organized chronologically, and are given literally with no regularization of spelling and minimal modernization of capitalization and punctuation, primarily to indicate beginnings and ends of sentences. The editors have, however, silently corrected some inadvertent errors for clarity. Datelines, which are based on Louisa's own and sometimes cover many days or even months under a single date, have been standardized. Paragraph breaks have occasionally been added to improve readability. An ellipsis in brackets indicates an unreadable word or words. Words printed struck through represent cancellations in the original that the editors have restored because of their interest. Omitted sections of the texts are indicated by scotch rules (double bars). Illegible material is supplied, where possible, by the editors in roman type within square brackets; bracketed comments in italics are editorial insertions included to clarify Louisa's meaning or to identify names and places. Editorial notes at the beginnings of chapters and periodically throughout the book provide context and explain or identify events or personalities mentioned.

The manuscript originals of all of Louisa's diaries are held in the Adams Family Papers manuscript collection, given by the Adams family in 1956 to the Massachusetts Historical Society, whose mission since 1791 has been to collect, preserve, and make accessible material related to the history of Massachusetts and the United States.

A Traveled First Lady

·[CHAPTER ONE]·

"All Was Joy and Peace and Love"

Youth

Louisa Catherine Adams began her first piece of autobiographical writing in the summer of 1825, only a few months after moving into the White House. Addressed to her three surviving children—George Washington, John 2d, and Charles Francis—she entitled this memoir "Record of a Life." She hoped her sons "may be amused with it," promising to confine herself "to those events which are worth recording only." In "Record," she covers the period of her youth and young adulthood but cuts the narrative off at a point shortly following her marriage, just as she was first establishing herself as a diplomat's wife in Berlin. She would not resume full-scale autobiographical writing again until 1840, when she began drafting her "Adventures of a Nobody." Unlike her other diaries, which are divided into dated entries, "Record" is a straightforward narrative. But because it was written over twenty-five years after the fact, Louisa's recollections are not always entirely accurate, nor do they necessarily follow a precise chronological order.

At the time she was writing "Record," Louisa was unhappily serving as first lady of the United States. John Quincy's presidency got off to a rocky start when he failed to win the election of 1824 outright. Instead, it was thrown into the House of Representatives, which selected John Quincy, despite the fact that his main challenger, Andrew Jackson, had received a plurality of both the popular and electoral votes. Jackson's camp accused John Quincy of enacting a "corrupt bargain" with Henry Clay to get the necessary votes in the House, and Jackson's followers in Congress were determined to thwart John Quincy's legislative agenda at every turn. Louisa was an accomplished hostess, but even her talents could not counter Washington's poisonous political atmosphere.

Not surprisingly, Louisa begins her memoir with a brief history of her parents. Louisa's father, Joshua Johnson, was a Maryland merchant who went to London on business in 1771 and there met the Englishwoman Catherine Nuth.

*They began a relationship and had their first child together in 1773. Unbe-
knownst to Louisa, the couple did not legally marry until 1785. Louisa writes
with great warmth about her parents, whom she loved dearly, downplaying
their shortcomings. Her recollections of her childhood suggest that, despite
the impact on the family of the American Revolution, which forced them to
move temporarily from London to France, this period of her life was by far
her happiest.*

As some day or other my Children may be amused with it I will endeavour
to give a slight sketch of my life until this time confining myself to those
events which are worth recording only. They may perhaps think on this
principle, that I need not write at all but a review of past incidents may have
a good effect upon myself. I shall only write when in the humour or to speak
learnedly when the Cacoëthes Scribendi [*insatiable desire to write*] has
siezed me and my flights will probably be excursive as I have no pretensions
to be a writer and no desire to appear any thing more than a mere commonplace personage with a good memory and just observation enough to discover
the difference between a man of sense and a Fool, and to know that the latter
often do the least mischief of the two.

My Father was the descendant of an English Gentlemen who emigrated
to this Country in consequence of a marriage with a Miss Baker of Liverpool
then an Heiress and a Ward in Chauncery— As she was not of age to avoid
the pursuit of the Law they came out to the State of Maryland and established themselves in Colvert among the Colvert family— They were wealthy
and respectable and left one Son who inheritted the property and who married a young Lady from the Eastward or connected with the Sedgwicks she
bearing the same name— My Father was one of eleven children and early in
life was placed in the Counting House of a very respectable Merchant from
Scotland a Mr. Graham the Father of Major Graham of one the most distinguished families of Scotland— He had not the advantage of a Classical education My Grandfather retaining many of the English prejudices in favour
of the eldest Son on whom was lavished all the expence to make him an
object of consequence in the Country— At the age of two or three and twenty
my Father entered into partnership with two Scotch Gentlemen by name
Wallace & Muir and in consequence removed to London as second partner
in the Firm— There he became acquainted with my Mother of whose family

I knew very little as some misunderstanding had subsisted for some years indeed ever since the death of my Grandmother which had cut off all communication between my father and Grandfather whose character was I am sorry to say very indifferent— My Grandmother was a Miss Young extremely beautiful and I always [*heard*] her represented as possessing qualities and virtues of the highest order. My father loved and respected her to the hour of his death and always spoke of her to *us,* as an example of exalted goodness.

My Sister Hellen was born in the December of 1773 and I was born in February 75. In 78 or 9 in consequence of the American Revolution my Father took his Family to France finding it no longer safe to live in England being in heart and Soul friendly to the Independence of the Country and my earliest recollections are French; for the little knowledge I had of my own Language was soon obliterated by the acquirement of a new one— All the scenes of my infancy come with such faint recollections they float upon my fancy like visions which never could have had any reality yet like visions of delight in which all was joy and peace and love. I perfectly remember the elegance of the mansion in which we resided the school to which I was sent the strong impression made upon my imagination by the Roman Catholick Church the heartfelt humility with which I knelt before the Image of the tortured Jesus and the horror I felt at the thought, of mixing with heretics. The veneration with which I entered the Convents the great affection I bore to one particular Nun who used to bring toys for sale to School all these shadows of early life have flitted before my minds eye but without the possibility of fixing names or even remembering a countenance which then was so familiar— One of the events which I recur to most distinctly was the marriage of my fathers Coachman to which we were permitted to go. The Bride was a dark complexioned rosy looking woman dressed in a large flowered Calico with a most enormous bouquet— They went to Church in my fathers Carriage and had the use of it for the day. My father gave them a handsome Supper and Ball and I still seem to see the Bride and Bridgroom opening the Ball with all the gaiety of french sprightliness— One of the events most strongly imprinted in my memory is a great inundation in Montz [*Nantes*] which obliged the people to sail in Boats through the Streets. oh! with what glee we children beheld it shrieking with pleasure when the servants would get into the boats from the basement windows without an idea that that which was productive of such fun to us was the cause of misery to thousands— Is not one of the great blessings of infancy its thoughtlessness its aptitude for every thing like enjoyment and its total unconsciousness of danger? Yet what is idiotism in an adolscent is it any thing more than mere Childishness or rather a mind immatured? Can we must we believe that mind grows with our growth and decays with our wasted forms— Is not mind or what we call spirit an etherial spark an emanation of the Deity and can any thing so pure an essence so divine suffer decay or be liable to desease— How profound the mystery how wise the Creator— Are we not called upon, forced to have faith in this mighty wonder and dare we say vile worms as we are that ought with the Omnipotent is impossible? From whence is the word impossible with whom does it originate? in those only whose power is limitted who are taught by God himself "thus far shalt thou go and no farther." Will all the wisdom that philosophers teach will all the learning to which the mind of man can attain teach what is death? what sleep? what the soul? all all is dark and God Almighty God alone in his own time can shed the light which can clear our understandings— But where will this theme lead me— I am bewildered and afraid and must still cling to that blessed being who in mercy stands between me and my God to pardon thoughts which I cannot controul.

The last year which we passed in France was full of pleasure and being more at home I was more familiarized with the acquaintance of my Mother which was very large. Among them I distinctly remember many of her friends with whom I have renewed acquaintance in other Countries. My Father was intimate with the celebrated [*John*] Paul Jones but I have utterly forgotten him if I ever saw him.

Louisa had eight siblings, seven sisters and one brother, of whom all but one lived to adulthood. Her older sister Ann (1773–1810) was commonly called Nancy. She married Walter Hellen in 1798. After Louisa came Carolina Virginia Marylanda (1777–1862)—named in a fit of patriotism shortly following the beginning of the American Revolution. She married first Andrew Buchanan in 1807 and, following his death, Nathaniel Frye Jr. in 1817. A daughter, Mary Ann, followed who lived only a few months, then the one boy of the family, Thomas Baker (1779–1843), who never married. Sister Harriet (1781–1850) married George Boyd in 1805, and Catherine Maria Frances (1786–1869),

called Kitty, married John Quincy's nephew William Steuben Smith in 1813
while they and Louisa all were living in St. Petersburg. The two youngest sib-
lings were Eliza Jennet Dorcas (d. 1818), who married John Pope in 1810, and
Adelaide (1789–1877), who became Walter Hellen's second wife in 1813, after
Nancy's death. Growing up, Louisa was closest to Nancy and Carolina, since
they were all so near in age, and they shared schooling, social activities, and
other adventures but also a fair amount of sibling rivalry. Because Louisa is
writing these memoirs in 1825, she frequently refers to her sisters by their mar-
ried, rather than their given, names.

In the Month of Feby 1783 I was attacked severely by a Pleurisy which left
me in so weak a state of health as to cause great apprehensions in my Dear
Parents for my life as they feared that Consumption would ensue— In April
83 we left Nantz on our way to England. The family had much encreased as
my Sister Boyd and My Brother were added to the Stock and our number
was four when we left Mrs. Hellen myself Mrs. Fry and my Sister Mariane
who died soon after my Mother settled in Nantz in consequence of the great
fatigue which my Mother had undergone on the journey— Of our journey I
do not remember any thing until we arrived in Paris. There we had elegant
Apartments in one of the best hotels and a day or two after our arrival the
Children at the request of Mr & Mrs. [*John*] Jay were all sent to pay their
respects. Mr. Jay was then in Paris I believe as Minister [*peace commissioner*]. Mrs. Jay was a very Lady like looking woman and she had two daughters children like ourselves but dressed in the plain english fashion white
Frocks and Pink Sashes which appeared to me much prettier than the fine
silk dress and hoop which I was used to wear. Their establishment was
handsome and their kindness unbounded and I have always looked back
with pleasure to this visit which is the only thing that occurred during my
stay in Paris which has stamped itself upon my mind— The sufferings we
all endured on our voyage from Calais to Dover the Bustle of our embarka-
tion the Packet itself were all objects of wonderment and fixed themselves
as objects of admiration and dread never to be forgotten—
Of our arrival in England and London nothing materiel remains— We
were sent to School to a Mrs. Carter a Maiden Lady and one of the greatest
Ladies in England more especially as She was in every respect one of the
largest and fattest that England ever produced. We were recommended to be

placed under her care and tuition by Mr & Mrs Hewlett the latter of whom had been a very particular friend of my Parents having been the Wife and Widow of an American Gentleman of whom my father was very fond. Mrs. Hewlett was a very excentric Woman of strong mind and still stronger passions of course susceptible of equally strong attachments. In the confusion and general derangement incident to the removal of a large family from one Country to another it is natural to seek assistance from some person already established and they by this means frequently acquire a degree of influence which they could never have obtained under any other circumstances— My two Sisters and myself were immediately sent to Shacklewell where in consequence of our extraordinary dress and utter ignorance of English we became objects of ridicule to the whole School which consisted of forty Young Ladies from the ages of seven to twenty— To this cause I am convinced I owe the haughtiness and pride of character which it has been impossible for me to subdue; to the sufferings I then underwent living in a state of constant torment, and being perpetually punished or mortified for those very things which had always before been subjects of admiration— A child is to a certain degree a reasoning animal; it can observe and strongly mark the differences and changes in its situation; but it cannot seek the why or the wherefore from whence these difficulties spring. This was my case and I became serious melancholy and almost gloomy—which caused me to be called Miss Proud by my schoolfellows, and placed me in a more painful situation than ever—

Among many of these unpleasant scenes those occasioned by my religious feelings were the most powerful— The first time I was forced to go to Church at Hackney I perfectly recollect my horror when my Governess obliged me to kneel down among what I had been taught in France to call the *hereticks;* which was so great that in the very act of Kneeling I fell as it were dead upon the floor and continued so ill although only eight years old that my father was obliged to take me home and to vary the scene I was sent to stay sometime with Mrs. Hewlett— After two Months I returned to School with strict orders from my parents that I should not be harried or urged too much upon the subject of going to Church; and that if it should again affect me in the same way, I was to be accustomed gradually to the prayers of the school, until my fears wore off.— In consequence of my again fainting at Church and being obliged to be taken out the judicious plan adopted by my

beloved and ever amiable father was put into execution and I quietly con-
formed to the usages and forgot insensibly all the prejudes which I had so
early and so strongly imbibed— As I am writing for amusement and as we
all love to dwell on that age of innocence and thougtlessness when all is
fresh with hope, and even our sorrows are like rainbow clouds dispersed
ere they are seen; you will probably find my prolixity very tedious; but it is
easy to skip what we do not wish to read and view it only as a blank.

Every Vacation we returned home to my fathers house; the very thoughts
of which was so delightful that we no sooner arrived at school than a List of
the Months and days was made, and our greatest pleasure consisted in tear-
ing one off every morning with a view to shorten the lagging of time; and
this occupation seemed to bring us nearer home— O home! sweet home!
thou ever wert to me the joy of life, and the domestic felicity for many years
almost uninterupted of my beloved Parents placed a picture constantly before my eyes truly enviable—and in no one instance during my life have I
ever met such an example. My Mother had been beautiful; she was at this
time very lovely, her person was very small, and exquisitely delicate, and
very finely proportioned. She was lively; her understanding highly cultivated, and her wit brilliant, sometimes almost too keen. My Father was the
handsomest man I ever beheld. His eye or the power of his eye was indescribable: its usual expression was sweetness and benevolence; but when
roused to anger, or to suspicion; it had a dazzling fixed severity that was
absolutely aweful; and which seemed by its vivid scrutiny to dive into the
very depths of the human heart— His temper was admirable; his tastes simple; his word sacred; and his heart pure and affectionate as that of the most
unsophisticated Child of Nature. The greatest fault he had was believing
every one as good, as correct, as worthy as himself— His establishment was
large, not sumptuous or extravagant, but such as the first Merchants in
London at that day usually had: he kept a neat Carriage and one pair of
Horses, and every thing was conducted in the family with the neatest order
and regularity— His entertainments when he made any, which was not often,
were handsome; but his usual way of receiving company was unceremoni-
ously social, and almost limitted to his own Countrymen who resorted to
England, for business or pleasure; these found a home and a Friend in him
at all times— In Religion or creed he was a Unitarian; but as those opinions
were at that time much decried; he took particular pains to educate his

Children in the Episcopal form as in regard to women he always said there was little danger in believing; there was *destruction* in doubt.

When I was about nine years old I was siezed with what was then called a one and twenty day fever which is very much like the Typhus, if it is not the same— Well do I remember my sufferings! the almost exessive tenderness of my indulgent parents! who watched me night and day with unwearied patience, and cheerfulness: and fondly supported my weary head, and soothed my aching brain. All the acquaintance of my father appeared to vie with each other in showing kindness to *me:* and every hour brought forth presents in toys and fruit, to charm my drooping spirit. My Mother while the tears ran down her cheeks sat by my bed anxiously noting every change: seemingly busied in dressing my doll, and making its clothes to amuse me— In sickness I was always patient, quiet, and manageable; and in this long and severe illness I was so in all points but one— My Sister Harriet was not three years old and a most lovely child on whom I had always lavished my affection: but this time, while devoured by this deadly fever, the sight of her would almost throw me into convulsions, and if my Mother looked at or spoke to her it reduced me to deaths door. To the poor child this was anguish; as my room furnished a most attractive spectacle, being filled with playthings of every description that could fascinate a childs attention; and it caused great affliction and wonder to my parents; my disposition was so affectionate; I had always clung with such ardent fondness to my brother and my Sisters, that this antipathy could not be accounted for: I had always been liberal even to extravagance; it therefore could not be avarice! but no matter what it was it occasioned great affliction—

I was particulary fond of the Gentleman who attended me—he used to come three times a day to see me; his manner was so mild, so quiet, so soothing, that I always saw him with joy— It was on this occasion that Dr. Letsom was called in; my case was deemed hopeless. He sat by my bedside—he was a tall thin man; his countenance was agreeable and his conversation lively. He asked me many questions which I was too weak to answer; but I remember perfectly that he drew a pigeon with a pen and Ink, and gave it to me; which pleased me very much, and made him a great favorite with me— A Blister was ordered and if it drew it would augur favorably; if it failed my fate was decreed: at twelve o clock at night the blister was to be removed but my poor Mother was overcome and unequal to the task; and Mrs. Hewlett was to perform the operation— I had been very low all day and have little recollection of any thing until I was roused, by seeing Mrs. Hewlett fall upon the floor, and feeling the smart of the cold air upon my back— The Blister had drawn favorably and the sudden joy had deprived her of sense, who never had fainted before. I cannot express the extasy with which I saw my dear Mother return to me; and from that hour I got well—

As soon as I could bear the fatigue my good Dr Letsome who took a great fancy to me, invited me to go and see him at Camberwell where he had a very beautiful place to which I afterwards went with my Mother— Again was I sent to Mrs. Hewlett for two Months Country air, and gentle exercise being recommended: and I shall never forget the kindness with which they treated me particularly Mr Hewlett who from that time I looked upon in the light of a father— The weakness and delicacy which ensued in consequence of this second illness; left me for several years very weakly, and I became a pet as is usual in such cases. Both my Sisters who enjoyed fine health were very lively and had little of that sensitiveness for which has always I was distinguished and which has proved so great an obstacle to my happiness—

Many traits of character I could recite, few of them would do me much credit— Pride and haughteur were my predominant failings, but they had the good effect of keeping me out of bad company, for I too thoroughly despised the vicious to associate with them. Dr. Parkinson used to attend the School as Dentist, and one day he insisted upon taking out two of my double teeth—the idea of it was so horrible that I refused to undergo it— After much vain entreaty, my Governess called the man Servant and told him he must hold me in His arms— This succeeded; for rather than be thus *poluted* I submitted, exclaiming "do you think I will be held by a servant—" The good old Lady was so amazingly struck by the look and manner in which these words were said, that instead of using the rod, she always used to say she was sure I was intended to be a very great personage— At School I was universally *respected,* but I was never beloved. The girls feared me because I would not enter into their schemes and intrigues—and always dreaded me knowing my horror and dislike of their plots and plans, lest I should betray them— One only young Lady could I become attached to: she was as remarkable in her temper and manners as myself: we slept in the same room; we read together, and were almost inseparable: she was an East Indian very dark, with long black indian hair; not handsome, but looked up to by all the Teachers and scholars as a girl of uncommon talents—

Miss Young was head teacher a most extraordinary woman. Her Uncle had her educated with boys for many years; and obliged her to wear boys clothes: and in this way she had in a great measure acquired something like a Classical education knowing some Greek and the rudiments of Latin. Miss Edwards and myself were her decided favorites and as we were both apt and quick in learning our different lessons, and very fond of reading; she took much pains to improve us and conversed freely with us upon the books we read, pointing out and selecting, the most beautiful and striking passages, and cultivating our taste by her judment— Her person was masculine and her manners were forbidding; so that unless she took a particular fancy to any one; fear and dislike kept the young Ladies aloof. Her heart was excellent, and her mind full of the highest qualities—

In the course of the year I was removed to the parlour, and allowed many privileges. Among the number was that of walking in the Garden; but there was an express prohibition concerning the fruit which we were forbidden to touch— One Evening, like Eve I met with a tempter, who persuaded me that there was no harm in taking some Grapes, as there was such an abundance the old Lady could not use them— I hesitated a long time; but the example of my companion soon produced its effect, and I not only eat some but put a number of bunches in my pocket, to distribute among my friends— The bell rung for supper; and I was obliged to go immediately into the parlour, like a thief conscience stricken— I was restless and uneasy; but when my Governess began to read Young's Night thoughts of which was to prolong our stay above an hour; I felt in perfect torture— While she was reading one of the finest passages, my Sister Nancy screamed out, that there was a great Spider on my Gown, and I began to jump and beg, that they would take it off, as I had a natural antipathy to this species of Insect, which nothing could ever conquer— Again we all sat down to listen to the reading, when again the alarm was given, and in my agony to get rid of the Spider, I pulled the grapes out of my pocket, and threw them on the floor, vowing that no earthly thing should ever make me steal again, as these creatures must have been sent as a punishment for my fault—

My feelings on this occasion were indescribable and I long thought nothing could wash out my disgrace. The reprimand I received was severe; but the spiders and the exposure they produced, proved a much more efficacious Lesson, which stamped it in never to be forgotten Letters on my mind— I hated the fault, but I hated much more the Girl who had induced me to commit it; unjustly attributing to her the act which had alone been caused by my own weakness— How frail is our Nature— How easily does the human heart throw off its own depravity, and cling to every straw in its deceit— Had I not a will of my own? did I not know I was doing wrong? committing sin? then what was this girls example to me! Was I not a creature endowed with reason, and did I not at the very time despise *her* for the Act? and yet I did it; and hated her *not* because I had committed the act, but because she had shown by this act of my own, that I did not possess the proud superiority over my companions, to which I had pretended; and that my resolutions were as weak and as unstable as those of my neighbours— This was a proof that good may sometimes be extracted from evil! I no longer held my head so high; and was much more lenient to those who I had hitherto considered far inferior to myself; I was no longer a standard in my own eyes; and from this hour the unbending harshness of my Nature, began to be subdued—and I to learn, that Charity for others, which I so much needed for myself—

In a short time after this my father removed us from School altogether— Three more daughters had been born to him, and the expenses of his family were heavy; but as our education was by no means complete, he engaged a private Governess to superintend our Masters, and to instruct the little ones. My Sister was in her fifteenth year I a year younger. My fathers establishment was so perfectly regulated though large, that every thing in it moved like clock work; his household consisted of eleven Servants; three of whom had lived with him from the time of his marriage; and all of them were devotedly attached to him. He was a very indulgent Master although strict, and as every thing was methodical, every thing was easy— My Mother superintended the whole establishment though her health was so delicate she was often obliged to trust to a substitute in whom she was obliged to place unlimitted confidence— At this time our old and valued Butler removed to France with his Wife, and we lost two faithful Servants and solid friends, which produced an unpleasant change in the family routine— The loss of an old confidential Servant however we may pique ourselves upon our independence, makes itself felt for years if not for life; more especially when we have grown old together, and formed the same habits and acquired in a great degree the same tastes; and we insensibly rely on them for our comforts— This change produced other changes, and in some measure altered the face of things— I am thus minute because, I derived some benefit from the circumstance of the New Cook becoming so very fond of me, that she insisted upon teaching me all she knew; and she could do nothing in her Department, without consulting Miss Weser [*Louisa*]— From this time my father insisted upon our taking turn each alternate week, in the superintendance of the House keeping, which was very beneficial to us all; and early initiated us in all the labours and troubles of family eoconomy—

My Fathers house as I have already observed was open to all the young Americans, and among them we formed some very agreeable acquaintance: two of these Gentlemen being in my fathers Office (he was Consul General from the United States appointed by General Washington) ate at my fathers house; and this naturally produced a great degree of intimacy, although they were nineteen and twenty, and we were so much younger— My attachment to Mr. David Sterrett was very great— His character his manners, his person were all excellent; and his disposition was such as to ensure the esteem and affection of all who knew him. He was equally fond of me, and always termed me his little Wife: and every body delighted to teaze me about him until a sentiment was forming in my heart, which no one doubted, least of all myself— Our time was all marked out for different studies; and in the Evening we joined my father and Mother in the parlour, and there were few which did not give rise to some frolick in which they joined, and all the family partook— Whenever we did better than usual as a reward the Carpet would be rolled up and they would join the dance; and lend their aid to add to the merriment of the Evening: and home was thus rendered so delightful we did not dream of any pleasure beyond it, unless it was an occasional visit to the theatre—

On the New Years day after we left School my father presented us a guinea each with a desire that we should expend it in whatever was most agreeable to ourselves— With what delight we went to the Shop each calculating how much they would get for their money! and fancying it an inexhaustible mine of wealth, never having possessed more than a Shilling at a time before— But alas! what a disappointment! when I found that Milton's Paradise Lost and Regained, with Mason's Self Knowledge, was all that my guinea produced. These however were treasures to which I had long aspired, and I was proud of reading, "that all our knowledge was ourselves to know." It was a curious selection for so young a child; but this book had been put into my hand by the teacher, and I had become very fond of its serious and contemplative subject. How often since that time have I thought it injured me; by teaching me to scrutinize too closely into motives, and looking too closely at the truth— Much, much depends upon the reading of our early life— Children appear to read carelessly, and to note little of the subjects which are placed before them. But the impressions which are made on them are durable, and though apparently lost for years; frequently stamp the taste and mark the character of the mind at a later period of their lives—

It was during the following winter that we were introduced into what is called society— The difference in the ages of my Sister and myself was so little it was thought proper to introduce us together— I have described her already and have but a few words to say concerning myself. I was timid to shyness reserved and cold—When pleased delighted to ecstacy and attached with ardour— My disposition inclined me to read the countenances of all who approached me with extreme care and my judgment of character was almost immediately stamped upon this investigation— Sense and talent I almost worshipped. Mr. Hewlett during my frequent visits had done much to expand my understanding and by his serious conversation had led me early to think— There was an old Gentleman by the name of Edmund Jennings who was likewise constantly at our House who was a man of fine sense whose conversation I was very fond of— Mr Granville Sharp David Hartly Tom Payne and many others whom I have forgotten— Society at home was ever delightful to me upon the footing on which it was received in my fathers family and our little unceremonious suppers were the very essence of social festivity— My Mothers conversation was brilliant. She was fond of reading and her manners were polished and the tone she gave to his company was easy and what the french call spirituél— My father seemed to hang on every word she uttered and gazed on her with looks of love and admiration "as if encrease of appetite had grown by what it fed on" never did man love woman with a devotion so perfect— His sparkling eye beamed on her with an excess of tenderness and his smile seemed to blend all those good and amiable feelings which spring spontaneous from a faithful and benevolent heart— She was his pride his joy his love and in her and his Children was concentratd all that made life desirable—

In disposition I was not half so amiable as either of my Sisters but it was my fathers idea that I was more steady and this induced him to treat me as if I was the eldest and to put much trust in my discretion. To me this proved often a very painful distinction exciting much justifiable jealousy but it gave me a habit of measuring my own actions by a pretty severe rule as I soon learned that any lapse on my part would be met with great severity in all quarters. I had not the advantage of possessing the personal attractions which adorned my two Sisters— I was so entirely happy I never looked or dreamt of any thing beyond the hour, and thoroughly detested every thing like society beyond my own home unless it was an occasional visit to the Theatre. So decided was this trait in my character that I would shed tears for hours previous to going out to a party never open my lips while there and return to my home in such glee that my father used to think himself oblged to rebuke me by showing me the contrast between my downcast looks my trembling knees and my awkward gate which he used to say made me appear as if some crime was heavy on my conscience— These lessons encreased my aversion and destroyed even the wish to be seen out of my own doors—

In writing thus of self I am betraying a degree of unpardonable egotism— It is true and I acknowledge the fact most humbly but in looking back to myself or to the happy period of my early days my memory is filled with reminiscenses so delightful it revels in scenes of such kind affectionate attentions such heart bestowed tenderness that I must be pardoned; for little in after life can compensate for such privations— Is a young woman thus situated a fit object to enter the world? Ever the first object of attention at home every fault pardoned, every virtue loved, a consequence given to every action with a constant desire rather to elevate than to depress her, with a system of reward and punishment calculated to perfect and expand every good feeling of her heart; can such an education fit a young artless creature for an entrance into a corrupt world?

Do not my children read this as romance for every word is true— Our family consisted of seven daughters and one Son as children they were remarkable for beauty and as it was my Mothers delight to dress them all exactly alike on a Sunday when we walked in couples to Church we were objects of general curiosity and permit me to say admiration to the publick— It was a goodly show and well I remember it—

Time rappidly flew our education was progressing and we had the best masters to teach us those accomplishments which properly used are an ornament to female loveliness— At this time my father received a singular Letter from Govr. [*Thomas*] Johnson who he looked on as a father telling him that he had heard much of his daughters and desiring him to be useful that they should "form connections with none but *men of note* and distinction in his own Country." This Letter produced a great effect on him and induced him to limit as much as possible our acquaintance among the English— Mr Thorp's family whom you knew in England were all boys and had been intimate in the family as children but they were the only young men of that Country with whom we had any intimacy— Our Evenings I have already described; but alone or in company my father required me to sing and nothing but sickness could furnish an excuse for non complyance; he listened with delight to our performancs which seemed to soothe his soul to peace and harmony after the labours of the day—

It was now that we continually heard annecdotes concerning the American Revolution the risks my father had run ere he was obliged to quit England. He would talk to us of Dr Franklin of Mr [*Henry*] Lawrence whom he had visitted in the Tower of Col [*John*] Trumbull who had been confined in Bridewell of Stephen Sair of Mr Jay of Paul Jones and of Gen Washington of whom he spoke with a degree of enthusiasm which fired our young hearts with the purest love and admiration. My Sister Frye had been named after the states of Maryland Virginia and the Carolina's in compliment to their acquiecence with the declaration of Independence as she was born in the October of the year which fixed this great event as a proof of his strong attachment to his Country and his zeal in her cause. Many were the Americans that he saved from imprisonment while residing in London at his own risk furnishing them with clothes money and passage on board vessels owned by him or his friends which convey'd them safe from danger either to their homes or to France—

The "Col Smith" mentioned below refers to William Stephens Smith, a colonel in the Continental Army who had married John Quincy's sister, Abigail (Nabby), in 1786. When the Smiths lived in London from March 1792 to early 1793, they socialized frequently with the Johnsons, and Louisa and Nabby became especially close. Little did the two women realize that they would eventually become sisters-in-law—or that Nabby's son William Steuben Smith would one day marry Louisa's sister Catherine.

The portraits for which Louisa recalls sitting below may have been those done by the American artist Edward Savage around 1793, that of Louisa being the only full-length portrait of her taken before her marriage. As a prosperous merchant as well as the U.S. consul in London, Joshua Johnson was in a position to have these paintings done, and to hire Savage, who was in England at the time studying the works of Benjamin West. It is unknown how many of the Johnsons sat for Savage, but portraits of Louisa, Nancy, Carolina, and Harriet, as well as Joshua and Louisa's mother, Catherine, all survive. Another set of paintings, miniature portraits of all of the living Johnsons except Thomas Baker, were likewise prepared sometime around 1792. Done in oils by an unknown artist, they can be seen in the illustrations following page 166.

I cannot pretend to mention all the Gentlemen with whom we were acquainted. I can only say that in consequence of my Uncle's [*Gov. Thomas Johnson*] silly Letter although we lived in the midst of the city of London we were kept almost entirely out of English society and visitted only one family in the street in which we lived— My Sister Caroline was just entering into society. Her form was light her complexion dazzling her manners arch and playfull and her disposition sweet— Timid to a fault it was only among our most intimate friends that she displayed her real character and all those became extravagantly fond of her— She was the most admirable mimic and

afforded us constant amusement by this talent but my father tried his utmost
to check it although he seldom could restrain his mirth at her performance—
Col Smith almost lived with us and was the mediator with our parents in all
our little troubles— At this time Mr [*Henry*] Gibbs of Carolina proposed to
my father for my Sister Caroline— he was very wealthy a great dasher and a
great Beau. This latter quality operated so unpleasantly on the old Gentle-
mans feelings that he quietly rejected the advances and we saw Mr Gibbs
no more—

My Brother was at School under the especial care of Mr. Hewlett with
Mr Ben Ogle the father of the young man with whom you are acquainted
who returned to America in the course of this Summer— He was received
among us like our brother and I never was aware that the young Gentleman
had any predilection for my worthy self until my residence in Washington—
Alas how unthinking and childish I must have been never to suspect the
power of my charm's but so it was and I have heard of a number of ardent
admirers that I had at that time since I have grown old the rumour of which
never reached my ear in my youth— There was a Mr John Taylor a Gentleman from Masstts. whom I disliked more than I can express Who was the
only one that I was at all conscious of having smitten but my feelings towards
him were always those of disgust. It was at this time that the family portraits
were painted or rather began. Most of them were thought good likenesses
but mine never gave satisfaction to my friends nor indeed any one that ever
was painted in those days— The one George has was thought the best and
that squints—

In the Summer we went to Lymington and in the course of our journey
had a fine opportunity of seeing a number of beautiful seats and of visitting
the Isle of Wight. Six weeks passed most delightfully and we returned home
in fine health and spirits from our tour in which we were accompanied by a
Mr West of Baltimore one of the most really amiable men I ever knew. Here
again my life was endangered by a singular accident as well as my Mothers.
We were riding in a large four wheeled Chaise and Mr. West was driving
when we met two large Waggons laden with Hay— The drivers were walking at some distance behind and did not notice our situation and as the road
was bordered by two high banks it was impossible to get out of the way—
The consequence was that the Waggons advanced on us threw down our
horse and was literally coming over us when Mr. West at the risk of his life

jump'd out and endeavoured to stop the Horses while my Mother scrambled over the Shafts of the Waggon and made her way safe out; the Horses still pressing on to me, and I too lifeless to move: fortunately the men came up and I was taken out of the carriage more dead than alive— I never shall forget the agony of the poor young man. He was in a deep decline and I think the shock he underwent at the idea of our horrid danger hastened his death which took place not long after— As neither he nor my Mother could see any thing of me after they had extricated themselves from the peril; and as I neither spoke nor move they both expected to find me crushed to atoms, and you may conceive their astonishment when I came forth coolly saying to the men pray take care of my Wig which appeared to be the only object of my concern my head having been shaved in consequence of a severe illness and my vanity not admitting of so cruel an exposure of my bald head—

It was at this time that my father took a french family into his House that is a man and his Wife by the name of Gallement french Emgrants in great distress and professedly Nobles. He was to be Tutor to my Brother She Governess to us Females for although the three eldest were introduced into company we were still obliged to attend to all our school duties— The French Revolution was then blazing in all its fury and the Emigrants became objects of general pity in England— My father had lived so much in France and so happily that he felt a sympathy for these poor people and was liberal in the services he rendered them— He had known the King [*Louis XVI*]; he had been graciously received by the beautiful Queen [*Marie Antoinette*]; had rejoiced with the Nation in the birth of the Dauphin; and he could not however he admired the *cause of freedom* witness or hear of the enormous cruelties of the period, without execrating its authors— Until this time Lafayette had been an object of idolatry like Genl Washington; but now we knew not what to think— Was it weakness? was it want of judgment? or what caused the unfortunate seizure of the King and Queen which brought them to the block with such unheard suffering? Something mysterious has ever attended this circumstance which no time can reveal— He is good he is amiable he is ambitious and in this instance he was unfortunate for I will not believe that he was capable of adopting the Stateman's horrible doctrine that we may sometimes do evil that good may come of it— But I will endeavour to believe that as creatures of circumstance he was prevented from saving the wretched beings who clung to him for existence by unforeseen accidents beyond his power to controul—

Genl [*Thomas*] Pinckney was Minister to England from the United States and our families became very intimate— Mrs. [*Elizabeth*] Pinckney was a truly lovely Woman and I became very fond of her. My father contrary to his usual custom allowed me to stay at her House very frequently and I there became acquainted with a number of young Carolinians among whom was Mr. Huger and their singular relation Mr. [*Daniel*] Horie who however only made them flying visits as he was too much devoted to France to be able to stay in England— On one of his flying visits he took the trouble to ride down from Cumberland place to show me [*Johann Caspar*] Lavaters Angel; which he assured me was my exact likeness at which I was very much surprized as he was one of the objects whom I most unmercifully quizzed— Col Smith was gone to France and our society had entirely changed—And we moved in a more fashionable world through the medium of Mr Pinkney and Mr John Barker Church's family then living in a very splindid style in London and at Chiswick. Through them we became acquainted with three most beautiful American ladies Mrs. Falconnet and the Miss Hunters of Rhode Island— One of them was blind; and they were in search of some Occulist in the hope that Miss Hunter might recover her sight—

Col and Mrs. Smith arrived in England and again our acquaintance was enlarged and I will say improved— The very familiar footing on which we lived made their society delightful to us. Whenever the Col dined from home Mrs. S. would bring her Children early in the morning and pass the day with us and as this happened very frequently it brought us together continually— It was my delight to dress her and I was often employed in making up Articles of Millinery which I used to insist upon her wearing and in which she looked beautiful— She was one of the most placid quiet beings I ever saw; very cold in her general manners; but when she laughed or entered into the spirit of our gaiety which was very often, she seemed to be the life of the party— She would romp or dance and partake of all the jokes like one of us and she was perfectly adored by the family— The Col's manners you perfectly remember were irrisistable and we seldom sat down to our favorite Suppers without him—

Thus years rolled on and we were too happy to think of the lapse of time—
In the Summer the Col and my father took a house between them at Brighton
where we lived together six weeks but the air disagreed so much with my
Mother we were obliged to leave it and we all returned to Town together—

Mrs. Smith was one of the most really amiable women I ever saw, and
under the appearance of coldness and reserve was very affectionate in her
disposition— She became very much attached to my Sister Frye during her
residence in England, and I believe retained that attachment to her death— I
loved her then and still better after I became her Sister— At that period we
had little idea that such a circumstance could ever happen— We had changed
our Governess in consequence of the encrease of the family of our french
one; who however lived in our neighbourhood and was an object of constant
interest as well as expense to the family— My Brother left England for America under the protection of Major [*William*] Jackson and Mr [*Thomas*] Francis; my father fearful lest he should imbibe european Notions was anxious to
give him an American education and thus fit him to live among republicans
a thing very difficult to people who have lived in the European cities as I
have found to my cost; for a Republick in theory and a Republick in practice
are two essentially different things as many wiser people have found as well
as myself— It was in the autumn that Mr. Jay came over to make the Treaty.

*George Washington sent John Jay to England in the spring of 1794 to negotiate
an Anglo-American commercial treaty and to attempt to address the many issues that remained unresolved following the 1783 Peace of Paris. Jay concluded
the negotiations on 19 November 1794, and the treaty, which became known as
the Jay Treaty, was sent back to the United States for approval and signature
shortly thereafter. Jay himself remained in London with his family until the
following spring.*

*Around the same time, in late October 1794, John Quincy arrived in Lon-
don with his brother Thomas Boylston, en route to The Hague. John Quincy
was going there to take up his appointment as U.S. minister resident to the
Netherlands—his first diplomatic assignment. Thomas Boylston would be
serving as his secretary.*

As I write without attention to dates many errors will be found in my relation of events as to the exact time of their occurrences: but until the eara of

my marriage or rather my engagement; time flew on unheeded and as I never knew what trouble was I had no data to make a strong impression on my mind— This is the real blessing of happy youth, and alas it vanishes while we are insensible of its enjoyment—

Mr Jay as I have before said came to England and while he was there Mr Adams and his Brother Tom arrived in London on their way to Holland. Col & Mrs. Smith had returned some time to America— Mr Jay and your father and Uncle were invited to dine with us the latter were to leave England immediately, and they were asked on account of the former acquaintance of the two families when your Grandfather was Minister in England— Your father was engaged: but your Uncle dined with us and so far were we from dreaming of a future connection in the family that from some strange fancy my Sister Nancy nick named your Uncle Abel and of course the brother whom we had never seen was called Cain. I mention this merely to show how little idea or desire there was in the family to plot or plan a marriage between the families— I also had a nick name in consequence of my habit of warning my Sisters if any thing was likely to go wrong; they called me Cassandra because they seldom listened to me until the mischief was done— My Sisters both possessed great vivacity and much playful wit; and every person who visited in the family were either objects of admiration or severity—

Col Trumbull [*Jay's secretary*] was our constant visitor and as a man old or young who visits frequently in a family of young Ladies must be supposed to be in love; I was selected as the object of his partiality. He was old enough to be my father I was therefore very much at my ease with him, it never entering into my imagination that he could think of me but as a favorite child— This I knew he did for he took every opportunity to mark the distinction between myself and my Sisters— He gave me some instruction in painting but I was a poor pupil and did not profit as much as I should have done from so good a preceptor— Once in his life he said he wished he was a young man for *then* he should certainly pay his addresses to me; and this was the utmost that ever passed between us that could be tortured into love or what we fashionably term a belle Passion— In consequence of our being at Mrs. Churchs the first Evening that Mr. Jay and his Son [*Jay's nephew, Peter Jay Munro*] and the Col was introduced he also bore another name among us Girls— The Servant a frenchman announcing them as Mr Pétéràjay and Col Terrible— You may suppose this was too good a joke to lose and it attached itself to them as long as they remained in England—

If I ever had any admirers no woman I can assure you ever had fewer lovers than your Mother— In all this time not a shadow of an offer was made to either of us excepting Mrs. Frye, who refused Mr Buchanan the Gentleman who afterwards married— My Sister Hellen had got over her penchant for Mr. Jennings [*an American student in London*] as all the news we received concerning him proved him utterly unworthy of her affection; and the scandalous chronicle had so thouroughly affiched [*publicized*] his vices that it was impossible to regret his loss— That there was much truth in these reports I have since had reason to know for all his prospects were blighted by his conduct and his chief support has been the favour of the wealthy married Lady who seduced him. We were too entirely happy to make marriage a *want* and we only looked forward to it as an evidence that we were not devoid of those attractive qualities which generally are the operating causes of affection in such connections; more especially as my father had always told us that the fortunes he would be enabled to give would not be large enough to prove a motive for an offer— We were constantly taught to believe that we should have five thousand pound Sterling a piece; and so thoroughly was my father convinced of possessing this Sum, that even when all his calamities came so suddenly upon him; he still believed could he have found one single friend in his distress that his children would be amply provided for—

It was about this time that a Gentleman called on my father a small neat looking man in a very handsome chariot with livery Servants &ce. He walked into the Office entered into conversation very agreeably and then presented some papers to my father which concerned some American business to be done before the Consul— My father returned the papers for signature and stood to see the name when to his utter surprize he discovered that it was the Traitor [*Benedict*] Arnold, and he deliberately took up the *pen* with the Tongs and put it into the fire— The gentleman sneaked off endeavouring not to notice the act— This trait will give you a real insight into your Grandfathers character— He was a perfect Gentleman in his manners and universally respected— The American Sailors adored him and his house was their refuge on all occasions— Noble in his sentiments; noble in his Acts; he was ever ready to befriend the unfortunate, and his temper was so open and confiding he soon became the victim of fraud and hypocrisy—

Mr. [*Walter*] Hellen was sent to America as his Agent, and his Commissions amounted to three thousand dollars a year; my father relied upon him to collect the moneys due to him and to settle all his concerns independent of the partnership with Wallace & Muir— This was not done to his advantage but to the astonishment of many who knew that his Agent was dependent on him, Mr. H. came out as a Merchant with a handsome capital having Ships &ce without any visible cause for his prosperity. At the same time the partnership was dissolved by mutual consent and terms entered into with all the Creditors for a settlement of their debt— It was their wish that my father should have come over to this Country in person and left my Mother and some part of the family in England as hostages— Happy would it have been for him could he have done so. The Ship was prepared for his departure and every thing was ready but my Mother could never be persuaded to consent to it— She had never been separated from him and the responsibility attached to the care of so large a family was too great for her nerves— To this however all my beloved fathers misfortunes must be attributed as all the Lawyers whom he had employed assured him that his presence was essential to prevent the utter destruction of his property in the hands of Mr. Muir, who was even then attempting to embezzle the profits of the concern— My poor Mother has been severely reproached for this act by those who ought to have treated her with Respect; but if we consider her situation, many allowances must be made for her. The charge of so many young women to whom any connection in England was positively forbidden; who were never permitted to be out of sight a moment was not easy; and had any misfortune happened she would have been too great a sufferer—

In October 1795, John Quincy, still U.S. minister resident at The Hague, was asked to travel from the Netherlands to London to exchange the ratifications of the Jay Treaty. The trip proved fruitless in one respect: the ratifications had been exchanged by the time John Quincy finally reached England. But his visit to London had unexpected benefits. There he met the young Louisa at her father's home on 11 November and quickly began courting her. As Louisa relates below, his overtures were apparently subtle enough that Louisa, her sister Nancy, and their mother were not entirely sure which sister he favored. But by February

1796, he had made his feelings for Louisa known publicly, and they subsequently became formally engaged.

In the Autumn of this year Mr Adams was introduced by Col Trumbull. The first Evening he supped with us he was in high spirits conversed most agreeably and after he retired all the family spoke well of him. His dress however produced some mirth as it was completely dutch and the Coat almost white— Col Trumbull was to leave town immediately after for France he being concerned in some speculation in which he was principal actor— He joked us and said Mr Adams was a fine fellow and would make a good husband but his dress did not impress us agreeably as it made his person appear to very great disadvantage and Col Smith was the great model that we young Ladies most admired—

After this introduction Mr Adams came frequently to see us and as his devotions were supposed by every body to be paid to my Sister Nancy we all became very intimate and I rattled on quite unconcerned on the subject— He was a great favorite of my Mothers but I do not think my father admired him so much— He always had a prejudice towards the *Yankees* and insisted that they never made good husbands. When Mr Adams passed the evening with us my Sister and myself were regularly called upon to play and sing to him which we did for two or three hours. My father never would retire to his chamber without requiring what he called the same indulgence and it in fact became a habit almost as regular as our meals— I never observed any thing in Mr Adams's conduct towards me that indicated the smallest preference but used to be surprized some times at his dislike of some of the songs which I used to sing— All those which he knew to be favorites of Col Trumble were so disagreeable to him he would immediately take his hat and bid us good night when I began one of them. Hearing that he was a poet I told him that I expected he would write me a Song— This was a subject of perpetual banter between us and as I have before said being convinced by the observations of many Gentlemen that visited the family besides bets which were made on the subject that my Sister was the object of his preference and being likewise aware that she thought so I never dreamt of the possibility of drawing on myself his attention or regard—

You will probably think this was a great degree of stupidity or simplicity whichever you may please to term it but it is the sacred truth and it proceeded from the habit of thinking myself less attractive than my Sisters owing in part to the consequence which my father always gave me and which I could only account for in a manner not flattering to my personal vanity however agreeable on the score of mind— In addition to this my Sisters had even assumed a tone of superiority towards me which had contributed to produce a constant doubt of my power to please— My Mother was always talking to me of my awkwardness my father of my bashfulness my Sisters made me the block on which all their fashions were tried and in this way I was constantly exposed to the ridicule of the whole— Indolence of disposition and a settled indifference made me careless of every thing and music and reading were the only things in life I thought worth living for excepting to laugh at all the oddities which fell in my way—

As an evidence of my silliness one day when we were going to a Ball my Sisters sent for a very fashionable hair dresser and as usual there was some difficulty about who should be dressed first. My Sister Nancy whose influence was irrisistable pursuaded me to sit down— At all times this hair dressing was perfect torture to me and I generally fainted before it was done but this unlucky day I supported the torture with great philosophy entirely unconscious of what was going on— When the curl papers were taken out the hair dresser announced that he was going to dress me en téte de Mouton [*in sheep's head*] and you may conceive my horror when I found all my hair cut short and curl'd close to my head in imitation of a sheeps wool and powdered quite white and both my Sisters laughing as if they would kill themselves at the beautiful appearance I made. My mortification was extreme for I was very fond of being well dressed but there was no remedy for the evil and bon gré mal gré [*for better or worse*] I was obliged to submit to the evil. Circumstances of this kind had however often happen'd I resolved no more to be the but. This matter occurred long before the period at which I am arrived but my eldest Sister always took delight in adorning Caroline and never even on my wedding day would in the smallest degree assist my toilet— But what where these troubles of an hour fleeting and evanescent as a morning dream leaving no trace behind—

I think it was in the month of november that we first saw Mr. Adams. Time flew on its lightest pinions and I looked not beyond the hour.— I rattled and laugh'd then heedless of harm and never dreamt of change— Matters went on thus for two or three months my father, my mother and all my friends being persuaded my Sister was the object of your fathers visits: when one evening at Supper he handed a paper across the table to me saying it was the song he had promised and I immediately opened it and began to read out; when Miss Henning the children's governess who sat next me whisper'd to me to stop and took it out of my hand— This as you may believe caused me to blush and behave like a fool; and as I have often since thought stamped a meaning on the verses which Mr A. never intended to give them, and which I never should have dreamt of had it not been for the act of that Lady, which for many days put the whole family into confusion— Long did I contend against the possibility of such an affection existing in the heart of your father—for but this woman argued so strongly that she had discovered it all the winter and that had foreseen how it would end that my vanity was enlisted and without a particle of affection. At the time I suffer'd myself to be coaxed into an affection that lasted probably much longer than would have done love at first sight— The winter roll'd over we were engaged and on the 12 of Feby. as usual my father allowed me to give a Ball and at this ball Mr A. first made his attentions decidedly publick which brought much trouble on my head; as both my Sister and Miss Church were my rivals, and they contrived to make me suffer so severely that even my first lesson's in the belle passion were pretty thickly strewed with thorns— Love seemd to chill all the natural hilarity of my disposition, and those hours which had been spent in cheerful mirth were passed in gloom and anxiety in a sort of consciousness of some thing wrong without knowing to find the error— Shun'd by my Sisters, the unforgiving silence of Nancy made me wretched, and it required all the entreaties of Miss Henning to prevent my telling Mr Adams how I was situated—

In the Spring we made a party to go to Ranelagh [*Gardens*] and Mr. Adams was to accompany us— I had jokingly told him that if he went with us he must dress himself handsomely and look as dashy as possible—not aware that on this subject he was very sore, and that some enemy of mine had made him believe I laugh'd at him. The night previous to the party he took leave very coldly and desired if we went that we should call for him at the Adelphi [*Hotel*] on our way, as he had engagements and could not see us sooner to which we readily agreed. Accordingly we took him up at the Adelphy and I obser'd immediately that he was very handsomely dressd in blue that he had a large Napoleon hat and altogether looked remarkbly well.

As I had dressed myself very becomingly as I thought both my Sisters and myself being exactly alike we drove off in high spirits expecting a delightful evening. On entering the Rotunda our party naturally separated and Mr A offered me his arm and while we were strolling round the room I complimented him upon his appearance at which he immediately took fire, and assured me that *his* wife must never take the liberty of interfering in those particulars, and assumed a tone so high and lofty and made so serious a grievance of the affair, that I felt offended and told him that I resign'd all pretensions to his hand, and left him as free as air to choose a Lady who would be more discreet. I then drop'd his arm and join'd my mother with whom I staid the remainder of the evening—

On our way home apologies were made and accepted but if lovers quarrels are a renewal of love they also leave a sting behind which however apparently healed reopens on every trivial occasion; and the smart frequently felt inspires the mind with a secret and unknown dread of something hidden beneath the rosy wreath of love from which we would in vain turn our thoughts; but which like the faint sunbeams through a dense fog only produce a momentary gleam of light to make the darkness which surrounds us still more impenetrable. Such is the obscurity which envelops a young mind under the influence of a first affection; the momentary flashes of reason which lead us to look to futurity are too evanescent to light us on our way, and only produce those weak and imperfect presentiments which inspire fear of some unknown and overhanging evil without guiding to the point by which the danger threatens— Thus it was with me there was a sense of unnecessary harshness and severity of character presented to my view which often led me to fear something I knew not what, and cast a damp upon my natural spirits which I never overcame— I loved with all the affection of a warm and untried heart, and the trials I underwent in the disatisfaction of a sister with whom I had always lived in love and harmony, taught me to reflect and to judge myself with sincerity and I often thought all had not been towards her as I could have wished—

The time arrived for Mr. Adamss departure to Holland and he took leave of me stating that our engagement was for an indefinite term and he could name no period at which our marriage would probably take place: and desired that I would correspond with him. He recommended to me during his absence to attend to the improvement of my mind, and laid down a course of study for me until we met, which might be in one year or in seven— I urged him to give me a right to his name before he left me as I always had a horror of the banter and jests to which a young woman is exposed who is known to be engaged; and wish'd that he would have the marriage take place just before he left the house and leave me at my fathers, for I knew no happiness out of his house— You will smile my children and think this very romantic but I had the idea in my head that as the principal reason assign'd for our marriage not taking place was the then state of Holland, that as soon as things in that Country were sufficiently settled I could have join'd my husband without impropriety, and not have had the constant dread on my mind of being obliged to accompany my father to America, and thus add to the difficulty and lengthen the distance which was already between us.

I dwell on all these perticulars because however innocent my conduct and my thoughts; circumstances arose in the course of a few Months which gave a colour to every incident which blighted all my after happiness; and gave a cast to my mind and character which amounted almost at times to a derangement of understanding— I shall never forget the anxiety with which I awaited a letter from Mr. Adams and the terror which assailed me at the idea of answering it.— I felt my folly and my insignificance with a degree of inexpressible mortification and I vainly endeavoured to write. My officious governess however undertook to correct my letters and to give them such a tournure as she thought would be most elegant— It is true I was not young enough to need such assistance, but never having had a correspondent and at school having always undergone this process, I was too much afraid of trusting to my own performance to venture to write any thing without her approbation— Our correspondence once begun was continued very steadily; but although I counted the hours that must elapse ere letters could arrive, when they came they oftener caused me the most undefined and uneasy sensations than pleasure, and I faded in health and appearance so rapidly that my father became alarmed and without my knowledge in the fullness of his affection and earnest anxiety for my happiness, sat down and wrote a letter to Mr. A. in which he represented my situation; and offered as he had business in holland which required his attention to go over himself with me and my Mother, that we might be married and I be restored to health and happiness— His intention was to have left England altogether to return to his own Country. I never saw this letter but I so well know my beloved fathers heart and principles that I am perfectly convinced it was written under the impulse of the most honourable feelings; and if he overstep'd the most rigid bounds of delicacy, it was only occasioned by those best of all human feelings the ardent hope of promoting the happiness of a child so dear to him— By return of Mail he received an answer so severe, so cold and so peremptory, that his feelings were bitterly wounded and all the pride of my nature was roused. I adored my father and I was proud— For the first time I gave way to my feelings and I wrote without assistance. I scorn'd the trammels I had borne with for I felt all and more than I could say— So many many years have elapsed since that period that I have forgotten how the matter terminated but once more every thing went smooth—

At the time these events took place I was utterly unsuspicious of evil, and every appearance as I have long since learnt was against me. My prospects in life appeared so fair I never dreamt of any thing that could arise to give a colour to improper motives, and I went on in the path I had adopted with all the guileless simplicity of unsuspecting and fearless youth— I had attain'd to the age of twenty but in knowledge of the world I was not fifteen— My husband was the first and only man with whom I was ever left alone or who ever dared to take a liberty with me and *he* never till after our engagement was sanction'd by my parents— If there is any thing to be proud of in such a boast I can swear before the living God that I came pure and virtuous to his arms, and that to this hour I have remained so; and that though the scorpion tongue of political slander assailed me ere I had been a wife a year; my Sons may look up with proud and unsullied honour to the mother who bore them who as far as chastity goes was pure as the azure of an unclouded sky. This is no boast as 'tis the boast of thousands of my sex— I had nothing to resist, I was without temptation—

George Washington arranged for John Quincy's promotion to U.S. minister plenipotentiary to Portugal some months prior to John Adams's election to the presidency in late 1796. Shortly after John Adams took office in March 1797, however, he changed the appointment, sending his son to Prussia instead. Around the same time, the Johnson family decided to leave England for the United States, ostensibly to allow Joshua Johnson to attend to business matters in Maryland. Rather than be separated for even more time, and with John Quincy now feeling he had reached a financial status sufficient to allow him to support a wife, he and Louisa agreed to marry in London in July 1797. The Johnsons left for America a short time later.

But the Johnsons' departure proved the beginning of new troubles for the young Adamses. Joshua Johnson had defaulted on various debts and left England with numerous creditors demanding satisfaction. John Quincy was forced to respond to these requests, and Louisa was deeply traumatized by what she believed to be the unfair labeling of her father as a debtor and possibly a fraud. She would be haunted by these events for the remainder of her life—convinced that John Quincy blamed her father for the loss of her dowry and for her family's financial disgrace—and would return to it frequently as a subject of her writings in the years to come.

It was during the Spring that Mr Adams wrote to announce his appointment to Lisbon and to request that I would be ready to receive him that our Nuptials must take place immediately after his arrival as he could only spare a few days to me and my family as he must proceed to his post without losing any time. Several letters came on the same subject and my Mother began to prepare my wedding finery which was all got ready for the expected occasion. Weeks rolled on however without any further intelligence and considering it as a false alarm every thing was locked up and all the preparations concealed with as much care as if I had committed some crime in having made them. Time ran on until July when Mr A again wrote to beg my father to procure him a passage on board some vessel bound to Lisbon, and repeating his desire that he might not be detained in London— My father and I understood him literally and he accordingly fitted up a small vessel of his own with every thing that could make us comfortable to take us to Portugal whenever it suited Mr. Adams's convenience. He arrived and owing to some trifling accident on his route could not come to see me until the day after when I met him with feelings of mortified affection more bitter than I could express; and with a dread at the idea of my immediate parting with my parents that almost broke my heart. Under all the impressions so strongly received by his Letters and wishing that some days after I became a wife might be passed with a mother from whom I had never been separated; when he asked me to fix a day for our marriage I named a very early one without hesitation; naturally supposing that it was what he most desired. I dwell on the topic my Sons to show how the most simple acts may bear upon future events even when we cannot look into futurity, or in any way imagine the good or bad fortune which may be about to assail us—

At this moment every thing seemed to combine to make my prospects brilliant— My father had entered into the most favorable arrangements with his creditors and was allowed to fit out a Vessel to convey his family home; he was to return in two years to England to wind up all the business of the house, and he expected to give each of his children a small fortune and to retire himself upon a handsome property without owing any man a shilling— We became acquainted with Mr T[homas] B[oylston] A[dams]— who accompanied his brother who soon won the hearts of all the family. On the Wednesday 26 of July 1797 I became a bride under as every body thought the happiest auspices— I must here observe that my mother expressed her surprize at my having fixed so early a day and rebuked me for not having consulted her; and I felt ashamed at the idea of being thought so indelicate the more so as it seemed to me upon reflection that Mr. A appeared surprized also— Two days I think it was before I was married we went on board the Vessel to see our accomodations and I think soon after Mr. A. received Letters not to go but to wait for further orders and the Vessel sailed without us—

Two happy weeks passed swiftly away, when suddenly I was overwhelm'd by a blow that prostrated my pride my pretensions I will say my happiness for ever— The man who had pretended to be my fathers best friend, in whom he had confided his trust for five and twenty years, brought the heaviest calamity on his head and stamp'd a wound upon that heart and that honour, which through life had been proverbial for rectitude— He was obliged to stop payment for the sum of *five hundred pounds* in consequence of the failure of a remittance, and the non arrival of a large East India ship, and to quit the Country with his family in a very different manner and under very different circumstances than he had ever expected— Conceive my Dear Sons the shock I underwent, every appearance was against me; actions proceeding from the most innocent causes looked like deliberate plans to deceive; and I felt that all the honest pride of my soul was laid low for ever— I removed to your fathers lodging and too forcibly learnt that I had forfeited all that could give me consequence in my husbands esteem or in my own mind— No vindication could be offered on my part; appearances were too much against me; and all I could do was to mourn over that which could never be undone and which could only be aggravated by any effort to prove its falsity— In this I will say extremity of affliction; my mind seem'd rapidly to grow old and the bitter knowledge of real life was acquired in almost all its varied forms of agony and mortification— Never have I, never can I blame Mr. Adams for his feelings on this trying occasion, for I felt that thus situated my impressions would have been too strong to admit of either doubt or paliation; for he found himself exposed to a situation full of difficulties and as he thought disgrace and utter disappointment: from that hour all confidence was destroyed for ever in me and mine— My marriage was not gay as acquaintance was very limitted; but the very exertions my poor father made to do us honour were afterwards set down to shameful extravagance—

Mr. R[*ufus*] King was then Minister in London but had left Town on a journey to Wales. I think he did not return until after my family had left England. He was so good so friendly had he been near perhaps this overwhelming ruin had been spared and I save from the pursuit of a phantom which has unceasingly followed me through every stage of life and which will follow me until the heart then so deeply wounded has ceased to throb— Never never as long as sense shall last shall I forget the worse than brokenhearted look of my adored father the last Eveng he passed with me in my own house: my poor Mother too I was not aware that they were to leave me so soon; but ere morning broke they had already left that Country in which all his children were born, and in which he had so long lived honoured and respected— When I arose and found them gone I was the most forlorn miserable wretch that the Sun ever smiled upon— I loved your father with the utmost sincerity but I learnt too quickly in spite of his utmost exertions, & how low I was sunk in his estimation without a hope of ever recovering the standing which was irreparably lost. It was strict and rigid justice and I had nothing to complain of— Such was my honey moon. I was found to be incompetent to the management of the family concerns: and they were put into the hands of Mr [*Tilly*] Whitcomb [*the Adamses' servant*]— Every rap at the door made me tremble as every rap produced a dun to my father; and to me they appealed for payment believing that my father had left the means with me to settle them: and to crown my sufferings a Letter of the most barbarously insulting character was put in to my hands calling on my husband to save my fathers forfeited honour.

In the midst of such really heavy afflictions I had no one to turn to but Mrs. Court an old friend of my family who by her unwearied kindness saved me from despair. Your Uncle Tom was kind and affectionate and to him I opened my heart and assured him of perfect innocence. As soon as Mr. King returned he came to see me and from him and his Lady I received all the consolation that could be offered under such circumstances— Until we quitted England my time was chiefly spent at Mrs. Courts when I could go out; but my Health was dreadfully impaired and I was in a situation in which there was little probability that it would mend— Two days after my fathers departure the fatal remittance arrived and the villain [*John*] Maitland bribed the bookeeper in my fathers Counting house to give it to him which he did and thus took the sum which had been destined to settle all my fathers current debts; every one of which it would cover— Thus things rolled on until our destination was changed and we were ordered to berlin—

CHAPTER TWO

"An Object of General Attention"

Prussia

Following their marriage, Louisa and John Quincy left London for Berlin, where John Quincy was due to take up his post as U.S. minister plenipotentiary to Prussia. The couple sailed from Gravesend aboard the Danish ship Frans on 18 October 1797, landed in Hamburg on 26 October, and continued overland to Berlin, the Prussian capital, arriving on 7 November. Before they could leave London, however, John Quincy had to continue to address the fallout from Joshua Johnson's financial collapse and removal to the United States. All of these events are covered in the final section of Louisa's "Record of a Life."

Accompanying the couple to Berlin was Thomas Boylston, John Quincy's brother, who had been secretary to the legation during John Quincy's entire term as minister at The Hague. Louisa had met Thomas Boylston briefly when he and John Quincy passed through London on their way to the Netherlands in the fall of 1794, but this was her first opportunity to become better acquainted with yet another member of the Adams family. Because Thomas Boylston later served as chief justice of the Massachusetts Circuit Court of Common Pleas, Louisa occasionally refers to him in these writings as "the Judge." As she describes below, Thomas Boylston was of considerable assistance to the young bride, who found herself ill prepared to serve as a diplomat's wife at a foreign court.

Owing to a long detention at the Duke of Portlands [*British home secretary*] we did not reach Gravesend until after the Vessel had sailed and though late in the Evening we got into a boat and rowed some miles down the river to overtake her and I got on board just in Season to get to bed being very sick— Here we began to breathe more freely— Objects of novelty to me occupied my attention and the affectionate kindness of your father and Uncle once more cheered my drooping spirits and warm'd my sinking heart into something like hope. Amid all my distresses it was delightful to me to think I had incurred no new obligation for to my knowledge not a shilling was ever paid on mine or my father's account therefore the injury which Mr. A received by his marriage with me was the loss of the five thousand pound which my father had intended to give me and the having connected himself with a ruined house— When I first engaged myself to Mr. Adams I think my father had not lent his name to the speculation into which Mr. Maitland had plunged. At any rate he had entered into no responsibility therefore their could have been no intention on his part of palming his daughter upon any one and his misfortunes were as unexpected as they were sudden— Never as long as I have being will I cease to defend your Grandfathers character from the foul aspersions of those who have accused him and no sense of after obligation can ever obliterate the pain I have endured when I have been forced to hear them—

We had embarked in a Danish Ship which fortunately for us was heavy enough to stand the tremendous storm which assailed and in which the Packet was nearly lost the Passengers being obliged to pump the Vessel during the whole of the voyage. Our Bark weathered the tempest and we crept on with a snails pace and after eight days hard sailling reach'd the port of Hamburg— Our stores were excellent and we at least had the privilege of living well as far as good eating goes— Every Evening and morning the Crew were rung to prayers and it was in this vessel that I first saw in practice the dutch eoconomy in the use of Sugar. There was a piece of white sugar Candy tied to a string which was passed alternately to each who suked it and then sipped the tea. We took up our residence at Hamburg for a week or ten days having to prepare our Carriage for the journey and here I became acquainted with [U.S. consul] Sam Williams his brother Frank and Mr. [Charles] Ross.—

We received several visits I went once to the Theatre and I passed the day at Mr David Parish'es then English Consul and immensely wealthy— His Country house was very prettily situated on the banks of the Elbe and both he and his wife were kind and hospitable scotch people whose manners were such as to make you feel like old acquaintance after a visit of half an hour— Hamburg is a dreery looking City the Streets very narrow and the houses like described by travellers in Edingburg of many stories high— They are dirty and gloomy and the narrow canals which intersect some of the streets have a dirty gloomy and disagreeable appearance— One [*of*] the peculiarities which struck the most unpleasantly was the spouts which lead from the tops of the houses to carry off the water. As they nearly meet in the centre of the street the rain is conducted in distinct channels from the Roofs and produces a continuation of streams which falling from such an elevation cause a horrible sound of rushing waters which look at the same time like a threatening deluge—

Our time passed agreeably enough and we left Hamburg in company with Mr S Williams Mr. Ross and the party who commenced the journey from England. What creatures of prejudice and circumstance we are and how seriously trifles sometimes affect us— You will laugh at me as much as I now laugh at myself but when my liveried footman was ordered to take a seat in my Carriage with me I felt as if the greatest insult had been offered to me and set it down as another consequence of the downfal of my family— An American can never understand the sensation of mortified pride which I endured but an Englishman would blaze at the idea and you must remember that even my father had never seen America since she had become a Republick. Our journey was dreadful the accomodations as bad as possible and the roads such as to make our Carriage a very dangerous conveyance and we were very thankful when we arrived at the beautiful City of Berlin as we had not met with one object of interest on the route— Berlin is a beautiful City and as we took up our residence at the most fashionable hotel in the Linden Strasse we had a constant opportunity of seeing the best part of this famed City—

Louisa was pregnant by the time she reached Berlin, but shortly thereafter she suffered a miscarriage—the first of many over the next twenty-five years. The details of Louisa's medical history are elusive, but her own writings make clear that she had considerable trouble carrying pregnancies to term. Her repeated miscarriages and one stillbirth took an enormous physical and emotional toll, especially on Louisa but also on John Quincy, who keenly felt these disappointments.

In Berlin, Louisa found a number of close friends, including Miss Dorville, the daughter of the court's master of ceremonies, and Pauline Néale, one of the queen's maids of honor. Queen Louise, wife of the newly crowned King Frederick William III, took a particular interest in Louisa. She, in turn, thought that, in the queen, "every thing was combined that can shed loveliness on female beauty." Also part of the royal court were the princesses Henry (Wilhelmina of Hesse-Cassel), Ferdinand (Louise of Brandenburg-Schwedt), Louis (Frederica Sophia Carolina of Mecklenburg-Strelitz), and Radziwill (Frederica Dorothea Louise Philippine, sometimes called Princess Louise), all of whom were commonly called by their husbands' names.

A presentation at court was an important moment in a diplomat's life and that of his wife. Louisa describes below the complicated process she endured in Berlin to meet the king and the dowager queen, Frederica Louise. Once the introduction was accomplished, however, the person presented was then free to participate fully in court life—a necessary aspect of any successful diplomatic mission.

By contrast, the Brown family—Dr. Charles Brown, his wife (whose name is unknown), and their four children, Margaret, Isabella, Fanny, and William— British neighbors of the Adamses in Berlin, provided a happy, comfortable social alternative to the rigors of court activities.

The fatigue trouble anxiety of mind and sea sickness in the very delicate state in which I left London brought on a very serious illness and my life was despaired of for sometime. It is almost impossible to imagine a situation more truly distressing for a woman of refinement and delicacy than the one into which I was thrown— Just arrived in a foreign land only three months married having suffered in that short space of time every calamity through others which can afflict the human heart excepting the pang inflicted by death thrown into the society and on the protection of young men without a female friend but a young servant girl of seventeen who was as wretched as myself and lying in the most helpless condition from sickness and disappointment with every sense of delicacy shocked by the disgusting and to me indecent manners of the people who attended me and in a noisy and publick Hotel. Never before having been parted from a father and Mother to whom I had been a darling child and sick unto death!!! An English Physician was sent for and this I believe saved my worthless life— As I lay gasping on my rude bed of agony after eleven days of dreadful anguish I heard Mr T B. A come into the room and ask if I was dead.— As it was reported in the house that I had expired— This was a new and a cruel scene for Mr. Adams and called forth all his kindness and most gratefully do I remember his tenderness and his affection during a trial so severe— I recovered my health very slowly and I think (as I write from memory without notes or help) it was three long Months that elapsed ere I was able to take that rank in society to which I was entitled— In that period no ~~one~~ female visited me and though I constantly heard of Mrs. Brown and her daughters as the most amiable good people still they never came near me.—

During this Interval the King [*Frederick William II*] had died the present King ascended his throne his lovely Queen had been crown'd and Mr Adams and his brother had been presented at Court— We removed from the Hotel to a small House at the Brandenburg Gate. Were I writing a book of travels I should certainly endeavour to describe this splendid object which may be termed the pride of Berlin but as it is I will only say that I had taste enough to admire it although I knew nothing of its architectural proportions— Immediately under my Windows was the Guard room and few days nay even hours passed without my ears being assailed and my eyes shocked by the screams and blows which were bestowed on the soldiers who inhabited them, and my weak nerves were not strengthen'd by the constant repetition of this scene of suffering.— My husband was now launched into the sea of dessippation which followed the coronation and it was only owing to the kindness of Mr. T. B. Adams that my lonely hours were cheered by the pleasure of society— We kept no Carriage and as I have already said no female had yet paid me a visit— At last however I suppose from curiosity Miss Dorville afterwards the Wife of Mr. [*Francis James*] Jackson came to see me and she was [*followed*] immediately by the Countess Pauline Neale to whom I owe all the comfort and all the respect I ever enjoyed during my residence in that Country. Expressing my astonishment to her at the difficulty I found in making acquaintance she told me it was because I had not been presented and that the Queen had said unless I was presented soon that she should suppose I was not married— This was the first intimation I had had of the necessity Mr Adams never having suggested the propriety and I supposing in the then state of my feelings that it was owing to his mortification at his marriage that he did not wish to take me out— This however was a new and bitter stroke and I resolved to appear in publick—

A party was made to the Theatre the first Eveng. that the Sovereigns went there and I, poor I, as timid as a hare became an object of general attention— Never shall I forget with what inexpressible admiration I saw the

Queen of Queens— In her every thing was combined that can shed loveliness on female beauty— Grace affability sweetness amiability and the most irrisistable beauty formed a combination of loveliness to which no language can do justice and which the painters art never could depict— Years have elapsed and I still see her in my minds eye moving in all the majesty of youthful royalty and followed by the admiring gaze of thousands who thought themselves blessed if they could catch a passing smile or have a glance of her beautiful form.— This may be enthusiasm but if it is it is the honest enthusiasm of grateful affection for kindness received at the hands of this angel which can never be obliterated from my recollection while the life blood animates my frame.— Much have I seen in the lapse of fifty years which have dragg'd over my weary head but never before or since has an object so unique met my sight—

Arrangements were immediately made for my presentation and I waited on the Marquise Parella [*Sardinian minister's wife*] to request her to introduce me and to patronize me on my first entrance into society— My acquaintance Miss Dorville was one of the court belles and at that time very celebrated as a beauty tho' not for discretion— I understood from Mrs. & the Miss Browns who now called on me that this young Lady had given a most curious account of my person and manners and represented me as having a face like a horse and being very ugly— This was however no disadvantage to me as people being prepared to see something very disagreeable were more inclined to be indulgent when they found me pretty much upon a par with my neighbours— Madame Parella according to appointment carried me to pay visits to all the Grande Gouvernates of the different Courts which then consisted of the Queens the Queen dowager Princess Henry's Princess Ferdinands Princess Louis Princess Radzivils and the Princess of Orange. Cards were left at all the great houses and among the Corps Diplomatique. My good little friend the Countess Neale gave me instructions concerning the dress and I was finally prepared for the eventful day—

It was on a Sunday Eveng. that I was appointed to be at the Palace I think at about seven o'clock when I was usherred into the private apartments of her Majesty— My extreme debility and the terror incident to the novelty of my situation and the formidable appearance of Madame Voss in her great hoop and her tall upright person had such an effect upon me that I could not proceed as my knees seemed to refuse their Office and I trembled from head to foot— The Queen perceiving my great embarrassment and pitying my situation waived all ettiquette and came forward to speak to me kindly telling me how much she had been interested for my situation which she had heard of very fully from my physician. She asked me many questions in the most soothing tones and then observing my weakness and that I looked pale kindly dismissed me saying she hoped to see me again in the evening on which I curtsied and retired— I accompanied Madame Parella to the drawing room and was there presented to all the Corps diplomatique—

I was delighted to return to Mr Adams and his brother from whom I had been separated as they were my world and I felt utterly lost when without them— When the Queen appeared and the circle was formed she again spoke most kindly to me and I was formally presented to all the Princesses of the Royal family and met with a most kind and friendly reception. To the kind offices of my good Dr Brown and to my little friend the Countess I was indebted for my reception which was flattering beyond my most sanguine hopes.— The scene was so entirely new to me my senses were perfectly bewildered and when I was invited to stay supper and told that my husband could not stay I was distressed beyond measure. But the Marchioness Parella engaged to take me home and to sit next to me and in this way I was enabled to get through my difficulty— The Queen spoke to me several times during Supper with great sweetness and I was treated generally with the kindest attention— When I got home I had a great deal to tell as the novelty of the scene had exhilarated my spirits to a great degree and I thus afforded great diversion to both the gentlemen to whom these scenes had become quite familiar— From this time I was launch'd in the giddy round of fashionable life as successive invitations followed most of which were orders from the Courts as in strict ettiquette people are not allowed to refuse unless sickness prevents the acceptance.

Louisa ended her "Record of a Life" with a short description of some of the people she met in Berlin but carried the story no further. It was nearly fifteen years before she resumed her memoirs of her life in Berlin, this time in a work she named evocatively "The Adventures of a Nobody." Louisa began the project in July 1840 at age sixty-five, directing it to her only living son, Charles Francis, and his wife, Abigail Brown Brooks Adams. At the time, John Quincy was serving in Congress, and he and Louisa lived most of the time in Washington, D.C., with regular summer visits to Quincy.

Louisa wrote much of "Adventures" in a diary format, with substantial portions based on (and even copied from) her husband's private diaries, which he had maintained steadily since he was a young boy. Louisa, however, was considerably less methodical and precise in her writing than John Quincy; her datelines, especially for the first portion of the work, are sporadic, and her recollection of precise details sometimes questionable, though she vividly and accurately captures the spirit of events. As with "Record of a Life," Louisa never intended for "Adventures" to be published but rather meant it for the amusement and edification of her family.

I was pleased at the receipt of your last Letter my Dear Charles as from a recent one written by Abby I was led to believe that you could not spare time to write to me under the pressure of your business avocations. The Letter itself was therefore an agreeable surprize and its tone altogether gratifying being indicative of repose and contentment two things utterly and entirely out of my reach— My temper is so harrassed and I am I fear so imbued with strange and singular opinions, and surrounded by persons with whom it is decidedly impossible for me to agree, I feel that I am a torment to myself, and a still greater torment to your Father, who bears with me with the patience of Socrates; but who like Socrates glides smoothly on in the course which he has laid out for himself enjoying the turmoil, the very reflection of which is to me perfectly insupportable— Conscious as I am of all his fine qualities, his easy temper, his quiet home habits, and his indefatigable powers of application; I am for ever ashamed of my-self for suffering my heart to crave for some social comforts; some soothing influence to fill up the lagging hours, which at my age in consequence of weakened faculties, and want of *essential* resources; hang with a tedious weight upon my time, and leave me to a too vivid and too painful contemplation of the past: where infancy and youth were fraught with bliss in the bosom of strong and unchanging Parental affection—

The faults of my character have never been corrected, owing to a happy, but alas a visionary education; which have made the disgusting realities of a heartless political life, a source of perpetual disappointment—

It has been asserted that I am inordinately ambitious! In what the evidence of this fact consists, it would puzzle any body to say, if by ambition is meant the thirst for place and mere worldly honours— Of such honours most assuredly as the Wife of your Father, I have had a large share— But such *honours* have never been sought by me; on the contrary they have been purchased at a most *bitter* expence of duty to my children, personal suffering to myself; loss of health and freedom of thought; and with all the cruel and stinging mortification of National pauperism, which most of the Foreign Missions present at the Courts to which they are sent—and the effects of which fall most heavily upon the Women; who dependent upon their Husbands, are obliged to make every sacrifice of pleasure, and often of comfort, that the paltry Salary may prove adequate to the necessities of her husband, to enable him to appear with due *decorum;* to accomplish the Mission on which he is sent!

Louisa's memoirs make reference to the wide range of individuals active at the Prussian court in the late 1790s. Numerous princes and princesses, as well as diplomats from all over Europe, haunted the scene. The Prussian empire had become an important force in Europe under Frederick the Great in the mid-eighteenth century, and in the late 1790s it remained a significant counterweight to the influence of France and Russia. Nearly every major European power had a diplomatic representative in Berlin, one of the reasons the U.S. government was anxious to have strong representation there itself.

January 1798

My house was within a few doors of Dr. Browns—and with them we formed a most intimate and friendly acquaintance— All the English Strangers of distinction or respectability assembled there every Eveng. when there were no great parties, to partake of their bread and Cheese Suppers; and the whole entertainment and establishment was conducted upon the simplest, and what in this Country might be termed, the most really democratic footing: and their guests always returned with delight from the Courtly scenes of the great world, with renewed zest, to the enjoyment of this unaffected, friendly, and charming society—

Dr. Brown was a very handsome courtly gentlemanly man; in his own person highly aristocratic, and almost constantly in attendance upon the different Members of the R[*oyal*] F[*amily*]; with a very extensive practice among the Nobility and Gentry of the place— Showy in his manners, proud of his daughters, and fond of distinction; he was attentive and amiable to his patients; and generally esteemed and beloved— His Wife was a Welsh *lady*—accustomed to a Country life; I *think* but do not exactly recollect, the daughter of a Welsh Curate: her means of education had been very limited, and her superstition enlarged in proportion— She was the beau idéal of a good, honest, simple minded, kind hearted old Lady, of the old School; always decked in her close Cap, her dark Silk gown, her neat muslin neckkerchief, and her *apron*—always at home, busy with her housekeeping, or at her needle work; ready to hear the news, or to delight in the amusements of her girls; who she thought paragons, in their different lines of perfection— She would laugh continually at the impossibility of her ever acquiring the German language, and relate her mistakes with an irrisistible comic humour, that defied gravity, with all the simplicity of a Child—

One day having called in the morning, I found her with her Servant giving orders for her dinner; and she was repeating with earnestness, "that she wanted her to make a bitch and boy" to the great diversion of her daughters, who laughed till the tears rolled down their Cheeks: and at last translated pigeon pie into such German, as the Servant could understand— Many a time and oft have I laughed at my own equally comprehensive knowledge of the language; when necessity has compelled me to *affect* to know what I could not even understand; and wondered how I have been extricated from similar difficulties, in situations of actual necessity, at a later period of life— Margaret Brown was not handsome—though what is styled well looking— She was a very dark brunette, with sparkling black eyes and an expression too intellectual for feminine beauty: her education had been that of a youth, and her quick capacity, steady application, and retentive memory; had garnered large stores for future use more suited to a maturer age, than for the epoch at which we had become acquainted—; amiable but firm in her character, she was deficient in what is termed softness; though never course— Girls were afraid of her, and young men dreaded to converse with her, because they *felt* her superiority, and their

own insignificance— She was her fathers special friend, and counsellor—
her age 22.

Isabella was very handsome—also a brunette; but a perfect contrast to
her Sister: the hair and the eyes were a shade lighter; her features more
delicate, and the character of her countenance, and its general expression
was less intellectual, but much more pleasing; more especially as it corre-
sponded with the gentle and unassuming tone of her manners, adding interest to her timid and unobtrusive attractions— She was my particular and
devoted friend until her death; and while I write this little tribute of sincere
and long felt affection to her memory; the tear glistens in my eye while I
exclaim, "when shall I see her like again." Her Sister Fanny, but who could
describe Fanny!! She realized the Poets dream of golden hair, a complexion
of lilies and roses, fine features, eyes like the large and melting as the gazelle's;
of the softest blue; a head placed with beautiful symetry on her Shoulders,
and with the Hebe elasticity of joyous fifteen— The pet of the family, and
the admired of all— She was very amiable; and being in the first blush of life,
happy innocent and yet a child, was one of the loveliest girls I ever met with—
One handsome boy made up this charming family, with whom I passed the
happiest and most cheerful period during a sojourn of three years and a half
in the City of Berlin.

In old age we look on the past days of our youth, with a degree of rapture,
and howe're the sorrows of life may have assailed us: there is a cheering
hope that buoys us up in youth in spite of ourselves; to hail a future change
for the better— Forty two years and a half have elapsed since this period!—
and with the garulity of age, I dwell upon the picture in all its freshness; and
if it is tinted with *romance;* remember, that to me life was *new;* and with a
mind so depressed by the fate of my family of whose safety I had not even
heard; it was natural that the kind sympathy of such a family should have
produced emotions in my heart of both affection and gratitude.

My little friend Countess Pauline De Neale was not handsome, but full
of animation and ésprit, and perfectly amiable, with all the bonhommie and
sincerity of the German character— Well educated, and well read; a Maid
of honour at the Court of Princess Louisa; full of anecdote, and gaining
hourly experience in the busy world; she was to me a sort of Mentor ever
ready to instruct me in the usages and customs of high life, and to assist me
in the duties of its performance— Whenever we met she gave me an insight

into the characters that passed before us; and this peep behind the Scenes, was always amusing, beneficial, and instructive— Ever the same, we lived in perfect harmony; and many of my pleasantest hours were passed in her society both at home and abroad. Her Father and Mother treated me with the same constant kindness during my stay at Berlin—

Miss Dorville was the Daughter of the Maitre des Ceremonie of the Queens establishment; and as I have already said was a *beauty*. She was tall not very fair, had a good deal of easy assurance; and being *un peu* passé [*a little past (older)*] betrayed rather too great an anxiety to obtain a Matrimonial settlement; the great object of her ambition, to which however the English Ambassador Lord Elgin, the main object of the day, turn'd a deaf ear, and while elegantly trifling with her hopes, allured only to disappoint. Her features were prominent and of the roman Cast: but somewhat too masculine, and her air was altogether too *prononcée* to excite either love or respect— The Scandalous chronicle of the day was already busy with her fame, and many light jests were made at her expense; to which her after life unfortunately gave pretty strong credibility— Lord Elgin assured of his conquest, made a *bet* with some young Roué like himself, that he would invite a large party, and that *he* would present her with a pair of diamond Earings, on condition that she would allow him to kiss her in the presence of the whole company; to this she readily agreed, and went through the ceremony in the most gracious manner, and to the delight of his Lordship, and all the quizzers of Berlin—

As it is necessary to give you a Carte du Pays [*map*] ere we can complete our travels—I must introduce you to the Corps Diplomatique of that day, a Season prominent in history, as the close of the reign of William Frederick; and the beginning of a new era under the present King Frederick William— who so recently left this earthly Scene; and who if not the *greatest* King, was certainly one of the most suffering and the most worthy of the age in which he lived— I do not make this trifling eulogiem on selfish principles, although the distinction and kindness with which he treated me, during a residence of nearly four years calls forth my gratitude to his memory— Throughout the time of my residence there, his attention was unvarying and never failed to the hour of my departure in sickness and in health— I never saw him but on publick occasions— I owed all this to the effect produced by Mr. Adams who was universally liked—

Monsr Caillard was an old Gentleman formerly known to Mr. Adams in St. Petersburg; Minister from France— Baron Rozencrantz with a Wife who had for several years lost the use of her limbs—Minister from Denmark— The Marquis and Marquise Parella from Sardinia (not Naples) a little sprightly vulgur Italian, speaking but little french— Lord Elgin English; very handsome and equally presuming. Count and Countess Zinzendorf, Saxon, who had been residing there twenty two years; an excellent couple of the old School, stiff and formal as old Portraits; and with faces exhibiting about as much variety of expression— The Viscount Anadia of Portugal; fat, good humoured, and *half* agreeable— Baron Ompteda a man of doubtful reputation from Hanover. Count Panin and Lady of Russia; since become famous as one of the conspirators in the reign of Paul [*Tsar Paul I, assassinated in 1801*]— Baron Shultz von Ascheraden Sweedish Minister— The Marquis de Musquits Spanish; do Prince Reuss austrian—

I have already mentioned my presentation at Court to the Queen, at a private audience, and the numerous presentations at the Circle to the different Princesses. Our means being small, my dress was of course simple— It consisted of a pale blue Satin Robe, a white Satin Skirt, and the body and Sleeves trimmed with blond—my hair dressed and a couple of Ostrich Feathers—white Satin Shoes, kid Gloves, and a Fan— I was not worth an ornament, and such things would have been injudicious— The only article of the dress bought for the occasion being the Robe; my Father having supplied me handsomely with clothes suited to the calls of fashionable society— When Supper was to be served, to my utter consternation, I was to remain, and Mr. Adams was informed that to avoid questions of ettiquette, the Ministers never dined or Supped with the King— You can easily conceive my consternation when I found myself seated opposite to the King and Queen as a mark of honor shown to all Strangers of distinction; and obliged to converse, or rather to answer to the questions of their Majesties during the Meal. This Presentation took place on the 20th of Jany 1798.

The next day paid visits to all the *great* and their *seconds* in command; and thus was launched into a world altogether new to me, and little to my taste; being totally unfitted by circumstances, disappointments, character and education to fill a sphere so novel, and so unsuited to the station to which I was born, and to the *then* fortunes of my family—

23 January 1798

The Marchesa di Parella sent me word early this morning that the Queen Dowager would recieve me between 1 and 2 o'clock; and that I must *wear mourning*— Countess Neale my Maid and myself literally *basted* up a Dress; and although it barely held together while I wore it; by the aid of a long black Veil I was ready when the Marchésa called for me, and went through the audience with more success than could possibly have been anticipated: thanks to the affability of her Majesty, who received me with the kindest distinction— Conceive my astonishment at the sight of this singular looking old Lady— She wore *Widows* mourning; a Bombazine Robe and Skirt, trimmed with white Cambrick up the sides like *weepers;* the Collar and Cuffs and body to match— Her hair was scratched out on each side in the manner of my old picture, only more á lá crazy Jane; with a long String of splendid diamonds fastened up in the front, then brought into a deep festoon on each side upon the hair; and over this a black Crape Veil, falling to her feet— Being seated the effect was altogether extraordinary—and it was with the utmost difficulty that I kept my sérieux, with the dignity suited to the Wife of a foreign dignitary— When I got home the Judge laughed with all his heart at my recital of the Scene, and the gravity assumed by Mr A. who terribly dreaded some indiscretion on my part, could not controul our mirth— He was always kind as the most affectionate brother, and being less interested, was of course more indulgent to my follies or my griefs, than Mr. Adams; whose very anxiety for my success, rendered him uneasy, lest by some gaucherie I should fail—

24 January 1798

Went to sup at the Prince Ferdinands with Mr. Adams and his brother— reception of extraordinary kindness from the Princess; her daughter the Princess Radzivil, and the Landgravine of Hesse Cassel— The Princess Ferdinand was old, and her manners were rather abrupt— She invited me to sit by her, and began asking me how long I had been married? and how *old* I was? I told her, and she said she had not thought me *more* than sixteen— She then called across the room to the Prince Radzivil, a very handsome and gay young Spark; who had married her daughter a charming woman, but seven years older than her husband. "Prince Antoine venez ici!" [*Prince Antoine come here!*] He came up to her and I thought she was going to introduce him to me—but she fixed her eyes on my face and said to him, "regardè là, come elle et joliè?" [*look at her, how pretty she is?*] He laughed; but I was so *raw* I blushed Scarlet, and then she cried out "Ah! voyez la? comme elle rougit.—" [*Ah! do you see that? how she blushes.*] This capped the climax and I felt as if I should *cry* for very shame— The Landgravine saw my distress and kindly relieved me, by occupying the attention of both her Sister and the Prince; and from that hour took me under her peculiar protection, as long as I remained within the circle of her acquaintance— She was a superb looking woman, who had been very beautiful in her youth; and whose tastes appeared to be of a more simple and quiet order, than those of her Sister the Princess F——.

The Party was small; no dancing, and the Supper was plain and unceremonious— My little friend Countess Neale, with her Father and Mother contributed by every kindness to remove the restraint naturally experienced on such occasions, to a novice like myself, altogether unlearned in the way of Courts, and naturally timid among Strangers—in addition to which that most corroding idea, that I had entered Mr. Adams's family under circumstances so inauspicious, and apparently so unfavorable to my own character, who alas, was one of the proudest women existing; acted upon my mind as a bar to all happiness; tho' I have no doubt that it produced an excellent effect, by checking the natural love of admiration existing in all women accustomed to the flattery of mankind; and to the doting love of warm hearted Parents; who had always gazed on me with delight as the ideal perfection of beauty and loveliness—

At my age when all the illusions of youth are over, and when the contrast between what *once* was, and what *is*, is so self evident; there can be no vanity in relating mere facts of the past age, from which I can derive no benefit— In my own eyes I never possessed beauty; and yet strange to say, I was so familiarized to the idea of possessing it; that when I was often mistaken as I rode or walked for one of the most celebrated women in London, Lady Elizabeth Lambert; it never excited either surprize or vanity; as to my own eye there was no resemblance— Accustomed to consider both my Sisters superior to myself; surrounded by a beautiful growing family, and remarkably handsome Parents, it never appeared to me to possess intrinsic value; and though I ranked it high among the blessings which I had received from heaven, it seemed *too natural* to excite a puérile vanity in my mind— Haughty to excess my vanity was of a different character, and was not founded on so just a basis—

The qualities of the heart and of the mind, excited a higher aim; and a romantic idea of excellence, the model of which seemed practically to exist before my eyes, in the hourly exhibition of every virtue in my almost idolized Father; had produced an almost mad ambition to be like him; and though fortune has blasted his fair fame; and evil report has assailed his reputation; still while I live I will do honour to his name, and speak of his merit with the honoured love and respect which it deserved— As long as he lived to protect them, his Children were virtuous and happy—amidst poverty and persecution; and it is only those who have lost such a Father, that can measure, or re-alize the destruction which such a loss brings upon his Orphans— If when I have thrown off this mortal coil, one single virtue; one amiable or deserving quality should ever have found favour in the eyes of my children let them see, feel, and understand, that amid all the trials of a suffering life; all the afflictions, calamities, and disappointments which have assailed me; that it was *his* watchful eye, and his protecting care that developped and strengthened that little, but abiding good; which has preserved me from the snares of evil; the meretricious fascinations of gorgeous Courts; and the more trying intrigues, insults, and gross contaminations of political struggles; in the cause of heartless and soul corrupting Ambition—

Let this fact impress itself upon your hearts as it is not confined in its action to me, but to all the children who he lived to see grow up; on *whom* never was cast a reproach; one of whom lived and died in the performance of every virtue, as Daughter, Sister, Wife, and Mother [*Nancy Johnson Hellen*]; and another who in the exhibition of a long life in poverty, in affliction; in almost every trial of mind and body that can exercise the soul; has *proved* an example to her Sex in the practice of every virtue, that the purest christianity can exact [*Catherine Johnson Smith*]. It is forty three years since I became a Wife and yet the rankling sore is not healed which then broke upon my heart of hearts— it was the blight of every future prospect—and it has hung like an incubus upon my Spirit— It has been my reproach; but it has preserved me from temptation in this guilty world; and now at sixty five I can say to my Son; for my Children alone I valued reputation; and that through all my follies; all my inequalities of temper; that I have never commited in any sense an act, that should call a blush into their Cheeks for the conduct of their Mother, from the day of her birth to this hour— I had nothing but a fair reputation to bequeathe to them; and though in this Country such ideas are trivial, I have been differently schooled, and deem it a fair inheritance—

My next Sortie was to Princess Henry's; a very stiff old Lady who never went to Court, but always received at home— In consequence of a weakness of the Spine, she wore an iron collar, to support her chin and throat, which made her look like a stick—but her dress was so contrived with a quantity of Lace, as to conceal this appendage entirely— Hers were always Card parties, and immediately after my presentation I was siezed upon by two old Ladies and an old Officer to play Whist— Mr. Adams foreseeing the event, had furnished me with a Purse with some gold; timid, and a very indifferent player, the result was easily foreseen, and after fleecing me unmercifully; in despite of truth and justice, they made me pay for the lights and Cards; a perquisite as they said to the Maitre d'Hotel, and emptied my fine purse of its contents—

Just before Supper to which I was invited to stay without being able to say no; and without Mr Adams; I was introduced to Lord Levison Gower, one of the handsomest men in England about my own age, and Mr. Frere one of the most agreeable and the most talented men I ever knew— His Lordship was sent as Ambassador to congratulate the King on his accession to the throne—Mr. Frere Secretary— As his Lordship and myself were the two Presentations of the Evening, we were honoured with the Seats of distinguished Strangers, and I fear that neither the Ambassador or myself behaved with the dignity or propriety exacted on such an occasion: and the scene was altogether so novel to us, and so contrary to English usage; that Lord Gower and myself being equally struck with the *novelty;* became quite intimate; and having the liberty to talk in (to the company an unknown tongue) amused ourselves without hesitation with the Scene displayed before us— The Supper was termed elegant— It consisted of all the delicacies of the Season in lavish quantities: but the style of the service produced in us almost irrepressible mirth— Conceive of four huge joints of Meat roasted, and adorning the four corners of the table!!! With every thing else in proportion, on a table laid for thirty Persons—

Among the guest's there was an old Lady who seemed to fix the attention of my astonished neighbour; and he busied himself with counting the number of dishes of which she partook; during which time he was obliged to watch the Princess, so as to answer any question which she might put to *him;* and then *I* was to remember the number, while he did the same for me in my turn— He got up to *nineteen,* when the thing became so irrisistably ridiculous, we were thankful to rise from table, lest we should commit some gross bévue which would have stamped our ill breeding, and shocked the whole company— Fortunately the Princess was nearly blind; therefore escaped the sight of our nonsense. Mr. Adams was quite dismayed when I showed my purse; and we agreed that I should go as seldom as possible to Princess Henry's as I could not afford to lose, and could not avoid playing when there— The moment I appeared there the harpies would sieze on me; and whenever I was so unlucky as to stay, the same result was produced, and I was afraid to show the deficit in my purse made at an expence of all pleasure to me, and of real pain to my husband— Cramped as we were in our circumstances, these were heavy taxes, but unavoidable to the Station which we filled—

The first private party at which I participated was one at General Kunheims at which there were assembled between four and five hundred persons, among whom I found myself almost a stranger— Judge Adams accompanied us; and as he was as much a Stranger as myself, we naturally remained together while Mr. Adams mixed in the throng of Nobles, with whom he had become intimately acquainted— The Ball began with english Country dances, and the Judge led me out to make my dèbut— The dance was long and fatiguing, but I was so extravagantly fond of the amusement, that the Strangers were forgotten and he danced so well and with so much spirit, I was quite delighted— Prince Radziville then invited me; and Prince Vitgenstein for the next dances; and I had a succession of partners until two o clock in the morning—when I returned home perfectly exhausted— It was thus that the Judge made me the fashion—and I became a *Belle*—

Unsuited to a life of almost constant dissipation, these incessant parties became very irksome to me; and I availed myself of every opportunity of excuse, where public duty permited me to remain at home, without giving offence— A most social and agreeable intercourse existed between us and the Families of Count [*Karl von*] Bruhl, Dr. Brown, and Count Neale; and we met almost constantly without form or ceremony at tea, taking a Supper of the most simple kind, of cold provision, often of bread and Cheese (English) there deemed a great luxury— The House of Dr. Brown was the resort of all the English foreigners of distinction; and there we formed some of the most agreeable and distinguished acquaintances we have ever made, upon the easy terms of social familiarity; the only terms on which you can know the peculiar character of that Nation to advantage— The utter exemption from all the ettiquettes of idle pageantry; and the playful simplicity that pervaded the conversations, and amusements of the younger branches, were a source of continued enjoyment to the elders—and seemed to *youthify them,* while they participated in their innocent sports; and while I resided in Berlin; that house seemed the centre of attraction, as a relief from the formal monotony of the Courtly Assemblies; where

> Gewgaws shone with regal splendor
> and eyes of envy oped to wonder
> Not to approve fair beauty's smile
> But youthful innocence beguile—

the dazzling diamond seeming to posses a Circean charm, whose witchery could lure the passions of the young and lovely to their destruction—

We kept no Carriage as our stay was doubtful; but our Lodgings were so inconvenient in sickness; the Drums incessantly beating morning, noon, evening, and night whenever the Royal family or any Officer of Rank passed through the Gate; in addition to witnessing the corporeal punishment of the soldiers, without the possibility of avoidance; we sought and found a house a few doors from Dr. Browns in a fashionable and central quarter of the Town; but at a rent very unsuitable to our finances— Our Furniture was of course of the very plainest and cheapest description; and my good friend Mrs. Brown who was very plain spoken, taxed us with *meaness* sans cérémonie—

You will laugh at the minuteness with which I dwell on subjects apparently of little importance—but one of the objects of my writing this little history of past events, is to show you that *stations* that call forth the spleen, acrimony and jealousy of the multitude; are not the Bed of roses on which you may sleep, undisturbed by the scorpion care; but on the contrary they are *schools,* to teach forbearance, under the most bitter mortifications; and of perpetual and necessary privation in the midst of temptations, almost impossible to contend against— Few like your Father have resisted them, and persevered in a line of undeviating duty through life, with an unshaken purity and integrity beyond all praise; appreciated in every Country in which he has served, and from whom the highest tokens of respect and admiration have been loudly, unceasingly and honourably awarded— My love and respect for him was so unbounded; my keen regret at having become an added burthen to his cares so unpropitiously; my extravagant admiration of his superior talents, and his amiable character, had taught me to venerate his motives; though I often shrank from the severity of his opinions in passing judgment on others, less gifted than himself: and although the change in my life was *extreme;* taken from the midst of luxury, from a family who thought me almost,

"The faultless monster that the world ne'er saw"

and almost broken hearted, at the harshness of feeling elicited by their misfortunes, without the means of vindication, or the knowledge of the cause— the agony of believing myself suspected of connivance in knowing all the circumstance of my Fathers commercial difficulties; all bore upon my spirit; and bereft me of that greatest of all comforts; the talking of the absent, the joys of the past, and the fond affections which had blessed all the roseate hours of infancy— To condemn was impossible; and to destroy the gratitude and affection of years of unremited happiness, was equally impossible; and would have been unworthy: and nothing but the ardent affection I bore *him* made me think no privation too great, no mortification too severe, in mitigation of his disappointment— The mere loss of the very small property that I should have possessed I knew could not be the cause of so much bitterness— It must therefore have been the unfortunate *period* of my Fathers difficulties, owing to a protested bill; a misfortune to which every Merchant is liable in peculiarly hard times; that made the stroke so bitter; as his Station was sufficiently prominent to produce publick attention, and to shock his pride; and I am perfectly conscious that to a mind like *his* the wound could never he healed—

In Mr. Adamss Library we had a List Carpet; pine wood bookshelves; a mahogany writing desk, a second hand Sopha; and a few Chairs— My bed chamber had *no Carpet;* a Bedstead with white Cotton Curtains of the coarsest quality, bordered with a strip of Calico cut from a striped print; and made by myself, with window Curtains to match; a very common pine wood Toilet Table, with a muslin Cover; and an equally plain Toilet glass— No fire in the Winter; and half a dozen Chairs— The two drawing rooms I have already described one of these served for a dining room. They were very pretty—

Remember I was the *Wife* of a Foreign Minister, and daughter in law to the President of the United States—always addressed as your *Excellency,* and sometimes called *Princess Royal—*

Louisa's complaints about John Quincy's salary were common to American diplomats, who routinely received far less monetary support from the U.S. government than did ministers from other countries. Congress set government salaries and believed it was exercising republican frugality in keeping compensation for all government officials relatively modest. But most members of Congress had little understanding of the difference in cost of living between the United States and Europe, or the expectations for entertaining and appropriate dress placed on diplomats at royal courts. Still, Louisa was mistaken in her belief that John Quincy was particularly penalized. He had received a raise when he was promoted from minister resident to minister plenipotentiary and transferred from the Netherlands to Prussia, and would have received the same salary whether he was posted to Lisbon or Berlin.

May 1798

Mr. Adams now purchased a plain Chariot, and a pair of Horses; and my household now consisted of Whitcomb, my Maid [*Elizabeth*] Epps, who afterwards became his Wife; a footman, a housemaid, a Coachman, and a woman Cook—

My ill health was a perpetual tax upon Mr. Adams's feelings—but his kindness was unremited in promoting my comfort— The perpetual anxiety which he displayed however had a tendency to defeat his wishes, and to keep me in a state of disquietude beyond my strength— My nervous system became affected, and the slightest agitation produced the very consequences which he so constantly apprehended—

Happy indeed would it have been for Mr Adams if he had broken his engagement, and not harrassed himself with a Wife altogether so unsuited to his own peculiar character, and still more peculiar prospects.— When we were married every disappointment seemed to fall upon us at once— My health was already injured by the anxieties by no means trifling attending my engagement—and the change of destination was as unfavorable to my constitution as possible— The consequences of our detention were likewise much more injurious to *me* even than the Climate to which I was removed— For a long time Mr Adams in his Letters had urged me to be ready to accompany him at the shortest notice after the reception of his appointment to Lisbon; and had even informed me that a residence was already procured for us in that City, and I had been so accustomed to the idea; and these directions were so peremptory, that my Father had a Vessel prepared to convey us, which had been kept in waiting one Month so as to accommodate our removal— My wedding clothes had been prepared a *year,* and not an article was added to them when the event took place—so that there was ample time for deliberation, and for a thorough investigation into the character of my family, and my connections, which should prevent the possibility of deception: and I had had more than one misgiving as to the *fitness* of my *temper* to cope with the difficulties which presented themselves to my imagination—

Educated in england I had already discovered that our views of things were totally different in many essential points; and that there was a severity bordering on injustice in some of the opinions which I heard expressed; for want of a more enlarged acquaintance with the customs of my Country: and more especially with those peculiar to *my* Sex—and on some points alarming to a young and inexperienced girl, a sensitive fractiousness about the minor concerns of life, which might occasionally create serious uneasiness; and a rupture of our engagement had nearly taken place in which I had at least evinced sufficient spirit to prove, that my *affections* were not to be sacrificed to my pride, or to any desire of ambitious *exaltation*— Brought up a *republican* and living in a Monarchy; I had learnt to consider the boasted greatness of ephemeral dignity, from which most of the Ministers with Whom I had been acquainted, had either returned impoverished, or involved in debt; were not worth much: and my own father had suffered too much in the cause of his Country, to raise any very great expectation— An American Minister was to *me* a very small personage; and in my eyes *is* so still, in as far as place goes—and the only superiority he can ever claim in any Country of Europe; *is,* the possession of superior talent to ensure him a real standing or reputation in those Countries—

Mere place in our Country, can never give even artificial rank; while the Salaries are too mean to place you on a level with your Colleagues, and *too* narrow to admit of your surrounding yourself with those appendages which through a little gilding, cover many little flaws in the understanding, and deficiencies in the manners— Talent acquirement, information and learning, is the only passport which will ensure respect, and claim and maintain its station all over the world; and this was the sterling gold to which I bowed in the choice of my husband, and which in every position in which he has been placed in this world; has been *felt, understood,* and *granted* in the midst of trial, persecution, disappointment and affliction— Such greatness bears its *own* stamp, and is the reward of *years.* With the consciousness of such powers, we cannot wonder that his measure of others less gifted, has often been unduly severe; and in early life, when the suffering which *experience* brings, has not taught us leniency to the casualties, the changes, and the calamities which no care can prevent, no forethought assuage, we are too apt to inveigh against the *effects* of misfortune, without a just appreciation of its causes, and all the concomitant circumstances attending it; and to censure without mercy those ills which have deserv'd compassion and sympathy—

I am induced to make these observations from a perusal of Mr. Adams's Journal—In which I find many allusions to my fathers difficulties conveying an idea altogether injurious to *him,* for want of a freer explanation— Mr. Adams was in England a long time without even an invitation from them my parents— It was therefore his own choice that led him to seek *us;* while it is evident that some kind friend had warned him of his danger, and had carefully opened his eyes to *any* thing that might follow— Besides *his* Father, *his* Mother, and *his* Sister, had known us for years; and our marriage was not so hurried as to prevent their timely interference to prevent the connection— Letters from America announcing the arrival of my Father and the family in America— The information contained in them and the expression of acute suffering so evident in their tone, which forced themselves upon my memory, though so many years have elapsed, and they are laid in the peaceful tomb; have induced this painful retrospection; and as this recital of the past is not intended for the eye of any but my Children, I write freely and under the dictation of Truth; visible in almost every line in the accounts detailed at the time, concisely; but reviving all the links which have laid dormant on the tablet of memory, to be renewed with the vividness of present reality—

Mr. Garlick the english Chargé D'affaires became very intimate; and fortunately for me, many young Ladies constantly visited me at my own home, in the most social and agreeable manner— Some amused me with the Superstions of the Country—

Where Ghost's and Goblin's formed the tale

others the scandals and peccadillo's of their neighbours—some annecdotes of the late Kings reign; an era prolific of themes of

Quere and strange romancing, yet too true—

Many of the Hero's and heroines being then at Berlin; having been principal performers in the guilty scenes; such as Madame Rietz (I think that was her name) Monsr. de Bishoffswerder the leader of the Illuminiti; and many others who soon after made their last appearance on the Stage, to give place to better rulers— The Lady abovementioned was the favorite Mrs. [*mistress*] of the late King, who was banished [*from*] the Court; and much of her property unlawfully gained, was siezed and resumed by the young King— Among the Stories *told* to me, was, one, which I think I can repeat, and which was current— The late King before his death being very low, and on whom every species of deception was practiced; had for some time resisted the extortionate demands of this Woman, and his Minister Bishoffswerder: and a *vision* was planed so as to shake his nerves, and thus atchieve through the terrors of religious apprehension, the base purpose which they so nefariously prosecuted— At the dead of the night, a figure representing our Savior, as risen from the dead, appeared to him; and commanded him to grant the prayers of his most *deserving* Minister, and most affectionate *friend;* and a failure to perform this *duty,* was to be punished everlastingly in the world to come— This scene was of course dramatized to suit the occasion; and fainting under the fears of an excited imagination, and the operation of power-ful opiates, the King promised; and swooned— In the mean time the mystic paraphernalia was removed, and when he recovered all was as usual— In the morning he related his vision to one of the high Officers of the Court, and remarked "that he did not know before that *Jesus* wore a Watch Chain"!!! This observation led to the discovery of the imposition and banishment was the consequence— A queer anecdote!!!

Louisa's time in Berlin proved one long series of illnesses, mainly caused by complications arising from a number of pregnancies and miscarriages. Her memoirs give no explanation for the five-month break here, but John Quincy's diary indicates that she suffered another miscarriage in July 1798.

A loss for Louisa was Thomas Boylston's departure for the United States in the fall of 1798. He had already stayed in Europe three years longer than he had initially planned when he first joined his brother in the Netherlands in 1794. He returned to Philadelphia in early 1799 and resumed his law career, eventually moving back to Quincy in the early nineteenth century. There he married Ann Harrod in 1805, and served briefly in the Massachusetts state legislature.

Replacing him as secretary was Thomas Welsh Jr., a distant relation to the Adamses and recent Harvard graduate. Some years before, John Quincy had lived in the Welsh household in Boston while launching his legal career. In 1799 Welsh returned to Boston, where he too pursued a legal and political career.

October 1798

After a lapse of five months I again took my place among the great world of Berlin, and again went through the same tread-mill round of ceremonious heavy ettiquette— At the Princess Henry's my greeting was polite— Again the vultures preyed upon my devoted purse, and though chagrin and spleen beset me, I endured the sight at Supper of the ruthful cuts upon the depart-ing joints; and inwardly mourned at the want of capacity in myself, to enjoy with the delicious gusto of a *fasting* taste, the eates so amply set before me. Madame Eichstadt a Lady of eighty, who had done such honour at a former mentioned supper Lord Gower appeared with a splinded suit of diamonds new set, of a most costly description, and did her duty on this happy occasion, with equal fervour and unsubduing zeal— The wicked girls who let me into the secrets of the lesser lights, that shed their little rays on such occasions, had informed me that on these publick days; *dinners* were omited; lest the acuteness of the appetite should be blunted, and its keen edge be destroyed for the performance of the honors due to the Royal Viands— It is true that the amiable Lady above quoted was found dead in her bed supposed of an *indigestion,* after a supper of this kind at the same palace—

My next appearance was at Bellevue, the Country house of Prince Ferdinand (I never saw the remarkably famed Prince Henry) and there the Princess extended her arms to embrace me, and from hers I passed to those of the Landgravine of Hessé Cassel who greeted me with the affectionate warmth of a Parent. Here I felt at *home,* The Landgravine made me sit by her at her work Table, and those who prefered work to play, sat with her and plied their needles; while a few Gentlemen joined in the conversation which was always light and agreeable— The Prince never sat down to Supper and the Princess prefered her Whist— Princess Radziville did the honors. Easy, and graceful, affable in her manners, she possessed that greatest of all *arts,* the power of ensuring the respect due to herself, while she gave a tone of social independence to her guests—

The Chanoness Madlle. de Bork was an elderly Lady of a great reputation for sense, observation, and reading— She possessed a great talent for drawing, which had been very highly cultivated; with a peculiar tact for siezing the likeness or expression of any features that happened to strike her fancy— With a small Card and a Crayon She would hold it under the Table, and while apparently conversing very animatedly, would perfect her sketch: The object of her work being utterly unconscious of the Act, and without suspicion of the fact— When the Supper was concluded I saw a large Card presented to the Princesses which seemed to fix all eyes on *me;* and much to my discomfiture I found she had taken what was generally pronounced to be a fine likeness of me: but I was not permitted to see it until it was completed, a process always performed in her own apartment— A book of these likenesses was shown me at Princess Radzivilles; and a group of herself, her husband, and their little Child of three years old placed between them; gazing up in their faces with its lovely ringlets, and cherub Cheeks, as fresh as rosy morn, was one of the prettiest things I ever saw—

After these parties when I returned home I missed the Judge beyond expression— If he accompanied us, he had always something amusing to relate; and we would compare notes

And o'er, and o'er again the past enjoy—

but Mr *Welsh!!* the contrast was complete! In appearance a perfect Cub—Stout, athletic, short necked, coarse complexioned, *raw!*—his manners abrupt; his conversation brusque; his voice vulgar; and exquisitely self-sufficient, th'ough very good tempered: the change was too much for my philosophy; and I could not help regretting, and perhaps making him sensible, how much *less* I thought of or admired *him* than his *"illustrious predescessor"*— An inveterate Yankee; every Fish was a Pickerel—Every Duck was a Brant; and like Cymon [*an unsophisticated character*] he wanted some bright *imagination,* to rub his newness off— Whitcomb was his choice companion! and he soon made acquaintances out of our line—and we saw but little of him— Mr Adams recommended to him to take a french Master and he studied so assiduously, that in three months he could talk it fluently, and enter into society; corrected in many points and fashioned to appear in company— Somehow or other he did not succeed in the Grand Monde, and though I grew to like him better, I never could learn to like him much.— He never attained the lustre of the diamond, or the polish of pure gold, but like french or birmingham gilding the brass would show through—

---

13 December 1798

Prince Augustus [*of England*] and his Family; Lord Talbot, Mr Garlick, Secretary of the English Legation; The Hanoverian Minister Baron Ompteda; His Cousin The Chevalie Ompteda; a very remarkable person, measuring seven feet in height; A very Gentlemanly man of high Rank in the Military Service; but so embarrassed at being *so tall,* that it made him quite unhappy. I had much trouble with my Household arrangements my Cook being so intoxicated that she could not Cook; and dinner being delayed and spoilt in consequence— The Browns and Mr. Sloper an Englishman of fortune completed the company— The party was social and after dinner the Prince said he would stay to *Tea,* he found himself so *comfortable;* if I would order my Servant, to desire *his* Valet to bring his dress Clothes, that he might make his toilet at our house, previous to his visit at the Baron D'Alvenslebens, where we were all invited to Meet the King and Queen— Every thing was arranged to his fancy, and I did the honours of the Tea Table in the old fashioned style— As at this period much was said concerning the quarrel between George the 4th. [*then Prince of Wales*] and his *Queen* [*Caroline of Brunswick*], the Prince was standing at the Table talking to me, when Mrs. Brown very abruptly, and in her off hand manner, asked him (much to my confusion) "if *he* thought the Queen so *bad* as she was represented—" He hesitated a Moment; and then said "my Dear Madam" my brother is a *Beast!!!*— It was quite late in the Eveng when the party broke up, and then I had to dress for the Ball. When I went up to pay my respects to their Majesties, the King said to me "so Prince Augustus dined with you to day"? I mention the fact to show you how well they were informed of every thing that passed.

19 December 1798

Went to dine with the Queen Mother; I was alone! She was very kind to me. I forgot to mention a visit made to her on a former occasion, at what they termed a Court of *Condolence.* The Ladies all went in full dress of deep Mourning, but without Veils— The Gentlemen full suits of black, Swords, &ca of the same— The Queen was Seated on one side near the Centre of a long Hall, hung with black— Her attendants in a half Circle behind her; and every one in deep black: herself in the deepest Widows weeds, with a Crape Veil flowing round her, and reaching the Floor— The Ladies and gentlemen passed very gravely, stopping before her; making a low obeisance, and then passing onward to give place to others— Not a word was spoken; not a smile seen and this mummery lasted two or more hours! Although it was a well known fact that this poor Woman, had been a wretchedly neglected and miserable Wife,— Her husband having installed two favorite Misstresses in high rank; and fortune; who lived more courted and admired than herself;

because more able to obtain favours for the parasites who hang upon the smiles of Royalty—

---

1 January 1799

Began the year with the usual routine of congratulatory visits; the Eveng at Prince Ferdinands—but we did not stay to supper— My friend the Landgravine always kind—Sat at *her* table where Mr. Graves was very amusing, and quite in *ecstacies* with the exceeding beauty of the Queen—bantered him; because he had positively declared that he *would not* think her handsome!!

Had a small party at our House; the same as at Lord Talbots—Count and Countess Panin, Mr & Madame Bacounin, Count and Countess Golowkin, and their Daughter; all the English, and several of the Prussian young friends, with whom I was intimate— Prince Augustus sent an excuse—he was *obliged* to go and play at Blindsmans buff with the King and Queen; a diversion that the King was particulary fond of; but only play'd with the R[*oyal*] family or any foreign Prince who might be at Berlin— Ettiquette he said made it impossible for him to accept any other invitation however agreeable— He had accepted our invitation conditionally, anticipating this *call* which was often repeated— Prince Radziville and Mr. Sartoris came to supper, Count and Countess Bruhl and their daughters were of the party, and we danced until four o clock in the morning— Next day Mr. & Mrs. Errington were introduced to me at my own house— Lord Talbot introduced an elegant man to us Mr St George—quite a Sir Charles Grandison—

At a large party at Count Shulemburgs—heard strange whispers of Princess Louis— The King and Queen both sick— The Princess Louis has made a faux-pas, and the result is so apparent, that she has confessed a private marriage to the King; but the Clergyman cannot be found who performed the ceremony— Her *Husband* is the Prince de Solms, an Officer of an inferior grade, without fortune, but handsome— They are ordered off to Anspach a Garrison Town on the Frontier— It is said that she cannot reach the Station before her confinement— Something was suspected from the change in her dress— She had suddenly become very modest and precise— This Lady is the present Queen of Hanover— The Queen has had no Court— She is dreadfully distressed at the conduct of her Sister— The amusements at Court postponed— The Princess Louis was confined at a poor miserable inn on the road, on the first night of her Journe'y— Three nights before I had seen her dancing the whole Evening, Waltzes and Country dances until eleven o'clock; the only difference in her *appearance,* being the extreme simplicity of her dress—in which hitherto she had always vied with the Queen in her ornaments, and in the richness of her apparel— Whispers running round at the same time concerning one of her Maids of Honor, a very beautiful Woman, with whom rumour said the King was much smitten— She had had Twins supposed to be his Majestys; and this Winter had been married off to an Officer in the Army near the Kings person; who was promoted suddenly on the occasion—

At Court a Ball! not intending to dance, I wore a train; and when my Princely Partners asked me I declined dancing; and was quietly seated by one of my friends, chatting very pleasantly; when I saw Madame de Voss the Grande Gouvernante of the Queen, coming across the Hall; and while every eye was on her She advanced and stood immediately before me; "and announced to me, that the King intended to dance the first Country-dance with me— That I must sit still until I saw his Majesty take his place; and that I must then walk up alone and take my stand opposite to him—" Conceive my situation! Madame de Voss no longer was the object of attention; She sidled off with her hoop shaking under her mincing step, erect as a may Pole; and every eye was on me, who being under the necessity of looping my train, thus betrayed the message, even before I was to go through the most painful part of the ceremony— The dance formed; the King took his place, fortunately for me next couple to the Queen, and I marched up ready to faint, and took my place—

The King walked up and spoke to me, and the Queen with her usual loveliness; took my hands in hers, and stood and talked some minutes until I recovered myself— She told me I looked so pale she must make me a present of a box of rouge; I answered that Mr. Adams would not let me wear it— She smiled at my simplicity, and observed that if *she* presented me the box he must not refuse it, and told me to tell him so. She then beckoned to the King, and told him to begin the dance in the middle of the line, at the same time that She began it at the top; and *we* began the dance at the same moment— Prince Augustus and his Gentlemen all encouraging me, and kindly complimenting me when I returned to my Seat, upon the marked distinction with which I had been treated— My accustomed *partners,* who had claimed the engagements entered into for the Winter complained that although I was engaged to them; I could dance with the King; I got so flurried that Mr. Adams took me home before Supper—

I told Mr. Adams what the Queen said; but he said I must refuse the box, as he should never permit me to accept it— At this Ball I saw Madame D'Harlberg a Lady from Vienna, who had formed a liáson with Mr. Graves, and had quitted her *Husband,* to follow her chére Ami to Berlin.— Her conduct displeased the Queen; and though she was a Lady of very high rank, she was treated very coolly— My health being again very delicate I staid much at home—

4 April 1799

Mr Grenville and Suite, Mr Arbuthnot, the Browns, Lord Talbot, and Mr Sloper dined with us— Mr Grenville was a brother of Lord Grenvilles, then Minister of Foreign Affairs in England. He was one of the mildest, most agreable and most amiable men, and distinguished as a diplomatist— I knew so little concerning politicks, I seldom heard, and never enquired what was going on— I only knew that it was a period of great events, which I did not understand; and in which I individually took no interest— Mr Adams had always accustomed me to believe, that Women had nothing to do with politics; and as he was the glass from which my opinions were reflected, I was convinced of its truth, and sought no farther—

When my health failed the House of Dr Brown was my refuge—

At Mr. Cohens we saw the Barbier de Seville, and the Somnambula; a private performance: the first tolerably well performed— The party very large and crowded—

Mr. Mrs & the Miss Sanfords were introduced to me—An english family of great respectability and wealth— The Husband a complete English Squire of the old School; a regular Tally ho!!! Mrs. Sanford a most beautiful Woman; Young and apparently very ill, mismatched, and very unhappy— They requested me to present them at Court, and we arranged to call upon the Grande Maitresses of all the Courts, amounting to six; and to ask an introduction to the Queen and Princesses: This was a ceremony always performed in *person,* from which no one could be exempted; An arrangement was then made between us in regard to their dress &ce and that I would accompany them at the time appointed. The two young Ladies were very pretty, but quite eclipsed by the beauty of their Sister— Mrs. Sanford was one of those exquisitely sensitive, and lovely creatures; that appeared like the sensitive plant, to shrink at the gaze of man, and to tremble at the rough tones of her husband, and his boisterous ways— Delicate to fragility; apparently far advanced in consumption, with all the elegant polish of the highest refinement; It was impossible to be acquainted with her, without feeling admiration and love for her fine qualities, and her lovely disposition: and compassion for her *lot,* which evidently was not of her own seeking: and you could not see her without feeling a conviction that she had been sacrificed by some dire necessity, most likely to the shrine of Plutus the God [*of wealth*] to whom so much of the adoration of this life is paid— We all went to Court where the Ladies were well received, and Mr. Garlick presented the Ursa Major, that accompanied them; much to the diversion of the Court, to whom such a character was new— Madame D'Harlberg on this Eveng. was so indelicately dressed; that the Queen sent her Mistress of the Ceremonies to request; that she would retire and make some change in her arrangements, *or go home*— This unblushing Woman who was very handsome, returned into the Hall—and danced the whole Eveng— The Queen herself Waltzed with Mr. Graves, wherever she met him—

A night or two after they went to the Queen Mothers— The Queen told Madame D'Halberg in the morning, that she had invited Mr. Graves on purpose to meet her— She was glad to see them so well together and hoped it would last!!! This Speech she made at a breakfast which her Majesty gave in a Green House at about a mile from Berlin— The Sanfords also there— The poor old Queen was about half crazy—

Count Zinzendorf who had been Minister at Berlin for 22 years, was recalled to be Minister of War at Dresden— We were invited to a Féte given to him, prior to his departure—

At Count Panins; a party on her recovery from an illness two french plays; la Gageure imprevu and le Sourd— They live in a Palace in which there is a regular built theatre:—very handsomely fitted up— Count Caraman a great performer—and Count Galatin—

At Count Zinzendorfs party— He gave it himself upon taking leave— It was a Ball and Supper. The young Ladies crowned him with flowers— I thought it was given to *him*. With the Sanfords I went to Prince Ferdinands; as usual I sat with the Landgravine, and we stayed Supper—a new *Rule*. At the Princess Henry's, with the Sanfords having presented them— Mr. Adams was invited to Supper— The Sanfords and I played Cards together—

While standing at the Window in the library I saw a child run over by a Cart— He was taken up dreadfully injured, and I fainted and fell— The consequence was a sudden illness full of disappointment, and ruinous to my constitution— The wretchedness of Mr. Adams aggravated the evil and only made the suffering more distressingly excruciating; At such seasons women want every solace, for they endure both corporeal and mental anguish— He was kind and affectionate in his attention; but his feeling of disappointment could not be subdued—

Following yet another miscarriage, Louisa and John Quincy embarked on a three-month tour of Dresden and the surrounding area. They planned to take the waters there in hopes of restoring Louisa's health and also to give themselves a break from the exhausting rounds of state functions in Berlin.

May 1799

Count and Countess Gowlofkin called to take leave of us ere their departure for Teplitz, to which place they urged us to go, as they thought the bath's would be of great service to me—

The illness which had threatened me so long again occurred and I was kept at home 4 or 5 weeks— My Nerves were so terribly shattered by this last illness, that Dr Brown recommended a journey; and on the 17th of July, I was lifted into the Carriage, and by the time we arrived at Dresden, I had gained sufficient strength to participate in the pleasures, which the journey presented—

Went immediately after dressing to see my friend Mrs. Errington, who I found with a sweet little Girl, who she had named Dresdina— Almost as roughly handled as myself, she had narrowly escaped with her life—but she was blessed with a fine Child, while I only lived to witness the pangs of disappointment, which so bitterly distressed my poor husband, and destroyed all the comfort of my life— The Letters from America weighed me down with sorrow, and mortification; for anguish will have vent, and the heart will breathe its sorrows to the loved ones who have participated in our blessings. It is a trite saying "that it does no good" but it is not true; for even the momentary relief, assuages the heaviness of grief, and softens its asperity— We dined with Mrs. Errington, and there met two young Englishmen, Mr Thompson, and Mr. Wright— I accompanied Mr. Adams to the [*Royal*] Picture Gallery— I will not discuss the Paintings; but will only say that some of them inspired me with delight almost adoration— On returning home met Madame De Berg and the beautiful Louise her daughter—

24 July 1799

At four o'clock in the morning we started for Töplitz— The Geyersberg is a mountain so steep, that we could not descend in the Carriage; I was placed in an arm Chair, supported by two poles, and carried down gently by two men— On the side of the Mountain about half way down, stand the ruins of a Castle, said to have been magnificent in its day, and owned by a feudal Baron of a desperately wicked character— This Man having commited every crime, like the far famed Don Juan we were informed; had sold his Soul to his Infernal Master, for the privilege of a lengthened career; which was granted on condition, that the catalogue of his crimes should be complete— The Bond was signed in form; but the penalty was exacted in the midst of his successful triumphs; and his Lordship was siezed, and dashed from one of the loopholes of the highest turret, which caused a frightful gap; at the deriding laugh of the unrelenting spirit; who with malignant joy delighted in the agonies which he occasioned— 'Twas in this ruin that we were assured, that his Satanic Majesty revisited the Scene of his former glory, at a periodical Season; and that during his *stay,* the Ruins were brilliantly illuminated with most unholy fires; and that he kept up his Orgies with the most horrid sounds, and diabolical language, till the Cock crew; when he and his Satellites disappeared to renew the clamour at the dark hour of midnight; when the awful Tragedy was again rehearsed; the body thrown out, the shrieks and curses; and the laugh reechoing its horrid sounds, for miles around—

We arrived safely at Töplitz—having met Madame de Castel, who informed us that our Lodgings were all ready; and immediately on our arrival took possession and found ourselves quite comfortable. Töplitz is situated in a deep Valley, through which runs a Stream of Water of different temperature, from hot to cold; seemingly graduted by Nature in its different degrees, to suit the temperaments of different Invalids— The Baths are built very roughly, immediately over the Stream; at intervals; and the Physician of the place prescribes the degree of warmth proper for the complaint of the Patient— The debility under which I laboured was such, he would not permit me to attend the publick Bath's; and the Water was brought to the House and the bath's were prepared in my Chamber in Tubs, until I should be strong enough to bear the fatigue of the bath, and the exercise together— Three times a week the bath, and every day a bottle of Pyrmont Water taken while walking in the gardens of Prince Clary, always open for the benefit of the Publick— Our Lodging was quite near them, and close to the Catholick Church; the Music from which we found a perfect treat, during our stay; as it was remarkably good, and well performed—

In the Eveng. we went to the Tea Party at the Salon in the Garden; a sort of reception Room, where all the fashionable company met, and the Tea is given by different persons every Evening— This Evening the party was given by Countess Kollowrat; to whom we were presented by our friend Countess Golowkin, who likewise presented us to the Grand Dutchess Constantine, and to her Father Mother, and Sisters; the Prince and Princesses of Sax Cobourg family: and to Prince Reuss, the Father of the Austrian Minister our acquaintance at Berlin; besides meeting some of our Berlin friends— We made a short stay, and returned to our Lodgings— The Country round Töplitz is magnificent, and we walked about to look at the magnificent prospects from the heights— The Tea party on the next Evening was given by Madame de Malnitz a Saxon Lady, and afterwards we went to the Theatre a small building in the Gardens.

August 1799

Our residence was very agreeable while at this place— The Evenings at the Gardens dancing or walking; sometimes at the Theatre—Often meeting our Berlin friends, and forming new and agreeable acquaintance among the daily arrivals— Mr & Mrs. Hildprandt of Prague we became very intimate with— We accompanied this family to Kloster Osegg a Monastery about six miles from Töplitz— They being well acquainted with the Prior, he treated us very handsomely, and shewed us all his Apartments, gardens, &ce. The Monks appeared to be very illiterate, having no library, and nothing worthy of curiosity; excepting a small Island in the middle of a Pond, in which were a number of small black Turtles; and on the Island a small *Fort* called Turtles Fortress—A number of small huts with thatched roofs containing turkish Ottomans, and Sophas, and two sets of machines for different Sports, for gentle exercise— We took tea in a Summer house at the bottom of the Garden, from whence we enjoyed a superb prospect; with various kinds of fruits; and then examined the Church; large, and full of fine Paintings and we returned home much pleased with our little tour at eight o'clock in the evening—

The next day we went to look at the famous ruin on the Geyersberg [*the castle of Dobrawksa Hora*] which we passed on the road from Dresden— This ruin was then very Ancient; and its Owner we were informed had been the mortal enemy of the Baron of the Schlosberg Fort—though the latter must have been a family of much more modern origin— We returned home to dine, and at 4 o'clock in the afternoon we sat off again on an expedition to *Dux,* the seat of Count Wallenstein— I went in a Chaise with Miss Hildprand; the rest in a Carrige peculiar to the Country— It is called a Linée and is open, without a top; and consists of one long bench on which the Gentlemen sit across; it is very low and runs on four wheels— Count Wallenstein to whom Mr Hildbrand introduced us, shewed us his Stables; containing a hundred Horses of which he is very proud— They form the great obect of his care, and of his amusement— We did not see the inside of the Castle but walked through the Gardens, which are not very inviting— The prospects in every direction lovely and magnificent— That next day Count Bruhl called to invite us to a Tea Party given by Baron Krudener, the Father of the Minister of that name, who has since been in this Country; but we were too much fatigued to go; it being at Dopperlberg— In the Evening saw the Opera of the Zauberflöte by Mozart— The Princesses of S. Cobourg handsome—

Baron Hildprand and family called to take leave of us. They return home, and gave us a warm and urgent invitation to visit them at Prague—

1 September 1799

I was too sick to go out— Count Panin called, and in the Eveng. Mr. Adams went to the Tea party given by Princess Reuss.—

A visit to Count Panin's— Appointed Vice Chacellor of the Empire; and he is preparing to leave Töplitz, which is beginning to thin very fast; another englishman by the name of Garvey called. Went to the Hall in the Eveng and saw a play performed by the company of Ladies, and Gentlemen— It was not worth, much; and we staid later than usual— The Piece Jerome Pointu—

Walked with Mr. Adams to the Schlosberg, and ascended the mountain, having derived much benefit from the Pyrmont Waters; disgusting to the smell and taste— Did not go out in the evening, but received a visit from Mr. Garvey—

At the Schlosberg again, took new milk on the top of the mountain, and amused ourselves with reading the names of the visitors carved on the walls; some of which were written upwards of a Century ago. Wrote our own to pass down like the rest— Saw Countess Panin ascending the mountain in her *Carriage;* a proof of what the wealthy and great of this world can accomplish— At home in the Even.

Took our leave of the Schlossberg— Count Bruhl having kindly made arrangements for our journey, and procured a Boat to take us down the Elbe on our way to Dresden, to avoid the Geyersberg Mountain, and to vary our route— Madame de Huernabine takes our Lodgings—The Lady of the Twins—very beautiful—

The 9th of September having in a great measure recovered my health, and taken leave of most of my kind friends at Töplitz; particularly our kind Doctor; we had taken an early dinner and were ready to step into the Carriage; when Countess Panin came to introduce Countess Ozarowska a Polish Lady of distinction— We started in our own Carriage at two o'clock in the afternoon, and arrived—at Ausig, were we stopped for the night; while our Carriage was shipped, so as to proceed early in the morning— Commenced our Water excursion at five o'clock—Mr. Adams, Epps, Whitcomb, and myself— Epps had proved a treasure during the whole time of her Service in my family; almost educated by my Mother, she had been so accustomed to my habits, and manners; and was so attached to me, I always found her faithful and affectionate; and she attended me with the most unremitting care and attention— She was housekeeper, Nurse, Seamstress, Mantua Maker, and Clearstarcher and; thus saved me from a heavy burthen of expence— She afterwards married Whitcomb, who treated her ill, and the unhappiness which she endured, changed her habits and her character, which soon destroyed her constitutuion; and she died leaving a family of five Children— As a foreigner she had no friends; her crafty husband was pitied and approved; while the censure of the *honest* should have been his portion— Mr. Whitney was the only person who declared this *truth*, and it did him honour in proving his discernment—

Arrived at Dresden we proceeded to our lodgings procured for us by Mr. Errington at the Hotel which they occupied, and they received us in the most friendly manner— We went to the Fair it being about to close and made some purchaces of table linen famed for its beauty and cheapness in Saxony— Mr. Adams sent some to his Mother— The Eveng Mr & Mrs Errington spent with us we called at Count Golowkins at the Hotel de Baviere and there we met Madlle. Bishoffswerder and her Mother with a large party of our Töplitz friends—

Mr & Mrs Greathead, and their Son Bertie, called on us and asked us to Tea in the Evening. He was a gentleman of family and distinction, to whom Mr. Errington had introduced us. As we went in we met Mr. Hugh Elliot, the English Minister at the Saxon Court; a remarkably handsome and elegant man whose history I had heard before I had left Berlin— He had married a very beautiful German Lady, who after living with him a year or two had eloped with a Noble Countryman of her own, and taken her only child, a daughter with her— A few months after, Mr Elliot contrived through the medium of secret Agents, to steal the Child in its Cradle, and immedeately set out for England with her, where she was educated by his family—

14 September 1799

In the morning we walked in the Gardens of Count [*Heinrich von*] Bruhl, a Man well known to history as the enemy of Frederic during the seven years war: and in the Evening we again strolled out after being at the Gallery of Pictures an hour or two— Another day was lost to me as I was too ill to go out— The Evening Mr & Mrs Errington called, but I could not see them—

At Mrs. Erringtons where I met Mr. Elliot— We called at the Countess Worthern's one of our Töplitz friends; but she was out.

15 September 1799

Mr. Adams was presented by Mr. Elliot to the Elector of Saxony, and his Dutchess, the Princess Mary-Ann, Prince Max his brother, and his Wife a Princess of Parma— In the Evening he went to a Ball at the Governors: I stayed at home—

The Evening passed with Mrs. Errington and met a Mr Artaud. Dined with Mrs. Errington; Mr. Greathead and family, Mr Prescott, Miss Elliot, the stolen Child now grown up, and very beautiful; accompanied by several young Gentlemen, came in to spend the Evening— She was engaged to be married to Mr. Payne the Son of a great Banker in London— The next morning a Mr Oliver of Baltimore, brought Letters to us. We went to the Gallery and then remain quietly at home all the Evening— Mr & Mrs. Errington and Mr Oliver dined with us, and Miss Elliot joined us at Tea—

The next day we dined and spent the Evening at Mrs. Greatheads. They are very agreeable— She an elderly Lady of very pleasant manners and conversation—

Accompanied Mrs. Errington to the Catholick Cathedral— There is a grandeur and awful sublimity in these buildings very striking to the imagination of young and ardent minds—and the Music, the Paintings, and ornamented Alters; with the Showy paraphernalia of the Priests; and the frank Incence; all sieze upon the senses, and steal insensibly upon the heart with rapt enthusiasm— The Arts are all called into action; and you gaze in wonderment at the works of man; while if you are of a reflecting mind, are led to think; if man can atchieve so much, how surpassingly wonderful must the Creater be; who combines all that greatness, and all that we behold of the great Waters, of the deep, and the lustrous magnificence of the Celestial Heavens, and all created things so full of might and glory!— So dazzling with perfection in all their vast variety; the same for ever; yet forever new!!! In the Evening we were at Mr. Elliots—

The Adamses returned to Berlin in mid-October and resumed their regular schedule. As Louisa noted in a part of "Adventures" not printed here, "I have been thus particular to give you an idea of our routine while at Dresden; which was nearly akin, to that which I led in Berlin: the only difference; here; it was all social, and that in Berlin when I was well enough to visit the great world; it was all State and very laborious."

In January, Louisa suffered her fourth miscarriage since arriving in Berlin. John Quincy commented in his diary, "I can only pray to God, that there may never again be the possibility of another like event— A better hope, it were folly to indulge; for in cases like this hope itself is but an aggravation of misery."

November 1799

Received a Visit from Madame Ursinus to return thanks for an accidental service which *she* said I had rendered to her— Her husband was a Physician— They had not been long married and had one Child, an Infant about eight Months old— The Child was siezed with convulsions, and they were dreadfully alarmed. They lived on the floor over us, and they sent in great haste to me, to know if I could do any thing for them— The day or two before; I had heard that Madame de Mussow's Child when apparently *dead*, had been restored by an application of Oil of Amber, gently rubbed up and down the spine, and held to the Nostrils to inhale— I informed them of this Case, and advised them to try it— It had proved successful, and she came to return the thanks of her Husband and herself; stating that he was quite ashamed of having so lost his presence of mind; as he well knew the efficacy of the remedy— I mention this fact as there may be instances in which the remedy might prove useful, where convulsions are not the consequence of prolonged desease— The Baby was sent down to me full dressed, in a pink silk slip with a Gauze frock over it, and numerous bows of Pink ribbon—

This reminds me of the astonishment that siezed upon me at the sight of my housemaid, the first Sunday after my return— She came up to me dressed in an elegant Satin Cloak of pale Blue, trimmed with Fur—A National Cap, the Crown embroidered in colours; flat to the head; with a very broad lace border, put very much off the face, and something in the form of the front of a bonnet, only put on in large fluted quils, like the portraits of Mrs. Washington— She was as proud as a Peacock; and in perfect ecstacy at her finery— As she had been accustomed to go almost without necessary clothing, and I had had great difficulty to make her wear Shoes and Stockings; and she had been a very good Girl; I was frightened lest she should have done Something wrong, to enable her to make the purchace: and I hastened to Mrs. Brown to relieve the quandary into which I was thrown— She laughed, and told me, there was no cause of alarm: as it was the uttermost height of the ambition of these poor Girls, to own a fine Cloak, to sport at Church, and in the Deer Garthen on a Sunday; and they would deprive themselves of every internal garment, and even their Tea, to save their money to procure such finery—

December 1799

Went with Mrs. Ofarrel [*Spanish ambassador's wife*] to visit all the Courts; after which we went to a very large party given in honour of the marriage of the young Countess Shulembourg, with Prince Hadzfeldt—a Lady since so celebrated in the history of Napoleon; which was said to have given rise to the famous Piece, called Trajan, in compliment to the Emperor for his clemency— She was a charming woman; but I did not admire her husband Prince Hadzfeldt, and thought him a cold, supercilious, haughty, flashy personage. What College youth's call "all sufficient" the qualifications necessary for the completion of the character existing *only* in their own conceit— Mrs. Ofarel was standing immediately before me, when one of the Grandee's asked me to present him to her— I tapped her gently on the shoulder, and in turning she fell as gently on the Carpeted floor, and exclaimed that she had broken her Leg— I sank on one knee immediately, and rested her head on the other; when she fell into a dead fainting— She had barely recovered, when she again said she had broken the limb; which being heard by a Gentleman, who said it was only a sprain he took hold of her foot, and turned it; upon which she screamed and fainted again— Her husband had gone for a Surgeon, who raised her gently on a Sopha, and she was carried into another apartment, to which the Doctor desired me to accompany her. He then examined the *hurt,* and declared the bone to be fractured in two different places; and ordered me to cut the Stocking off, the leg being very much swolen; He gave me a pair of very sharp Scissors, and though I trembled like a leaf, I succeeded; and on examining the limb, he prefered to have her carried home as she lay, prior to the operation while he would prepare Splints and all the necessary apparatus—

I tried to find Mr. Adams that I might get home; but ere I could succeed, I fell down in a deep fainting fit; and was carried home—being attended by three or four Ladies who were alarmed at the length of time which the total insensibility continued: A succession of these fits continued nearly all night, and they kindly staid with me until I was thought out of danger: but my recovery was slow, and though I was able to go and sit with Mrs. Ofarell, and assist to nurse her; at the end of a few weeks I suffered all the ill consequences of the fright, and again had the misery to behold the anguish of my husbands blighted hopes. Why do we so bitterly repine at evils, if such they really are, which are so utterly beyond our controul; and which probably are sent to soften the asperity of our natures, and to teach the high unbending spirit of man, submission to a Will too mighty to contend against, and which exacts for our sakes, that we may abide in the right path; with implicit and patient obedience to its decrees—

On the 19th of Janry. 1800 I again was able to take a ride and move about among the living—

The Old Queen Mother held a Court to Perform a Play in which she acted herself— Mr Adams did not go; I too weak to go out even to my friend Mrs. Browns— Mr. Adams became quite sick from anxiety, and want of Rest—

An American by the name of Ellison introduced to us—For ever at our house—a very disagreeable man—

1 February 1800

Went to Dr. Browns to pass the Evening, and to get rid of my disagreeable companion who staid late in the Evening whether Mr. Adams was at home or not: the former event being very rare. He became perfectly insupportable to me, and I forced myself to go out, to get rid of him— Received the News of the death of General Washington— Mr Adams was much affected by it. Col Swan of Boston came to See us; and Mr. Adams after remaining at home several days, took him and presented him to the King—

Went to the Opera—but was not so pleased as at Dresden where the Music and the Acting was exquisite— The Opera was Tigrane. On the 6 went to the

Ridotto— Being more than usually pale I ventured to put on a little rouge, which I fancied relieved the black, and made me look quite beautiful— Wishing to evade Mr. Adams's observation I hurried through the room telling him to put the *lights* out, and follow me down; this excited his curiosity, and he started up and led me to the Table, and then declared that unless I allowed him to wash my face, he would not go— He took a Towel and drew me on his knee, and all my beauty was clean washed away; and a kiss made the peace, and we drove off to the party where I showed my pale face as usual—

The Adamses continued their usual round of social activities throughout the spring of 1800, and again in the summer decided to travel, this time to Silesia. They left Berlin in mid-July, returning in late October. While away, they visited various churches and galleries, purchased art, and attended the theater. John Quincy also used the opportunity to see some of the textile mills for which the region was known. By the fall, Louisa was once more expecting, or, as she would say, in "delicate" health. While the pregnancy was not without its scares, this time she and John Quincy were destined for joy: George Washington Adams was born on 12 April 1801.

October 1800

On the 23d of October after five weeks of lingering sufferring at Leipsic—We set off for Berlin, impatient to be at home once more; Mr. Adams being in very bad health, and I in a situation to create perpetual alarm, and anxiety. We hurried on as fast as prudence would permit, and on the 21st we found ourselves once more at our comfortable home. Whitcomb having preceded us to make all necessary arrangements— Again I was surrounded by my loving friends, and was soon as much spoilt as ever— I was sick almost unto the death, and sadly wearisome to every one; but they bore with me with the patience of Angels, and never by look or word, made me feel the pang of *mortification,* by the most trifling indication of ennui at my complaints: but expressing the tenderest sympathy, and the most persevering and delicate attention, to an unfortunate creature; who as Mr Adams remarks in his journal "never knew what it *was,* to be well a whole day"—

I was obliged to make some visits of ceremony after my return, and I formed some new acquaintance, one of whom proved most valuable to me;

Lady [*Elizabeth*] Carysfort, wife of the English Ambassador [*John Joshua Proby, Lord Carysfort*], and the Sister of Lord Grenville, and Mr. William Grenville, who had recently been here on an extra Mission— She was one of the finest women I ever knew—of very superior mind and cultivation: having received a Classical education like her Brothers— She was very plain in her person; somewhat masculine in her manners; and an premier àbord made one feel timid and afraid— But she took a fancy to me, and was so uniformly kind, and affectionate at all times; her conversation so instructive, so entertaining, and at times so delightful; I clung to her as if she had been my own mother, and loved her with equal sincerity— Mrs. [*Melesina Chenevix*] St George a gay and dashing widow with Mr. Kinaird also pleasant—

1 November 1800

Obliged to renew my dissipation—took Tea with Mrs. St George with the Browns, Lady Carysfort, and the Bruhl family, and Mr. Kinaired (the present Lord Kinaired).

At a great Ball at Madame D'Engerstroom's [*Swedish ambassador's wife*]—3 hundred there—Supper superb. Next Evening at Mr. Ofarels— The night after at Tea at Mrs. St. Georges—at Supper at Prince Ferdinands— As soon as the Princess saw me she as usual caught me in her Arms; and then called one of her Chamberlains, to put a Chair near her; all the company excepting myself standing; I was scarlet with susrprize—but you can never resist Royalty— The cause of this mark of distinction was too evident— We excused ourselves from Supper, and I passed the Evening as usual at the Landgravines Table— Prince and Princess Radziville had returned from Poland that morning.

Evening again at Dr Browns to meet the Carysforts, the Bruhls, Mrs. St. George, and Mr Kinaird—

31 December 1800

I have already mentioned that I had determined not to go out in public. I have not told you the why and the wherefore— The truth was, that I had dressed to go to Court. The everlasting teazing about my pale *face*, induced me to make another trial of a little rouge; and contrary to my first proceeding, I walked boldly forward to meet Mr. Adams— As soon as he saw me, he requested me to wash it off, which I with some temper refused; upon which he ran down and jumped into the Carriage, and left me plànté là! even to myself appearing like a *fool* crying with vexation— As Soon as I had composed myself, I very cooly took off my finery; *re*dressed myself suitably: and stepped into the Carriage to joined my friends the Browns; who never guessed that I had made myself so ridiculous— In those days Anger seldom lasted with me more than ten minutes, and once over all was forgotten— When Mr. Adams returned from Court, he came over to Mrs. Browns, and we returned home as good friends as ever— I never went to any of the Courts after that—

6 January 1801

We had a little party at home a dance and Supper. I was too much exhausted—two oclock in the morning before the company separated— Nevertheless I went the next evening to a party at Mrs St Georges, where Mr. Adams and myself taught them to play Rerversi [*Othello*]—

The Carnaval set in most brilliantly— It opened with a Court in Hoops, and was particularly splendid— As the political feeling of the Country was all French, Lady Carysfort seldom took the trouble to attend— The manifestation of marked coldness, to any particular Diplomatist, always being sufficiently decided to make it not only unpleasant, but painful— Her Ladyship was alone, and received me in her Boudoir—a sort of Sanctum Sanctorum as she informed me, into which she never admitted any body, but her husband, and Children—and that *I* must consider my reception *there*, as one great proof of her affection— Here she sometimes gave way to her private sorrows—and *here only* she could talk to me of her private history; of her afflictions; of her own peculiar opinions; both religious and literary— This was too flattering from a woman of sixty, to a young woman of little more than five and twenty—and I used to sieze these occasions almost at the expense of my life— They were so impressive, and so interesting. She told me how intensely she had suffered at the loss of her only Son! How long she had been before, even her strong sense of religion, her duty as a Christian, had brought her mind to the proper degree of unrepining submission, to the Will of her Almighty Father; and how she repented, and prayed that the rebellion of her heart, might be forgiven, by that merciful Father, who knew best what was good for her— She kindly said that she did not know why she thus opened her heart to *me;* it was an indulgence of which she rarely availed herself, but she could not help it—and she hoped I should consider it as a proof of great attachment and respect— She then told me to apply to her on all occasions when I wanted Motherly advice, and that she would be with me in my hour of trial, if I wished it—and asked me to come and see her again, when ever we could find an opportunity for an agreeable Causerie—

The Queen this Winter was more lovely than ever— Like myself, she was in *delicate* health; but she always danced and Watzed until the last moment, and made no change in her dress, excepting fancy Scarfs falling in draperies, tastefully thrown over her— Josephine of France loaded her with superb presents, and she literally reigned over all hearts. Her Sister the Dutchess of Hildeburghausen was on a visit to her very handsome, but not so beautiful as the Queen— Princess de Salms (late Louis), at a Garison Town on the Frontier— Her brute of a husband is said to receive all his Officers while in *bed* with her at five o'clock in the morning, Smoking a Meer-shaum: What a change produced by unbridled passions!!!

The King and Queen were both ill: so that the amusements were suspended.

The Hereditary Princess of Mecklenburg Shwerin a daughter of the Emperor of Russia likewise on a visit to the Queen, to spend the Carnaval; very handsome and distinguée—

The Browns passed the Evening with me, and Miss Bishoffwerder; the latter told me that at one of the Ministers Evenings; the Minister Werder had introduced two of his daughters to their Majesties— These Girls had been *reared,* I wont say *educated,* in the Country; and had never seen any thing like a town life, or the refinements of a Court. They were coarse, rough, boisterous girls; romps, talking loud, without an idea of the requisite formalities which enforce propriety, in a Circle of Courtly society— The Young Men very improperly, instead of giving the poor things Lemonade; had plied them with punch, until they were perfectly intoxicated; and one of them while turning the Queen in the dance, was so overpowered, that her

Stomach suddenly rejected the *stirring* beverage, and to the utter consternation of the Court, the royal Robes were *sullied,* and the Queen was obliged to retire— The young Ladies were sent back to the Country, next morning; and the Poor unconscious Minister the Father, came very near being punished for this *gross* offence—

The length of time it took for correspondence to travel across the Atlantic meant that John Quincy did not learn of the death of his brother Charles on 30 November 1800 until early February 1801.

1 February 1801

Mr Adams at Court— Fanny Bruhl with me—

2 February 1801

Mr. Adams to day received the painful information of his brother Charles's death at N.Y. He was Deeply grieved—

3 February 1801

News of the Election of Mr. Jefferson and that the President Adams was ill of a Fever—

Put on mourning, but Lady Carysfort came and forced me out to ride with her— My Situation more and more *critical*—

Mrs. [*Elizabeth Orby*] Hunter and Miss Jones called to take leave of me— She said "mine was the *only House* in which she was *not* received, with chilling frigidity"— She was to leave the City on her way to France next day— This Lady had bought a Carriage on purpose to carry her Parrot; and Miss Jones, and her Maid, were to ride in it by turns, to take care of it. When she *died,* she left a Legacy to this *Parrot,* of five hundred pounds a year— Young Caulfield kept a first rate Valet de Chambre, and a Chariot, for the especial use of his *dogs*—

We went to the Opera—And I there saw the Grand Dutchess. This has been the most splendid Winter since we have resided here—

Dined at Lord Carysforts only the Viscount D'Anadia beside the family. We stayed also to supper—

Dined again at Lord Carysforts to meet the Turkish Chargé D'Affairs and his Interpreter— They had their dinner all brought ready cooked, and would taste nothing on the Table excepting a small piece of Salmon, of which they took a mouthful out of compliment to the Host— After dinner he came and sat by me, and gave me his Snuff Box to look at on the lid of which was painted a very ugly Ladies face, which he informed me was his favorite Wife— He talked a great deal to *me;* and Lady Carysfort quizzed me after he was gone, about his distinguished preference of my Ladyship.

Before I had retired from the Court Circles; Madame D'Engerstroom had taken it into her head, to make a Claim at Court; of a higher distinction than was customary as to the Seats at Supper at the Kings Table— As the Ladies of Foreign Ministers had the most distinguished Seats at Table; I could not imagine what it meant— She had paid me a formal visit to request my support, and I had told her that I had always been so kindly treated by their Majesties; and as the Wife of the Representive of a Republick I had no especial claims to press; that I therefore declined altogether having any thing to do with the subject—That Lady Carrysfort was a more proper person to apply to— She left me somewhat piqued; but insisted that I should aid *her,* in introducing the fashion of *Pockets,* as she was determined to wear them— I told her that my situation was such, that I doubted if I was of consequence sufficient to introduce *any* fashion, although I might follow one when it was established— She took her leave very coolly.

Lady Carysfort sent for me to sit with her in the evening; and I mentioned the circumstance of Madame D'Engerstroom's visit, and asked how I should have acted. She laughed and said, "that she had gone through a similar Scene; and that she had positively *declined* to interfere in the established arrangements of the Court, which were highly satisfactory to the Corps Diplomatique; and she did not believe they desired any alteration or amendment—" She laughed heartily about the *Pockets* and turned the whole affair into complete ridicule. Madame D'Engerstroom was a very flighty, and extraordinarily weak Woman; and her whole aim was to *magnify* herself into some *super-eminence,* for which she did not possess one satisfactory quality— Superior beauty, Superior attainments, or superior virtues, may sometimes elevate themselves to great prominence in the World: but always blended with respect or admiration— Superior wealth may *enforce* attention, but without other accessories in *Europe,* it does not yield positive respect— It is a concomitant, but not the prime requisite—

To finish this silly affair which—I mention in detail; because it was a useful lesson to *me,* when Mr. Adams was S[*ecretary*] of State, with a restless Diplomacy of Foreigners at Washington— In spite of every advice, all the other Ladies of the corps refusing to participate— The first Court Supper she attended after making this pretention; the *other* Ladies were escorted to the usual Seats, assigned to them by the King; Every Lady holding any place at Court, when *she* attempted to move up; politely, but positively told her, that her *rank* did not entitle her to a seat above them; and thus *alone,* without her *Husband,* she was thankful to get a place, through the intervention of the Master of the Ceremonies; at the very foot of the Table; being at the same time informed, "that a rule had been adopted by the Kings Ministers to prevent all disputes on the subject of Precedence, to assign to each Lady a *place* by *courtesy,* as distinguished Strangers—" Her situation was mortifying in the extreme: for she had wilfully brought it on herself; and the opportunity gave universal pleasure— Lady Carysfort enjoyed and laughed heartily at Madame's complete discomfiture— The punishment ceased with this exhibition, I *suppose* by order of the King; and at the next Court supper she was received as usual— This Lady has since been pre-eminent in Sweden—

While Louisa and John Quincy were at a far remove from the contentious politics of the U.S. presidential election of 1800, its outcome affected them directly. After one of the most vitriolic and divisive campaigns in American history, Thomas Jefferson emerged as the winner over John Adams and Aaron Burr. John Adams accordingly recalled John Quincy from Berlin, believing it appropriate to give Jefferson the opportunity to appoint his own diplomats. News of the recall reached Berlin in late April 1801.

The timing could not have been more difficult, as Louisa had given birth to their son George just two weeks earlier. Not surprisingly, given Louisa's medical history, the birth proved difficult, and she was ill and weak for some time thereafter. But by early June, the Adamses began to prepare for their departure. They left Berlin on 17 June, traveled by carriage to Hamburg, and sailed from there on 8 July aboard the America. They would arrive in Philadelphia on 4 September.

24 March 1801

Mr Richards wrote a Note to Mr. Adams informing him of the death of poor Isabella Brown—After an illness of two days of congestion— Prejudice of an unconquerable character, and not to be overcome, caused her so sudden dissolution; How careful Mothers ought to be, in early youth to familiarize their children to changes of circumstane and custom in life—and to prevent that local tenacity of opinion, which only sanctions the customary usages which hourly surround us— She was lovely in her character and her mind only wanted *expansion,* to render her all that could be wished— She in her last moments rejected the tears, the entreaties, the experience of her agonized Father, and the loss of life was the fatal consequence— Her strong attachment to me was evinced in her last moments— After taking leave of her Parents and Sisters She left a kind assurance of her affection for me, and desired that a Cap which I had presented and made for her, should be given to her— She laid it by her with a solemn request, that she should be buried in it, as the last proof of her love— All I loved seemed to be deserting me— This was a severe stroke— After the Funeral Lady Carysfort called to see and console me— Once I called at Mrs. Browns to see her after the loss of her dear daughter, but my health totally failed after that sad event; and on the 12th day of April, I was blessed with a *Son*—but under circumstances so distressing; and treatment so cruel on the part of the Drunken Accoucheur [*male midwife*], that my life nearly became the forfeit; and I rose from my bed of agony, a *cripple,* with the loss of the use of my left leg—

For five weeks my life was despaired of and in the hope of saving *me,* and to keep the fever from the Brain, I nursed my boy, and a little Girl of six months old—The daughter of a kind english woman, then resident at Berlin— She never would nurse at her Mothers breast afterwards— The sixth week in a state to excite pity I was lifted into the Carriage— Mr. Welsh and Whitcomb carried me down in a Chair, and Mr. Adams from within the Carriage lifted me in— I went to Lady Carysforts, she and her husband having stood Sponsors for poor George, when I was too weak and ill to attend the *Christening Service* on the 4th inst. [*May*], which was performed by

Mr. Proby, the Chaplain of the English Embassy; and when I got there, I was kindly lifted out and carried into the House by Major Casa Major— Here I attended the morning Services—went through the ceremony of Churching, and received the Sacrament, with feelings I sincerely trust of devotion, and gratitude for the blessings bestowed on me— I was a *Mother*— God had heard my prayer.

Through my miserable confinement, the King had the ends of the Street barred up, that no carriages might disturb me; and the Queen sent every day to enquire how I was— In the situation of my health when I left my chamber; I was altogether unable to take leave of them, and express my grateful thanks for the unusual kindness shewn to me; and only through Dr. Brown and Countess Pauline, was I enabled to offer them after I was gone— All this was complementary to America—Not personally to *me*—

1 June 1801

Preparations were making for my departure as Mr Adams would not stay after his recall—

4 June 1801

George was innoculated with the [*smallpox*] Vaccine Matter preparatory to our departure.

8 June 1801

Went to Charlottenburg could not walk without assistance attended the Services by Mr. Proby.

15 June 1801

I went to Lady Carysforts not having been able to go the day before, being again very ill; and after dinner took my final leave of her with bitter tears— When it was thought on the 4th day of my confinement that I was dying; that a mortification had taken place—I had entreated her to *take* my Child, until Mr. Adams should leave the Country; and she had faithfully promised to perform every duty to him, as I would myself—and I have not the slightest doubt at this moment that She would have consciensciously fulfilled the promise—

16 June 1801

We dined at Dr. Browns and on taking leave of me he entreated me to persevere in nursing my Child for six Months; at that period my *constitution* might change—but he considered me in a deep consumption, and only trusted to this crisis to save my life— I had been fully aware of my situation and was rather pleased to learn that I might live to see my Parents, and perhaps die in their Arms—

CHAPTER THREE

"Had I Steped into Noah's Ark"

United States

In the summer of 1801, Louisa and John Quincy with their young son George sailed from Hamburg to the United States. For Louisa, this would be her first time encountering her father's homeland. As she recounts below in the continuation of her "Adventures of a Nobody," she found the experience disconcerting, especially the sharp contrast between her life in the major cities of Europe and the small-town world of Quincy, Massachusetts. In her words, "Had I steped into Noah's Ark I do-not think I could have been more utterly astonished."

The family arrived in Philadelphia on 4 September, thoroughly worn out from the long transatlantic voyage. They almost immediately separated, John Quincy heading directly to his family in Quincy while Louisa went to meet her own in Washington, D.C. They would reunite there in October and travel together to Massachusetts, where they stayed first at the Old House (also called Peacefield), the family home in Quincy, before ultimately settling in Boston in a house on Hanover Street. John Quincy resumed his legal career. But he was hardly going to stay out of public life for long. He was elected to the Massachusetts General Court in April 1802. The next year, the Massachusetts legislature named him a U.S. senator, and Louisa once again found herself playing the role—often uncomfortably—of wife of a public official.

Another challenge confronting Louisa on arriving in the United States was facing John Quincy's past, most notably his former amour, Mary Frazier. While Louisa managed to fully convince herself that John Quincy still loved Mary and would have been happier married to her, the reality was quite different. John Quincy had long before broken off his relationship with Frazier, commenting to his mother in the summer of 1796 that their "separation was not merely the result of necessity, or of an angry moment, it was a mutual dissolution of affection: the attractive principle was itself destroyed. the flame

was not covered with ashes, it was extinguished with cold water." But no
amount of reassuring convinced Louisa that John Quincy was not comparing
her, unfavorably, to Mary.

8 July 1801

Went on board of the Vessel in the Evening; having left Hamburg in a
Lighter, and settled ourselves as comfortably as we could— My poor Babys
Arm was very bad, and I was quite frightened at the appearance of it—

Sixty long and wearisome days passed over us— My Babe had the Dis-
sentery so badly I feared we should lose him— No advice; inexperienced,
and so ill and feeble I could scarcely drag myself about; the first half of the
voyage was dreadful— My boy got well, and the Sailors had him constantly
in their arms; and he throve so rapidly that *at* Sea, and though only three
months old when we sailed, I had to set to work, and short coat him, lest
some accident shou'd happen through his long Frocks— Epps loved him as
if he was her own, and she was an admirable Nurse—

On my voyage I heard for the first time of Miss *Frazer;* and all the history;
and my curiosity was much excited to see her— I candidly confess however,
that poor faded thing as I was; the elaborate but just account which I heard
of her extreme beauty; her great attainments; the elegance of her Letters;
altogether made me feel *little;* and though I was not *jealous,* I could not bear
the idea of the comparison that must take place, between a single woman
possessing all her loveliness, and a poor broken consumptive creature, almost
at the last gasp from fatigue, suffering and anxiety— It is true I had every
confidence in my husbands affection, yet it was an affair of vanity on my
part; and my only consolation was, that at any rate I had a *Son*— This was
all very foolish no doubt, but is it not human nature?

On the 4th of Septb. we landed in Philadelphia; the weather was
intensely hot, but it was of service to my limb, not yet perfectly re-estab-
lished— With pain my old friends recollected me; and Tom Adams was
shocked and distressed when he saw me— Here I first saw Mrs. Quincy
and Mrs. Tudor— And I went out several times though scarcely able to
crawl; to dinner, and to Tea, and this continued as long as I staid— Dr
[*Benjamin*] Rush attended me—and was very kind to me—

12 September 1801

At eight o'clock in the morning, Mr. Adams put me into the Stage for Baltimore, with Epps, my Bably, and Whitcomb, to visit my poor Father and my family in Washington. We had never been parted before; and though this Country was to be my home, I was yet a forlorn stranger in the land of my Fathers; and I could not reconcile myself to returning thus sick and desolate, among those who had so loved me— Mr. Adams felt the same anxiety to see his Parents that I did; and I could not complain of the feeling which occupied my own heart; When I arrived after a tedious and dangerous journey, my Father was standing on the steps at the door of the house, expecting his Child, yet he did not *know me*— After he had recovered from the shock at first seeing me; he kept exclaiming that "he did not know his own Child," and it was sometime before he could calm his feelings, and talk with me— Whitcomb remained a day, and then returned to Boston—

Unaccustomed to the American Stages, I was perfectly exhausted, and the next morning waked in a high fever. A Physician was sent for, and he decided without a moments hesitation that early in October, I must wean my boy or he would not answer for my life— The kind care and affectionate attention of my Mother and my Sisters restored me in a few days to my usual state, and on the 12th of October I weaned my boy by absolute compulsion, against my will, and with great bodily suffering— Two little months escaped rapidly before Mr. Adams came on, and I had the misery to see my father fearfully changed; and delighting only in his Grand children Johnson [*Hellen*], and George, and shadowing visions of brightness for future times— Mr. Adams arrived on the 21st of October and was warmly and cordially greeted by the family, with delight by myself— Thus we were all once more united—

27 October 1801

My Mother, Mr. Adams, Epps, the Child and myself, went to visit Mrs Washington at Mount Vernon— My Father was unexpectedly called to Anapolis— There I saw Mrs. Lewis the celebrated Nelly Custis [*Martha Washington's granddaughter*] a beautiful woman—

28 October 1801

At ten o clock the next morning we took leave, and returned to dinner at 1/2 past three— Mrs. Hellen come to stay there while her Husband was absent— I was better than I had been for a long time—

Caught a violent Cold and could not travel on the 31st the day appointed by Mr. Adams—

We were out a great deal while we staid at Washington— Dined at Mr Jeffersons, Madisons, Smiths, and many other places— Never at Mr. Galatins—

On the 3d of Nover. we started for Frederic; I with a dreadful Cough, at 1/2 past two in the morning, accompanied by my Father, Mother, and two youngest Sisters— Caroline was to accompany *me*— About half way my Father, was taken very ill; so ill that it was with the utmost difficulty that he could reach Frederic, where he was immediately put to bed and a Physician called in— I staid with him a couple of days at the Hotel; and was then forced to go to my Uncle Governor Johnson's, at Rose Hill, about a Mile out of the Town— All my relations received us with the utmost kindness, and treated Mr. Adams with the most marked attention and respect— Their Horses, their Carriages, Their Houses, all were at our command, and we were *petted* in every possible way during our stay, which was in every way painful, in consequence of my dear Fathers dreadful illness— Mr. Adams sat up with *him*— His danger was great— Our dear Babe became very ill with the Summer complaint—

11 November 1801

At four o'clock on this day I was obliged to leave Frederick and my dying Father—My Baby being very ill of the Bowel complaint; and I not permited to take leave of my suffering Parent, lest it should agitate him; and me *so* much as to incapacitate me for the journey; Mr. Adams being anxious to proceed to Boston, lest the Winter should set in— Caroline would not leave my father in such a state, and remained to nurse him faithfully, on that dreadfull Bed of sickness, from which he was removed to his brothers; Baker Johnson's to die, after a lingering sickness of Six Months of intense and unremited agony, away from his home, and from the most of his family— I never saw him

more— We travelled all day only stopping once; the Child constantly shrieking so that we could not pacify him; by the Lancaster road, and arrived at
the Ferry at 7 o'clock, so dark, that we were in imminent danger of running
on the rocks in a very small Boat, and lodged at Columbia on the Eastern
Shore— I had no proper Clothing for such a journey; and I cannot describe
my suffering of both mind and body—

At two the next morning, we again started from Columbia, and for 12
Miles we were alone in the Stage, over a very rough Turnpike road— We
then took eight Passengers, and travelled 76 miles without stopping, and
arrived at Philadelphia at 5 o'clock in the Evening; I extremely overcome
and very ill—and my darling George not much better— Next day I was apparently better, and was taken to the Theatre— I was so severely ill, after
this that Mr. Adams sent for Dr. Rush— Could my spirits be otherwise
than bad; my situation was doubtful, and my fathers state enough to cause
every apprehension— Mr. Adams remarks "that my Spirits were more depressed than myself *really* ill"—

15 *November 1801*

I was a little better but still very poorly and remained quietly at home.

16 *November 1801*

At two o'clock we again set forward and went as far as Trenton where we
arrived at eight in the Evening— Here we were all obliged to lodge in the
same chamber, and the Child was so restless and uneasy, we could get no
sleep—and soon after 4 o'clock, we resumed this dreadful journey, breakfasting at Princeton, dining at Elizabeth Town, and arriving at Newark at 4
in the afternoon at Giffords Inn— Then I was obliged to walk to see Col
Smiths *Mother,* who insisted upon our staying and passing the Night at
her House— Abby Adams, afterwards Mrs. Johnson [*Charles Adams's
daughter*] then a Child was with her— The *evening* was very stormy with
heavy rain— Mrs. Smith an immense woman entertained us with a dismal
family history—

18 November 1801

At nine in the morning we rode to Pawles Hook, the roads dreadful, in a pouring rain; and then crossed the Ferry in an open Boat called I think a perogue, the Storm of wind and rain being so severe, that only *one* man could be found, who would cross with us—without even an Umbrella, dressed in a pale blue Satin pelice trimmed with black lace, and without one particle of covering, under which we could Shelter our devoted heads— We waited in the doorway of a house drenched to the Skin, while Mr. Adams got a hack; a thing difficult to procure at that time—and we drove to Mrs. Smith's [*Nabby*], who was too much shocked when she thus saw me drenched to the Skin, so ill, and weak, without stopping to ask any questions, she led me into a bed room, tore off my things, and insisted upon nursing me up in the kindest and most affectionate manner— What I had been and what I was!! the contrast was too great and my temper, my character entirely changed— Dearly did I love her—

19 November 1801

The next day I was better, that is able to get up and received some of my old friends— In the evening She had company and I sat up quite late I was a favorite of the Col's—

20 November 1801

At four o clock in the afternoon we took passage in the packet Cordelia weather very Cold— Many passengers—

22 November 1801

We went ashore at Newport and Lodged at Mrs Brentons, and

23 November 1801

the next morning to Providence and continued our Route in the Stage to Boston, where we arrived wet and tired; and fortunately for me and my babe, too late for the Quincy Stage, in which I was to have proceeded immediately— These were my first impressions of America! No one can wonder that they were not agreeable— Suffering and sorrow, sickness and exhaustion, with anguish of mind, all combined to harrass me; and hitherto I had been the spoilt Child of indulgence; could I realize the change? Impossible! and under such circumstances could I appear amiable? Mrs. [*Hannah Carter*] Smith the Wife of Mr W[*illiam*] Smith of Boston received us very kindly, and we passed the night at her house, and breakfasted there in the morning— At ten o'clock we started for Quincy, and arrived there just at Noon— Both Mr & Mrs. Adams received me very kindly, and were much pleased with the Child: for whose sake I had been thus hurried on from the South to gratify their wish and the necessity of Mr As entering into business— In the Evening Miss Beale came to see me (late Mrs. Wales)—

26 November 1801

Was thanksgiving day— We appeared at Church or rather Meeting— Mrs. Smith, Mr T Welsh, and W[*illiam Smith*] Shaw dined with us— Mrs. [*Mary Smith*] Cranch [*Abigail's sister*] called in the afternoon—Capt Beale and Mr Peter Adams [*John's brother*] in the Evening— From this period my Cough and breast were in a most distressing state, and Mr Adams could get no rest— The Quincy visitations were almost insupportable, and I longed for my home, with an impatience that made me completely disagreeable— Mr. Adams bought some of his Old Uncle Quincy's Furniture for our house—And I went with him to see the House in Hanover Street which he had purchased—

On the 21st. of December we took up our residence in Boston—in Hanover Street, Epps, and Lydia Pray with us— Very ill— Mr Hall and Mr. Smith called on us—

1 January 1802

Mrs. Doble, Mrs. Wilson, Mrs Payne Mrs. Bartlet and Mr Boylston called on us— In the Evening was obliged to go to a small Tea party at Mrs. Smiths, met the Welsh's; the Storers &ce—Mrs Storer a fine woman. Went out to Quincy—Weather so severely Cold could not endure it, and was very ill all the time I staid— Quincy! What shall I say of my impressions of Quincy! Had I steped into Noah's Ark I do-not think I could have been more utterly astonished— Dr. Tufts! Deacon French! Mr Cranch! Old Uncle Peter! and Capt Beale!!! It was lucky for me that I was so much depressed, and so ill, or I should certainly have given mortal Offence— Even the Church, its forms, The snuffling through the nose, the Singers, the dressing and the dinner hour, were all novelties to me; and the ceremonious partys, the manners, and the hours of meeting 1/2 past four were equally astounding to me—

In England I had lived in the City of London—In Berlin at Court! But the ettiquettes of Court society were not half so burdensome— I had promised Mr Adams at his particular request never to talk about Berlin, and I faithfully kept my word—but we could not silence Epps, and she would make ridiculous observations; and the consequence was unfavorable to me— This was forty three years ago and forty three years in America is equal to a Century any where else; and do what I would there was a conviction on the part of others that I could not *suit,* however well inclined— This I necessarily *felt,* and the more particular the attentions that they thought it necessary to show me, the less I felt at *home,* and the more difficult my position became— I had a separate dish set by me of which no one was to partake; and every delicate preserve was brought out to treat me with in the kindest manner— but it always made me feel as if I was an apàrté in the family; and though I felt very grateful, it appeared so strongly to stamp me with unfitness, that often I would not eat of my delicacy, and thus gave offence— Mrs. Adams was too kind and I could not reject any thing— Louisa Smith was jealous to excess, and the first day that I arrived, left the Table crying and sobbing, and could not be induced to eat any dinner— No wonder that I was anxious to have a house—

The old Gentleman [*John Adams*] took a fancy to *me,* and he was the only one— I was literally and without knowing it a *fine* Lady— No qualifications had hitherto been demanded of me— Mr. Adams had made Whitcomb his Steward and had no confidence in any body else—but I had nothing to do but to see that the orders given were executed; and Epps, was the Housekeeper, as she kept the Linen, the Plate, and our Clothes in order— I had no private expences; because I had no means, therefore I had no responsibility! Could it therefore be surprizing that I was gazed at with *surprize,* if not with contempt— The qualifications necessary to form an accomplished

Quincy Lady, were in direct opposition to the mode of life which I had led—and I soon felt, that even my husband would acknowledge my deficiency, and that I should lose most of my value in his eyes— My dreadful ignorance ~~sickness~~ excited no sympathy, and I saw, and knew that I was totally unfit for my duties, and that I ~~could no longer please~~ under such circumstances could not be useful—and this *idea* added so much to the difficulties of my situation, that I became cold and reserved, and seldom spoke at all—which was deemed pride— All this was perfectly just; and I could not complain of any body but myself— I tried by every means in my power to *work* as they call it; but my strength did not second the effort, and I only made matters worse— Mrs. Adams gave me instruction and advice, but I did not readily learn—and in fact on my part all went wrong, and the more I fretted the worse things grew— Our pecuniary means were small; and of course eoconomy was essential. My people soon saw through my ignorance and took advantage of it, and in short I was in every respect any thing but what I should have been—

Mr. Adams could not hear these things eternally, without seeing my faults; and questions of expenditure and mismanagement highly merited on my part; caused perpetual uneasiness of a character painful to both, yet impossible to avoid— I state this merely to show how imprudent it is for a woman to form a connection in a foreign Country— I was a burthen to my husband; I felt it, and I grieved because I loved him; for what I could not repair— You all see my deficiency at this moment of writing—

In Boston I met with the most decidedly flattering reception— Every body talked to me of Miss Frazer as if they were afraid that I did not know the tale; and Mrs. W Smith told me the whole history, until I was perfectly convinced of the truth of the french Song

> "Qu'on revient toujours à ces premieres amours."
> [*We always return to our first loves.*]

and that it would be impossible for me in any way to compete with this Lady; and that it was a great misfortune that so sickly as I was, I should stand in their way—

Mr. Adams could not afford to keep Epps, and offered to pay her passage back to England— This was a bitter stroke but I knew it was unavoidable—

She declined the passage and married Whitcomb, and they set up in business [*as proprietors of the Boston Concert Hall*] which proved successful— I was sorry but I too well understood the necessity either to grieve or complain—

The Charge of my darling boy then devolved upon me and the sleepless nights of Mr. Adams soon taught him to regret the loss of his loving and faithful Nurse— He was the great blessing in my cup; and he made up the sum of my joy—

All the élite of Boston called on me, and entertained me most handsomely, and it never entered into my head to regret Europe—

The situation of my Father was dreadful, lingering amid the pangs of poverty and agonizing sickness, for six long Months; it is true receiving all kindness from his Brothers—but far from his home, when a crisis took place and hopes were entertained that he might overcome the desease—but the news arrived that Mr. Jefferson had taken his place [*in the Treasury Department*] from him, and he sunk rapidly into his Grave; knowing that, that *place* kindly and mercifully given to him by President Adams, contrary to the advice of all his nearest friends; was the only support that he had for his numerous and distressed family— He died on the 14th of April, leaving a large property which has been totally lost to his family, in consequence of the want of Means to administrate upon the Estate of himself, and his Partners—Lands in Georgia to a large amount situated in the neighbourhood of Augusta, and at this moment recorded and registered in every Court House in the Counties; where the Lands lie—In addition to large Sums, which have furnished fortunes to the Children of the Lawyers, in whose hands the Moneys had been collected—

I mention this *fact,* only as a proof, that my Fathers were just Claims; and to exonerate his memory from every charge calculated to injure his character— Kindly and affectionately treated by Mr. Adams's family, could I have enjoyed health, and fitted myself to perform the duties required by my change of life, I should have been happy— But I hourly betrayed my incapacity; and to a woman like Mrs: Adams; equal to every occasion in life; I appeared like a maudlin hysterical fine Lady, not fit to be the Partner of a Man, who was evidently to play a great part on the Theatre of life— These ideas will be called romantic.— They were so when young; but they exist to this hour— The moment in which my Fathers misfortunes occurred, gave a colouring to my future days, which could never be eradicated— It overtook *me* in the *zenith* of my happiness; at that peculiar period of life which marks a future destiny; and that colouring appeared to stamp my character, with a base deception which my Soul utterly *scorned,* and no evidence could ever be brought forward in my favour afterwards, to *prove* the perfect innocence of my conduct—

The loss of Fortune so small as the best to which all knew I could have pretended to, was scarcely a consideration—but the apparent dishonour of palming myself upon a family under such circumstances, was a baseness from which my spirit has revolted; and it has and still does make the wretchedness of my life— It has turned every sweet into gall—and I have never thought it *possible* however desirous, and willing; to make a reparation for the bitter misfortune of a connection with a family so uncongenial, and so unfortunate as mine has proved to Mr. Adams, both in his private and publick situation—

This is a sentiveness carried to excess many will think, but to a man in a public career in this Country a woman should be like Cæsars Wife.

John Quincy's legislative career necessitated yet more movement for the young family. Initially, from 1802 to 1803, his service was only in the Massachusetts state senate. But after a failed bid for a seat in the U.S. House of Representatives in the fall of 1802, he was appointed a U.S. senator in the spring of 1803 as a member of the Federalist Party. Thereafter, he was obligated by his position to spend winters in Washington, D.C., though he continued to return to Quincy and Boston in the summers, and Louisa, sometimes together with their children (a second son, John, would be born in the summer of 1803), accompanied him for the winters from 1803 to 1805.

Louisa Catharine Smith, whom Louisa Catherine mentions above as being "jealous to excess," was John Quincy's cousin, the daughter of Abigail's brother William Smith Jr. Abigail and John had taken cousin Louisa in when she was still a young girl and raised her. She never married and attended to the elder Adamses until their deaths, after which she continued to live with various Adams family members until her own passing in 1857.

Another of John Quincy's cousins, William Smith Shaw, also spent significant time in John Quincy and Louisa's home. Shaw had previously been John

Adams's private secretary and later became a lawyer and librarian. He would socialize regularly with all of the Adamses, and even lived with Louisa and John Quincy for a time.

12 April 1802

My darling boys birth day passed almost unnoticed— He was a fine Child, and *I* was *too vain* of him— But the name which we had given him was not liked, and perhaps we ought to have given him the name of his Grandfather—

15 May 1802

On this day I went out to Quincy, I had not seen any of the family; and George went with me— Here I remained till the 24th. and Mr. Adams came out on the Saturday and remained till Monday—

26 May 1802

Mr & Mrs. Adams came to Town and passed the night at our house; my health and spirits both wretched— My fate was sealed—and all hope of my Fathers affairs being settled gone for ever—

28 May 1802

Mr. Adams was now in the Legislature, and of course with so much business, was not much at home. The old Gentleman was in Town; Mr. Adams did not see him, and I was very ill—as I had been so frequently in Berlin— Mr. Adams delivered an address before the [*Massachusetts Charitable*] Fire Society, I was too ill to attend it. The Ex-President and Mrs. Adams attended the performance, and came to our House to Sleep— It was very successful—

Mr & Mrs. Adams left us and Louisa Smith staid— She had already made me a long visit in the Winter—

2 June 1802

Mrs. Adams came into Town and dined with us and in the Evening returned with Louisa Smith to Quincy— Went to walk with Mr. Adams and looked over a House on Beacon Hill—

On the 25 of June Mr. Shaw came to live with us— My life was very quiet and agreeable— The family from Quincy often dined with us, and I went out there to stay from Saturday to Monday, whenever I was well enough; sometimes to stay a week. Every care was taken of me, and every kindness shown to me; but I was changed; I had lost my spirits and my health equally; and under such circumstances how could I please any one?—

22 June 1802

Charlotte Welsh who had been on a visit to me left me this day and my Mother and Sister Caroline arrived this Eveng— I was *too* happy—

26 June 1802

Mrs Adams came to Town and took us all out to Quincy— We stayed over Sunday—and My Mother and I and my boy returned to Boston, leaving Caroline there who Mrs. Adams was very fond of— We lived almost constantly at home, occasionally walking in the Mall; and Mr. Adams read to us in the Evening— My Mother had a great many friends in Boston—Mr. David Sears, Sheriffe Allen, Col Bradford, Capt Scott, husband of Mrs. Hancock; Jos Hall, Fitch Hall, the Appleton's now dead; Stephen Higginson, and William Gray of Salem; besides many others that I have forgotten—

I forgot to mention that Mrs. Murray, Wife of Dr Murray with Miss Mary Frazer called on me, and I found the latter *all* that she had been described— She was engaged to marry Mr. Daniel Sargent— This visit took place much earlier than I have mentioned—

The Month of July passed without any event of consequence and our lives were altogether Monotonous— I much prefered it to a roaming restless life, and the Society of my Mother and Caroline, left me little to wish for— The Nature of the illnesses to which I was so constantly exposed, required repose; a thing almost incompatible hitherto with our situation; and even now, not approved: but my mourning authorized it, and it was of essential benefit to my returning strength—

My kind Sister took upon herself the cares of Housekeeping and released me from a thrall heavy enough to break the spirit of a Tyrant— My Experience's in this *line* in consequence of ignorance had been peculiarly painful; and my blessed Sister saved me from unspeakable discomfort— How singularly things turn out in this wonderful world! I had been the only *one* in my family who had gone through a regular *Cooking* education, in consequence of having been a favorite of a very superior Cuisiniere in my fathers family; and who was always delighted to have Miss *Weeser* with her, to learn her mysteries; and for several years my two Sisters and myself had been *compelled* to keep house weekly, for a very large family, under the judicious instruction of Mrs. Nowlan and my Mother— But English housekeeping did not qualify me, and such a tàlànt was worth nothing in my circumstances—

My Father was a Merchant, and a Stipulation was entered into by the Partners of the House, that he was to *entertain* the Americans who visited London; and of course to *receive* an equivalent for the expense thus incurred— It was the settlement of this question, that involved him in difficulties with his Partners when he returned to his Country; and which so materially contributed to his ruin— His house was always open to his Countrymen from every part of the Union; and those who have most cruelly censured him; made no scruple of enjoying its welcome pleasures, and social greeting; as long as it suited their convenience; although I have known but few that would speak in his favour when misfortune overtook him—

Mrs. Smith the amiable and loved Sister of my husband constantly at his house during her residence in england; and was invariably the same; and never changed in her conduct to my family nor the Col— She always wished that my Sister Caroline had been the object of my husbands choice— She knew *him,* and I was so much with *her* that she knew *me* almost as well; and her judgment was probably formed upon some striking characteristic, of which we were not aware—but so it was—and she was right— I am what the french call "àltiére"—She *firm* and *mild*— Few have laboured harder to correct the defects of their character than I have, or have studied their faults so keenly but there is a constitutional irritability about me of late years, trying to my friends and painful to myself, which is I know so disagreeable to

all who live with me; it induces me to live much alone, that I may not burthen those, whose happiness I most desire in this life, and for whom I would
willingly make any sacrifices to promote their welfare— This is written
with the sincere consciousness of the defect—

*Contrary to what Louisa writes below, the Adamses and the Johnsons had
generally cordial relations with one another. Abigail wrote regularly and
warmly to Catherine Nuth Johnson, and had encouraged John to give Joshua
Johnson an appointment as superintendent of the Stamp Office in the Treasury Department, which John did in the spring of 1800.*

*By this time, Louisa was again pregnant. Her second son, named John for
his father and grandfather, would be born on 4 July 1803.*

November 1802

This Month passed away almost entirely at home; My poor Mother was to
leave me, and the trial under all its circumstances, was *very, very* severe—
My eldest Sister had kindly invited her to live with her, and Mr. Hellen;
and she had accepted their invitation being left destitute— Washington
seemed to be her home, and she made the journey in company with Judge
[*William*] Cranch [*John Quincy's cousin*] and his family— Mr. & Mrs.
Adams had paid her much attention—but she was excessively disliked by
the Latter, who never could overcome the sentiment— Too earnest in her
entreaties for the place which the old Gentleman had granted to my father,
against the decided judgment of Mrs. Adams, and her Son Thomas; He
had indulged the kindly feelings of his heart contrary to the interests of his
future prospects; and this generous but imprudent act, of kindness; laid the
foundation for Mr. Adams *future course,* from the moment we returned to
America— My own sense of the injury to himself, was as strong as that of
Mrs. Adams— and though I [decidedly] suffered from its consequences, I
could never condemn a sentiment, in which my own soul had fully accorded—
I would rather that he had kept a Hotel than have resorted to such a means
for a subsistence— This was the first and last time My Mother ever was in a
house of Mr. Adams's— Caroline staid with me— I was again in a very bad
way— We passed all our winters with her at Mr. Hellens in Washington but
one from that time—

I have been forty three years married and I have been but once since our first visit to Frederick and Mr Adams has never been there from the day that we left my Father— My poor Mother was no favorite with her husbands relatives. She had been the spoilt Child of excessive indulgence and her change of fortune came hard to her in her old age— Many and many a time when she was sick, have I seen my Father roll papers round the handles of the Knife and Fork, and lay them before the fire to take the chill off, before she was allowed to touch it; and no matter how busy he might be, he always sat by her to cut the food which was presented to her, and gave it to her with his own hand, with the kindest looks and words— Hamlets description of his Fathers love for his Mother, is the only one which I have ever seen, that could realize the picture ever before my eyes, presented by my Parents— and I was twenty two ere I married: and he was as a Father what he hourly proved himself as a husband— Was it wonderful that she should pine at the change in her situation? when she saw herself forced to *cook* and do all the drudgery of the family? and when that family so reared and educated, actually wanted the very necessaries of life?— It was too severe a trial, and she who I had always known, the most domestic, quiet, unobtrusive Mother; always at home, always at work for her children, all of whose Clothes she made with her own hands? Who had taught those children to help themselves by the work of their own ingenuity, and even under the greatest difficulties to maintain the appearance suited to the station in and in a Slave Country! could she be happy or contented?

Although Louisa only mentions it in passing below at the entry for April 1803, the failure of the London banking firm of Bird, Savage & Bird had a significant impact on the finances of not only John Quincy and Louisa but most especially John and Abigail, who lost virtually all of the money they had put aside for their retirement. Since John Quincy had recommended the bank to them, he felt responsible for their losses and was determined to make them whole. As they would not except his charity, he instead agreed to purchase property from them—the Penn's Hill farm, which contained two cottages known today as the John Adams Birthplace and John Quincy Adams Birthplace—in exchange for the cash they needed.

7 January 1803

Had the first Party I ever gave in Boston—between forty and fifty we danced until one in the morning— The House being small I opened all the Rooms; and sat small Tables prettily ornamented in every direction and two larger ones in the Centre of the Chambers up Stairs: all covered with refreshments— This broke the formality of a Supper and seemed to please generally—

11 January 1803

We had a Tea party of our friends—always stiff and cold—

13 January 1803

We went to the Ball and bought home Miss Morton— These Balls always lasted until morning, or rather between one and two o'clock— They were generally pleasant— Mr Charles Bradbury was a devoted Beau of Mrs. Frye's; but never popped the question—

23 January 1803

We observed a great smoke in the Bed chamber of my Sister; and particularly in the China Closet; and were very much perplexed, no fire being ever made in the apartment but on occasions of sickness— A small fire had been made a week or two before and Caroline became so much alarmed on seeing the smoke issue from under the hearth, that she called Mr. Adams to look at it— On sending for the Mason it was found that a large beam under the hearth, was nearly burnt through; and that if we had not fortunately poured a quantity of water down through the Cracks, it would have blazed out, and probably destroyed the poor old Rat hole; for the benefit of a future Generation, but seriously to *our* loss—

28 January 1803

At a very large and handsome party at Mrs. Gardner Greens— Mr Adams did not come there until late in the Evening— His avocations were so constant we saw but very little of him—

31 January 1803

Caroline left me to spend some days with Mrs. Dexter at Roxbury. Louisa Smith had spent some time with us and enjoyed herself much—

3 February 1803

Mr. Adams was elected to the Senate— Here again was to be a change in our Situation tolerable in perspective but requiring great sacrifices of domestic comfort— My establishment was very comfortable and I longed for quiet. Every thing had been so new to me on my arrival I had had so much to learn so much to be *reconciled* to; Even my Religious opinions were adverse to those of all the friends of Mr. Adams a thing altogether new to me as from the first moment of my acquaintance with him he had apparently known no creed but mine— The change was so inconceivably great, it required time, judgment, and patience to realize; things of which I had never dreamt; and which were altogether contrary to that *fixedness* of opinion, which has proved through life one of the strongest traits of my character— Gradually they became familiar and although I could not sacrifice the sentiment which had

"Grown with my Growth, and strengthened with my strength";

though until I became a *Mother;* perhaps not properly weighed and considered; one more of precept, habit, and example than of meditated reflection— Yet since that period I had become a Member of my Church by reason of preference, and conviction; and my faith was fixed and unalterable— Between my husband and myself there never existed a moments difficulty— He ruled his Children and I quietly acquiesced to his right of controul, on a point so materïal; and I likewise joined in the Duties of his religious exercises as a tribute of respect to him, and as an example to my little ones— convinced that where the heart is true, and faithful in its worship, God will mercifully accept the adoration of a Sincere believer, through whatever form it may be offered with heartfelt humility and decorous devotion—

My health became more and more delicate every hour, and suffering appeared to be *my* lot, and cruel anxiety *that* of my husband; He was now necessarily a man of active business; and I could no longer expect to be the engrossing object of his care as I had been; and like a petted Child I pined at that, which ought to have gratified me— I knew nothing of Politics, and of course was without ambition: and domestic life seemed to be the only life for which nature had intended me— The prospect of the birth of another Child, made every idea of change unpleasant; and under all these circumstances his election to the Senate yielded me no satisfaction— But there was no help for it—and such feelings were warmly disapproved by the family—

I think it was sometime in the Spring of this year, that I went with Caroline and Mr. Adams to pay the Wedding visit to Mrs Daniel Sargent [*Mary Frazier*]; but I am not sure— She looked beautiful, and I believe that this was the last time that I ever saw her— Her married life was very happy and very brief, and she left but one Child a daughter—

April 1803

Mr. Adams received the News of the suspenstion of Payment of the House of Bird Savage and Bird— This was another severe stroke to him—and it confirmed his dislike to Commercial Houses— To prevent the possibility of loss to his Father he immediately began to dispose of his property so as to secure his Father from loss— The energy and decision with which he acted on this occasion was highly honourable and meritorious.

12 April 1803

My Darling boy was two years old, precocious and full of promise— How many prophecies of his future greatness I heard!!! Bishop Chevereux used to dwell upon his features, and then exclaim that he was born to accomplish great deeds of intellectual brightness. Did not I defeat this promise by my desertion of my children, to suffer exile amid the pomps and vanities of a Court, at the expense of every feeling of my Soul, and of the sweetest affections of the heart? and O how bitter has been the punishment— When woman, poor feeble powerless Woman, is called upon to act; what can she, what ought she to do, between conflicting duties— Should she desert the helpless Creatures who God himself has placed in her keeping, to follow the fortunes of one, who is in his strength, and master of his Will?

Friends however near or however well disposed, cann'ot perform the duties of a Mother, unless the life of a Mother is extinct; In that case a Child has but one person to look up to, as its guardian; and its affections are fixed upon one object as they are when the Mother is living— No substitute on the face of this Earth can be found for the Mothers attachment, or the Mothers devotion if she is virtuous; and if the strong and powerful instincts of her Nature have not been perverted by some unholy and worldly master passion— When this is considered; when the average portion of harmony in connubial life is measured; when the loss of youth and health, the rapid decline of beauty, the satiety of habit, and the constant and alluring temptations of a captivating and dangerous intercourse with Society render a Mans home insipid, what can compensate to a Wife, but the companionship, the cares, the tender caresses, and the fond love of her Children? Nearly Four years of lingering hope, of repeated disappointment, had rendered this *great* blessing dearer to me than it is to most women; and my religious opinions had rendered these continued frustrations of a sanctified hope, still more painful.— You can then easily conceive with what ardent love I regarded this my first born Child, and with what earnest anxiety I watched his growth; and with what delight I traced each little thought or expression, that indicated brightness or promise of mind— He was at this period the delight of his Father, whose great ambition to have a Son had thus been so fully gratified—

Our time was pleasantly spent, sometimes in Society but more frequently at home; where Mr. Adams used to read to us every spare hour that the Evenings admited, or with visits from the family at Quincy— Constant faintings and violent attacks of illness short in their duration, prevented my visits to Quincy; as Dr. Welsh's assistance was always necessary, these attacks being incident to my situation and always alarming as to their results— One of the most painful peculiarities attending me in these situations from the period of my marriage, was the loss of the use of my hands which generally caused such agony, that they were obliged to be often tied up in laudnum poultices—

---

4 July 1803

Nothing very material happened until the last Evening— Charlotte and Hariet Welch took Tea with Caroline and myself— Mr Adams at Quincy. Mr. Shaw out; My Nurse not to be found. My two girls out and only the little girl at home— I made all my [*preparations*]. At ½ past ten my Nurse came home. Shaw also had gone to bed— But he went for Dr. Welsh who came at twelve and at three o'clock in the morning just as the first Guns fired my Dear John entered upon this world of care— He was laid upon the Carpet and took a violent cold; the young women in our service not thinking it *delicate,* to afford assistance to a fellow creature in such circumstances; but Caroline jumped out of bed, and ran into the room almost undressed, to assist; and took the Child immediately— Charlotte and Hariet Welsh had run away from the Tea table— I mention this as an example of the *false* delicacy, which is too often practiced even at the expence of life—

I recovered very slowly but as soon as I could crawl came out to Quincy to see Mrs. Adams, who was so dangerously ill that she was not expected to live— My Boy was named *John* after his Grandfather as soon as he could be carried to Church; and Long before I was able to rise from my bed— He was beautiful, and I fear I was too proud of being the Mother of two fine Children—

We made our preparations for our removal to Washington and although I was going to my relations I knew that my home could never be what it had been; and that the situation in which I returned, would be productive of uneasiness every ways— But the course was to be pursued, and it was met without Question—

The extreme kindness with which I had been received in Boston made it painful to relinquish my establishment—again to become a wanderer; and I surely did not behave with either the fortitude or the patience, which might have been expected—

Ambition was not one of my Sins and as I have observed before I felt that my husband should have had a Wife fond of display, with a soaring mind and qualities, of a much higher grade than those of a woman, who was content to live at home and nurse her tender babes.

September 1803

My Father and Mother Adams treated me with *too* much distinction—and whenever I met my Sister Mrs. W Stevens Smith, she treated me with the kindest partiality and affection. She had known me in England and there I had learnt to love her— In America that love and admiration encreased to enthusiasm— For here I saw her under every change of fortune, from the height of affluence and Station, to the misery of poverty and obloquy; sustaining herself and her family with a degree of persevering fortitude; uncomplaining sweetness, and patient resignation, with the Christian devotion of a Saint— Col Smith was a very elegant Militaire; a Man of the World to whom money seemed as dross, and to be used only in the promotion of every taste, and every gratification that it could purchase. Up in the Clouds when prosperity cast its Sun gleams oer his head; or in Prison bounds when wanton recklessness had

Strewn his golden fleece & scatter'd it away—

He was always the gay deluded toy, that wanton'd with the wind and good fortune was to him but the ebb and flow of a changing tide— He was a delightful companion; one of those beings who are born to be the charm, and the plague of doating Woman,

Who feels the ill yet fondly loves the aggressor;

What he possessed he shared too liberally with all that he loved and that liberality was dispensed with a courtesy a *heartiness* cordiality does not imply enough to describe the *manner;* that it won all hearts until repeated follies turned the scale, and left him nearly friendless— Mrs. Smith loved this Man with the purest devotion; under all circumstances; and all, and every trial that wayward fortune could inflict; and was the most untiring exemplary Wife, that I ever saw without any possible exception. She possessed great strength of mind; Gentleness of disposition, unswerving fortitude and deliberate and reflective firmness of religious principle, which bore her triumphantly through Scenes of difficulty and perplexity, to which few are equal in this world of trouble; and she left a reputation as free from reproach and as highly cherished, as that of the Infant Cherub whose pure and unspoted innocence had fitted her for the heaven to which she was so recently called—but whose memory lives in the hearts of all who were susceptible of love and admiration for her, alas, too precocious loveliness.

Col Smith was a brilliant rather than a solid man; but still he possesed powers which ensured him a high Rank among publick men, and has left in this respect a fair and handsome reputation—

September 1803

Mrs. Adams continued dangerously ill— My baby bore his Grandfathers Name—but she grieved that he did not bear his likeness, and that was a grief to one so sensitive as myself—

Under the necessity of procuring a Nurse to take care of my two little ones I had twenty young women apply for the situation—and alas! for this Land of good or bundling habits—every one had *had* a *Misfortune* and had a young lady or gentleman to provide for, and were thus obliged to condescend to take a Service, even far from home— This however did not suit me, as I felt afraid I might have to provide for more; and I selected a very staid looking *Lady,* sent to me by Mrs. Otis with a recommendation— I engaged her, and fixed the time for her entrance upon when I received another a second Note, stating that this person could not suit me; as She had a Child by a coloured Gentleman, and was altogether an improper character— I immediately declined to take her, and engaged Patty Milnor, who I was obliged to send back early in the Spring, as *she* was constantly in hysterics, *because* she could not see her *Sweet-heart*—

Our residence in Boston I have already said was very pleasant—and I grieved to give up my House: a fact I fear too strongly evidenced when I gave up my house, and signed the deed of Sale— I cordially approved of the Act; but I sadly regretted its necessity—

I had no right to feel so it is true; for it was not my property and the total beggary of my family took away all claim— But to a Woman, her home is a blessing under every circumstance; and it is the only element in which her happiness should be fixed—

1 October 1803

At last we departed, leaving Mrs. Adams recovered— We rode to Milton and there took up Mr. Allyne Otis, and from thence went to Providence and lodged at Mr. Ammidons—Caroline Patty the two Children Mr. Otis Mr Adams and myself—

2 October 1803

The Fever in New York made it difficult to procure a passage across as all intercourse was suspended and the Capt of a small Packet called the Cordelia agreed to take us and Land us at Powles Hook— The wind not being fair we remained in Providence—

4 October 1803

We sailed. A Singular being named James Brown forced himself upon our attention and soon convinced us that he was one of those Crack-brain reformers who fancy that they can change the whole system of the World and new create the Age— These characters are a sort of pest when you are closeted with them as in a Packet at Sea and until the weather became so bad that we were confined to our Cabins or elegantly termed State Rooms by that most inexorable of all sickness le mal de Mer we were bored beyond all patience— Mr Otis left us to go on by Land—

The Weather being bad and the Wind very heavy we landed at Newport and Lodged at Mrs. Brinton's— Mr. Hore a young Englishman went with us— Here we found a French family from St. Domingo—Dirty beyond conception.

5 October 1803

As my poor George was playing in the Garden he nearly trod on a Snake and narrowly escaped its sting— The weather still continuing bad we could

not sail and contented ourselves with our very kind hostess who I still remember with pleasure—

6 October 1803

Again we took possession of our Berth's I and my two Babies in one State
Room. My Sister and Patty in the other both too sick to move— The Night
and day were dreadful. My Baby only three Months old would not leave the
breast one moment— My poor George sick almost to death; but "saying
nerver mind Mama;" I shall soon be better; myself so weak I could scarcely
crawl and almost as sick as the Children— Even the boy who waited on the
Cabin Passengers was constantly wanted on Deck, found it impossible to
attend to us, and "our sufferings *was* intolerable"—and at last we were obliged
to put into the Port of New London—

8 October 1803

Mr. Hoare took my George, washed and dressed him, and carried him on
Shore; and offered me every assistance in his Power— He was a very elegant
young man, only 24 and apparently quite unaccustomed to such services,
but performed them admirably— We landed at eight o'clock in the morning
and got a comfortable breakfast; and then laid down to rest our exhausted
frames— In the afternoon My Sister myself and Mr. Hoare took a short
walk to see the Town, and at nine o'clock we all undressed and went to bed,
in the hope of getting strength to renew our voyage—

9 October 1803

At eleven I was waked; and had to wake my Babes, and dress them to go on
Board, out of their warm and comfortable Beds, and at twelve we again set
Sail upon this tedious and really perilous voyage—for the Sailors told
Mr Hoare while I was in my Berth with the door open to the Cabin, "that
the Rigging was so rotten, it would not bear them to the Sails"— George
was now much better and sat in the Berth with his playthings— I did not
observe that the window was open just wide enough to put his hand
through; but when about to land he told me he had thrown the Keys of all

our Trunks and his Shoes out of the Window, and they of course had fallen into the Sea— Here was a new embarrassment added to which I was in a raging Fever, and during our ride to New Ark of ten miles over a log road, quite delirious— Arrived at Giffords I was put to bed; with all the Family in the same chamber; and every one shrinking from me in the apprehension of the Yellow Fever—

10 October 1803

Continued dangerously ill— Dr. Johnson attended me; but he was afraid to come near me, and made me stretch my arm out as far as I could for him to feel my pulse, and would not look at my throat; such was the panic occasioned by that frightful desease— Mr. Adams and my Sister Nursed me; and every thing was done for me that was possible to promote my comfort under such circumstances— Mrs. Smith Senr. and Mrs. C[*harles*] Adams took George with them to pass the days, and brought him home in the Eveng.— On the day that we started from Quincy we had heard of the death of Mrs. Hellens Child, and she lay in a very dangerous state not expected to live— This delay was therefore very painful and distressing— Col Smith called.

12 October 1803

My Fever having subsided I was lifted out of Bed, and put into Mrs. Giffords Carriage; and we rode six miles to Elizabeth Town. The exertion appeared to revive me and my medcines were all prepared and punctually administered— We remained at Elizabeth Town very much in the same way; and with the same alarm as at New Ark— At Princeton and at Frankfort we were received on the same conditions as heretofore dining and sleeping in the same chamber, children and all-together; lest *I* unfortunately should carry this plague out of my immediate family, who were to derive all the benefit of infection from the dreaded yellow Fever; without a possibility of escape, if they sought protection under the roof of *Christians*

"Lord what is Man, that thou shouldst be mindful of him"—

when in the hour of tribulation he has so little feeling for his fellow creature.— We did not enter into Philadelphia; but travelled round the outskirts and arrived safely at Washington then a scene of utter desolation— The roads were almost impassable and Mr Hellens house lonely and dreary and at least two miles from the Capitol— Judge Adams came to us here—

Throughout their time in Washington, D.C., in the first decade of the nineteenth century, Louisa and John Quincy stayed with Louisa's sister Nancy Hellen and her husband, Walter, at their K Street home. The city was still very much a work in progress, with poor roads and many federal buildings only partially completed. It compared poorly to London and Berlin. Louisa also found the social situation awkward; she believed that democracy led to "a perpetual struggle for a position," which in turn caused social tensions, unlike in European courts, where status was clearly delineated.

October 1803

Mr. Adams was now a Senator of the U.S. Thus a distinction was immediately created between my *station* and that of my own family with whom I boarded; and though this fact produced a difference *out* of doors in this equalizing republick by the distinction shown to a *man* as a *Senator* by all the Officers of the Government &c; still this very distinction pointed the fact of a difference, and often occasioned unpleasant feelings very painful to myself, and not a little galling to others— Having lived abroad, all this operation of mere circumstance was new to *me;* and it had a very depressing effect upon my spirits— In other Countries *Station* is so defined, and the rules of Society are so clearly understood; *feeling* is seldom unpleasantly shocked by changes which stand on the firm and fixed basis of common custom— But with us, jealousies are immediately awakened, and even your children and your nearest and dearest connections, are *fearful* of being *supposed* to play a minor part on the great theatre, and despise the idea of a *secondary* place, even to age combined with dignity and wisdom— This is not the puerile observation of six and twenty; but it springs from the long tried experience of six and sixty, after a varied life of good and evil; and from the mind of one who never valued what is termed greatness by a vulgar world; but who being accustomed through her connection with a family whose real *greatness* emanated from great minds, morals, and qualifications, has raised a standard from which almost all others shrink; by which alone her judgment can be satisfied—

The Winter was severe; but we frequented the parties, the dinners, the Assemblies, and all the routine of a Metropolitan Season at a Congressional Session, almost at the risk of life, in consequence of the difficulties of intercourse— The City not being laid out; the Streets not graduated; the bridges consisting of mere loose planks; and huge stumps of Trees recently cut down intercepting every path; and the roads intersected by deep ravines continually enlarged by rain—

Mr. Jefferson was the President of the day—the ruling Demagogue of the hour— Every thing about him was *aristorcatic except* his person which was ungainly ugly and common— His manner was awkward, and excessively ineligant; and until he fairly entered into conversation, there was a sort of peering restlessness about him, which betrayed a fear of being scanned more closely by his visitors, than was altogether *agreeable* to his self complacency— While conversing he was very agreeable, and possessed the art of drawing out *others* and at the same time attracting attention to himself— The entertainment was handsome—French Servants in Livery; a French Butler, a French Cuisine, and a buffet full of choice Wine and Plate: had he had a tolerable fire on one of the bitterest days I ever experienced, we might almost have fancied ourselves in Europe— Mr. Madison and his Lady were present; and the French Minister Tureau; and among others whom I have forgotten John Randolph, who gave us a specimen of his wonted rudeness, in an attack which he made on the wine—

Mr. Madison was a *very* small man in his *person,* with a *very* large *head*— his manners were peculiarly unassuming; and his conversation lively, often playful, with a mixture of wit and seriousness so happily blended as to excite admiration and respect— I never saw a man with a mind so copious, so free from the pedantry and mere classical jargon of University Scholarship—but his language was chaste, well suited to occasion, and the simple expression of the passing thought, and in harmony with the taste of his hearers— Mrs. Madison was tall large and rather masciline in personal dimensions; her complexion was so fair and brilliant as to redeem this objection, in its perfectly feminine beauty— Dressed as a Quaker with all the nâive simplicity of the sect; there was a frankness and ease in her deportment, that won golden opinions from all, and she possessed an influence so decided with her little Man that She was the worshiped of all the Idol-mongers, who hang on tinsel greatness— Genl. Tureau was one of the Revolutionary Hero's of France in its worst era in La Vendéé [*a 1794 massacre*]; who still retained such a love of *fight,* that he and his fair Lady often gave to the public fine specimens of Battle, which necessitated an interference from *neighbours,* and even constabulary *force* to protect the frail conquered party— Of John Randolph what shall I say? Among some of the theories broached by mankind the World is said to be haunted by *Dæmons;* and if this idea could be re-alized, surely John Randolph in person, face, manners and mind, might have been the prototype of this *imaginary* monster, created to torment and bewilder mankind—

The dinner was agreeable enough—but when we retired to the Drawing Room in the *french* fashion, Ladies and Gentlemen together; We found a Grate of small size in the vast Circular Room, the fire not rising above the second bar of this coal grate, and the coals what there were of them barely kindled; in fact in such a State, that one of the Guest's said "he could have amused himself *'by spitting out the fire'*"; Shaking with cold the company reduced to a state of silence, we were under the necessity of keeping our teeth close shut, lest their chattering should proclaim that, "our sufferins was intolerable." while the gallant President drew his Chair close into the centre of the hearth, and seemed impatiently to await our exit; which was sadly delayed by the neglect of the hackney Coachman; although we were countenanced by the blustering french hero, who amused himself with a gallopade backwards and forwards in the apartment, until relieved from the same inconvenience as ourselves— After a long and dangerous ride, over the *glacier's* between the Presidents and the lone house by the river side occupied by Mr. Hellen, we had a hearty laugh at the events of the day—and a cheerful Cup of Tea, that most welcome of all restoratives round a pleasant family Table in social chat, measuring the present by the past, thus brought in contrast to my view—and I saw but little to choose between the vulgar aristocracy of German Courtiers, and the time serving democracy of the borrowed luxuries and the stately assumption, of the Parvenue triumph of a political *hypocrite,* denominated the Leader of a faction—

1 January 1804

According to the fashion of the day Mr Adams paid his visit to the President— A day which draws out an unruly Crowd of indiscriminate persons from every Class; peculiarly annoying to the Corps Diplomatique, whose fine clothing, Carriages &ce, become the gaze of the curious vulgar, only to be satisfied by tangible means, exceedingly trying and unpleasant to aristocratic feelings and education— Tom Jefferson as the founder of democracy; was obliged patiently to submit, and to *permit* these indignities: and to have his wardrobe ransacked that the People might admire his *red breeches* &c &c and amuse themselves at his expense, and *not a little* annoyance—

5 January 1804

My little boy was very ill of a fever and my time and cares were too necessary to his recovery to admit of my leaving him— Among the acquaintance which we made none were more kind than Judge [*William*] and Mrs. Cushing— They seemed to belong to a patriarchal age; strongly imbued with the puritan spirit softened by that benevolence which a free association with men generally produces through observation and experience, when we have passed the age of the passions; and ambition been gratified by established popularity— Their persons, dress, manners, and the manner of their lives; equipage; all spoke of a primeval age; exciting astonishment in the mature; and risibility in the young; who under the idea of their *freedom,* are apt to make a use of *liberty* not exactly accordant with the rules of good breeding—

Gayéty was the order of the day and the House was thronged with visitors— My Sisters were very pretty and attractive and their education and accomplishments rendered them objects of general admiration— My manners were frigid, cold, and repulsive; and being naturally timid, and educated under much restraint; much was attributed to pride which was caused by fear of giving offence, or clashing with some usage which I did not understand, or some omissions of ceremonial with which I was totally unacquainted— At the Courts of Princes you get written instruction's to teach you the forms and ettiquettes—you are therefore seldom liable to give offence by erring— In a democratic government where all are monarchs; although *one* yourself, there is a perpetual struggle for a *position,* which gives rise to constant feuds, and demands utterly impossible to satisfy; & which lay the foundation for absurd enmities that can never be reconciled— A man intent upon business walking to his department, passes by a Gentleman who *bows* to him— *He* does not see it; but the consequence resulting therefrom, is an exaggerated enmity so violent; that howerver gifted by talents, knowledge or experience for Office; a vote is for ever cast against the offender however fit for the Office in question—

Many pretend that the Government of Moses was a *Republic.* But the people did *not* create and select *him,* and enforce obedience to him and to Aaron: It was the Almighty who ordered his course; and who sustained him in Power; and without this special and divine support Moses would have been no better than common *men:* excepting from the education which he had recieved miraculously to fit him for the purpose— How could that be a Republick which had the King of Kings for a Ruler?

Louisa remained in Washington, D.C., with her children over the spring and summer of 1804, while John Quincy traveled to Massachusetts to see his family and attend to business. He made the trip with Louisa's nurse, Patty Walin (sometimes called Patty Milnor in Louisa's memoirs), who had been in perpetual poor health over the winter. John Quincy returned to Washington in October in time for the opening of the new session of Congress.

During the summer months in Washington, many of the regular social activities were suspended. For instance, the president's weekly drawing room— a social gathering that included light refreshments but not a seated, formal dinner—ceased during the congressional recess when so many government officials left town. Likewise, Louisa was spared for a time the onerous duty of making visits, traveling to ladies' homes to leave her calling card.

2 April 1804

The winter passed under much uneasiness and anxiety of a domestic character: and the time having arrived for Mr Adams's departure we prepared every thing and he left us taking my Nurse Patty Walin with him under the most disagreeable circumstances She, having been subject to fits all the Winter

and obliging to vacate his writing room besides many other inconveniences.—
Mr Allen Otis accompanied him and I remained with my two little ones at
Mr. Hellens a fearfully responsible situation on account of the Climate to
which none of us had been used—

This was the first long separation I had ever been exposed to since my
marriage and my health and spirits were sadly depressed.

May 1804

I weaned my boy which he appeared to bear very well; but he soon sicken'd
and I was kept in a state of deep and constant anxiety under the apprehension that I must lose him—

The unintermiting care and attention which he required Night and day
prey'd, upon my health spirits: and the active and ever restless spirit of my
eldest Son who was ever in danger in consequence of a careless Nurse rendered cares almost beyond my strength to endure and the responsibility
heavier than I can express although every kindness was shown to me. One
day when I had sent my George out to walk his Uncle coming home from
his Office thought he saw a Child alone on the wharf. He approached very
softly behind him; and when he had fast hold of him he asked him what he
was doing? He was pulling his Shoes and Stockings off he replied "to get
into the water (the Potomac) to see how *deep* it was!" At another time his
curiosity was roused to go down into the Garden by the Porch leading out
of the third Story instead of going down the Stairs— He was not five years
old yet this thirst after knowledge seemed to pervade every thought and
action and I knew no peace—

The health of my Children was the sole object of my life and I was continually moving from the City to Bladensberg or to Clarksville about half
way to Frederick for the benefit of change of Air which through Gods great
mercy succeeded in restoring him and he gained so rapidly in the [*fresh
air*]. Occasionally I saw Mrs. Madison Mrs. Merry [*British minister's wife*]
and some of the Ladies of the District and attended at the Episcopal Church;
but I had no Carriage and the distances were too great to walk—The Church
being in the upper part of George Town—

My Sister Hariet since Mrs. Boyd was a ministering Angel in my distress
and never left me alone night or day.

November 1804

In November when Mr Adams returned to Congress I had the happiness to present his children to him in high health beauty, after seven Months of absence to pass thro' another winter of dissippation and fatigue—

---

1 January 1805

At this period of time 1804 & 5—only the *elite* of Congress entered into what was termed the best Society.— And the consequence was that the Society was quite select:— It consisted chiefly of the heads of Department and those Families or Residents whose independent fortunes enabled them to live handsomely and sometimes to entertain their friends and acquaintance— Luxury was unknown except in the Houses of the Foreign Ministers and there were very few who aimed at great and ostentatious display— There were no Confectioners &c or French Cooks and the Ladies prepared there own entertainments at the expence of much labour and anxiety but generally with success—

As there was no Lady at the Presidents there were no Drawing Rooms so that dinners were the only mode of entertainment— The aspect of the House *below* Stairs was very handsome— Up *Stairs* there were strong indications of the want of female inspection— Mrs. Madison so well known and so much admired usually officiated on these occasions and was universally popular for the amenity of her manners and the suavity of her temper— She seemed to combine all the qualifications requisite to adorn the Station which she filled to the satisfaction of *all:* a most difficult performance.—

Col [*John*] Tayloe's family were wealthy and their House with his kind and amiable Wife [*Ann Ogle Tayloe*] and daughters to grace it was one of the most elegant in the City— Mrs. Ogle of Annapolis was an elegant Woman and greatly admired when she visited at Mrs. Tayloes her Daughter—

To follow the routine of the day would be monotonous— Miss Wheeler was a great belle. Miss Murray Miss Lee the Misses Chace Mrs. Caton & her daughters the eldest engaged to Mr R. Patterson—Miss Spear Miss M Smith and a number of others with the Merediths Daltons &ce and Miss

Dearborn formed a Centre of attraction which gave great eclat to the City and Georgetown in which was also a number of beautiful Girls. The Miss Worthingtons Mason's Jennifers Stodarts &cc too numerous to mention—

Col Boyd was paying his addresses to my Sister Hariet; and the french Secretaries of Legation were often at the House of an evening the family being musical and speaking French— Mr. Adams health was not so good as usual and his application to business was incessant— I was much occipied with my young Children and could not go out much with my Mother and Sisters—

Mr [*Albert*] & Mrs. Gallatin I did not know— He was Secretary of the Treasury— Genl. [*Henry*] Dearborn Secretary of War.— His Wife was one of the kindest hearted beings in the world and his daughter was a St Giles's beauty of the most Showy Class— The poor old Lady was for ever pining for the Chickens and Cows that she had left in Maine: and mourned for the loss of her occupation of Cheese making almost with tears of sorrow— Yet she entered with real glee into the routine of parties of pleasure and rendered her very agreeable by the general bon homie of her receptions— He was a pompous Militaire of the Democratic School and was full of annecdotes of his own martial experience. He one day was recounting to me his having been taken prisoner by the Indian's and been kept among them a long time—And he observed with great gravity—"It was really astonishing how soon we lost the habits of civilasation; in *two* months we became as savage as any of them."— I could not help smiling and thinking that in regard to polish there was not much to lose: for the Secretary's education had not been very finish'd— He spelt Congress with a K. always and when his Wife lay hopelessly ill he met the Physician who asked him "how she was?" he answered almost with a sob, "Oh dear Doctor she is *convalescent!*" He was a kind family man a little puffed up by the Station into which he had popped: or according to Shakespeare into which

"Fortune had thrust him."

As I interested myself very little with the Congressional business I can write very little about it— Mr Adams was almost always immersed in the business and passed much of his time in his room writing— We saw Mrs. Merry frequently and I think that it was at a Ball at her house that she brought the Secretary of Legation Mr. Foster and asked me to open the Ball with him, because she "said *I* had seen something in Europe." This will serve as a specimen of her manners— She was a prodigious favorite of John Randolphs— She never favored her company with her presence at her Supper Table; but used to make some of the members of Congress fetch and carry what she [*wanted*] a service which they always appeared to perform with great gusto as Gentlemen in waiting—

3 March 1805

Congress sat this day it being the day for adjournment although it was Sunday.— Mr. [*Aaron*] Burr took his leave of the Senate in a most elegant and even pathetic address delivered in the most graceful and touching manner, and Mr Adams who had never liked him came home quite affected by his manner, appearance, and sentiment— O! how winning is refinement and polished decorum! I fear it will ever white wash many Sin's which morality must condemn. I hated this man for his duel; but I had no acquaintance with him; and never spoke to him. My trial was to come— At half past nine in the Eveng. Congress adjourned—

6 March 1805

Mr Adams having some leisure from his Congressional pursuits examined my Fathers Papers and found them all in the best order being regular until within 4 days prior to his leaving Washington in company with us on my journey towards Quincy. He would have Administrated on the Estate had not the Securities been to heavy and the Affairs too complicated— I never could blame him.

14 March 1805

My Sister Boyd was married on the evening of this day I having requested that the wedding should take place previous to our departure The families of the Bride and Bridegroom only being present.— Balls and parties ensued when she went to reside with his Mother—

We prepared to return to the north and my Sister Eliza was invited to accompany— My Children were both sick and I had no nurse so that I started on the rout with great apprehension as to my strength to accomplish the charge of them on such a journey—

19 March 1805

This day Mr. Adams my Sister Eliza myself and my two Children left Washington in the George Town Stage for Baltimore in which Seats had been secured for Col Burr and Com Preble— They however had concluded to go in a private Carriage and we went on without them— I at that time felt a sort of loathing for this Col Burr who had recently killed Genl Hamilton in a Duel and I felt quite relieved when we were informed that he would not go— Arrived at Baltimore without we got the best apartments [we] could the Col having secured the best apartments at Evan's and here we met Judge and Mrs. Cushing kind as ever loading George and John with *goodies* and assisting me in all possible ways—

The Children were both quite unwell and of course very troublesome. It was the first time that I had the entire charge of them and my anxiety was proportioned to my want of health and strength—

My Sister was not at a time of life when Girls are willing to devote themselves [to] such confinement when circumstances of pleasure and excitement are for ever calling forth expressions of admiration and flattering attentions— When we arrived on board the Packet we found Mr. Burr and Com Preble already there and I took possession of a State Room with my two Children— When I returned into the Cabin Mr. Burr the Vice President was already there and I was formally introduced to him— He was a small man quite handsome and his manners were strikingly prepossessing and in spite of myself I was pleased with him— He appeared to fascinate every one in the Boat down to the lowest Sailor and knew every bodies history by the time we left— He was politely attentive to me devoted to my Sister— At Table he assisted me to help the Children with so much ease and good nature that I was perfectly confounded— We had a very rough Passage and to the astonishment of Com Preble fell out of one of the high Births and rolled upon the floor— At about twelve at Night we landed and it was diverting to see Mr Burr with my youngest Child in his arms; a bundle in his hand and leaning on his other arm to walk from the Wharf while my Sister Mr Adams and George followed us to French Town [*Delaware*]— Yet it was all done with so little parade and with such entire good breeding that it made you forget that he was doing any thing out of the way. He talked and laughed all the way and we were quite intimate by the time we got to Philadelphia where he called to see us, and this the first and last occasion on which I ever saw this celebrated man—

At Philadelphia we remained some days the Children as we found By Dr Rush having the Whooping Cough and Chicken Pox; so that I obliged to engage a girl to attend to them with me: more especially as he insisted on my accepting several Eveng. invitations from his friends there with he wished me to become acquainted— Old Mrs. Roberts the good Quaker with whom we boarded undertaking the charge of my little ones while I was absent— It was under these circumstances that I first became acquainted with Mr & Mrs: [*Joseph and Emily*] Hopkinson a charming family with whom we formed a lasting friendship which exists to this hour—with her; and which continued with him as long as he lived— He was a most delightful companion—Intellectual learned gay and witty it was impossible not to love and esteem him. The anxiety of my mind rendered me a tedious guest but my Sister made friends wherever she was seen.

We were at a great Ball at Mrs. Tench Coxes in the highest style of elegance— Many beautiful girls shone brightly at this gay party where wealth and luxury reign'd triumphant— I was obliged to leave it early much to the regret of my Sister—

How many charming families I then knew The Willings Francis Jacksons Peters Meredith's Mc. Pherson's Bishop White and Daughters the Harrison's Powells and how many others as Cox's Bird Hare &c &c— And here I met Nancy Smith a connection of the Adams family—

And where are most of them now?— This Lady Mrs Masters the only one of that branch of the family left!!

We arrived at Quincy after a tedious and unpleasant journey and our House not being ready we remained a week or two with the Gentleman's family— Mr Thomas Adams was married and himself and Wife resided with them with a Niece of Mrs. Adams Miss Le Smith and her Grand Daughter the Child of her Son Charles.— The Family being so large we removed as

soon as possible and not being able to procure any Servant or more properly *help* I had to cook and perform all the duties of the house with the
assistance of my Sister who was more successful in milking the Cows as I
confess with all my labor for want of *knack* I could not get a drop of milk.—

Never did we laugh more heartily than while thus occupied our perpetual blunders rendering the whole scene so ridiculous; but we were highly
gratified when Mr Adams pronounced his Meals excellent— One of my
Neigbours kindy relieved us of the milking department: and at the termina-
tion of three days we began our usual routine with the assistance of a boy
and two females with my assistance occasionally and superintendence—

*From April to November 1805, the Adamses visited Quincy, accompanied by
Louisa's sister Eliza. Following some renovations to the small saltbox cottage
where John Quincy had been born on the Penn's Hill farm, the family moved there
in late April 1805, with plans to return each summer when Congress was not in
session. Shortly thereafter, on 16 May, Thomas Boylston married his longtime
sweetheart, Ann Harrod, in Haverhill; John Quincy and Louisa did not attend.*

*That winter, the couple returned to Washington, D.C., without the children.
George and John remained in Massachusetts under the care of relatives—John
stayed with his grandparents, while George spent the time with John Quincy's
aunt Mary Smith Cranch and her husband, Richard. Louisa found Washington largely unchanged and unimproved; she wrote that they returned "to spend
another Winter in the midst of political intrigue and party cabals in which
I could not take the smallest interest."*

*Louisa also found herself pregnant again. When the congressional session
ended in April 1806, John Quincy returned by himself to Quincy, leaving
Louisa with the Hellen family in Washington. On 22 June she gave birth to a
son who lived only a few hours. Her memoir resumes on 26 July as she and her
sister Caroline are preparing to return to Boston.*

26 July 1806

On the 26 of July I started with my Sister under the protection of Com Hull
for Boston and passed night at Baltimore— We there went to the Methodist
Church where I witnessed a scene that was perfectly undescribable—and

I will not attemp to paint it— The House was the best I ever was in but I do not recollect the name of it— My wedding day.

Sometime before the birth of my Child Mrs Merry introduced at our house the celebrated Thomas Moore The Author of Anacreon and a number of very beautiful Songs The loves of the Angells L'alla-Rock &c &c and the Judge Family— I heard him sing many of his Songs and two or three Evengs. sang with him— He said that I sang delightfully but I wanted *Soul*— He appeared to be the [*avatar*] of Love and his style was so full of sentiment it would not have been very becoming or suitable for Ladies generally to echo his tones or the expression of his words or his manner! Warmed by his devotion to music and to his worship of the Muse delicacy appeared cold and propriety formal and he could find no pleasure in the modesty of judicious restraint— As a companion he was delightful and we regretted that his stay was so *short*—

27 July 1806

At Baltimore we met Mr William Duer who was lodging at Barney's and Dr. Davis and there was one other Passenger all of whom joined our party and we travelled together to Philadelphia— Overcome by fatigue and weakness I fell into a succession of faintings which made it neccessary for me to remain a day.—

Towards evening I was so much better that I insisted upon continuing our journey the next morning and decided to pass the night at Princeton—

29 July 1806

Arrived there very weak and exhausted and President and Mrs. Smith [*of Princeton College*] and her daughters a delightful family came to see me at the tavern and insisted on my going to their house and would take no denial— Every kind attention was shown to me by these excellent persons and I can never forget the attention and sympathy displayed towards me by Mr. Duer throughout the journey to New York—

31 July 1806

In the morning after a good Breakfast we took leave [of] Mrs. Smith and the young Ladies one of whom was engaged to be married to Mr Duer and arrive at my Sister Smiths who immediate recieved us my Sister and myself and was as ever lavish in her attention and care of the poor weak invalid— We remained with Mrs Smith four days. I very quiet but my Sister Caroline in the enjoyment of all the sights that New York produces—

8 August 1806

We sailed in the Packet for Newport and had such a stormy and dangerous passage that Com Hull to[ok] the management of the Vessel out of the hands of the *Capt* who he threatened to put in irons for his bad behavior and we did [not] reach Newport on account of the Storm until very late on the night of the 7th. and to remain there till the next the whole of which was passed in beating up to Providence— There we passed the Night under the care of Mr Jarvis and proceeded as far as Walpole [*Massachusetts*]

10 August 1806

and the next day arrived in Boston and passed the night at Whitcombs at Concert Hall— Mr Adams was glad to meet us and I was in an agony to be restored to my Children—

11 August 1806

We went out to Quincy and were kindly greeted but my Children recieved me as a stranger and I was almost forgoten. After dinner we moved to our own house and arranged every thing as well as we could for our accommodation— Little or nothing had been done even in the arrangement of the Furniture and we had only a small boy to do anything for us for two or three days— God gave us strength and we soon became comfortable— Mrs. Judge Adams who lived with the Old Gentleman had given birth to a daughter [*Abigail Smith Adams*] on the 29 of July and of course they could not accommodate *me*.

John would go back to his Grandmothers and it was with great difficulty that I could keep him at home—

14 August 1806

Three or four days of labour and I was able to accompany my husband to
Cambridge when he attended his Class [*as Boylston Professor of Rhetoric
and Oratory at Harvard*]. It was very fatiguing but the success of an experiment which I had not approved and very much mistrusted was a sufficient
reward— On one of thes occasions I saw several of the Proffessors; and
Mr Hedge spoke very highly of my Brother as a Scholar; and expressed his
regret that he had left the College; as he would certainly have left it with the
highest honors had he completed his education— It was singular that Mr
Johnson had not called on the Proffessor: but he felt the sting of poverty too
bitterly to expose himself

"To the prouds man's contumely"

So often exhibited in that said Institution of Harvard: where assuredly the
purse strings of the wealthy are closely watched: and where Scholars are
only *made* through the worship of the Golden Calf—or for some political
magnanimity towards an old established *power*. This union of politics and
purse is very *weighty*— The Idol set up are of a very vaccilating character:
but on the *main* point they are always true: and their significancy is felt and
understood by the devotees—the Gold ever in Statu quo.

But enough! Such digressions are useless.

16 August 1806

We were much alarmed at a fall that our dear boy John had out of bed; in
which he bruised his head sadly, and cut his lip— He soon went to sleep
afterwards and we hoped that he was not much hurt—

Mrs. Adams was quite ill— And the colored man [*William Abdee*] in returning from Boston was thrown from his Cart, and run over—Fortunately not
much hurt— He was an old Servant of the family—formerly a Slave— The
time passed very quietly— Often at the Old President's where we met the
Family and were much with the Judges Wife, who was a very fine woman—

They had a pretty little girl of whom they were very proud— It was the first Child—

27 August 1806

At six o clock accompanied Mr Adams to Cambridge through Boston— Arrived at Dr [*Benjamin*] Waterhouses where we met the Judge and Caroline— We went to the Chapel and took our Seats— The performances began at eleven and closed at three: literally to me on the stool of *repentance*— Then went to dine with Mrs. T K Jones; an elegant dinner; laid out under a large Canvass Pavillion in honor of her Son, who had graduated that day with destinction— There were about 300 Persons— My Sister returned to Boston with Mrs Danforth her friend. We returned to Dr Waterhouses where we passed an agreeable Eveng.

28 August 1806

Mr Adams took me to see the Library; Philosophy, chamber (I picked up nothing that ever served me) and to the museum— And at 12 o clock went to the Phi Beta and heard a Poem from Mr Whitwell and an Oration by T B Adams his manner always good but his voice not loud enough— When the exercises were finished we dined at Dr Waterhouses again— Never was a greater Original seen! He always put me in mind of the Mountebank Quack Dôctors that I had seen so often in England; with a Clown playing tricks to amuse the people; while the Charlatan sold his wares and filled his pocket— He was a man possessed of great learning but full of Paradoxes—full of wit, satirical, mordant in his invective, he yet was kind hearted, charitable, and beneficent— And his name stands recorded next to Jenner as a Saviour in the distruction of the direful Pestilence Small Pox which was so destructive in various forms to mankind— His Lady was a superior Woman of sweet manners: but she had the anxious look that all women who have married men who stand out as marks of singularity before the Public: and who always have something about them *out of Place.*

September 1806

"For the rain it raineth every day with a High ho!"

Went into Boston with Mr Adams on business returned in the Evening took George with us— The weather dreadful—

8 September 1806

Went in the Even to a dancing masters Ball— I went as *I* thought very *smart:* but my toilet did not please— It was much too simple for the occasion; as I found many elaborate Costumes very different from what I expected; and in a *taste* altogether new to me— The Dancing Master himself appeared as a Zéphir; and wore a suit of the lightest colored Nankin; with a broad Pink Persian Sash across his Shoulders, fastened at the side with a large bow, Silk Stockings, black Shoes with large Rosettes the color of the Sash!! A short time after my entrance, wearing a small white french lace Cap ornamented on one side with a delicate bunch of Morss Roses; with a simple white India Muslin dress; a pink belt to match the flowers in my Cap and bouquet; & pink Satin Shoes. A Lady of about sixty without a Cap and dressed in a Lace Veil worn as a Nuns; was handed in at arms length by the dancing Cupidon; and I felt quite abashed by the ecstacies of admiration thus excited, in contrast to my negative appearance— My Sister and I however hid our blushing heads (to laugh) and got through the dance as well as we could with the contemptuous glances cast at us.

For two or three days after I had some lectures, and apologized for not knowing better— The error was utter *ignorance* on my part— The time was dull: frequent stiff set parties; my youngest Child sick: and was very uneasy about him: but his complaint was worms and he got better though his health fluctuated.

Mr & Mrs. [*Robert Goodloe and Catherine Carroll*] Harper, Mrs Caton, her two daughters, Mr Rogers, Mr. Shaw, and Mr Bowdoin & Mr R Sullivan—came to see me.

I was making and baking Cake, and was obliged to *dress* before I could appear— The rooms of my house were literally too small to hold my company.— These Ladies were the elite of Baltimore— There was something truly ridiculous in my position— The shaking off of the kitchen drapery for the parlour finery; and the assumption of the fashionable manners of my Station: was such a transition: as robes Cinderella as a Princess; and I could scarcely fancy that the smoke spots had left me *fair;* when I presented myself to the company— Mrs. Harper had lived with my family in England and knew full well what I was used to— My boy was so beautiful he took all the shine off his Mother, and she felt no jealousy on the occasion— My Sister was much acquainted with them: and had often staid at Mr Carrolls at Carrolton—

I undertook to drive my Sister Caroline to Weymouth to pay some visits. The two Children were with us. We were going very gently up a Lane when a man came by with a red Wheelbarrow.— In an instant the Horse started and flew right up the bank; when we all found ourselves lying in the Road— Fortunately the horse satisfied with his *noble daring:* stood still, and I flew to my Children to ascertain their state. George had recieved no damage; but John had a heavy blow on his head which made him cry fearfully. My Sister and myself recieved severe contusions on the arms, and I one on the side of my face— As the accident occurred near the house of Dr Tuffts, we went there and had our bruises examined; and poor John got some cake and ceased crying, although the hurt on his head was considerable— The Man took George and my Sister so that they arrived at our house without farther trouble— Mr. Adams came to the Doctors and took John and myself home—

28 September 1806

Went to meeting and afterwards dined at the old House accompanied by my Sister, children and husband— We returned early in the evening. Mr. Adams is quite a Gardiner; and we are all learning to *bud* and *graft*—

30 September 1806

The month ended with dreadful weather— It was varied by occasional Parties: one at our *own house,* and others in the town— They were always *full* dressed; plenty of Cake and fruit; a number of Ladies; few Gentlemen; and Mosquito's in abundance: and they usually broke up at nine o'clock— Mr Adams spent most of his Evenings at his Fathers—

In the fall of 1806, Louisa decided not to return to Washington, D.C., when John Quincy left again in November. The family had moved to a house on Poplar Street in Boston, and Louisa was unwilling to be separated from her children. She was also once again pregnant. Shortly before John Quincy returned from Washington in March 1807, the family moved within Boston, to a home at the corner of Frog Lane and Nassau Street. As Louisa notes below, when he arrived he was accompanied by his sister, Abigail (Nabby) Smith, and Nabby's daughter, Caroline, and son John Adams Smith. The "uncomfortable reception" stemmed from disorder caused by the recent move and illness in the family.

The "new occupation" Louisa mentions for John Quincy on 16 July, below, was serving as a commissioner appointed by the Boston town selectmen to negotiate the filling of the Mill Pond. This would create a substantial new tract of land for settlement in Boston.

18 March 1807

And on this day when Mr. Adams arrived from Washington he met with a most uncomfortable reception and the return to his family under such circumstances was any thing but agreeable— He immediately however sent for his Sister and her daughter and we accomodated her as well as we could— In the morning they left for Quincy—

A great part of our Furniture had to come from Quincy and we could make no final arrangement of our house until they arrived—

My situation was very delicate— Threatened with Consumption and with great and constant pain in the side and most violent Cough I was almost unfited for severe duty and the fatigue and exposure was very trying to my Constition— Thus afflicted; with sick Children to take charge of I was almost entirely confined to the House until June, and it was two or three weeks before my husband could get any quiet— His attendance at Cambridge was constant and he with my Sister participated in the pleasures of society— and passed almost every week at Quincy going early Saturday afternoon and returning on Monday— My poor John was very sickly in consequence of an Emetic having been administered to him by Dr Welshs own hand which caused him to throw up blood.—

1 June 1807

Mr Andrew Buchanan a Widower in Baltimore made an offer of marriage to my Sister which she accepted; and he was invited to come on and stay with us; where the marriage should take place when he should have made the necessary arrangements to recieve his Wife at home— My house was so small I could not invite the family and my situation made it impossible for me to make any show about it— The bans were published all the forms settled— My time passed in occasional visits to my friends: and from them as well as from the family who sometimes staid three or four days at a time—

16 July 1807

Mr. Adams the Judge came to pass the day and night— As he was leading me down to dinner my foot slipped and I fell; but fortunately for me he caught me by the Arm and saved me from going to the bottom— The jar however proved very injurious. He staid the Night with us and left us next morning— Mr Adams had a new occupation and his time was still more absorbed—

I became very ill in consequence of my fall, but recovered soon— My sister passed a week at Quincy with Mr Tom Greenleafs Family Kind and excellent persons for whom I have ever felt the since-respect and regard— Mr & Mrs. Adams passed the day and night with us. The Child is very sickly— They returned to Quincy in the morning— Mrs. Adams is a woman whose mind has been highly cultivated and is celebrated for beauty— Versed in all the duties of a *bon Menage* she forms a most striking contrast to poor me; who know but little of it— And it was certainly not in London or at the Court of Prussia that I could learn the management of a Quincy establishment— I did the best I could and God mercifully requires no more of us if we do it with faith and good will—

19 July 1807

Mr Buchanan arrived from Baltimore— He passed the Evening with us and the next day all was arranged and the day fixed— He could not dine with us but promised to stay with us every day at meals until the event took place— He was a most amusing and good humoured being—but I feared that my Sister was taking cares upon herself which she would find too oppressive; he having four children by his first Wife the daughter of Gov Mc.Kein and Sister of Madame Yruco; and not being in good business— But he had offered himself to her when she was a beautiful girl of sixteen and she had rejected him—and it was natural that she should be flattered by an affection which so tacitly acknowledged her worth—

21 July 1807

The Judge and his Wife with Mrs. Smith and her daughter were invited as well as Mrs Adams and the Ex President— Between eight and nine in the Evening Andrew Buchanan was married to my Sister Carolina Virginia Marylanda Johnson— Miss Welsh was bridemaid— Mr. Hall and Mr Shaw, ~~their attendants~~ Miss [*Caroline Amelia*] Smith, and Susan Adams; Mr [*William*] Emmerson the Clergyman with Dr Welsh and his Lady were the company present at the Ceremony; and John [*Adams*] Smith was the groomsman—and the house was full of Company during the Eveng— All the Quincy friends staid the *Night* as well as the Bride and Bridegroom.— No presents were offered or recieved— Our supper was pretty but the accommodation *every* way small—

Louisa and John Quincy's third child, a son named Charles Francis, arrived safely on 18 August 1807. As she makes entirely clear in her memoirs and diaries, Louisa's children were central to her life. She took great pride in their accomplishments and worried constantly about their well-being. She also held herself responsible for their troubles—frequently out of all proportion to what she could actually control. The separations from her children were especially traumatic, and she believed they were to blame for George's and John's struggles later in life with alcoholism and financial failure.

7 August 1807

As I was sitting alone in my Chamber towards Evening, my poor George came into my Chamber looking deadly pale: and said, "Mama! I have been thrown out of a swing as high as the Poplars by the Otis boys." And he had got up all *alone* and come to me—!!

I examined him but could only percieve a bruise on his hip to which I immediately attended: and then took him and made him lay his head on my lap; until the Dr could come: to whom I instantly sent— The poor fellow moaned piteously every now and then, and I was much alarm'd. Mr Adams was dining out— The Doctor came and said the Shoulder was a little swoln, but he thought there was no material injury— The Child began to play and seemed almost to have recovered— His Father came home and I told him of the accident, and what the Doctor had said and then proposed to take the Child to the swimming bath: they went and returned in about an hour and as he appeared much exhausted I had him put to bed— He was very restless and uneasy, and cried and sobbed almost all night— His Father sat by him and tried to soothe him: but it was impossible, and in the morning early the Dr was sent for again— The Shoulder was so much swoln that he said he could do nothing at that time but put the Arm in a Sling—but still thought it was a *jar* and nothing serious— He gave him something to compose him and he fell asleep and when he waked he was as lively as a bird— His arm did not appear to hang naturally and I felt very anxious: but my fears were laughed at, as I must not bring up *my* boys to be delicate—

12 *August 1807*

Mr & Mrs. Adams came into Town to see us— As soon as they saw the Child they told his Father to take him to a famous bone setter to examine him; and the moment Dr. Hewit saw him he said that the Shoulder was dislocated and the collar bone was broken: and he set the one and fixed the other; before my poor boy knew what he was about— When he came home his Grandfather gave him a quarter of a dollar as a reward for his *bravery;* and as soon as he got it he ran on the common, and meeting one of his School "told him to run and spend it all in Gingerbread for the boys, and when *he* was *President he* would make *him* Secretary of State"— This was a most amusing joke to us when the boy came with the Cake and informed us of the promise—and my poor fellow distributed it with the utmost delight to all the Children standing round him; having only one hand and keeping but a small piece for himself— He was but little turned of six years old!!

18 August 1807

Unable to do any thing time passed heavily— I walked in the Mall until ten o clock— At two in the morning I disturbed the family; My Nurse towards morning was so alarmed at my Situation, that she burst in to tears and was sent away: and for the first time with my *fourth* Child Mr Adams was with me at the birth to see another *apparently dead Child*— In about half an hour the Child had recovered the play of his lungs, and my husband had witnessed sufferings that he had no idea of—

What a contrast to my last birth! 500 Miles away from my husband— Children; and a dead but beautiful Child only fourteen Months before!!

For two days we were in great fear for the Child who had not entirely recovered—but after that time appeared to thrive rapidly and all went on prosperously— Thanks be to God!!

30 August 1807

I had felt unusually strong and well and foolishly took the Child off the Bed and walked across the Room with it in my arms— He was very heavy and I was siezed with severe and dangerous illness which nearly cost my life and two weeks did not repair the mischief— Mrs. Smith kindly supplied the place of my Sister, and assisted me in the concerns of the family and in the care of poor George—who seemed born early to taste the ills of life.— A french Gentleman when he was three years old attached to the french Legation had playfully drawn the Childs horoscope without my knowledge and brought it to me— I declined taking it but he told me that he was threatened with a great *peril* at the age of *eight* and *twenty* but that if he escaped it he would be one of the most extraordinary Men in this Country— I would have nothing to do with it for I had no faith—

5 September 1807

George was siezed with a fever; and Mr Adams was almost worn out in a day or two. The Child grew better but my own situation was very critical— Mrs. Smith came to us and all began to grow well. Mr and I was able soon to ride— My youngest Son was brought from Quincy to see his new Brother but he would not look at him and seemed to think the little stranger was a *usurper*— His Grandmother was obliged to take him home—

12 September 1807

Was able to ride out for the second time and we made preparation to have the babe vaccinated on account of our coming journey to Washington—

13 September 1807

Our Boy was baptized this day by the name of Charles Francis—after a Brother of my Husbands who died before I came to this Country, and Judge Dana with whom Mr. Adams went to Petersburg as Secretary at the age of four-teen— The Baptism took place in the first Church Chauncy['s] place [*taken*] by Rev Mr Emmerson— I was not able to get out of the Carriage: ~~but my Sister held the Child~~ and the Nurse brought it back so that I could immedi-ately return home. Mr [*Joseph Stevens*] Buckminster the far famed and extraordinary Preacher returned from England.

Alexander Everett entered Mr Adams's Office as a Student— A young man of great promise—

In October the Adamses once more set off for Washington, D.C., leaving son John with the Cranches while George went to Abigail's other sister, Elizabeth Peabody, in Atkinson, New Hampshire, to continue his education. The congressional session was an especially momentous one for John Quincy, who broke with the Federalists to support a trade embargo proposed by President Thomas Jefferson and designed to punish Great Britain and France for violations of American neutrality. Enacted in December, the measure was wildly unpopular in Massachusetts, as it prohibited American ships from traveling to foreign ports and even limited movement of ships between American ports, substantially undercutting New England's profitable trade economy. John Quincy's decision to endorse the policy despite this opposition led to his eventual expulsion from the Federalist Party.

December 1807

We lived very quietly as the fashionable Season had not commenced until
to day, when we attended at a great Ball given by Mr Elias B Caldwell a company of more than 200 and very gay— We returned home between eleven
and twelve at night— Mr Caldwell was of a great Revolutionary family, and
had married Col Boyds Sister— She was a very pretty Woman and he was a
very amiable Man— Politics were growing very hot and Mr. Adams was
very busy and very anxious— The Whigs began to be jealous of him, and
the old Federalists hated him: so that we were fast getting into hot water—
Mr Jefferson took but little notice of *him* and of me none at all— Christmas
day we spent together and Genl Van Cortland dined with us— In the Evening
a small party at Mr *[British minister David]* Erskines Music and Supper:
but few guest's: Mr & Mrs Nat Cutting a very pretty French Woman— He
was a Doctor and a Poet— John Randolph was very troublesome and the
theme of general conversation—and there was a great fuss about John
Smith of Ohio *[charged with treason]*—but troubled myself very little about
them—

1 January 1808

Went with Mr Adams and my Sisters to pay the New Years visit at the
President's— It was very crowded with men women and Children and it
was difficult to find the President— Most persons disapprove of this sort
of company: but with all my *supposed* arristocratic tastes I think it is a privilege due to the *People;* to permit them to see their President in his house
once a year, that they may evince their respect for *him* and their homage to
the Nation that they love and cherish— And this cold brow beating Scorn
sits but poorly on the uppermost Class of Society in this Country where a
man can never feel sure of his Station for a year; and is up to day and down
tomorrow— Order should be observed and decorum required and then the
privilege would be esteemed— A Lady mentioned to me that at one of my
Drawing rooms; a Coachaman with a whip in his hand stood close to her
and that she feared he would spoil her dress— I had remarked this personage myself, and enquired how he got in— The answer that *he* made was that
he was the Coachman of a gentleman from New York who was there with

his family and of great wealth— *He* had been a driver; the man *said* and he thought therefore he had a right to be there also—

5 *January 1808*

We dined at Mr Erskines— Tolerably pleasant— England and America not on a very agreeable footing— We heard of nothing but the Embargo.

Mr & Mrs. Erskine took Tea with us— She is pretty and innofensive— He is gentlemanly and agreeable *et tout dit* [*and all said*]—

12 *January 1808*

A large Ball at Mr. Erskines. I could not leave my Babe so often. Mr. Adams and the family went—it was brilliant.

13 *January 1808*

A Ball at the Mayors: Mr Brent— All went but myself I staid with my babe who was quite sick— Mr Rose the New Envoy from England was there; and the party was large— My boy was quite ill all night— The North Chamber was so cold we were obliged to take my husbands chamber. A terrible change to *him*— He went with the family to a large party at Mrs. Duvalls— All three of us sick; Mr Adams a bad Cold: I an ague in the face—and the Child very ill— My Mothers old friend Col Jno Williams spent the Evening with us: My Baby better—

The family all went to a party at Mr Erskines and Mr Adams made me go with him— We staid a short time and then went to Mr Riggs's a house warming: but I was too unwell to stay; and we left the family at the Ball and returned home.

My baby was much better and I was better of course— Mr Adams had also got well and I took my boy and passed the day with my Sister Boyd; and staid as late as I dared—

A large Ball at Dr Worthingtons. It rained so heavily no one could go—

Again at Mr Erskines. Mr Rose was a mild elegant man; who I had heard much spoken of in Berlin where he was a favorite— His manners were charming and his conversation interesting though not brilliant— The

Mr Casamajors were the delight of the Girls; and were very pleasant men. They were quite an acquisition to our Society— Thus closed the Month of Jany 1808.

Louisa, John Quincy, and Charles Francis returned to Boston in May 1808 accompanied by Louisa's sister Catherine. One month later, the Massachusetts General Court met and named John Quincy's replacement as U.S. senator despite the fact that John Quincy had six more months left to his term. This action was a clear rebuke of John Quincy's support for Democratic-Republican Party policies, including the Embargo Act, and he resigned on 8 June, declining to serve out the remainder of his term. He subsequently turned his energy to his work as the Boylston Professor of Rhetoric and Oratory at Harvard University, a position he had held since the summer of 1806, and resumed his legal career.

8 May 1808

In the morning we left Providence in the Stage where we rode to Walpole and dined and then took a Carriage to our own House in Nassau Street— We found the House all ready for our reception— I was to have gone to Quincy with Mr. Adams but he was unwell—

10 May 1808

Went to Quincy with Mr Adams and Charles. Mr. Adams went to Mrs. Cranch's and brought my John again to my heart and arms. We dined and passed the afternoon there; and returned to Boston in the Evening.

 Mr Adams could not go out to Cambridge being quite sick and obliged to see a Physician. Mr Hall and Mr Dexter called— Mr Adams awoke quite ill but as usual in despite of all entreaty went to Cambridge accompanied by Dr Welsh— He delvered his Lecture performed all the usual business: and returned home stopping on the way to leave an excuse at Mr Austins not for not dining with him on the plea of indisposition and returned home so sick he was confined to his Chamber the rest of the day—was much better in the Evening—

14 May 1808

This Evening Mr. Adams though still quite unwell went to Quincy to see his Father and Mother with his brother who had come to town with Miss Welsh— Nothing about was settled and home was any thing but agreeable—

16 May 1808

Many visits from my Lady friends— All sick— The Judge and Mrs Adams and Child came to see us.

Dr Welsh and family came and spent the Eveng and Mr Degrand—

18 May 1808

At a large party at Mrs S Dexters— The company agreeable but people shy—

19 May 1808

Mr Emmerson was suddenly seized with a heamorrhage of the Lungs— It is thought that he can never recover— Mr Shaw promises to go to bring home my poor George— My Children are quite estranged already.

20 May 1808

Went to a large party at Mrs. Allen Otis's.

24 May 1808

Mr. Riply called and the old Gentleman came into Town to a Meeting of the Accademy [*of Arts and Sciences*].

25 May 1808

Our dear George reached home just before dinner. Mr Shaw brought him— They were detained by an accident which befel their Chaise and from

which they fortunately escaped uninjured. His health was miserable—
Once again we were a family—

Mr. Adams took the George out to Quincy to see his Grandparents and
brought them back on Monday. When he took them to [*school*] John would
not [*stay*] there either Morning or Evening—

1 June 1808

The time passed in this way occasional parties; visits to Quincy— A large
party at Dr Danforths which was gay and pleasant. On the eigthth of the
Month Mr. Adams sent in his Resignation to the Legislature as his policy
was not approved and it was accepted and Mr James Lloyd was chosen in
his Place on the 9th of the Month. Thus ended my travels for a time and
began a system of persecution painful to our Family but disgraceful to the
State of Massachusetts whose Citizens are ever Slaves to a handfull of
Men who right or wrong submit to their dictation— They [*are*] utterly incapable of an enlarged and noble policy: but with all their boasted independence hang on the Skirts of Great Britain, as Child Clings to its Nurse—
And with the true slavish spirit The more they are scorned the deeper
the worship—

*Having resumed his legal career, John Quincy went to Washington, D.C., in
January 1809 to argue a case before the Supreme Court. Shortly after President James Madison's inauguration in March, he offered John Quincy the post
of first U.S. minister plenipotentiary to Russia. (Louisa is confused below
about the timing of these events.) John Quincy was uniquely qualified, having
spent time in St. Petersburg in 1781–1782 as a secretary during an earlier unsuccessful mission to obtain Russian recognition of the fledgling United States.
The Senate initially rejected the nomination, believing that a minister to Russia was an unnecessary expense. But Madison persisted, and as tensions in
Napoleonic Europe grew, the Senate eventually agreed to the appointment in
late June. John Quincy promptly accepted without consulting Louisa and despite knowing of her strong objections.*

26 January 1809

Mr. Adams again left us for Washington. And we were left with all the political World frowning us down with but few friends to protect us. Catherine went out very frequently and I staid at home with my Children— We often heard from Mr Adams and I had the satisfaction to learn that the Senate had rejected Mr. Adams's Nomination to Russia a thing perfectly abhorrent to me and which I hoped was done with forever— O how unfit I always have been for the Wife of a *great Man* and a Politician— Content to glide on in the plain routine of domestic duty I seldom took any part in what was going on unless it was to loathe intrigue and persecution— How different had Mr. Adams married one of his own Country women—

15 February 1809

Went over to pay a visit to my Neighbour Foster— The Ice was thick on the Pavement and being exceedingly timid and having no one to help me—I slipped and fell with my back against the Curb Stone and an hour after I got home was taken very ill and being in a delicate situation and the consequence was inevitable and a sickness somewhat dangerous ensued from which I did not recover for three weeks— My Sister then had a Pleurisy and Charles had an ugly eruption both painful and troublesome—

Time wore on until the 26 March and on that day Mr. Adams returned and again we had a prospect of tolerable quiet.

1 March 1809

We went out to Quincy and I immediately went to see George who was placed there to attend to Mr Whitneys school— Was laid until Monday morning and returned to Boston with the Children.

Nothing occurred to vary our lives— The Fosters Mr & Mrs. W. and Daughter came frequently to see us. Mrs F was a french Woman and spoke but little English and they resided with the old People who spoke no french so that our house was quite congenial to them—

Visits to and from Quincy were frequently exchanged and these were the regular course of our lives— Mr Adams attending his Cambridge duties with great regularity—

16 April 1809

We went to the Theatre and took our Children for the first time. Hamlet was performed by Master Payne— We were more diverted by the questions of the boys than by the performance although young Payne greatly excelled the most favorable anticipations— He promises well—

22 April 1809

George went to the dancing School— His Father scorns the idea of instill-ing the graces. Why should not a man move well? is it preferable to be like Clown? Surely not when we have the means of improvement— Dr Johnson *mind* might have been softened and less brutal had he been mellowed by the polish of gentle and easy motion— Dancing may not be a necessary part of instruction: but in its association as we cannot dance alone: it has the ef-fect of subduing rude egotism and teaches the art of abstaining from that roughness which is an almost inevitable consequence of ill breeding—and by teaching persons how to associate with Familiarity and ease under judi-cious and proper restraint—

4 May 1809

Went with my Sister and Mr. Adams to hear Mr [*James*] Ogilvie's Lecture and was much pleased— It was against duelling— The boys had got a new idea and instead of playing Minister and preaching all the afternoon they played and buried Ophelia my Dressing Case being the Coffin and und[*er*] the Bed the Grave— And the Duel between Hamlet and Laerties always finished the performance—

4 July 1809

This day the news arrived of Mr Adams's appointment to Russia and I do not know which was the most stuned with the shock my Father [*John Adams*] or myself— I had been so grosly deceived every apprehension lulled— and now to come on me with such a shock!— O it was too hard! not a soul entered into my feelings and all laughed to scorn my suffering at crying out that it was affectation— Every preparation was made without the slightest consultation with me and even the disposal of my Children and my Sister was fixed without my knowledge until it was too late to Change—

Judge Adams was commissioned to inform me of all this as it admited of no change and on the 4 of August we sailed for Boston I having been taken to Quincy to see my two boys and not being permited to speak with the old gentleman alone least I should excite his pity and he allow me to take my boys with me—

Oh this agony of agonies! can ambition repay such sacrifices? never!!— And from that hour to the end of time life to me will be a susession of miseries only to cease with existence—

Adieu to America—

CHAPTER FOUR

"The Savage Had Been Expected"

Russia

Despite her manifest unhappiness at John Quincy's appointment as U.S. minister to Russia—and especially his decision to leave their two eldest sons, George and John, in the United States—Louisa reluctantly complied with this new test of her constitution. The couple and Charles Francis set off on 5 August 1809, accompanied by Louisa's sister Catherine Johnson and three aides: John Quincy's nephew William Steuben Smith, Alexander Hill Everett, and Francis Calley Gray. Louisa strongly objected to Catherine's joining them, both fearing the added expense of caring for her sister and concerned that an inappropriate situation might develop between her sister and one of the three young men, all single, who were also in the party. But again, Louisa was overruled. The group sailed on the Horace, *an American ship, and encountered no difficulties until they became caught up in naval tensions between Great Britain and Denmark connected to Napoleon's ongoing effort to control all trade in Europe.*

The material on the Adamses' years in Russia again comes from Louisa's "Adventures of a Nobody," in which she carried her memoirs up to September 1812. In the sections below, Louisa sometimes begins writing about herself in the third person. This occurred not for any literary reason, but because she was copying directly from her husband's diaries and forgot to change names and pronouns. Likewise, some of the more clumsy grammatical constructions come from inaccurate transcriptions of John Quincy's original writings.

5 August 1809

We went to see on the 5 of the month to undertake this long voyage to me painful in every possible shape for many more reason's than I can mention— Mr. W. S. Smith was Secretary Messrs. Gray and Everett as attachès— I had urged every thing against my Sisters going— She was entirely dependent with out one sixpence in the world not even clothed properly when she started and I *knew* that *I* could never supply her— But it would not do against my Mothers and my pleadings: the temptations on the other side were too powerful to be resisted and fate was settled by the privation of my Children— Before we had been a fortnight at Sea with three young men—Squabbles and jealousies commenced and the future was laid bare to my eyes as clearly as if it had passed— Broken hearted miserable, *alone* in every feeling: my boy was my only comfort— I had passed the age when Courts are alluring— I had no van- ity to gratify and experience had taught me years before the meaness of an American Ministers position at a European Court— Nothing but mortifica- tion presented itself to my imagination with the loss of all domestic comforts to give me fortitude to support the change—

If it was to do again nothing on Earth could induce me to make such a sacrifice and my conviction is that if domestic separation is absolutely nec- essary cling as a Mother to those innocent and helpless creatures whom God himself has given to your charge— A man can take care of *himself:*— And if he abandons one part of his family he soon learns that he might as well leave them all— I do not mean to suggest the smallest reproach— It was thought right and judicious by wiser heads than mine but I alone suf- fered the penalty— They are known only to God—

Our voyage was very tedious— All but Mr Adams and Mr Smith very sick and as usual I having the whole care of the Child who suffered as much as any of us.—

17 September 1809

We had not seen a Vessel since we passed Fair Isle in the North Sea— We had had a heavy gale all day and night and the Swell was frightful— The Swell continued terrific— At about five o clock in the Afternoon a British Brig was discovered. She fired a Gun to the Leaward, upon which our Colors were run up: within an hours time she came up with in Speaking distance and hailed us:— Where from?— From Boston! Whither bound? To Russia! Let down your Boat and come on Board: After some minutes the order was repeated— The Boat was very small and the Capt thought it could not live in the Swell— The order was repeated and a Musket with ball fired ranging along the side of the Ship— It was dusk the wind blowing in Squalls like a Gale with a very heavy sea— The Mate went into the Boat with three men in her but cried out that she could not live and the Brig Shot a head and was out of sight in a few minutes— All this time the Boat and people were in the most imminent danger but got on board at last in safety.

18 September 1809

Another dreadful night— The Sea mountains high and the Vessel rolling and pitching as if she would upset— In the morning we made the Land on the Coast of Norway and at Noon were abreast of the Naze [*southern tip of Norway*]— The water became smoother and we got into the Sleeve so called between the Coasts of Norway and Jutland—and we had a quiet night—

19 September 1809

We were awakened this morning with the news that an English Cruizer was near us— She came along side of us and sent an Officer on board without speaking [*to*] us and four Men— She was in pursuit of a Danish man of War for two days— He said it was fortunate that he had not seen us last night as he should have fired into us supposing it was her— At about 7 in the Evening we saw another Brig under Danish Colours. She fired a Gun to bring us too and lay close beside us. She hoisted English Colours after she had ascertained the usual questions and sent an Officer on board of us with four Men— The Officer did not know as they the English were it [*at war*] with Denmark whether we might proceed or not— The Boat soon returned with an answer that we might proceed without interruption having a Minister on Board—

We sent for a Pilot and while considering which place to put in a small Craft with two with about 15 or 20 Men armed and a Swivel came under Danish colours fired a gun and ordered us to bring too. A Danish Lieut of the Marine by the name of Kauff [*came aboard*] and told the Capt he must go into Christiansand— The Capt became alarmed and declared he would not put any where and turned his Ship about to stand out to Sea— The Lieut immediately made a Signal and about fifteen men came from the Boat heavily armed and climbing up the rigging and took possession of the Ship walking the quarter deck while others from the boat were preparing to board us— The Lieut however made a signal to them to withdraw— He and the Pilot were afraid that the Capt would carry them out to sea— The Capt concluded to go into the harbour of Flecknore about four miles distant from Christian Sands.

I was perfectly indignant at being taken by this boat and was clear for, maintain our position as we had six Guns—

Mr [Peter] Isaacson an Agent for American Seamen a very Gentlemanly Man; the next day and we all had a charming dinner in this little nook in Norway. Mr Thorndike came on board the Ship and passed the night— Met Lawson Alexander and a number of Americans taken by the Danes—

We were detained on Shore by a heavy Storm and Mr Isaackson to his great inconvenience accomodated us all with lodgings where we were compelled to stay until the next Eveng. when the Gov's Boat was sent and Mr Adams obliged us to return to the Ship in a heavy Gale and that night we sailed for the Catigat [*bay between Denmark and Sweden*]— We saw four or five Vessels ashore.

25 September 1809

At Sun rise this morning we came abreast of Koll Point [*Sweden*] but the wind veered and came a head, and in the midst of the Passage of the Sound we saw a Ship of War at Anchor— And a Sloop with several other Vessels anchored near them— We made up directly to the Man of War; and a Lieut from her soon came on board—who on examining the Papers of the Crew was very troublesome and threatened to take one of them off— The Officer not understanding Mr. Adams Commission told him he had better go on board the Admirals Ship and see him himself— He went accompanied by the Capt and the young gentlemen and we were left under the protection of the Officer. We were nearing the Port of Elsineur when at about eleven o clock at night the Vessel was drifting up against the Man of War— The wind was fair for our progress. The wind was at the same time blowing fresh, and we put down another small anchor which however did not arrest the drift— At about five in the afternoon she began to drift again and we droped our third and last Anchor a very heavy one— We had drifted within the

Ships length of a large Brig whose bowsprit was threatening our Cabin windows and we were within a mile of the Shore. At the approach of Night I was anxious to send the Ladies and Child ashore for which purpose a signal was made at the Masthead—but none came out— Shortly before Sun set a boat from the British Man of War came out to us and gave some advice to the Capt— He told him that one good anchor, would be better than three and recommended to him in case the wind should change to cut his Cable and go out to Sea— He returned on board his Ship: the night came on.— The night came on with foul weather about midnight which hove in Channel off till about midnight— The wind then changed and continued freshening till morning.

27 September 1809

All the morning was employed in weighing the Anchors; two of them were successfully got on board— At this work all the hands were engaged and most of the Passengers part of the time with the rest— An American Vessel came in but was sent back by the Admiral. The wind came continually more a-head and the Vessel would not wear round and the Capt ordered the Cable to be cut away and we stretched out so that we hoped to get to Elsineur that Night— At the third attempt the Capt lashed down the helm put the Vessel under close reefed Mainsail Topsails Maine and fore stay sails but the fore Yard Arm had broken right in two in the middle and they were obliged to take it down— We were between the shores in a narrow see and expecting every instant to be dashed on Khol Point a fearful spot in the history of Wrecks. Fortunately it was not very dark and not cold and no Sea so— The next night the Storm continued. The light in the Binnacle went out and there was not a light to be had in the Ship— Mr. Adams got his tinder Box.

To go through the horrors of this most terrible and tedious voyage is beyond my streng[*th*]—

After a brief stop in Denmark, the Adamses finally landed at the Russian port of Cronstadt on 22 October 1809. From there they quickly proceeded by water to St. Petersburg, reaching the city the next day. They settled first at the Hotel de Londres on the Nevsky Prospect, where they were met by Levett Harris, the

U.S. consul at St. Petersburg. They later moved to the Hôtel de Ville de Bordeaux on 11 November, and finally settled into private apartments on New Street, near the Moika Canal, on 12 June 1810.

As at Berlin, Louisa had to go through the usual ceremonies of a court presentation to Tsar Alexander I; his wife, Elizabeth Alexeievna; and his mother, the Dowager Empress Maria Feodorovna—always something of a trial. But Louisa was a more mature, confident woman this time around, and she found the entire experience easier than in Prussia. Once this ritual was accomplished, Louisa and John Quincy could begin to participate in an array of social activities centered around the Russian court.

22 October 1809

At last we reached our destination though some distance from the [*Mole, a protected harbor*] and an Officer coming up [*in*] the Admirals Boat we dressed ourselves and accompanying him left every thing in the Vessel so as not to detain and landed perfect beggars though supposing that our Trunks would follow us immediately—

My Sister and myself wore hats which had been chosen at Copenhagen that we might appear fashionable—and we could scarcely look at one another for laughing: immense Brown Beaver of the most vulgar imaginable as much too large as our American Bonnets were too small— Thus accoutred fancy us immediately from the Ship usherd into an immense Saloon at the Admirals House full of elegantly dressed Ladies and Gentlemen staring aghast at the figures just introduced and with extreme difficulty restraining their risibility Maid and Child and all taking their place in the Farce and our Black Servant [*Nelson*] following— It was exquisite beyond all description and too ridiculous in the first moments to be mortifying as we naturally supposed it would only be momentary— Not a place could be be found to put our *heads* in (Bonnets not excepted) the Admiral politely urging us to stay at his as well as his Lady but which we could not accept being such a number and so situated— And at last the Vice Consul gave us apartments and a very nice supper and we went comfortably to rest—

23 October 1809

At Breakfast Mr. Sparrow informed us that a heavy [*wind*] had sprung up; the Vessel been blown many miles down (leagues) I mean and the [*ship*] she probably would not get back for ten days— Here was a position agreeably defined— Myself a *white Cambric* Wrapper; my Sister the same; A Child of little more than two years old with only the suit on his back, and the Minister with the Shirt he had on; solus!! We did [*not*] appear quite in the Garb of the Aberiginals of our Land but as near as possible to do it honor—

We embarked again in the Admirals [*boat*] all the Females the Child Mr Adams Mr. Everett and Mr Gray en suite and Nelson—at twelve at noon we started: and were two hours before to warp out of the Mole—and we were four hours more before we arrived at the Wharf at Petersburgh and had to wait until a Carriage could be procured to take us to and the water had already affected the Child very much so that it required to be more than a philosophic Squaw to bear up against our varied trials. Mr Martin an American Gentleman whom we met at Cronstadt accompanied us and kindly had a dinner served up and every[*thing*] as comfortable as possible in the horrid Hotel that could possibly be got—

Immediately after dinner Mr. Harris the Consul came and all the Shop keepers were set in motion to procure the requisites for ready use— And we had an outside garment and the Minister was dressed from top to toe much to his discomfiture in a superb style Wig and all to be presented to the Chancellor of the empire [*Count Nikolai Petrovich Rumiantsev*] when he should be ready to receive him—

25 October 1809

The Chancellor appointed seven o clock in the Even— Mr. Harris dined with us gave Mr Adams much instruction as to how many bows he must make— Almost what to say; and told him to be careful not to dwell upon business but to be careful to introduce something light and pleasant into the conversation as the Russians must be amused; and that he must immediately get a Carriage for the fact was that in St Petersburgh "Ill faut rouler" [*one must roll*].

At seven o clock in the Evening they departed—Mr Adams looking very handsome all but the Wig. O horrid! which entirely disfigured his countenance and not to his advantage— They soon returned as the visit was short but the reception courteous— Mr Harris passed the Evening with us.

26 October 1809

Mr Smith arrived with only a small part of the baggage and that was carried to the Custom— An invitation from the Chancellor for Mr. Adams to dine with him on Saturday. Mrs. [*Anna Dorothea Smith*] Khremer the Lady of the Court Banker called on me and was kindly polite— She entered fully into our situation and appeared to take great interest in the Child who was sitting on my knee when she came in— About an hour after her visit every requisite for our toilet was sent with a Note express[*ing*] a wish that we would make a free use of the Articles as long as they could be convenient—with a large supply for the Child she having one of the same age— The whole business was so elegantly performed that I felt very grateful and readily used the favour for the Child—

27 October 1809

We this day recieved our Clothes and baggage from the Custom House every article plumbed— We my Sister and myself went to visit Mrs Krehmer and accompanied her to some Millinere & Mantuamakers and Furniture— Mr. Adams looked over a suite of appartments very suitable but just engaged—

I was quite ill! The Water was dreadful in its effects and both the Child and myself suffered every thing— The Chamber I lodged in was a stone hole entered by Stone passages and so full of rats that they would drag the braid from the table by my bed side which I kept for the Child and fight all night long—and my nerves became perfectly shattered with the constant fright least they should attack the Child— We were all more or less sick.

Mr Crame and Mr Smelt paid visits— Mr [*Sebastian*] Krehmer invited us to dine. Mr Adams and myself were too ill to go— The young Gentlemen went. The Emperor sick can not recieve—

The dinner at the Chacellors at which Mr Adams attended was in the highest style of magnificence.

1 November 1809

The style of expense is so terrible here it seems as if it would be impossible for us to stay here— We are in pursuit of lodgings but can procure none— The Emperor signified through Count Romanzoff Chancellor of the Empire that he would recieve Mr. Adams as Minister U S A an hour after the Mass and afterwards to the Empress.—

The Commandeur [*Joseph*] de Maisonneuve [*master of ceremonies*] sent a gentleman to enquire when Mr Adams could see him that he might make arrangements for his presentation to the Emperor— Mr A sent word at eight o clock in the Evening— He came and we found in him an old acquaintance who had done the same service for us at Berlin—A most delightful old man.

Mr Adams was presented the Emperor in his Cabinet steping forward to meet him at the door when he addressed him in french "Sir I am happy to see you here."

8 November 1809

This morning Mons de Maisonneuve called and informed me that I must write a Note to the Chancellor requesting to be presented to the Empress Mother and to the Reigning Empress and that Mrs. Adams must also be presented and the time fixed was after the Mass and Te Deum on Sunday.

That it would be proper for me to call on the Countess Litta [*grand mistress of the court*] on Saturday Evening as Mrs. Adams would then be able to recieve such directions as would put her au fait of the ceremonial— In the Evening we went by appointment to the Bavarian Ministers Baron de Bray— We saw Madame de Bray. Madame de Bray was young and very pretty and the only Lady of the Corps Diplomatic besides myself— Several of the foreign Ministers were there and also the Mother and Sister of Madame de Bray who reside with her— Her account of the forms of presentation differed very much from those we had heard before.

11 November 1809

We entered our new lodgings to day—somewhat better but very bad—at the Hotel de Londre— Mr & Madame de Bray returned our visit just after we had got in— Just before seven o' clock according to appointment by Mr. De Maisonneuve we went to Countess Littas. The Count & Countess recieved us very politely— The Countess told me that I was to be presented the next day directly after Mass to the Empress Mother— But she did not know if I was to be presented to the Empress Elizabeth or Mr: Adams— He was to be presented before Mass— The forms of my presentation had been correctly given by Mr De Maisonneuve and were altogether different from those given by Madame de Bray—

12 November 1809

Mr Harris took Mr Adams to the Palace at eleven o clock and just as he was starting he recieved a Note from Mr de Maisonneuve with the words tres press's on it stating that my presentation was put off until 1/2 past two— Of this Mr Adams informed me and I was left alone to go through all the fears and frights of the Presentation perfectly alone at the most magnificent Court in Europe— Three or four messages arrived from the Palace changing the time for my presentation and I was obliged to hurry as the last ordered me to be at the Palace at 1/2 past one—

Off I went with a fluttered Pulse quite alone in this foreign [land] among people whom I had never seen dressed in a Hoop with a Silver tissue skirt with a train a heavy crimson Velvet Robe with a very long train lined with White body and sleeves trimed with a quantity of Blond; my hair simply arranged and ornamented with a small diamond Arrow—White Satin Shoes gloves Fan &ce and over all this *luggage* my Fur Cloak— I was attended by two footmen—and thus accoutred I appeared before the Gentlemen of our party who could not refrain from laughter at my appearance—

Arrived at the Palace after ascending with great difficulty in the adjustment of my trappings. I was recieved by a Gentleman and shown in a long and large Hall in which I found Countess Litta superbly dressed and covered with diamonds— She was the Niece of Potemkin and inherited all his wealth—Very handsome and very fat— She recieved me very kindly—Told me that I was to be presented to the reigning Empress first and then defined my position for the presentation— She placed me in the centre of the Hall fromting a large folding door and informed me that the Empress would enter by that door and that I must stand unmoved until her Imperial Majesty walked up to me—that when she came up I must affect to kiss her hand which her Majesty would not *permit* and that I must take my Glove off so as to be ready and take care in raising my head not to touch her Majesty— She then retired to the embrasure of a window and left me thus drilled to act my cue— Naturally timid I felt as if I was losing all my composure and with difficulty could command the tremour.

Two Negroes dressed a la Turque with Splendid Uniforms were stationed at the doors with drawn Sabres with gold handles— At the opening of the doors I saw a suite of long rooms at each door of which stood two Negroes in the same style and the Grand Marshall in a splendid Costume preceded the Emper and Empress who came up together with a long train of Ladies and Gentlemen following and as their imperial Majesties passed the door the Grand Marshall fell back and the door were nearly closed and they approached me— The Emperor was in Uniform and the Empress like myself in a rich court dress—

I went through the forms which the Empress made easy by her extreme affability and the Emperor assumed the conversation the Empress only joining in with a word or two— I think the audience was of about fifteen minutes ending with some complimentary words and they with drew as they came and I remained in the same position until the doors were re-closed— And thus ended act the first— Countess Litta who had never approached during the ceremony came up and congratulated me on the success of introduction and said the rest of it would be more simple—

We then went to the Apartments of the Empress Mother every thing superb but not so elaborate and there knowing my Lesson I was more at my ease— She recieved me very graciously and evidently expected to quiz my ignorance putting many questions to me as to the effect on me of the wonders that struck my eyes every where in Petersburgh— I expressed in strong language my admiration of every thing and mentioned that I had seen London Paris Berlin and Dresden—&ce but that I had certainly no City that equaled St Petersburg in beauty— Ah mon dieu vous avez tout vue!! [*Ah my God you have seen all!!*] and she appeared to regret it very much— The Savage had been expected!! She was wonderfully gracious and after an audience of twenty Minutes I was dismissed with a hope that she should soon see me again— It was beneath the dignity of Madame Field Marshall Litta to present me to the Grand Dutchess so I was transfered to Madame Lieven a fine old Lady and by [*her*] introduced to the Grand Dutchess [*Anna Pavlovna, Alexander's sister*] a girl of 14 of an elegant presence and most distinguished manner but not very handsome— The Audience was very short— At last I returned home with an additional budget of new ideas almost as oppressive and unsuitable as my Robes— I was very much fatigued with all this variety of agitation but Madame Litta gratified me by intimating that I had got through very well—

---

27 November 1809

This morning Mr Harris sent us a present my Sister and myself of an elegant Turkish Shawl— We wore them that Evening at the French [*embassy*]— Mr Harris had suffered agonies at the idea that american Ladies should appear without such indispensables and Mr Adams allowed *me* to accept it— We went at 4 oclock to dine with the Ambassador [*Armand Augustine Louis de Caulaincourt, Duc de Vicence*] and found every body there but the Duke of Mondragoni— My Sister was quite enchanted with all these parties but the want of variety of toilets was a dreadful drawback— What would have dressed one modestly was by no means competint for two more especially for a younger Lady and we had much to endure from the rigid parsimony of the Salary. Our expenses were very heavy and our difficulties encreased every hour at a Court so showy and every way extravagant—

The party was small divested of all cérémony— But I was not fitted for the sphere and "could not do as Rome does." The liason of the Ambassador was notorious and I could neither admire nor respect the Lady: and this circle of almost unrestricted gallantry did not suit my ideas of les convenances.

Princess Viazemski Madame de Vlodeck [*French ambassador's mistress*] and the Countess Tolstoy & her Sisters and two or three other persons of Rank with all the Corps Diplomatique attached to the french party were there— We were about two hours at Table and we returned to the Saloon. We found Mademoiselle Bourgoin a french Actress there who declamed parts from different plays Phedre—Zaire—l'Ecole des Maris and le Florentin— M de Rayneval read the alternate parts— This was very amusing— A band of musick was then introduced struck up a Polonaise which we walked round the [*hall*] and then we passed through a Suite of apartments to a Theatre where another Actor performed a number of tricks of slight of hand. We then returned again to the Hall and a dance began which lasted until Supper and we got home at 2 o clock—

14 December 1809

Thus we went on occasionally making visits and going to the theatre until this time when we all went to a fancy Ball for Children at the Duke de Vicenza's. We took Charles who I had dressed as an Indian Chief to gratify the taste for Savages and there was a general burt of applause when he marched in at which he was much surprized— There were forty Children admirably costumed from two to twelve years old some beautiful fancy dances performed by the elder and Charles led out Miss Vlodeck supposed to be the daughter of the Ambassader and they with the assistance of their Mamas opened the Ball— He was three years and a half old not quite— After the dance there was an elegant supper oceans of Champaign for the little people and the Mothers all stood full dressed behind their Chairs— When supper was finished there was a lottery of choice and expensive toys—but Mr Adams hurried us away when the Child left the table and would not permit him to take a chance— We all returned home together.

17 December 1809

Invited to dine with Madame Severin— We went and after dinner found that there was a Ball to which Madame Severin insisted on our staying— We remained until two in the morning when we sat down to supper and it was between 3 and 4. when we got home— I was quite knocked up—

23 December 1809

Recieved a Notification for Mr Adams and myself to attend at the celebration tomorrow Evening of the Emperors's birth day by the Empress Mother—to a Ball—

Having but one dress in which I had already appeared several times I declined on the plea of ill health and went to take Tea with Colombi Wife of the Spanish Consul and a lovely Woman who we visited most sociably— We passed a delightful Evening and I had gone to rest long before Mr Adams came from the Ball—

30 December 1809

Went with Mr. Adams to a small party at Mrs Krehmers but was so sick I was obliged to return home— My Sister had been quite sick for a week— I left him and the Gentlemen there—

1 January 1810

On this day I went with Madame de Bray and paid my visits— I was informed that her Majesty the Empress Mother having heard of my being out at Tea with a friend the Evening of the Ball to which I had been invited intimated that it must not occur again or I should be *omited* on future occasions— This was charming pour l'économie!! more especially as I had heard her tell a Lady who had worn the same gown several times that she "wished that *She* (the Lady) would get another for that She was tired of seeing the same colour so often."— Charles went with Mrs. Krehmer to pass the day with her Children—

Russia remained on the Julian (or Old Style) calendar when the rest of Europe and North America moved to the Gregorian (New Style) calendar in the mid-eighteenth century. Consequently, in the nineteenth century, Russian dates were twelve days behind their European counterparts, and the Russians celebrated the New Year on 13 January. Likewise, Epiphany—Twelfth Night—customarily observed on the sixth day of January, was celebrated by the Adamses in St. Petersburg on 18 January.

18 January 1810

The blessing of the waters took place this Morning. It is a grand Ceremony of the Church which takes place on the Neva right opposite to the Palace in the Presence of the Imperial family—the troops in the City and all the Foreigners and strangers of distinction— We obtained a seat in a window of a house in the Square and saw the Procession of Priests with the Archbishop at their head performing the Ceremony— Magnificent Furs covered the Balcony and The Emperor and all the Imp family attended by the Grandee's with all the Foreign Corps in superb costumes accompanied them— After they retired the Emperor and Caulincourt [*reviewed*] the Troops all in full uniform and on most splendid Horses drawn up in a hollow square and not deviating the breadth of a hair from the Line— This is the most splendid sight that can be imagined. G[*rand*] D[*uke*] Constantine [*Alexander's brother*] was in Command— Went to a Ball at Mrs S Cramers and at Supper the 12th. Cake was cut and Mr. Adams was made King; but declined the honor being a Republican— The Bean was transfered to Count Einsiedel and he chose Mrs. Krehmer for his Queen— We danced, and it was past five o clock when we got home— The Haute Commerce as it is termed live in a style of great expence and entertain continually once or twice a week beginning with dinners ending with Balls which do not break up until four in the mornings. Cards form a constant part of the amusement— The Foreign Ministers frequent them very much— Mr Krehmer was the Court Banker—

24 January 1810

A Ball at the Empress Mothers Her Birth— As usual enquired of Mr Adams why I was not there— He informed that I was quite ill and unable to attend being confined to my bed—

February 1810

Mrs. Krehmer sent for Charles and She kept him until after ten at night— This Lady is particularly kind and we are under great obligations to her— He is a Swede she is a German and a great favorite of the Emperors.— Gen Pardoe the Spanish minister is quite charmed with the Society of Mr. Adams and comes frequently to see and converse with him— He is a Greek Scholar an Author and very learned and full of Court annecdotes of this and the last reign—

3 February 1810

My illness encreased very rapidly and again I was afflicted by suffering and disappointment— This mode of life is dreadful to me and the trial is beyond my strength—

21 February 1810

Just getting about when Mr Adams was siezed with a violent Cold and was quite ill— Sent for Dr Galloway who ordered him to bed and to keep very quiet— I have omited to mention that Count Romanzoff came in State to visit *me*— He was in his State Coach with six Horses out Riders 3 footmen with Flambeau's all in full dress— Not being aware of the intended honor and our apartments very mean I did not recieve which was as great an oversight as that of politeness as could have been commited—

3 March 1810

Princess Amalia the Sister of the reigning Empress came to take Tea and spend the Evening with me. And the same blunder occurred neither my husband or myself ever having expected such distinctions— My presentation Madame de Bray informed us had been quite of the usual line: and I presume these honors were offered as compliments to the Country this being the first regular Mission from America—

Recieved a notification through Mrs. Krehmer to send my Boy to the Princess Amalias room in the Palace To see the Emperor and Empress who would be there on monday Morning at twelve o clock— Thus I was obliged to make him a suitable dress— It consisted of a white Satin Frock over which was worn a sprigged Muslin dress white Satin Pantelets—The Shoulders and bosom bare and the Sleeves tied up with Satin Ribbon with a white Satin Sash to fasten the waiste of the Frock and white Satin Slippers— He was about two years and a half old— Martha Godfrey [*Adamses' servant*] attended him— They were all anxious to see her in consequence of an impertinent Letter which had been intercepted and carried to the Emperor in which he was very disrespectly mentioned—

7 March 1810

Mr Adams who was confined by a violent Erysipelas [*skin infection*] in one of his Legs: insisted that I should go to a Ball given by the English Club to the Emperor and Empresses— I had had Blisters behind my ears which were not healed and I could not dress properly— But no excuse could be offered and I went with my Sister and the Gentlemen of the Legation and we could not return home until two in the morning— The Imperial Family recieved me with the usual distinction and exprest their regret at Mr Adams's indisposition— It was an elegant Ball—

8 March 1810

Obliged to go to a Ball at the French Ambassadors escorted by the Gentlemen of the Legation— We went at nine o clock the party brilliant as usual— Madlle. Gourief the Daughter of the Minister I think of the interior was dancing a Quadrille with Count Saxbourg— In waltsing round in the Chene des Dames She slipped and both fell on the Floor she being a very large coarse Woman: Her position was not an agreeable one as she found some difficulty in rising while her Partner stood and said Eh bien! Levez vous et ne faites pas des grimaces!!! [*Oh well! Stand up and don't make faces!!!*] This was too bad. Her Mother and I who was close by her led her to a seat and she soon after quitted the [*ball*]— Count Nesselrode was then a young man addressing [*her*] but it was not then supposed he would be permited to marry her by her Family— He was a young man of great promise but then not much known to the world— Supper as usual and dancing—

Nothing amused me so much as the instructions of our Consul Levet Harris— It was some time after we arrived before Mr Adams's Carriage was ready for us and Mr. Harris used to give me a Seat in his; while my Sister went with Mr. Adams: and during these rides he would favor me with Instructions as to my conduct and deportment &c— In the first place although I might take his arm on the Stair way where nobody could see it; *he* must drop it before he enterred the room and I must walk up to the Lady or Gentle-

man of the house alone—least our acquaintance should seem too familiar—
It was not ettiquette for a Lady to stand by a gentleman after the reception:
as it would be thought very improper— That a Lady must not go to the
Theatre with a Gentleman but only under the protection of her footmen:
and last of all that he hoped Mr. Adams would soon have his Carriage lest it
should [*be thought*] that *we* had an improper *Liaison!!* This was quite too
much for my gravity and I laughed in his face assuring him that whatever
fears he might have for *his* reputation I had none whatever for my own and
this entretien put an end to such discourse and to all future rides with Levet
Harris— He was a petit Maitre, with Quaker habits of exceeding neatness
and in his household, his furniture, his Equipage and his person there was
a refined elegance amounting to effeminacy in the best possible taste— He
had many amiable traits of character and I always regreted that association
with Men of corrupt habits had led him into practices which the strict principles of my Husband could not approve—

*Louisa's opposition to her sister Catherine's accompanying the Adamses to
Russia proved prescient. Catherine, called Kitty, quickly caught the eye of Tsar
Alexander I, creating an awkward situation in which Louisa risked either
allowing her sister to become the tsar's mistress—commonplace behavior in
the Russian court—or alienating the emperor and jeopardizing John Quincy's
position in Russia. Fortunately, the emperor, notoriously fickle, soon moved on
to other conquests, and the storm blew over. Less fortunately, Kitty also caught
the eye of John Quincy's nephew and private secretary, William Steuben Smith.
He and Kitty engaged in an affair, and John Quincy was eventually forced to
demand that they marry in February 1813. Like his father, Col. William Stephens Smith, William Steuben proved to have more charm than ability, and
consistently struggled to find employment to support his family. John Quincy
and Louisa repeatedly had to come to the Smiths' aid, especially when William
Steuben was imprisoned for debt on various occasions in the 1810s and 1820s.*

9 April 1810

Mr. Adams and my Sister (rather a breach) of rules went to the Ice Hill Party
at the French Ambassadors Caperoonage being deemed essential— It is a
very difficult thing for Americans to conceive of the restraints exacted by

European Society, and what are termed delicate proprieties— But I have found that we cannot reason upon mere forms with those who cannot or will not understand them when long established; and if we break thro' them we must submit to evil construction without asking the why or the where-fore— Custom is the Law—

14 April 1810

My health declines so much I could not go to Madame de Brays dancing party.— Besides which the expence of dress is too heavy for our apportioned Salary— I have tried every experiment even that of dressing in Mourning but it would not answer, and our motive was suspected— What mortifica-tions attend an American Mission!!!

Mr. Adams dined with the Dutch Minister Mr. Six—A real plain spo-ken Dutchman shrewed keen and very castic—An enthusiastic admirer of Napolean—Proud of his Station while he lives in perpetual fear of losing it— He took a great fancy to *me.* but his injudicious praises did me more harm than good—

29 April 1810

Easter Sunday is a great day at St Petersburg and we recieved Presents from some of our friends of painted and Cut glass Eggs without paying the Fee generally asked for the complement—as a religious ceremony and were obliged to accept them. They are very handsome and sometimes very costly— Every one even of the People have a right to kiss the Emperors hand on this sacred day. It is a privilege however mostly claimed by the Court which sometimes keeps him up until a very late hour of the Night— Ladies are not admitted or he would have no hand left— The Gentlemen all went to Court where there were grand doings—

My Sister and myself were accustomed to walk out occasionally when the weather was not too cold on the Newssky Perspective; and the Emperor would often stop and speak to us very politely— As my Sister was a great Belle among our young Gentlemen this circumstance though customary with the Emperor towards many Ladies whom he met gave umbrage to Beaux and occasioned so much teazing and questions that we left off our promenades for some time— But the weather being now very fine we resumed our walks and again met his Imperial Majesty who again stoped us and enquired "why we had left off walking out" and without waiting for an answer; turned to me and said "that it was good for my health and that he should expect to meet *us* every day looking at my Sister." that the weather was fine— This was a real Imperial command in its tone and manner; and he gracefully touched his hat and walked on— When we met at Table the usual question and sour looks greeted us from the young gentlemen and my Sister answered yes! repeating the order that we had recieved to vex them: they were all in a blaze and I related the conversation of the Emperor without exaggeration and precisely in the manner it had taken place

"Adding nought in malice as my Sister did"

The Minister looked very *grave* but said nothing— The young Gentlemen disapproved and hoped that we should not do it.

That however diplomatic usage did not permit and we continued our walks occasionally taking Charles with us who always had a kind greeting from his Majesty and a shake of the hand but the Emperor complained that he could not make him sociable—

10 May 1810

The Ice in the Newa broke up A handsome sight but perfectly delightful to us poor poor exotics—

12 May 1810

The Ice though broken takes time to float the Masses to the Gulph of Finland and still longer for it to come down from the Lake Ladoga— But it is a matter of great rejoicing to the [*People*]— The Gov of the City waited on the Emperor with a glass of the Water—and when all the Ice is gone the chain Bridge of Boats is put across the River and the Country is free to the Petersburg Public—

13 May 1810

It is customary to celebrate May day in Russia and the French Ambassador [*invited us*] to his Country House to see the Fete— All the Nobility Gentry and Citizens who can go out in Procession in their Summer dresses and Carriages Drozkis &ce &c of the finest kind of Horses which they cannot use in the Winter as they cannot bear the exposure to the Climate and drive to a Palace called Caterérimenhoff about two miles from the City at nine o clock in the Evening— Caulincourt had borrowed [*a house*] of a Merchant for the occasion— We did not go—the Gentlemen all went—

15 May 1810

Invited to dine with Mons & Madame de Laval de Montmorency of which family it was said he was a Scion— A Frenchman who had married a Russian Lady whose beauty had certainly not kindled the flame of love in his heart. Cupids arrow would certainly have been shivered in an attack on such charms— A Gentleman asking Count Eensiedel what the attraction could have been He coolly answered "Elle à une mine de Fér" [*She has an iron mine (or face)*]— The équivoke [*equivocation*] was delightful—

23 May 1810

Went to a Ball at the French Ambassadors in honor of the Marriage of Napoleon with Maria Louise of Austria— Obliged to go as the Imperial Family were to be there— The Palace (a Palace belonging to the Emperor in which he resided rent Free the Russian Ambassador in Paris having the same honor) was superbly illuminated; as were the Houses also of the Spanish Ambassador Pardoe and Count de Bushe Heinfeldt of whom I have said very little and Count St Julians the Austrian Ambassador but they made comparatively but little show—

The Emperor was remarkably gracious— He enquired of Mr. Harris where I sat and immediately came to me and tapped me on the Shoulder as I was talking to a Lady next to me and that *I* must walk or dance the next Polonaise with him— I was very much confused as I did not know what to do when a Lady of the Court came and informed me that as soon as I saw the Emperor take his place in the dance I must walk up *alone* and take my place by him— Naturally timid this idea almost overcame me but I got through ackwardly enough— He immediately took my hand and we started off— Fortunately for me the Polonaise was very short and I bowed when the music stoped intending to return to my Seat when he said "that the dance had been so short he wished to converse with me"! Imagine my confusion every Lady in the Hall was seated but myself. He did not hear well and I what with the flurry caused by the prominence of my position and the unfortunate loss of hearing which the Climate had could only betray my stupidity without being able to understand a word— Thus we stood for about five minutes when he bowed low and retired leaving plantè là until some one whispered to me to go and take a [*seat*].

The Music soon struck when his Imperial Majesty again came up and asked me "where my Sister was"? I told him I did not know but would go immediately and seek her. "He said no I must not as he would go and do that himself"— He sought Her and took her out himself to dance and she not knowing the ettiquettes began laughing and talking to him as she would have done to an American partner herself beginning the conversation contrary to all usages du Monde—and he was so charmed with the novelty that he detained Caulincourts Supper twenty five minutes to prolong the Polonaise— She had never been presented at Court so that this extraordinary distinction produced a Buz of astonishment and poor Madame de Bray being the only Lady beside myself of the Diplomatic [*corps*] was so distressed at not being noticed that the Emperor through the medium of Caulincourt took the Lady out and thus appeased the jealousies— The truth was the Emperor wished to become acquainted with my Sister and the honor confered on me was only a passport to the act— The Emperor Supper Table was magnificent and the wonder of the night was a gorgeously ornamented Bast of wrought gold containing Seven large Pears which strange to say had been cultivated in one of the Emperors Hot Houses and which his Imperial Majesty had treasured and guarded for the Fete of his Mother which would soon take place— Tho a little suspicious instituted enquiries on the next day and found that his pears were gone and that Caulincourt had paid one hundred Rubles apiece for them— We got home at two o clock in the morning and it was broad day light—

3 June 1810

At last there is a prospect of our getting out [*of*] this horrid Hotel where I cannot sing at my work or be accompanied on the Piano by my Sister when we think ourselves alone without hearing loud clapping of hands and brava's from the neigbouring apartments on one side and on the other the directions of a Gentleman for the finishing touches of the toilet which always terminates with Rouge— The looking Glass must hang near the partition door— The Emperor wants to have Nelson for his own Servant. He has fourteen Blacks who on entering the Service take an Oath never to leave him— They wait upon the Imperial Family alone wear Turkish dresses very rich and expensive and take their turns of Service— They have a handsome Table a Carriage and four at their service and as perquisites the remains of the Desserts of the Imperial Table—White Coachman Postillion's and Footmen quite in style— But he had tasted of freedom and the golden Pill of this new Slavery ~~the bondage became so bitter~~ he sunk and died under its operation.

We cannot get into our Apartments for a week—And I am harrassed to death; for the place is so inconvenient I have no suitable apartment for my Sister— Russian Houses have no Bed Chambers according to our ideas for *Lady* accomodation.

4 June 1810

Mons & Madame de Bray came to take leave— He is a kind hearted pleasant and gentlemanly man not a dangerous one from either the shrewdness or brightness of his intellect: but one of those Routine Diplomats so often employed by the European Courts who practice every rule of ettiquette punctilliously keep a most hospitable and liberal House without any pretention of magnificence; which forms a centre of Réunion for the Corps where the superior minds can collect the best information of passing events and use it accordingly for the advantage of his Government— We are all very sorry to lose them they are a charming family and I am the only Lady left—a sad substitute even if our Salary permited the expence—

Louisa, her parents, and her sisters sat for portraits around 1792. While now quite damaged—the image of Louisa's sister Catherine (not shown) is virtually destroyed— and although the identification of the sisters is sometimes conjectural, these delightful miniatures in oil show Louisa's attractive, well-to-do family during a particularly happy period of their lives.

(Courtesy of the Massachusetts Historical Society)

Joshua Johnson

Louisa

Catherine Nuth Johnson

Carolina

Harriet

Ann (Nancy)

Eliza

Adelaide

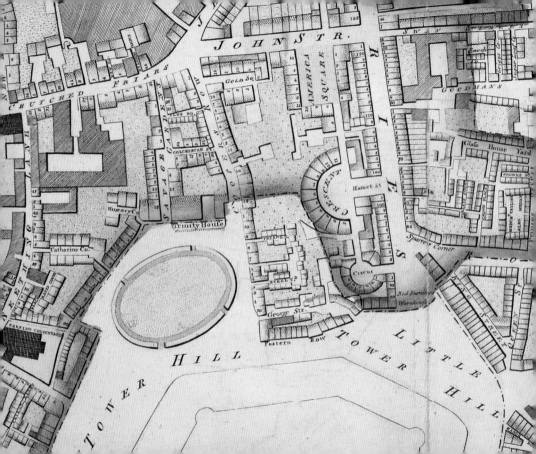

When Louisa and John Quincy went walking in the rotunda at the Ranelagh Gardens, the popular public space in the London neighborhood of Chelsea, they joined countless other couples who had used the inside location to court since 1741. Unfortunately, their visit was not entirely satisfactory: after a spat over clothing, John Quincy and Louisa went their separate ways. "On our way home," Louisa reported, "apologies were made and accepted but if lovers quarrels are a renewal of love they also leave a sting behind."

(© National Gallery, London / Art Resource, New York)

Louisa and John Quincy spent part of their time in Berlin living in the shadow of the Brandenburg Gate. This painting, by Charles Meynier, depicts Napoleon's entry into Berlin some nine years later. When Louisa returned to Berlin in 1815, she commented, "It was the same City that I had left in all its bearings The beautiful Linden Strasse! the fine Brandenburg Gate; the Bridges the Palaces, all spoke of former times; but yet it was cold, and flat, and there was a foreign air about it."

(© RMN–Grand Palais / Art Resource, New York)

When Louisa first arrived in Quincy in 1801, she and John Quincy stayed with his parents at the family home, known as Peacefield and, later, as the Old House. This illustration, entitled *View of the Seat of John Adams* by John Quincy's distant cousin Eliza Susan Quincy, shows the house as it appeared in 1822. Many years later, Louisa would make the Old House into her regular summer home, spending considerable time there when not in Washington, D.C.

(Courtesy of the Massachusetts Historical Society)

Gabriel Ludwig Lory the Elder's engraving *View of the Palace Square from Nevsky Prospekt* shows several places Louisa visited regularly while in St. Petersburg, including the Hermitage, the Winter Palace, and Nevsky Prospect itself. Louisa's first visit to the Hermitage led her to observe, "It is impossible to describe the Splendor of the Scene— All the Palace that is the two united the Imperial and the Hermitage with all its magnificent embellishments are laid open to the Public."

(The State Hermitage Museum, St. Petersburg. Photograph © The State Hermitage Museum / photo by Vladimir Terebenin, Leonard Kheifets, and Yuri Molodkovets)

Later in life Louisa viewed her journey from St. Petersburg to Paris as one of her crowning achievements. On this first page of her account of her adventures, entitled "Narrative of a Journey from Russia to France 1815" and written in 1836, she laments that "It has often been a matter of regret to me that I kept no journal of my travels." She suggests that her purpose in writing is to "show that many undertakings which appear very difficult and arduous to my Sex, are by no means so trying as imagination forever depicts them."

(Adams Family Papers, Courtesy of the Massachusetts Historical Society)

Narrative of a

Journey from Russia to France 1815 —

It has often been a matter of regret to me that I kept no journal of my travels from S.t Petersburg, to Paris — and having little to occupy my mind or attention, I will even at this late period endeavour to sketch some of its incidents; merely by way of amusement, to fill up an hour which might be less profitably employed. It may perhaps at some future day serve to recal the memory of one, who was — and show that many undertakings which appear very difficult and arduous to my Sex, are by no means so trying as imagination forever depicts theirs — And that energy and discretion, follow the necessity of their exertion, to protect the pui—ced weakness of feminine imbecility —

15. On the 12.th day of Feb.y at five o'clock in the evening of Sunday, I bade adieu to the splendid City of S.t Petersburg, where I had resided upwards of five years; in company with my Son Charles between 7 and 8 years of age; a french Nurse, who entered my service on that day, and two Men Servants, one of whom had lived with M.r Smith; the other a released prisoner from the remnant of Napoleons Army, who had been taken in that most disastrous Russian War, which terminated the career of that heretofore fortunate Soldier, in his transportation to the Island of S.t Helena —

AU NOM DU ROI.

Nous Envoyé extraordinaire et Ministre Plénipotentiaire
de S. M. le Roi de France près S. M. le Roi de Prusse,
prions les Officiers Civils et Militaires, chargés de maintenir l'ordre
public dans tous les Pays amis ou alliés de la France, de laisser
librement passer *Madame Louise Catherine Adams, épouse
de Monsieur Adams, Ministre des Etats unis près S. M.
l'Empereur de toutes les Russies, se rendant à Paris avec
son fils Charles François Adams, et ses domestiques*

et de leur donner aide et protection en cas de besoin.
Le présent Passeport délivré à *Berlin le 10 Mars 1815*.

Le Ministre Plénipotentiaire de France en Prusse

Le Cte de Caraman

Par le Ministre
Le S. de Légation
Le Cte P. de Vaudreuil

HELL HOUNDS RALLYING ROUND THE IDOL OF FRANCE.

Napoleon's return to France from Elba in March 1815 shook all of Europe, including Louisa, who was making her journey from St. Petersburg to Paris. This British cartoon by Thomas Rowlandson, entitled *Hell Hounds Rallying round the Idol of France* and published in April 1815, depicts an array of demons enthusiastically greeting Napoleon upon his return, with dead soldiers circled around.

(Bullard Napoleonic Collection, Brown University Library)

This French passport, issued to Louisa by the Duc de Caraman, the French minister at Berlin, on 10 March 1815, was instrumental in helping her to complete her journey to Paris. Identifying Louisa as the wife of the U.S. minister to Russia, it satisfied French officials loyal to the returning Napoleon and convinced French soldiers she was a sympathetic American.

(Adams Family Papers, Courtesy of the Massachusetts Historical Society)

The period from 1815 to 1817 when the Adamses lived in London while John Quincy served as U.S. minister to Britain was one of the happiest for the family. Charles Robert Leslie, a British artist of American descent, painted these portraits of Louisa

and John Quincy in 1816, capturing that sense of contentment. Louisa considered them both "striking likenesses."

(Diplomatic Reception Rooms, U.S. Department of State, Washington, D.C.)

During her years in Washington, D.C., Louisa visited the congressional galleries to hear debates on numerous occasions. This painting of the House of Representatives, completed between 1822 and 1823 by Samuel F. B. Morse, shows the chamber as it was reconstructed after the 1814 destruction of the Capitol.

(Samuel Finley Breese Morse, *The House of Representatives,* completed 1822; probably reworked 1823, oil on canvas, 86⅞ x 130⅝ inches. Corcoran Gallery of Art, Washington, D.C. Museum purchase, Gallery Fund)

George

John

Charles Francis

Charles Bird King painted Louisa's sons George and John in 1823. Four years later, King completed the portrait of Charles Francis. All three paintings show the boys near the age of twenty-one. King's studio was located quite close to the Adams home in Washington, D.C., and he also undertook paintings of several other members of the family.

(Courtesy of Mrs. Gilbert T. Vincent, Cooperstown, N.Y.; and National Park Service, Adams National Historical Park)

Entitled *The President's House from the River,* this hand-colored engraving of the
White House as seen from the Potomac River by William Radclyffe dates to around
1840, but is based on an earlier drawing by William Henry Bartlett. It gives a sense
of the views from the Executive Mansion when Louisa and John Quincy lived there.

(White House Historical Association [White House Collection])

The ball Louisa hosted to honor Andrew Jackson in early 1824 became the social
event of the season. This photoengraving, printed in 1871 in *Harper's Bazaar* maga-
zine, gives some hint of the elaborate decorations on the floor and the crowds of
people who attended. Jackson appears at the center, while John Quincy and Louisa
stand to the far right, greeting their guests. Both men's faces, based on portraits
made long after 1824, appear considerably older than they were at the time of the
actual ball.

(Harvard University, Widener Library. P 207.2F: Vol. 1, 2 November 1867, p. 168)

Thomas Baker Johnson, Louisa's only brother, worked as the deputy postmaster at New Orleans from 1810 to 1824. After that time, however, ill health, depression, and even paranoia kept him from holding any further employment, and he lived much of the remainder of his life in isolation until his death in 1843 at the age of sixty-four. This portrait has been attributed to Chester Harding, but little is known as to when or under what circumstances it was painted.

(National Park Service, Adams National Historical Park)

According to the inscriptions at the bottoms of these delightful silhouettes of Louisa and John Quincy, they were "cut by Master [William James] Hubbard in the President's House Washington 1828."

(Courtesy of the Adams Family)

Georgeanna Frances

These portraits of Georgeanna Frances and Mary Louisa Adams, Louisa's two granddaughters by John and Mary Catherine Hellen Adams, were created by Asher Brown Durand in 1835. Durand painted them "as a compliment" to John Quincy, who was helping to raise the children following their father's death.

(Asher B. Durand, *Georgeanna Frances Adams* and *Mary Louisa Adams,* Smithsonian American Art Museum, Adams-Clement Collection, gifts of Mary Louisa Adams Clement in memory of her mother, Louisa Catherine Adams Clement)

Mary Louisa

The Birth day of my

First born Son.

George Washington Adams

12 April 1849.

O God! who didst hearken to the prayer of my deep distress; and didst mercyfully grant me the blessing I so ardently craved: Pardon! pardon! the Sin of thy Servant for deserting the Children of my tenderest love, thy gifts, for mere worldly purposes; at that tender age when they most required a Mothers watchful cares. Forty seven years this day have elapsed since I first prest this treasured blessing to my breast with joy almost ecstatic! It was thy Will to take both my Cherished Sons from me, who knew not how to value thy blessed mercies ~~mercies~~, and left to others to perform those lovely duties, which thy goodness had called me to fulfil — My heart bleeds in sad repentance and I would humbly beseech thee to pardon my sins and manyfold offences — And spare me, and strengthen
                          God!
me gracious to better ... duties that are yet
           ^
left to me, that ... ope of the forgiveness of my ... Christ — Amen
This day 47 year ... poor lost Son!

                                        C Adams 12

Silver tea set

Henry Adams's warm memories of his grandmother Louisa come across in his description of her in *The Education of Henry Adams*. Writing sixty years after Louisa's death, Henry fondly recalled her "with her heavy silver tea-pot and sugar-bowl and cream-jug" at breakfast, pieces he ultimately inherited. Henry likewise compared her to the writing desk, shown next page, which, he believed, like Louisa, belonged not to Quincy but "to Washington or to Europe."

(National Park Service, Adams National Historical Park)

Topics of death and mourning permeate Louisa's later diary entries. In this one from 12 April 1847, offered as a type of prayer, Louisa remorsefully remembers her son George's birthday and expresses her guilt at not being present during his and his brother John's formative years. Another way to commemorate people's deaths in the nineteenth century was with mourning jewelry. The brooch shown here marks Louisa's own passing in 1852; it contains a lock of her blonde hair on black gros-grain under crystal. Her initials are inscribed on the back.

(Adams Family Papers, Courtesy of the Massachusetts Historical Society)

Secretary

6 June 1810

Thank God we now recieve Letters from our Children and friends in America— My Dear Sister Eliza was married to Mr John Pope of Kentucky a Senator of the U.S. All well—

12 June 1810

Moved into our Lodgings— My cares will now commence and where is my authority for any thing?— God help me— The licencious manners of this place; and the familiar habits of my Countrymen are not easily controuled— All eyes are on a Foreign Minister more especially on such an one as my Husband—a marked man everywhere for great ability and statesmanship and already so distinguished by the Emperor and his Minister—

14 October 1810

Invited to the Theatre at the Hermitage— The Emperor has given Orders as I am the only *Lady* of the Corps Diplomatique that my Sister should be invited also and this is considered one of the greatest honors ever confered upon a foreign young Lady; as well as the invitation to Minister of the second degree— This privilege is only assigned to Ambassadors and we owed this distinction to my Sister's dance with His Imperial Majesty as also to the great partiality of the Emperor for my husband— It is very kind.

23 October 1810

In the Evening I accompanied my Husband my Sister and my Boy who was dressed as a Bachus to a masked Ball— We went at about nine and were the first there always an awkward thing— The Empress Mother had a small party and the Duke was obliged to attend as a french play was to be performed: and the Actor who was engaged to manage his own Ball could not attend until released from his duties at the Palace and he did not arrive until eleven o clock— As however a number of Children were there they were set to dancing and amused as well as they could until the whole party had arrived consisting of about 150 Persons and between thirty and forty Children—

The Children walked the Polonaise danced English Country dances; and the Russian Golobalst or Dove dance and some others—

The Costumes were in great variety and admirable particularly Miss Pardoe who appeared as Madame de Pompadour and a young boy in the full costume of that age— She performed her part to admiration— Charles and Mad Vlodek opened the Ball they supped at eleven— The Supper was splendid and the animation of the bright and beautiful faces round the Table contrasted with the half anxious yet pleas[ed] countenances of the elegantly attired Mothers sparkling with Diamonds who stood around them formed a scene of the most glowing beauty where the purest affections of the Soul seemed to beam from Maternal love alone— The elegance of manners and the interest which he appeared to take in the general pleasure of the company consisting of the élite of St Petersburgh gave a high and finished grace to the Scene which exceeded all that I had ever met with— The Ombres Chinoise and a Lottery were to conclude the party and Mr. Adams not choosing that Charles should accept any *gift* we returned home much pleased and gratified but very tired at two o clock. I returned with my Sister and the Gentlemen being obliged to stay as Chaperone without waiting for Supper—

26 October 1810

The Empress Mothers birthday— Mr Adams and the Gentlemen at Court in the Morning— In the Evening we went to the Palace at half past six; at Seven we were ushered into the Hermitage Theatre— The Emperor and the Imperial family came in at eight and took their Seats in a row of Chairs in Front—Immediately behind the Orchestra— The French Ambassador in the same line with his Majesty took the Seat next the Grand Duke Michael [*Alexander's brother*]— Behind them sat the Ambassadors St Julian and Stedinck and all the great Officers of the Crown and their Ladies for there are no Boxes— The Corps Diplomatique sat on the right hand second row; and the Hall was filled up by the Noblesse the Men on one side and the Women on the other.— The Piece was Cinderella—The Music magnificent the Acting excellent and the Ballets beautiful— Some of the Songs were encore'd by the Emperor['s] order and every thing was splendidly gorgeous as it is almost every where in St Petersburgh in the Imperial domain— The distinction to Miss Johnson was a matter of wonder to all the world—

The incident Louisa describes in the entry for 5 December, below, in which Alexander I intercepted the Adamses' mail and then asked to meet their servant Martha Godfrey based on the letters she had written, was only a minor matter at the time. Eighteen years later, however, it became a part of the presidential election campaign of 1828. Supporters of Andrew Jackson, John Quincy's opponent, used it to argue that John Quincy had been in the habit while in St. Petersburg of procuring prostitutes for the tsar. These rumors circulated widely enough that some western Democrats tagged John Quincy with the title "The Pimp of the Coalition."

Louisa was pregnant again in the winter of 1810–1811. She would give birth to a daughter, also named Louisa Catherine, on 12 August 1811.

29 November 1810

Walked out with my Sister and Mr Smith— Being quite fatigued I saw the Emperor behind us hastening on with great strides: and not intending to do any thing rude: and far from supposing that his Majesty would notice it I beckoned to my Servants to drive up and with my Sister got into the Carriage and drove on— On returning up the Street we met the Emperor but his Majesty turned his head away and looked at the River and took no notice of us at all. I was very sorry but had no idea that *he* would be offended— The great distinction shown to my Sister, at the Invitation to the Hermitage had occasioned so much talk I thought it was injudicious to encourage it—

5 December 1810

My health became very precarious; and the Winter being bither, to very mild I rode in a Sleigh with my Sister and Child or with Mr Adams As I could not bear the fatigue of the motion of a Carriage and four over the Stone pavements. We rode every day wraped in Furs and this exercise was smooth and delightful—

Mrs. Krehmer and her Daughters came and passed the Evening with us.— In the course of conversation she told me that the Emperor had seen all our Letters to our Family; and that one from Martha Godfrey the Nurse of my Boy very abusive of Himself and Constantine had excited a great desire to see her; and that he had in consequence sent for the Child— That he did [*not*] think her at all handsome but that he was much please with the description and remarks which I had written of him to my Friends— I observed that it was very ungenerous of his Majesty after offering to send our dispatches by a Private and especial Courier to use the opportunity against *us:* for it was perfectly natural that with the idea of perfect safety attached to the conveyance of our Letters that we should describe our first impressions without disguise to our friends to whom they must certainly be very interesting— I knew that she would repeat this to the Emperor—

13 December 1810

Taken suddenly and severely ill—and continued so all Night.

16 December 1810

Convalescent; and resumed my rides— But as usual we met the Emperor but he turned his head away and did not look at us. I could not help laughing but was sorry when I found that he had taken offence—for I knew that Mr. Adams would feel unpleasantly about it: as the subject would become very disagreeable if the Court as customary adopted the same tone—and the first fine day My Sister and I resumed our walks— We met the Emperor on the Fontalka and he immediately stoped us and looked and spoke a little coldly addressing my Sister; but at parting turned to me and said that it was essential to my health that I should take such exercise and desired that *we* should walk every fine day when he should hope to meet *us.*— The Gentlemen had all been as angry at the want of notice as they had been at his Majestys attentions— It was quite diverting to me who was acting in the capacity of a mere duenna— The Minister took no notice—

22 December 1810

Charles was threatened with the Croup and I was in an agony of alarm—
I took him into my own chamber and Mr Adams was obliged to occupy
the Study— Dr Galloway staid and dined with us. I was quite sick myself—
There came a notification from the Master of the Ceremonies Inviting Mr.
Adams Miss Johnson and myself to a Ball on the Birth day of the Empress
Mother— Mr Adams informed him that my Child and myself were both
sick and that Miss Johnson according to Ettiquette could not go alone— He
replied that he was ordered by the Imperial Family to say that Miss Johnson
would be as already presented and be privileged to attend on all occasions
when notified— Monsr. de Maisoneuve also observed that if Miss Johnson
wished to be presented it would only be necessary for her to call on Countess Litta where the matter might be arranged when the Empresses came to
Town—

13 January 1811

Went to the palace with Mr. Adams and my Sister— The Emperor had
sent an order that we should be admited by the Petites Entree's only used
by the Imperial Family and the Ambassadors only and we were shown into
the recieving Room of the Emperor— Count St Julian alone was there
when we went in and the French Ambassador came in soon after us— We
were informed that this was a most extraordinary distinction ever granted
to a foreign Minister at that Court and that it was the express order of the
Emperor himself—

The Imperial Family soon came in and spoke very kindly to my Sister
and myself— They were preceded into the Hall by a small guard of the
Military and we followed by special order— On entering the Hall the Emperor called for the Grand Master of the Ceremonies order'd a Chair to be
set and turning to *me;* told him that he Mons de Maisoneuve (my old friend)
was to take me under his protection to sit or walk as most agreable; and not
to suffer the Crowd to press on me for turning to me "un malheureux coude
vous feroit un grand tort" [*a careless elbow could do you great harm*]— That
he was not to quit me during the Evening until he had seen me safe into my

Carriage— My astonishment and embarrassment was painful for I had no idea that my delicate situation had been observed by any one and it put me sadly to the blush—

The Emperor [*moved*] on and about an hour after still under the protection of my appointed Guardian we met the Emperor when he again accosted me and insisted that I should go and [*sit*] by the Empress who sat on an elevated Seat attended by her Ladies— I thankfully declined the honor— when he insisted and said dont you know that no one says Nay to the Emperor— I laughed and replied but *I* am a republican— He smiled and went on his way—

We soon went to Supper and then he came round and spoke to my Sister in English— He always spoke to me in French— I scarcely saw Mr Adams the whole evening or any of our party— Mr de Maisoneuve met me at the door of the Theatre again offered me his arm and we continued our Promenade until the Imperial Family had retired when I found our Carriage ready at the Emperors private entrance; and on taking leave of me the good old Gentleman said "that he hoped that he had faithfully performed the pleasant duty assigned to him by his Imperial and followed his orders punctually"— I thanked very sincerely as also all of the Imperial Family for such very great distinction for which I trusted they would be assured of my deep and lasting sense of gratitude— The old Gentleman had become acquainted with me on my arrival at Berlin many years before; who had been applied to by Mr. Adams for assistance in procuring *me* a Physician when I was siezed with a dangerous illness in consequence of the fatigues and anxieties which had suffered three days after my arrival; only four months married and without a single female acquaintance— The Empress Mother desired, he said, that Miss Johnson should for the future consider herself as presented— The motive of all this I presume is political and owing to the flattering partiallity of the Emperor for my husband— Caulincourt was siezed with a swimming in the head and left the Hall immediately—

24 January 1811

A Ball at Madame Lessceps I was too much exhausted to go—

Our Footman had a daughter born on New Years day and I was asked to stand God Mother with Miss Godfrey and Mr Gray as Proxies for the Duke of Oldenburgh and his Wife the Grand Dutchess Catherine. The ceremonial was of the Greek Church— A Pope was introduced heading the party who accompanied the Parents the Babe and their friends; a Table was set covered with a handsome white damask Napkin with Candles and a Camels Pencil— I was prepared with a Silver Cross; a Shirt; a Cap; and a piece of Showy Calico to wrap the Babe in— The Tub was half filled with cold water: and the Child was presented to me to hold quite undressed by the Nurse and we were ranged by the Priest around the Tub he standing by the Table and the Sponsors close to him— The Pope took the Child from me made a prayer in a sort of Chant and dipped it three times into the Tub at each interval making the sign of the Cross on its forehead very much as in our ritual and blessing it— Then with a wet sponge he made the sign of the Cross on its breast and Shoulders & Feet having used a Camells hair pencil for the forehead and head and then the babe was put into my hands by the priest with a short prayer while the second God mother presented me with the Cross and Chain the Shirt, the Cap and at last the wrapper and the Gold Cross presented by Mr. Gray all of which Articles blessed during the dressing of the Child— After which being ranged in order around the Tub the Priest put a consecrated Taper in each of our hands and we marched three times in procession round the Bathing Tub. The Pope or Priest as he is called when aproaching the Table with all the company turning their backs to the Water and chanting the service in three times circling round the Tub are ordered to *spit* out the Devil and all his works and the Service is terminated by the Priest cutting off a piece of the Babes hair rolling it up and throwing it into the water in which the Babe was baptized— He then folded up the Napkin and Candles as his perquisite and they all retired to feast on a collation prepared for them in their own apartments— The name Echaterina—

26 January 1811

I was taken very ill this day and Dr Galloway was sent for: the general routine of our lives was quiet— We rode out and walked accasionally— Frequently met the Emperor on the public walks who always stoped to speak to us very kindly and then passed on— My health was miserable and the family seemed to be broken up.

In fact we all pined for home and I scarcely endure a longer separation from my loved Children— This was burthensome to all, surely a man loses more than he gains by exacting such a sacrifice— I had thought that one year would have been the extent of my stay— How could we be happy under such circumstances— To give birth to another Child in a strange land after all I had suffered was a cause of incessant fear and anxiety; and my Sister was deprived of the pleasures which were so attractive to young persons—

23 May 1811

My situation precludes me from entering into the dissipation of the day and I only visit among my intimate friends.—

Mr Adams and my Sister were reading Letters just recieved from America in his Study; when I went in to see him as usual in the morning to ask how he did: and I immediately saw by their distressed countenances that bad news had come to us— They could not conceal it from me and my heart collapsed with agony at the sudden shock in a dead fainting fit— My loved Sister Hellen had died in Childbirth and the Infant and the Cousin of Mr. Adams also Mrs. Norton— The fright produced alarming consequences and a premature birth was threatened with dangerous symptoms for some hours. My Physician remained with me for many hours of intense suffering when a favorable change took place and perfect quiet was relied on for recovery—

Company was expected at dinner and apologies were sent to excuse us—

25 May 1811

After appearing better for the whole day of yesterday I was again siezed with violent illness and hope was nearly crushed both for my life and that of my Child— Laudanum was freely resorted to by my Physician but it at first aggravated my illness but a second dose judiciously applied produced sleep and on awaking I was quite composed the crisis had passed and hope blessed hope was renewed— It is at such moments that the heart is filled with fullness of joy: for in these moments the affections expand and all the best sympathies which lie dormant in the every day events of [*life*] rush forth uncontroul'd and give assurance of their reality—

27 May 1811

Slowly recovering God in his mercy has spared me— Recieved Letters from our Children— This was the best cordial in my weak State— They allayed my fears and assisted my recovery—

31 May 1811

Was able to sit in the Parlour the adjoining room to my Chamber and Mr. Harris kindly called to see me— He is very attentive—

26 June 1811

Went to see a large three Decker Ship of War Launched— The rail gave way and we were saved with difficulty from [*being*] precipitated into the Stream as She passed into the Water— The moment was fearful as the Crowd pressed down: but a gentleman caught me and pulled me back just in time to save me— I had not time to be frightened, but we were glad enough to get home—

28 June 1811

Mr. Navarro brought Madame de Bezzara and introduced her to me— She is a remarkably sensible Woman: full of that worldly knowledge which adapts a Lady for a political Station— Shrewed observant and practiced without any excss of sensitive delicacy; feeling her consequence and her great superiority to her husband a small man every way she is full of anecdote knows every thing that passes and is ready to offer advice wherever it is needed. He was Minister from the Court of Portugal—

July 1811

Mr Plinky came to inform us that our House was Sold and that we must move out of it as soon as possible: that is in thirteen days as the Emperor had purchased it.— This was rather severe: To look for a House: to find a suitable one and to move by the first of August which we thought to be absolutely necessary under the circumstances both trying and distressing to me who had never entirely recovered from my illness and was not very well able to bear the fatigue and anxiety of a removal—

5 July 1811

There was however no time to reason on the subject: and I accompanied Mr Adams in the search for Houses and we went to see one which was recommended to us opposite to the Palace at Kamini Ostroff— It is very pretty but too far out of Town being eith Miles from St Peterburg— Returned to town much fatigued to look farther—

The Adamses, having been forced to move despite Louisa's advanced pregnancy, found a new home on Apothecary Island, a few miles outside of St. Petersburg. The remote location offered a more tranquil setting than their previous apartments. But it also created significant difficulties for Louisa when she was required to participate in court events in the city and, most especially, when the time came for her to give birth. By October the Adamses had returned to St. Petersburg proper, as Louisa did not want to spend the winter in such a remote location. They settled back into another rented house on Voznesensky Prospect and Little Officer's Street, near where they had lived the previous spring.

25 July 1811

Mr & Mrs. Bezzara came according to appointment and I was obliged to accompany in full dress Mourning to introduce to Madame Litta at the Palace which was more than a Mile round from us as we had to cross the River— Countess Litta recieved us very kindly but begged that I would go home directly and not wait for Madame Bezzarras Presentation to the Empress. As however She had no Carriage but mine I was obliged to remain nearly an hour before I could get home: and when the Countess came back from the Empress She took my hand and sent me off saying while she laughed that she had never taken leave of any body with so much pleasure in her life— We reached home in safety and they staid to pass the Evening with us mourning for the loss of their Service of Silver Plate which was all worn in holes on the land journey— This was a killing life—

29 July 1811

Mr. Labouchere came and passed the Evening with us— He is a most agreeable man and his conversation is very pleasant—

At last for a few days we have obtained a little quiet— I go down to the end of the Garden; have a Chair on the Bank of the River with Charles; and we catch Fish not worth eating— It is an indolent sort of an amusement that just suits me for I *do not think*— When I look forward I tremble: but I bow down with trust in him who has mercifully saved me through a life of trouble and granted to me so many blessings—

11 August 1811

This was a day of great suffering and dreadful anxiety to my Dear Husband— My Nurse arrived: and as we were eight miles from [*St. Petersburg*] We were obliged to send to town for my requisite help. Mrs Keinche came out and remained through the day— Mrs Bentzpon here.

12 August 1811

Continued quite ill— Mrs. Heinche left me to go and see a Lady in the City taking my Carriage Horses and Servants and did not return until six o clock in the Evening— This indiscretion nearly cost my life— My Child a Daughter the first that I was ever blessed with was born at half past seven o-clock an hour and a half after her return— My Sister went and announced her birth to her Father and he soon came in to bless and Kiss his Babe— God was very merciful to me for I had been in great danger ever since morning—

9 September 1811

This day my lovely little Babe was Christened— We dared not ask the Emperor to stand as Sponsor least it should not please in America— Mrs. Bezzara, Mrs. Krehmer, and Mr. Harris stod Sponsors and she was named after *me* by her Fathers special desire contrary to my wish— The Service was performed by the Rev London King Pitt Chaplain of the English Factory Chapel— The Witnesses present were the Chevalier Bezzara, Gen Waltzdorf, Count Bushe de Hunnefeldt, Chevalier Navarro, Mr & Mrs. Bentzon, daughter of J J Astor; Mr & Miss Krehmer Com Bainbridge Mess Blodget, Fisher, Gray J. Harris Junr Jones and some others with the Family made up the company— The Sponsors were strangely selected Madame de Bezzarra Roman Catholick Mrs. Krehmer Episcopalian, and Mr. Harris Quaker— The Company dined with us and I got through the fatigue pretty well—

12 September 1811

Mr. [*Thomas Morton*] Jones and Mr. Gray took leave of us to visit Paris and London; Mr. Gray presented a Small diamond Cross to my little daughter— During his residence with us he was always kind and as affectionate as a Son— Our Family was now diminished to the Secretary of Legation and we sensibly felt the loss of the Society of our young friends who cheered many an hour by their attentions and agreeable conversations—

30 September 1811

Company at Dinner—Count Lauriston Mons Lonquerue his aid de Camp— Mons de Rayneval Sec of Legation; St Genet, Prevost, also Secretaries Madame de Rayneval Mr & Madame Lesseps Ct St. Julian; Messrs. Lebzeltern & Stummar Sec of Baron Blome & the Baron—Baron Schladon Prussian and Count Busche Hunnefeldt— They left us early—

10 October 1811

Moved into a House in the City selected by Mr. Adams, a miserable place but the only one that would suit our finances— The accommodations were altogether unfit for a family and it was in a very vulgar and unpopular part of the City— Debt or meaness is the penalty imposed by the Salary of an American Minister.

16 October 1811

When Mr. Adams returned from his walk he informed us that he had met the Emperor who had stoped to converse with him— Among the questions he had was whether I was confined yet. He answered that I had been confined in August! He then asked whether I had a Son or a daughter— My Husband answered a daughter the first he had ever had— What was she born in the Country? Yes Sire. He shrugged his shoulders and pretended he did not know it— He felt I suppose what a serious inconvenience he had put me to— He enquired if my confinement had been fortunate? answer perfectly so he thanked his Majesty— How inquisitive!!! As he is informed of every thing concerning foreigners he knew all about it before he put these questions— I had not seen him since I left the City— Every thing is changed since the departure of Caulincourt—

---

7 December 1811

Seized with a violent Fever— The Milk struck to my brain in consequence of a fright on finding that Charles had waked from his sleep and as I supposed ruptured a blood vessell: my fever ran so high and the delirium so violent that the Physician announced to Mr. Adams that if a change did not take place towards morning he must prepare for the worst— My Child was taken from me for the time— The Children were both very ill and our complaint was said to be the Grippe.

10 December 1811

Still considered in great danger but the head partially releaved— The Children severely ill.

18 December 1811

Myself out of danger and Charles better but my Babe very ill— All of us much reduced and very suffering.

28 January 1812

After a long protracted confinement by sickness and anxiety, I once again take my Station in the world for which I care so little— The aspect of Society is greatly changed— The Corps Diplomatique is no longer so brilliant and a Cloud has rizen to veil the future for a time— Mr Adams position is as high as ever with the Imperial Family and that is the *Sun-shine* of St Petersburgh—

29 January 1812

A Letter full of wo announcing my Mothers death that of my brother in Law Mr. Buchanan; Mr Adams's Uncle and Aunt Cranch within twenty hours of each other: and the dangerous and hopeless illness of his only Sister— God help us!! Yet are we always praying for Letters:

31 January 1812

The severity of the weather exceeds all calculation— Raumures Thermometer thirty two and a quarter below Zero— Full of mortal affliction— My Poor Mother! After ten years of poverty dependence and severe suffering which at this great distance it was so utterly out of my power to mitigate or assuage— How different will home appear should we live to return.— Gods Will be done! He afflicts us in mercy for here we are placed amid many sore temptations—

11 February 1812

My lovely beautiful Babe is very very ill— Ah! the fountain of her precious existence is sapped by these constant shocks and I look at her with fear and trembling— Every one who sees her stops her in the Street and they all say "that She is born for Heaven." The Russians are very superstitious and I fear that with the impressions already made upon my weak mind during my four years residence in Berlin I am too ready to fall into this error— Toward Eveng my babe was better— I am not naturally melancholy but my trials are heavy.

16 February 1812

Mr Adams & Charles dined out and my boy returned home highly delighted with a present which he had recieved of a Magic Lantern— We see the Americans frequently.

30 August 1812

Went into the Country with my sick Child.

9 September 1812

Took my Babe back to the City in Convulsions. Dr Simpson and Galloway both attend the Babe.

15 September 1812

My Child gone to heaven.

Louisa was utterly crushed by the loss of her beloved daughter. Even thirty years later, she was unable to continue to write her "Adventures of a Nobody" beyond this point. Five weeks after the child's death, however, Louisa began her only true diary from this time period—written solely for herself and intended for no audience. This short diary eloquently speaks to Louisa's intense depression—her sense of failure and guilt, her own desire to die and be buried next to her daughter. The long breaks between some entries demonstrate her inability even to find the energy to write. But the diary also shows how hard she struggled to move beyond her grief and, in time, find new hope and joy in her life.

22 October 1812

I have procured this Book with a view to write my thoughts and if possible to avoid dwelling on the secret and bitter reproaches of my heart for my conduct as it regarded my lost adored Child whose death was surely occasion'd by procrastination. Oh God I humbly bow myself in submission to thy allwise decree's and implore thy mercy to grant me strength to support the dreadful afflictions with which thou hast thought fit to try thy Servant—

23 October 1812

This day I have endeavourd to keep myself constantly employed but still my mind dwells on the past and nothing can fill the dreadful void in my heart. My babes image pursues me where ever I go bitter reflection adds to my pangs and in religion alone do I find consolation—

Humbly do I confess my sins great as is my punishment. I have a full conviction of the justice and mercy of my God who will not reject the petition of a contrite spirit but will grant me strength to correct the evil propensities of my nature and teach me to subdue that pride of heart from which all my errors spring—

24 October 1812

This day has passed without any thing to mark it and to relieve a little the sameness of my Sisters life I visited the Theatre. While I was there I was amused, but on my return to my home how cold blank and dreadful! My first object used to be my Child but alas now I see only the spot on which she died and every thing recalls her last agonies—

25 October 1812

This day Mr A. read prayers to me. It has been my practice for some time to teach Charles his prayers and the commandments. Mr A expressed himself dissatisfied with my method and I suffer'd myself to be hurried away by my temper in a very unbecoming manner. I am peculiarly unfortunate for what I undertake with the best intentions almost always turns out exactly contrary. I read I work I endeavor to occupy myself usefully but it is all in vain. My heart is almost broken and my temper which was never good suffers in proportion to my grief. I strive against it and humbly implore heaven to fortify

my soul and to teach me meekness and seregnation. He complains of my being suspicious and jealous. These were faults once foreign to my nature but
they are insensibly acquired by a perpetual coldness and restraint operating
on a naturally warm and affectionate disposition yet this is by no means
sufficient as an excuse and it shall be my study to amend such distructive
failings. I was taught from my earliest youth never to feel ashamed to acknowledge a fault and it always appeared to me to be a great meaness to
endeavour by falsehood or prevarication to conceal an error which I was not
ashamed to commit— For those I love no sacrifice will ever be too great for
me to make. All I claim is a little indulgence and if I at any time desire what is
unreasonable or improper affection and gentleness will always have full effect
upon my mind. It is surely enough to have the power of rejecting a request
without making a rejection more painful by harshness or contempt. I feel
what a burthen I must be to all around me and it is this which has made me so
solisitous to return home. There is something in an American life more active
and varied and the idea of seeing my children was an object on which my
mind could rest with real pleasure. In Mrs Adams I should have found a com-
forter a friend who would pity sufferrings which *she* would have understood—

6 November 1812

My thoughts have been so very gloomy that I have refrian'd from writing
some time and I dare not commit to paper all that passes in my mind. In
vain I strive to fly from them. My babes image flits forever before my eyes
and seems to reproach me with her death. Necesssity alone induced me to
wean her and in doing it I lost her. Oh God thou didst know the agonies I
felt e're I could bring my self to do it. Thou didst think to fit to take her
from me Oh Lord and I humbly bow myself in submission to thy will— I
struggle in vain against the affliction that consumes me and I feel that all my
wishes centre in the grave. I am a useless being in this World and this last
dreadful stroke has too fully convinced me what a burthen I am become—
Surely it is no crime to pray for death. If it is wickedness I implore thy
mercy Oh Lord to cleanse my heart and to teach me to bear my trials with
fortitude— My heart is buried in my Louisa's grave and my greatest longing
is to be laid beside her. Even the desire of seing my beloved Boys gives way

to this cherished hope and I look forward with joy to "that Bourne from whence no traveller returns."

———

5 December 1812

It is long since I have written. My mind has been in such a state as to render it imprudent to set my thoughts on paper— Kitty has been very sick and the Doctor kindly told me that if we did not make haste and return home that the Climate would kill us both. To me there is nothing frightful in this idea. I am only desirous of mingling my ashes with those of my lovely Babe. My only fear is that some one will take the place which I so ardently desire. As my senses are supposed to be affected I may be excused for expressing such a fear but I implore the friends I may leave should I die here to observe this my last request to lay me with my Infant and to let no one follow me to my grave. At the moment of making this request I am in good health and spirits therefore I trust my petition will not be thought to proceed from caprice or a distemper'd imagination. If I know myself I never was calmer or easier in mind and body than I am at this moment. Had I a Will to make it would be thought but prudent to make it in case of accidents. Therefore I indulge myself in the expression of this desire as my body is the only thing in the world over which I may pretend to have a right and that only conditionally. Even after death should I be ordained to be buried in this Country I again repeat as this will injure no one I hope it will meet with attention. I cannot help smiling at my anxiety on this subject as I fear it will only tend to confirm the idea of my intelect being impaired—

———

4 April 1813

We have at length recieved letters from America—Which bring favorable accounts of the health of our friends and my dear Children. To hear from them once in six or seven months is all that is left me as my prospect of ever seeing them more is now alas hopeless. My health the Climate and this dreadful War have added to the improbability of our return this Summer. For myself I scarcely can define my feelings. Much as I wish to see my Children my heart is torn at the idea of quitting for ever the spot where my darling lays and to which my whole soul is linked but my fears on Mr Adams's account render me desirous to leave a Climate in which he evidently suffers and which I fear will irreparably injure his constitution— Mr Harris joined me in the walk to day and made some observations on Mr A's looks which have contributed to render me more uneasy. I will trust in the mercy of heaven to hear my prayers for his health and to save him from all danger. He will listen to no advice therefore we must hope that the natural strength of his constitution and some striking event which may give an active occupation will remove the disease he is now threaten'd with— I have just closed a letter to Mrs Adams. It is the first I have written for many months and it has rent my heart afresh—

14 August 1813

What wonderful changes have taken place since I last took up this book. Even my health and spirits are so much amended that I scarcely know myself. I offer up my prayers and thanks to the Almighty disposer of events for his great mercy in having raised me up and comforted me in my severe affliction and will ever put my trust in him for in heaven alone can I find consolation and I look forward with the hope of soon being reunited to my Angelic Babe—

Another great crises is speedily advancing and life will soon become even more burthensome than it has been for the last twelve Months. In vain I ask myself what I apprehend. A sort of vague indefinite something tells me that I have still some heavy trials to go through ere I shall be released from this world of sorrow—

They say I am ambitious. If so why do not the vain projects of the world occupy my thoughts and fill my Soul. When I compare myself with those to whom I am the most nearly connected when I see every thought devoted peace happiness family every thing neglected for this one object my heart decidedly assures me that for this great end I was not made and that were I of consequence enough to be any thing I should only prove a bar in the way of attaining it. No! Life has lost its principal charm and all I wish is to quit a World for which I have long been conscious I was not fitted to live happy in this world. We must have something to soften the casualties to which the best of [*us*] are liable and without one being who will open his heart to you though bound by the closest ties cast such a dreadful restraint over the most trifling things as to banish and destroy all confindence and by this means render the greatest blessings unavailing in promoting that portion of happiness which we are allowed to enjoy—

·[CHAPTER FIVE]·

"The Memory of One, Who Was"

St. Petersburg to Paris

Perhaps Louisa's most compelling autobiographical piece, her "Narrative of a Journey from Russia to France," commences in February 1815 as she prepared to leave St. Petersburg for Paris with her young son Charles Francis. John Quincy had left Russia a year earlier, tasked by President James Madison with helping to negotiate a peace treaty between the United States and Great Britain to end the War of 1812. With the signing of the Treaty of Ghent in December 1814, John Quincy completed his mission. He wrote to Louisa, telling her he intended to go to Paris to wait for further instructions from Madison and asking her to join him there as soon as possible. She received the letter by early January and immediately began making arrangements to depart. She left St. Petersburg on 12 February with Charles; Madame Babet, a French nurse; a manservant named Baptiste, a former French soldier; and another servant, possibly a man named John Fulling. Together they would travel across Russia, Prussia, and France, finally arriving in Paris on 23 March.

The journey was divided into stops based on the European post road system. The roads, maintained by each separate nation, were divided into posts located roughly six to twelve miles apart (approximately the distance a carriage could travel in one hour). Travelers paid tolls at the post stations based on how far they planned to travel before the next stop; in exchange, they received fresh horses and local postilions (or post riders) familiar with the territory to accompany them. Usually attached to a tavern or inn, the post station also could provide overnight lodgings or a hot meal if needed.

Louisa wrote her "Narrative" in the summer of 1836 to amuse herself and, as she notes below, to "show that many undertakings which appear very difficult and arduous to my Sex, are by no means so trying as imagination forever depicts them." In many ways, this "Narrative" records what Louisa came to see as her defining moment, a time when, completely on her own, she demonstrated her ability to rise to the occasion and overcome the difficulties in her path. And difficulties there were. Not only was she a woman traveling almost two thousand miles by herself with a young child and several unreliable servants, a precarious proposition at any time. She was also crossing Europe mere months after the retreat of the Napoleonic Army, and her "Narrative" vividly describes the remnants of battlefields she encountered and the continuing fears created by the European wars. Interestingly, when Louisa first wrote about her journey, to her mother-in-law in June 1815, she downplayed the hardships: "My journey from St. Petersburg was performed with as little uneasiness and as few misfortunes as could possibly have been anticipated and I have really acquired the reputation of a heroine at a very cheap rate." Only much later did she acknowledge the true effort involved.

Because Louisa crafted this memoir completely from memory, without a diary or other records to aid in recollection, her "Narrative" contains various errors—misremembered routes, incorrect town names, inaccurate dating, and the like. Still, as a vivid account of a signal point in her life, it offers truths about Louisa that far outweigh these minor inaccuracies.

It has often been a matter of regret to me that I kept no journal of my travels from St Petersburg, to Paris—and having little to occupy my mind or attention, I will even at this late period endeavour to sketch some of its incidents; merely by way of amusement, to fill up an hour which might be less profitably employed— It may perhaps at some future day serve to recal the memory of one, *who was*—and show that many undertakings which appear very difficult and arduous to my Sex, are by no means so trying as imagination forever depicts them— And that energy and discretion, follow the necessity of their exertion, to protect the fancied weakness of feminine imbecility—

On the 12th. day of Feby. at five o'clock in the evening of Sunday, I bade adieu to the splendid City of St. Petersburg, where I had resided upwards of five years; in company with my Son Charles between 7 and 8 years of age; a french Nurse, who entered my service on that day, and two Men Servants, one of whom had lived with Mr. Smith; the other a released prisoner from the remnant of Napoleons Army, who had been taken in that most disastrous Russian War, which terminated the career of that heretofore fortunate Soldier, in his transportation to the Island of St. Helena—

To avoid the disagreeable and painful feelings of parting with friends with whom I had formed a friendship of some standing; I chose the above hour while they were engaged at their dinner; and Mr. Wyer put me into the Carriage and gave the last directions to my Postillions—

The weather was intensely cold; my Carriage on runners and the two Servants followed in a kibitka [*Russian sleigh*]. Every thing had been done by the Government, that the kindest politeness and interest could suggest, in the way of Passports to make the journey easy; for which I felt truly grateful and to this attention I owed all the facilities which rendered my journey so easy— Night and day we proceeded until we arrived at Narva, where I stopped to rest at the best Inn in the place. We had been there but a few minutes, when a Gentleman was announced, who informed me that apartments had been prepared for me at the Governors, and that he would wait on me in person to escort me to his house, as Soon as convenient to myself— Intending to proceed very early in the morning, I declined the invitation; but received the visit of the Governor; and one from the Count de Bray the Bavarian Minister, who was at that time on a visit with his Wife and family at her Fathers— The Count brought me also a very polite invitation from the family to pass a few days with them, which I also rejected; being without my husband I wished to be as short a time on the road as possible.

Very early in the morning I started *for* Riga, at which place we arrived in safety, and I found tolerable lodgings— Here we were overtaken by a thaw, and I was under the necessity of staying four or five days, to get my Carriage fixed and to dispose of my Kibitka— Our provisions were all frozen ere we reached the City, and even the Madeira wine had become ice— Here for the first time I had some reason to doubt the honesty of my Servant. A Silver Cup belonging to my little boy was taken from the Carriage and there was little Doubt that he had made free with it— I was however under the necessity of overlooking the fact, in consequence of the terms of his engagement, and I could not prove it—

We were barely settled in our Lodgings, when the Governor of Riga [*Marquis Filippo Paulucci*] called to invite me to his house and to offer the use of his Carriage during my stay— I declined the invitation to take up my abode with him; but accepted an invitation to dine, and pass as much time at his house as I could during my sojourn in Riga. This Gentleman was an Italian a great favorite of the Emperor Alexander, and one of the

most friendly, Gentlemanly men I ever met with— The Marquis had married a German Lady who spoke very little french; but who appeared to
possess all the amiable and domestic qualities of persons of that Nation—
During my stay I received every attention that politeness could offer— All
the most distinguished persons in Town were invited to meet me, and I was
forced to call up all the German I could muster, to answer to the kindness
expressed for me by the Guests—

After a detention of four or five days we proceeded on our journey, and
once or twice the Carriage sunk so deep into the Snow in Courland, that we
had to ring up the inhabitants, who came out in numbers with shovels and
pickaxes to dig us out— For this purpose the bell appeared to be commonly
used, and the signal readily understood— Without accident or impediment
of any other kind, we arrived in safety at Mittau, the Capital of Courland—
Here I stopped to rest for some hours with a determination to proceed one
stage more to sleep— The House was the best I had found: the people very
civil, and every thing comfortable— In about an hour after my arrival Countess Mengs, a Lady with whom I was slightly acquainted at St. Petersberg
called, and gave me a most kind and urgent invitation to her house; entreating
me to remain with her some days she desiring to show all that was worth
seeing in the Town to me, and to introduce me to some of her distinguished
friends— As however my Letters were urgent for me to proceed on my journey as fast as I conveniently could; I thought it my duty to decline an invitation which would have been very pleasant and agreeable; the Countess being
a Lady of great respectability, and superior attainments—

Immediately after my Dinner was removed, the Master of the House
[*Jean Louis Morel*], after carefully shutting the doors and watchfully noting
that no intruders were near; said he wished much to speak with me, upon a
matter which he considered of vital importance to me; who as a friend for
whom Countess Mengs had expressed herself much interested, he should
feel very happy to serve. I expressed my thanks to him, and assured him
I felt very grateful to the Countess, to whom I would certainly pay a visit if
I had time— I requested him to be seated, and to inform me on what subject he had asked this interview— He again examined the doors with an
appearance of great anxiety, and then sat down close to me, who felt not a
little uncomfortable at all this *apparently terrible preparation*— I however

assumed an air of great calmness and patiently awaited the *mighty tale,* which was to thrill my nerves with horror—

He began by informing me that the last night a dreadful Murder had been commited on the very road which I was about to take, and to urge me to wait until the next morning, before I determined to proceed— I told him very coolly and decidedly that the plan of my journey was fixed, and as I only intended to travel four german miles farther that night and was to start so early with two well armed servants, I concieved I had nothing to apprehend; as the Postillions must be in the habit of passing the road constantly which was a very publick one, and that I should reach the place of my destination by nine or ten o clock that night— He looked very grave, and shook his head— He said that he had mentioned this subject incidentally, that he did not wish to alarm me—That he was an old man, and that he had daughters of his own, and that he thought my situation such, as to entitle him to advise me, and to open my eyes to the danger of my position—

He then informed me that the french Servant who I had with me, was well known in Mittau; that he was a Soldier in Napoleons Army; and had remained in that City two years—That he was known to be a desperate Vilain, of the very worst character; and that he did not consider my life safe with him, if I suffered him to proceed with me— At the same time he begged most earnestly that I would not dismiss him at *Mittau,* for fear he the Servant should suspect that I had received information there, and he might burn the House over his head— I told him that the man had behaved very well so far; that I had felt a mistrust of him, and did not like him; but that the Gentleman who had engaged him had entered into a bond, that he should be taken to his own Country; and that I was not to part with him unless he behaved improperly— That I had no pretence to make any charge against him, as he had been particularly active and attentive; and that his conduct and manners were very respectful—

He observed in answer that the case was difficult; and suggested to me, that I had better appear to place unlimited confidence in him; to seem to rely on him in any case of emergency; and to accept his advice if any difficulty occurred, and then act as opportunity offered when I was among my friends— He apologized for the liberty he had taken; begged me not to believe that his desire to have me stay, was a mere innkeepers wish to keep his

company; but that his knowledge of the Man Servant had been the real motive of his conduct: and entreated that not a word of this conversation
should be whispered, as it would equally endanger us both— I promised a
perfect silence, and said, that I would willingly postpone my departure; but
as the hour had arrived for that departure, and the Carriage would be at the
door directly, I was fearful that a sudden change of purpose, would excite
suspicion, and do more harm than good; and I assured him I thought his
advice excellent, and should adopt it thro' the journey—

He rose to leave me, and I was immediately called to see the Countess,
who had left a gay party at her house about a mile from the Town, and again
urged me to change my mind, and to drive directly there, instead of pursuing my journey— All this I declined, I fear from a proud and foolhardy
spirit; and that conviction that however retarded, the difficulties of my path
must be conquered, and it was as well to face them at once— Finding me
determined; she took a very kind leave of me, and I got into the Carriage
and began my ride under the most uneasy impressions. After riding about
four miles, the Postillion suddenly stopped, and informed us that he had
missed the road—that the man who was accustomed to drive was sick, that
he had never been that road before, and that he could not tell where he was—
Until eleven o'clock at night, we were jolted over hills, through swamps,
and holes, and into valleys, into which no Carriage had surely ever passed
before; and my whole heart was filled with unspeakable terrors for the safety
of my Child, for whom I offered the most ardent prayers to the ever protecting
father of his Creatures— During this time my two servants were assiduous
in their service, watchful and careful to prevent by every possible caution
an overturn, or an accident to the Carriage— I consulted Baptiste frequently,
and took his advice as to the best mode of proceeding, and at twelve o'clock
at night the Horses being utterly worn out, and scarce a twinkling Star to
teach of living light; we determined that Baptiste should ride one of the
Horses, and endeavour to find a road through which we might be extricated
from our perillous situation—

He was absent about fifteen minutes, when we heard the trampling of a
horse, and voices at a short distance— The palpitation of my heart encreased
in its bounding motion until I thought it would have burst— My Child lay
sweetly sleeping on his little bed in the front of the Carriage, unsusceptible
of fear, and utterly unconscious of danger— Baptiste rode hastily up to the

Carriage door, and informed me that he had found a house quite near—
That he had awakend the family and that a Russian Officer had come to him,
and after inquiring what he wanted, had offered his services to take us into
the road, as it required great skill to keep the Carriage out of the gullies by
which we were surrounded— He came up to me while Baptiste was speaking, and again I was obliged to tell my story in most execrable German, and
as well as I could, express my thanks for the proposed service— Lights were
brought out; one of my men mounted *his* the (Officers) horse, and we proceeded at a foot pace, and reached the Inn in safety at about half past one;
where I ordered refreshments for the gentleman, and Coffee for ourselves—
He accepted a handsome present, made many polite speeches, and took
leave; recommending the Inn-keeper to be attentive, and to see that horses
should be ready at any hour that I might want them, he departed.—

The House was very indifferent in its accommodations; I therefore
expressed my satisfaction to my domestics for the prudence and discretion,
which they had shown through this singular accident; and bade them be
ready at an early hour with the Carriage and Horses; and after thanking most
devoutly the Almighty for his protection through this hour of trial, I sought
repose with renewed confidence in the persons attached to my service, and
determined not to listen to any more bugbears to alarm my nerves, and weaken
my understanding— I had contrived to conceal the bags of gold and silver
which I carried in such a manner that neither of my Men Servants supposed
that I possessed any; and as I carried Letters with me which I displayed, it
was believed I took up only as much as I wanted at one town, until I reached
another— I was likewise furnished with a Letter from the Government,
recommending me to the protection of all whom I called on, and that any
complaint should immediately be attended; to, as I was authorized to give
information to the Minister of the Interior throughout the Russian territory,
forming that portion of my journey—

What a pity that my romance should terminate in such a silly common
place! but so it was; and as I was neither young, nor beautiful; no skill could
colour it; or no varnish could heighten the tints, or add splendour to its
effect— It is the simple unadorned truth; and nothing but the fanfaronade
stories of the murder &c, which I had heard before the event, and immediately after, our relief from this fearful and harrassing anxiety; could have
given an extraordinary interest, to so trifling an incident— Tis often thus in

the realities of life, of themselves dull, straightforward, and simple; but made of painful importance by extraneous circumstances

> O'er which minds influence exerts; nor skill
> nor power to forsee.—

We proceeded on our journey early in the morning, and no event of consequence occurred until we crossed the Vistula—

It was four o'clock in the evening, and the ice was in so critical a state, I could with difficulty procure men and horses to go over— They informed me that I should have to make a very long and tedious détour, if I could not cross; that the passage over would be attended with great *risk*, if not danger; but if I had courage to attempt it, as there was no accommodation near, they would take long poles with Hooks, and attach the Horses to the extreme end of the Pole of the Carriage, and get over as well as they could— At five o'clock we started, the men going forward and sounding with their poles first, to find the firmest path; We got over and reached the other side of the River in safety, altho' the ice had given way on the border, and it required a violent effort in the horses, to prevent the coach from upsetting on the bank—

I have forgotten the name of the Town, but we crossed from a small corner of Poland which lay on my route; and where I saw the most filthy and beggarly Village that I ever had beheld in any Country.— At this Town to which we had crossed, I remained a short time, and proceeded with the same horses to the next stage; and no other incident occurred worth notice until we reached the frontier of Prussia. Here I had to wait three hours for horses, and the people were so much inclined to be impudent, I was obliged to produce my Letter, and to inform the Master of the House, that I should write immediately to the Minister of the Interior, and complain of his Conduct— The entrance into Prussia was about 3 or 4 Miles farther on— The Man appeared to be much alarmed, made a great many apologies; and said the Horses should be ready immediately, and very *politely* obliged me to take a couple more than the usual compliment, as he thought the Carriage very heavy— This is an exaction to which travellers were constantly exposed, and to pay the tax was an absolute neccessity if you wished to avoid delay.— At the Prussian Gate, I was obliged to go through the formality of showing my Passports, and answering all the customery questions too tedious to enumerate—

We came suddenly upon a view of the [*Baltic*] Sea, and were apparently driving immediately into it, when Charles became dreadfully alarmed, and turning as white as a sheet, asked me if we were going into that *great water*— The Postillions did not seem pleased to cross the Hartz [*Harz Mountains*], and said there was a House that I could stop at until morning— I enquired if there was any particular difficulty, but found that the principal objection was, that it would be *dark* before we should get across, and that it was a dreadful gloomy road— I asked at what time they expected to get in? They told me at about five o clock in the evening, and I immediately decided upon pursuing our route, as fast as we could— With much grumbling we again set forward, and as the Evening closed in, I began to repent my determination; for every thing around us looked blank and dreary, and the *terrible* [*depression*] without knowing why, or wherefore, seem'd to take its abiding place in our thoughts— Why is it that such thoughts appear to be annexed to peculiar situations? The ignorant, the learned, the romantic, the indifferent, alike fall into such moods, without any given cause; yet scorn the idea of superstition, or a thought of something hid beyond the ken of man— And yet how irrisistible is the pressure upon the strongest minds of this imperious spell; which

> Combats vain, 'gain'st reasons sov'reign sway
> And throws its mystic shadows 'thwart our way;
> Denying still her power to controul
> Subdues our Nature, and benumbs the Soul—
> O'erleaping learnings supercillious laws,
> The searching Spirit *seeks!* but where's the cause!

The Season of the year at which I travelled; when Earth was chained in her dazzling, brittle but solid fetters of Ice, did not admit of flourishing description, of verdant fields, or paths through flowery glebes; but the ways were rendered deeply interesting by the fearful remnants of mens fierry and vindictive passions; passively witnessing to tales of blood, and woes— Such are the graphic deleneations of Wars unhallowed march—that speak in thrilling language to the heart, where tongues of men are silent— Houses half burnt, a very thin population; women unprotected, and that dreary look of forlorn desertion, which sheds its gloom around on all the objects, announcing devastation and despair— These perpetual recurrences of lifes dire alarms; were the matters of in[te]rest which forced themselves upon our attention— Onward we travelled until we arrived at Koenigsberg where we stopped a day. I delivered my Letter of credit and made arrangements to proceed; also some trifling purchaces of Amber, and should have gone to the theatre if I had not been unprotected by a Gentleman.— The next morning it rained so much I was detained until three o'clock in the afternoon; when we renewed our journey to-wards Berlin—

Baptiste I believe that was his name (but no matter) began to assume a tone not by any means agreeable, and I began to be somewhat uneasy— I intimated to him that he might leave me as soon as he pleased, as I was in a Country where I was very well known, as I had lived four years in Berlin, and was acquainted with the King, and all the Royal Family— He said his great desire was to return to his own Country, and that he did not wish to leave me— That he understood I had *agreed* to take him the whole way— I told him that the performance of this *agreement* depended on his good behaviour, and that if he was diligent and attentive, I should have no wish to part with him— This conversation had a good effect, and he resumed his first tone, and was much more respectful; but there was something threatening in his look, that did not please me, but I was afraid to notice it— My other Servant was evidently much afraid of him, and avoided every thing that could put him out of humour—

We had gone about seven miles, when the fore wheel of my Carriage fell to pieces, and we were more than a mile from any assistance— The Postillions said they could not return, neither could they proceed— The evening was setting in, and they advised that one of the two should go to a small place that we had passed on the road, and get some conveyance for me; as the road was in such a state it was impossible to walk— To this plan I assented, and after waiting a considerable time, the man return[ed] with a miserable common Cart, into which we got, and accompanied by Baptiste, turned our steps towards the place— It was little more than a hovel consisting of two rooms and a blacksmiths shop. One Woman made her appearance dirty, ugly, and ill natured; and there were two or three very surly ill looking men, whose manners were far from prepossessing or kindly— Baptiste explained our dilemma, and enquired if by any contrivance they could convey us back to the City— They answered doggedly that they could do no such thing, but that if we chose to stay there, they could make a wheel, so that we could go on in the morning— I consulted with the Servants and they both thought it a pity to return to the City— It would be midnight before I could procure a Carriage to take me there; they were armed, and one could keep watch at the door of my chamber; and the other would sleep in the Carriage, and this would prevent any accident— According to this plan I had my little boys bed brought in, and while he slept soundly my woman and I sat up, neither of us feeling very secure in the agreeable nest into which we had fallen—

As I always had provisions in the Carriage we made out to eat something before we started, and at the next Stage we took our Coffee— Our wheel was very clumsy, and not painted, but it answered all the purpose to carry us through the famous road, which had been begun by Bonaparte from Kustrin, a fortress which we reached with much difficulty, and which bore the mutillating stamp of war, in all the pride of Bastion Stockade &ce that military skill atchieves, to give dignity to crime— On our way we met a travelling Carriage labouring through the mud— The Servant stopped our drivers to ask concerning the desperate state of the road; and the Gentleman inside, enquired very politely of me, how many times I had been upset? Informing me that he had seven times been exposed to this accident; I could not help laughing at his doleful account, and told him as I had not yet been so roughly dealt with, I hoped to escape the pleasure altogether— He informed me he was Count somebody I do not remember what, and that he was on his way to St. Petersburg— I wished him better luck and we parted— At Kustrin we found a tolerable house, but were not allowed to go within the fort— To my utter astonishment I heard nothing but the praises of the gallantry of Napoleon, and his Officers, and great regret at the damage done to this beautiful fortress; and learnt that from thence, I should travel over the most beautiful road in the world, which had been completed by his order, and that it would all have been finished in the same way, if the allies had not driven him away—

The desolation of this spot was unutterably dismal; and the guarded tone of the conversation, the suppressed sigh, the significant shrug, were all painful indications of the miseries of unholy Ambition, and the insatiate cravings of contaminating and soul corrupting War, with all its train of horrors— The Cossacks! the dire Cossacks! were the perpetual theme, and the cheecks of the Women blanched at the very name— We left Kustrin to pursue our journey, after the usual process of Passports &ce; and jogged on without any incident worth notice, excepting that one of the Postillions pointed out to us the small house, where that most lovely and interesting Queen Louisa of Prussia, had stayed with her sick Baby on their retreat from Berlin, after the French had taken possession of that City— My heart thrilled with emotion for the sufferings of one, whom I had so dearly loved, and I could not refrain from tears at the recital of her sufferings—

We arrived safely at Berlin and I drove to the Hotel de Russie, and established myself there for a week. The Carriage needed repairs, and our clumsy wheel to be painted, and Berlin was attractive to me—my poor and beloved George having been born there; independent of all these pleasant associations, which appear to re-connect us with the past; even when hope faints at the prospect of realizing the fearful changes produced by unrelenting Time— Memory; how ineffably beautiful is thy power! Years had elapsed; affliction had assailed the heart, with its keenest pangs of carking grief; disappointment had thrown its mingled hues of fear and care: and the loss of the loved and revered who had watchfully guarded youth *were* removed from us to greet our eyes no more, when we should return to the home to which we had looked with fond impatience; forgetting in the lapse of time and distance, that while we were participating in the luxuries, the pleasures, and the novelties of a Court, that desease and death might be crowning its work of destruction— Yet under all these impressions after an absence of forteen years, I entered Berlin with the pleasant recollections of the past; and youth seemed again to be deck'd with rosy smiles, and glad anticipations— and I wandered in the bright mazes of vivid recollections which every object called forth in fresher bloom, as if the scythe of time had left them glowing as of yore— I wrote a note immediately to one of my old friends, with a request to see her if disengaged, and waited with no little agitation to see one who had first known me as a young and blooming Bride, and who perhaps now might have lost all traces of the writer—

And now I must make a digression, and return to St Petersburg to relate a singular circumstance which occurred the night but one before I started on my journey— I went by invitation to the Countess [*María de Bodé y*

Kinnersley de] Colombi's [*Spanish consul's wife*] to take Tea with her and to bid her farewell— We had been very intimate— She was a charming woman and was apparently attached both to my Sister and myself— Much to her discomfort I found a Russian Lady there who had uninvited come to pass two or three days. Countess [*Ekaterina Vladimirovna*] Apraxin, was a fat coarse woman, very talkative, full of scandall, and full of the everlasting amusement so fashionable in Russian society, the bonne aventure— After Tea she took the Cards, and insisted as I was going a journey, that I should chuse a Queen, and let her read my destiny— I had never seen the woman before, and had never even heard her name until introduced on my entrance that evening— I assented and she began—

She said that I was perfectly delighted to quit Petersburg; that I should soon meet those from whom I had long been separated &ce &ce— That when I had atchieved about half of my journey, I should be much alarmed by a great change in the political world, in consequence of some extraordinary movement of a great man which would produce utter consternation, and set all Europe into a fresh commotion— That this circumstance which I should hear of on the *road,* would oblige me to change all my plans, and render my journey very difficult—but that after all I should find my husband well, and we should have a joyous meeting— I laughed and thanked her, and said I had no fear of such a circumstance, as I was so insignificant and the arrangements for my journey so simple, I was quite satisfied that I should accomplish it if I escaped from accidents, without meeting with any obstacles of the kind predicted; more especially as it was a time of Peace; and we were all very merry at the skill with which she had strung together so many improbabilities. I took my leave, she expressing many kind wishes for my happiness, and said she hoped I should *remember,* to which I responded I was certain I could never forget her— I note this because it is an amusing and undoubted fact, and I was called on to remember it every moment during the latter part of my journey—

Countess Pauline de Neale flew to meet me with all the friendship which she had formerly shown me— We made arrangements to visit the Princesses Ferdinand, and Louisa Radzivil, and also some of my old friends; and did not part until quite late with a mutual agreement, that she would pass as much time as possible with me while I staid— After a refreshing night I rose and prepared to make my visits, ordering a Carriage to be ready at the proper time, and gave all the necessary directions for the repairs of my *own,* to be dispatched as quick as possible, so as not to delay my journey— Every thing looked much as I had left it in the City, excepting the manners and the dress of the people— All the Nationality of Costume &ce had disappeared, and french was almost universally spoken— It was the same City that I had left in all its bearings The beautiful Linden Strasse! the fine Brandenburg Gate; the Bridges the Palaces, all spoke of former times; but yet it was cold, and flat, and there was a foreign air about it, which damped the pleasure I had expected, in revisitting the scenes of my youth— I missed many objects which had formerly excited my admiration, and the perfect stillness seemed to cast a gloom over all the scenes, which had once been so gay, and brilliant, while gladdened by the smiles and affability of the young Queen, who won all hearts by her manners and her beauty—

According to appointment we waited on the Princesses who received me with all their wonted kindness. The Princess Louisa invited me to pass every Evening with her while I staid in Town; and laughingly said that though she could not entertain as she had *once* done, she would give me two dishes for my Supper, and a hearty welcome— No toilet was necessary, and she would show me her daughter— Her husband [*Prince Anton Radziwill*] and Son's she told me were at [*the Congress of*] Vienna; and that the great people of Berlin had suffered so much from the War, that there was no pretention of style among them, and they were glad to see their friends socially— I expressed my thanks for the flattering kindness shown me by her invitation, which I should do myself the honor to accept, and at the same time mentioned my regret, that the King, and the Prince were absent; as I had wished much to see them, and to have an opportu[*nity*] of offering thanks for much kindness formerly shown to me, of which I retained a most grateful sense— I made my Congé [*requesting formal permission to leave*] and departed to meet again in the evening— The Princess was as little altered as possible, considering that time had not strewed roses in her path; but though the thorns had left some marks of their wounds, they had left traces of a softer shade of character on her face, than that which she possessed in the brilliancy of youth, and the entourage of splendid Royalty—

My friends greeted me with the most unaffected warmth, and my reception was that of long separated and beloved Sisters: each vied with the other in marks of attachment making my stay a succession of delights— I saw all that was to be seen new, but the object of most interest was the Mausoleum of the Queen [*Louise*] at Charlottenburg in all its beauty; decorated with a bower of evergreens; emblems of the undying love and respects of her subjects— How many interesting anecdotes I heard from the lips of the Princess concerning the War! more especially of the famed retreat of the suffering french— She rejoiced in their defeat; but she felt as a Christian, and she would permit no harsh and degrading language to be used in her presense; for the really great had fallen, and their punishment had overtaken them, in all the horrors that umitigated suffering could inflict; in addition to mortification and disgrace beyond the power of description—

She told me that one day she received a Note on a dirty bit of paper, earnestly entreating her to see a person who was in great distress; that if she granted his petition she must see him alone, and with the greatest secrecy, as his life depended on not being known— At first she hesitated; but knowing from experience how much misery lurked about; she asked where the person was? and was told that a *Lady* who appeared in much trouble, was waiting for admittance— In a few minutes the person was introduced, veiled and dressed in a blue Satin Pelisse; who immediately after she had dismissed her attendants, fell at her feet, and implored her assistance as he was almost famished, had no clothes to his back but the dress he had on, which had been charitably given to him by a Lady as a disguise— It was the Count de Narbone; with whom she had been most intimate when Minister at Berlin some years before, who was flying from the Armies, in this utter and abject misery, who had thrown himself upon her mercy, to obtain the means of reaching Magdeburg— Prussia had not then become the avowed enemy of the French, and she gave him money, and clothes, and food— He reached the Fortress of Torgau and was killed by a fall from his horse I believe during the Siege. He was one of the Master diplomats of the age, and famed for the elegance of his manners—

One evening She had invited the Princess Wilhelm. With a small party I was introduced. This Lady was very handsome. We sat round the Table with our work chatting; when the Princess Louisa asked me if I did not think the colour of her Gown was very gay— I acquiessed, and admired the richness of the Silk— She laughed, and observed, that she was rather *too old* for a bright couleur de rose; but she loved the dress, and must wear it, as it was a present from her Son [*Prince Wilhelm Radziwill*], who had purchased it with the first money he had been allowed to Spend; and had immediately on his arrival in Paris gone to a Magazin [*shop*] and selected it himself, as a first offering to a mother he adored.

Of my visit to Berlin I could write a Volume— The Brulhs; the de Néales; the Golofkins; the Zeinerts; the De Bergs; the Hardenbergs; the Hadzfeldt's; the Bishoffswerder, and many more, are names never to be forgotten by me, but always to be spoken of with affection— Count Caraman gave me a new Passport, as I was not satisfied with the one which the French Ambassador had given me at St. Petersburg, and I again prepared to sally forth on my journey, having settled my Cash accounts with Mr Shieckler, and engaged the sympathy of the Néales in favour of a Capt Norman, an American, whom I had found dying of a fever in the upper story of the Hotel, for want of care and attention.

Early in the morning I left the City of Berlin, for the last time with feelings both of gratitude and regret— There I had felt at *home;* all the sweet sympathies of humanity had been re-awakened; and the sterile heartlessness of a Russian residence of icy coldness, was thawed into life and animation— In Petersburg for five long years I had lived a *Stranger* to all, but the kind regards of the Imperial family; and I quitted its gaudy loneliness without a sigh, except that which was wafted to the tomb of my lovely Babe— To that spot my heart yet wanders with a chastened grief, that looks to hopes above—

The second half of Louisa's journey was marked by momentous events in Europe, notably the beginning of Napoleon's Hundred Days. Napoleon had been defeated by the Allied powers of Prussia, Russia, Austria, and Britain; forced to abdicate in the spring of 1814; and exiled to the island of Elba. He escaped on 26 February 1815 with nearly a thousand troops and made his way back to France. By the time he arrived in Paris on 20 March, his army numbered in the hundreds of thousands. But his rule was short-lived: he resumed war with the Allied powers and was finally defeated at Waterloo in June.

The roads were sandy and our course lay through Pine barren woods— We proceeded quietly on our route occasionly meeting small straggling parties of disbanded Soldiers, loitering home; which meetings were by no means relished by any of us— In the Evening after dark I used to put on my Sons Military Cap and tall Feather, and lay his Sword across the window of the

Carriage; as I had been told, that any thing that *looked* military escaped from insult— My two Servants rode on the box armed; and I was always careful to put away my *insignia* before I came to any house— My Friends in Berlin had advised me to avoid Liepsic, as I should have to cross the battle field so celebrated a year before [*Battle of Leipzig, October 1813*], and we went on a different route, to a fortified Town [*Eisenach*] in Prussia, the name of which I cannot recollect— It had once been strong: but was now in a miserable condition though still guarded at the Gates by Soldiers— Being much fatigued; I passed the night there and was exceedingly astonished to learn from the Master of the House, that a rumour had arrived of the return of Napoleon to France; which he said created many jokes, as he was *Known* to be very safe at Elba!—but such a *rumour* was abroad, and in every body's mouth— I started with astonishment— True or false the coincidence was strange; and the bonne aventure of Countess Apraxin forced itself upon my mind in spite of my reason—

I went to bed very tired, and for the first time left my purse with some gold in it upon the Table— My Childs Nurse who I had found perfectly honest; who had lived thirty years with Madame Colombi, who had given the strongest recommendations with her, slept in a bed with him, in the same room with me, had carefully locked the doors on our going to bed—but when I rose in the morning, the lamp was gone out of the chamber, my purse was there, but the gold was gone!— I ordered the Carriage immediately, and again we pursued our route to Franckfort on the Maine, to which place the Banker at Berlin strongly advised me to go, and gave me Letters to two or three families there— Wherever we stopped to change Horses, we heard of the return of Napolen; and when we arrived at Hanau, we found that it was received with less doubt, and measures were already supposed to be adopted, for calling the disbanded Troops together—

At about a mile before we entered the Town I had observed a number of mounds like Graves with Crosses at the feet, in the ditches on the sides of the roads— We enterred on a wide extended plain, over which was scattered remnants of Clothes; old Boots in pieces; and an immense quantity of bones, laying in this ploughed field— My heart throbbed; and I felt deadly sick ~~at my stomach~~ and faint; guessing where I was, when the Postillions pointed out a Board on which it was stated, that this was the Field of battle, where the Bavarians had intercepted the retreat of Napoleon, and that in this plain, ten thousand men had been slain— Conceive my horror at the sight of such a butchery! I could with difficulty keep from fainting, as fancy realized the torture, suffering, and anguish, thus brought before my eyes, with all the ghastly relics of the dead, exposed with savage barbarity to the view—

At Hanau a strongly fortified Town, I was much questioned; and with some difficulty procured Horses, which however I was obliged to wait for, three or four hours. During this time, the people of the House were very civil and talkative; they spoke French fluently, and took great pains to point out to me the wonders that had been performed by Napoleon, and his Officers— Three times they were beaten back from the bridge, but at last took it against a strong force, and obtained possession of the Town— They showed me where their house had been struck by three bullets or rather cannon Balls, during the Action; and informed me that the French Officers had quartered there, a fact of which they seemed very proud— It was a very remarkable fact that in the course of my journey, I heard but little praise of the Allied Armies, and unceasing admiration of the exploits of the French; yet suffering, and devastation, had followed their steps—but the renowned cruelties, and barbarities, of the Cossacks, seemed to have white washed all other crimes from their minds— At this place I observed that my Servants began to grow uneasy, and frequently talked about conscripts, and a renewal of the Wars—for which neither appeared to have any taste—

Soldiers were mustering in every direction; and there was a life and animation, altogether different from the dull monotony, which had pervaded all the former part of my travels— Feeling very uneasy; I pushed on with all the celerity that tolerable roads, and good Horses, six of which were always forced on me, would admit; and should have found many agreeable objects to attract my attention, if my mind had been more at ease— I arrived safely at Franckfort on the Maine, and sent my Letters to the Banker. A new dilemma of a very serious nature having occurred— My two Servants requested to speak to me, and informed me that circumstances having totally changed, since their engagement to attend me to France; in consequence of Napoleon's return, they must quit my service, and prefered to remain at Franckfort, to proceeding any farther; as there they would be likely to meet with opportunities of Service— *Here was a situation*— I could not compel them to stay; no bribe could induce them to go on in their state of Panic; and I was under the necessity of asking them to wait before they came to a final decision, until I had seen my Banker [*Simon Moritz von Bethmann*], with whom I would talk upon the subject—

He came to see me almost immediately after the receipt of his Letter, and I informed him of my difficulty— He was very polite; and urged me very strongly to remain a few days in the City, and he would endeavour to make arrangements for me— He said the consternation was universal, and that it would be very difficult to find substitutes for the Servants, who were determined to leave me; and that my position was so unpleasant, he thought it required great prudence in my arrangements— I insisted that it would be better for me to get into France as soon as possible; as I should probably meet my husband on the frontier, and every moment would add to the difficulty, should I delay— At present the panic itself would prove advantageous; as it would require time to ascertain events, before the Governments could take decisive measures— He agreed with me in opinion; but said Troops would be assembled, and ordered to the Frontier directly, by way of precaution— As most of them had recently been disbanded, it would require time to collect them, but there was always danger from stragglers— He advised on the whole that it would be best to proceed, but thought I should change my intended route for one more circuitous but safer; and more likely to be quiet; and he would try to find some person to go with me— I was to start at four o clock in the afternoon—

He returned in a short time with a boy of fourteen, the only creature he could find willing to go; and after arranging my money accounts, he put me into the Carriage and directed the Postillions as to the route to be taken— All went on very well— The boy was very smart, and active, and I thought it more prudent to take him withinside of the Carriage for fear of indiscretion— He had though so young been in the Russian Campaign with a prussian Officer; and told me a great many anecdotes concerning Napoleon during the retreat— Of his sitting among his Soldiers to warm himself! of his partaking of their Soup, when they had any! His kindness to them in the midst of their misery &ce &ce. At the same time he expressed great hatred of the man, with all the petulance of boyish passion— It was singular to watch the workings of this young mind, swayed equally by admiration and detestation, uttered in the strong language of natural feeling—

At Carlsrhue I stopped at a very good house intending to visit Princess [*Katharine*] Amalia [*Christiane Luise*], and Madlle. Bode [*maid of honor to Princess Amalia*]— I sent to the Palace to enquire if I could see them— The Servant returned, and informed me that the Empress of Russia, and her Sister, had left the day before for Munich—and the Grand Dutchess of Baden [*Stéphanie de Beauharnais*] was the only person at Court— As I had no one to introduce me, I ordered my dinner, and concluded to prosecute my journey in the afternoon— I was much disappointed; as I intended to obtain some information, which I expected would have been profitable to me on the road— While I was at dinner The Master of the Inn came in, and informed me, that Napoleon had been taken, and that he had been tried immediately, and *Shot*— He said the news might be relied on, as it had just arrived at the Palace— I heard an exclamation of horror; and turning round, saw the boy who I had hired, as pale as a ghost, and ready to faint— He looked piteously at me saying "O that great Man! I did not expect that!"— Fortunately the Inn Keeper had left the room, or he might have supposed me some violent Bonapartist, and the report would have been very unfavorable to my proceedings—

At four o clock I was again on my way, and pursued my course through the Dutchy of Baden, without interruption or accident— Waggons of every discription full of Soldiers, were continually rushing towards the Frontier— roaring national Songs, and apparently in great glee at the idea of a renewal of hostilities— What a mere animal man may become! A machine worse than the brutes; for the instincts of the Brute creation lead only to fixed objects; while those of men termed rational; may be perverted by mere accidental causes, to the worst and basest purposes, even without an adequate motive for such excesses— When I retrace my movements through this long, and really arduous journey, I cannot humble myself too much in thankful adoration to the Providence which shielded me from all dangers, and inspired me with that unswerving faith which teaches, to seek for protection from above— Thus far not a word or look had been unpleasant; and could I have divested myself of that restless anxiety for the future, which pervades all mankind, I should have enjoyed the perpetual varieties, and changes constantly offered to my view; and the retrospection, would have furnished me stores of anecdotes, and information, at this time worthy to grace my subject, with the embellishments of wit, and the ornaments of picturesque taste— As it is I can only give a brief sketch of the road, and I fear very often with a defective Geography, making

"Confusion worse confounded"

Research is not in my way— Indolence wars with exertion, and is too often victorious; and as I know nothing of style, or composition, those who may read this memento mori, must endeavour to extract light from the chaos which lies before them; and I wish them joy of the trouble—

Louisa carried four different passports with her on her travels: one from Russia, one from Prussia, and two from France. Three of these she acquired in St. Petersburg, including one of the two French passports, which was issued by Comte Juste de Noailles, the French minister at St. Petersburg, representing the Bourbon King Louis XVIII. Fortunately, however, given the changing political situation in France, Louisa acquired a second French passport while in Berlin. As she notes in the "Narrative" above, "I was not satisfied with the one which the French Ambassador had given me at St. Petersburg," so she obtained a new one from the Duc de Caraman, the French minister at Berlin, who had been a friend of the Adamses in earlier days. Unlike the first French passport, this new one (which can be seen in the illustrations following page 166) clearly identified Louisa as an American and the wife of the U.S. minister to Russia. When she later encountered hostile French troops, this passport—along with Louisa's fluency in French—proved vital in allowing her to reach Paris unharmed.

We reached the Fortress of Kiel opposite to Strazbourg on the Rhine, and here I was questioned, and troubled; and after some delay permitted to cross, which we accomplished with success, and landed in saftely— Here again I was stopped; my Passports demanded, my baggage taken off &ce— The Officer in command, recommended me to an excellent Hotel—and politely told me he would wait on me there— The House was excellent; and the Master of it came imediately to me, to receive my directions &ce &ce— I requested him to dismiss the Horses and Drivers, and that if he was at leisure I should be glad to consult him— He was a very respectable man of fifty years old or upwards, and in manners very gentlemanly— He told me the Officer would probably ask for Letters, and papers; and that as the moment was very *critical,* I had better cut the Seals before they took them,

and in that state they would not read them, but suffer me to retain them—
Here I found the Passport furnished me by Count Carnman of the greatest
service, as his name was popular and well know—That of Mons. de Noaille
being just the reverse—

The Officer came and informed me that my baggage would be allowed
to pass, and that my Passports would be endorsed &ce and returned to me
in the proper form— He said the Country was in a very unsettled state, and
that it would require great prudence and caution, in the pursuit of my journey to Paris— Strazburg was very quiet, but it was impossible to foresee
how long it would continue so— The Emperor had certainly returned; and
was then on his way to the Capital— I thanked him for his politeness; informed him it was my intention to remain at Strasbourg for a day at least,
before I prosecuted my journey—

The Master of the Hotel then came to me and I represented to him the
great difficulty I should find to travel without a Man Servant, and urged him
to seek a respectable and confidential person to go with me as far as Paris—
That I remunerate him handsomely, and pay his expences back; as the
moment I met my husband, I should have no occasion for his services—
That I must rely entirely upon the discretion of this person, in the management and arrangement of my route; and should depend on him for advice,
and assistance— He said such a person would be very difficult to find; but
that he had such a man in view [*named Dupin*], that he would see him directly, and prevail upon him to undertake the charge—

After dinner I took a walk with my Son— The Town is very pretty, and
I have sometimes thought that Wocester in Massachusetts looks a little like
it— In the evening the Master of the House I have forgotten his name, introduced a most respectable looking person, the man he had recommended;
and we immediately enterred into engagements; I requested him to see that
the Carriage was in order, and told him that on the next morning but one, I
intended to depart for Paris, and to go on with as much rapidity as possible—
He said he would be ready at the appointed time, and asked if the Boy was
to proceed with me—and I had him up to know if he would not prefer to be
discharged there, and to return home— He said no! his object was to find
his old Master in Paris, and that he would rather go on— As he had rendered
me good service, I could not refuse this; and a condition was made by Dupin,
that he was not to talk at any of the Houses where we might stay, and that

he was either to be under my eye, or his, at all times—to which he readily agreed— The Woman who was with me, Madame Babet was a quiet and respectable person, older than myself, and very plain in her person, and manners, and very steady— On the former part of my journey she had been very useful; but as she spoke no german she could not be troublesome—

The day at Strazburg was very tedious— My health was dreadful, and the excessive desire I had to terminate this long journey, absolutely made me sick— I had been a year absent from my husband, and five years and a half from my two Sons; and the hope of soon again embracing them, gave me strength to sustain the fatigue and excitement to which I was necessarily exposed— We pursued our route without impediment until one o'clock in the morning, when the Postillions insisted on my stopping at a very lonely house, to which proposition I acceded very unwillingly— My Servant made me a sign, and said he thought it would be adviseable to wait there until daylight—and I could procure some refreshment for myself and my Son— We drove up to a miserable place in which we found a long room, with a pine Table, several very surly looking men, and nothing but common benches to sit on— Here I was obliged to sit, while they procured us a little milk, the only thing we could get— Charles seemed very much frightened as these men asked him several questions, and I was obliged to tell them the Child was too sleepy to talk— Dupin took the opportunity to ask if I could have some chamber where I could put the Child to sleep, and a door was opened into an adjoining chamber even more uncomfortable than the one we left— In this Chamber my Maid and I passed the night without going to bed; and heard the threatening conversation in the next room, and the boasts of what Napoleon was to do now that he had arrived, to drive out Louis dix huit and his beggarly Crew— Our Postillions were vociferous in their exclamations; and there were many bitter anathema's against the Allied Powers and the horrible Cossacks—

I rejoiced when I found myself once more safely seated in the heavy Russian Carriage, and we renewed our journey with fresh spirits— I was much pleased with the conduct of Dupin, who appeared to me to be a very judicious and discreet person, possessing all the tact requisite to avoid threatened trouble, with a quiet smoothness of manner which enforced respect, and defied suspicion— At Nancy we stopped only to change Horses— The Square was full of Troops, who were mustering to express their delight at the return of the Emperor— Dupin told me that if we made good speed, we should keep in advance all the way; as it would require some hours for their preparation, and that we should reach Paris with ease before they could get half way there— On we drove, and at night we stopped at Chateau Thierry— We got good beds, and comfortable refreshment; but poor Charles was much annoyed by a Gen d'armes, who told him he must be a good boy, and not speak a word on the road, for that little children of his age often did a great deal of mischief— He was very inquisitive; expressed great astonishment at my travelling towards Paris in such a state of things, and seemed by no means contented with my answers, which were very simple—

The next morning we again set forward, every thing seemed propitious— The weather was fine; every thing quiet; the roads good, and all of us in renewed spirits; we thought we would stop to dine at Epernay— Here I was very comfortable; we had a capital dinner at one o'clock; and the Waiter said that I must have some Champagne as this was the fine Champagne Country and he doubted if I could find such in Paris. He was so urgent, I at last consented to have a bottle, which certainly was superior to any that I have ever tasted before, or since— In less than an hour we were again on our way— He told me that the people of the Town did not expect the Troops to pass until the next day, and that I need not hurry— We had gone about a mile and a half, when we suddenly found ourselves in the midst of The Imperial Guards, who were on their way to meet the Emperor— The first notice I had of my danger, was hearing the most horrid curses, and dreadful Language from a number of women, who appeared to be following the troops. Madame Babet was as pale as death, and trembled excessively; Presently I heard these wretches cry out, "tear them out of the Carriage; they are Russians take them out kill them." At this moment a party of the Soldiers siezed hold of the Horses, and turned their guns against the drivers— I sat in agony of apprehension, but had presense of mind enough to take out my Passports— A General Officer with his Staff, consisting of four or five, immediately rode up to the Carriage and addressed me— I presented my Passports, and he called out, that I was an American Lady, going to meet her husband in Paris— At which the Soldiers shouted "vive les Americains" [*long live the Americans*]—and desired that I should cry vive Napoleon! [*long live Napoleon!*] which I did waiving my handkerchief; they repeated their first cry adding "ils sont nos amis" [*they are our friends*]. A number of Soldiers were ordered to march before the Horses, and if we attempted to push on out of a walk, the order was to fire on us directly—

The General and his suite rode on each side of the Carriage. He told me my situation was a very precarious one; the army was totally undisciplined; that they would not obey a single order; that I must appear perfectly easy, and unconcerned; and whenever they shouted I must repeat the Viva's; that when we arrived at the Post House, he would use all his influence with the Lady of the House to admit me to pass the night, and advised that the next morning, I should delay my departure until the troops had all passed, and then take a circuitous route to Paris; as the whole Army would be in motion, to Greet the Emperor— I thanked him sincerely for his kind attention, and assured him I was ready to follow his advice. He complimented me on my manner of speaking french, and said that my perfect knowledge of the Language would contribute much to my safety, as no one would believe me to be a foreigner— My poor boy seemed to be absolutely petrified, and sat by my side like a marble statue— God in his great mercy seemed to give me strength in this trying emergency; for excepting a heightened and glowing colour in my Cheeks, there was no evidence of fear or trepidation: yet my heart might have been heard to beat, as its convulsive throbbings heaved against my side—

In this way we journied; the Soldiers presenting their bayonets at my people with loud and brutal threats every half hour— The road lined on each side for miles with intoxicated men, ripe for every species of villainy, shouting and vociferating À bas Louis dix huit! vive Napoleon! [*Down with Louis XVIII! Long live Napoleon!*] till the whole welkin rang with the screech, worse than the midnight Owls most dire alarum to the startled ear— At twelve o clock at night we reached the Post house— Genl Michell [*Claude Étienne Michel*] spoke to the Lady, and she refused to take me: At length he awakened her sympathy, and she consented, *provided* I would consent to stay in a dark room; have my people concealed; and my Coach stowed away in some place where it could not be perceived— O how gladly I consented may readily be conceived— I was almost spent with the exertions I had made to master my feelings, and could not of borne up much longer— I was put into a comfortable room; a good fire was made; the shutters were close barred; and a very kind old gentleman came to me, and encouraged me with the hope, that we should get through the night without farther molestation— The Genl had gone on with the troops whose great object was to reach Toul, where Victor [*Claude Victor-Perrin*] the Duc de Bellune then was; and that the cause of my detention, was the fear, that if he had information of their march, he would close the Gates against them, having refused to sustain the Emperor on his landing—

I was very ill all night; successive faintings, head ache, and sickness, made it impossible to sleep could I have divested myself of fear, which was out of the question; as the Soldiers were crowding into the house all night, drinking, and making the most uprorious noises— The Lady of the House came to my Chamber, followed by a woman with Coffee. She apologized to me for not being able to stay with me, but the moment was so *critical,* she had some Casks of wine opened, and brought out to amuse the gentlemen, and that she must be there, to "debiter des plaisanterie" [*make up some jokes*], or else she feared they might plunder her house— She was a showy pleasant faced woman, of about forty: of an assured and prompt spirit, and who seemed to possess that readiness, and playfulness of conversation, which is often so attractive in french women— Charles had fallen asleep—but Madame Babet really appeared to have lost her senses— She clasped her hands continually; while the tears rolled down her cheeks, crying out, that she was lost! for the Revolution was begun again, and this was only the beginning of its horrors— During my stay in my chamber, these ferocious creatures had attacked the poor boy, who was in my service with a bayonet, and forced him to burn his military Prussian Cap; and it was with great difficulty that his life was saved, by the dexterity of the Land-lady— Until five o clock in the morning it was utterly impossible to feel a moment of ease— After that time, the Doors were barred—and though stragglers frequently hola'd! and made a great knocking; no notice was taken, and we obtained refreshing repose—

At nine o'clock I was up, and ordered preparations to be made for our departure. The Master of the House advised me to go to Chatillon sur marne; and when there, I could make suitable arrangements for the remainder of the journey— I endeavoured as well as I [*could*] to express the high sense of obligation which they had conferred; to which they replied very handsomely; declaring that they felt a deep interest for me, and wished I would stay a day or two longer with them; they did not keep a house of publick entertainment, but would be happy to see me as a visitor— With most heartfelt thanks I assured them of my gratitude for their very considerate kindness, and after taking an excellent breakfast, set out again on our journey, which according to the irish adage we found "the longest way round was the shortest way home—"

We took our route to Chatillon, where we arrived in the evening— Here some passengers in the Dilligence informed me that I had better not go on to Paris, as there were forty thousand men before the Gates; and a battle was expected to take place. This news startled me very much, but on cool reflection, I thought it best to persevere, as I was travelling at great expence, and I was sure if any such danger existed Mr. Adams would have come to meet me, or by some means have conveyed intelligence to guide my course. Still as I had been under the necessity of changing my route, I could not be sure that he had heard from me at Strazburg,— I consulted with Dupin; and he suggested the best plan; which was to push on to the environs of Paris, and if the difficulty accrued, I could remain within the means of communication, and find some opportunity of informing Mr. Adams— He told me that in consequence of my being almost the only traveller on the road going towards Paris; that a whisper was abroad, that I was one of Napoleons Sisters going to meet him; and that this idea was so favorable to the promotion of my success, that *he* was *very mysterious* and only shrugged and smiled, at the suggestion— My six horses contributed somewhat to this notion, and proved very advantageous— It rained very heavily and the place was very gloomy—

On we went again the day follow to Sens, and from thence to Meaux, where I arrived the 20th of March— Here I dined— The Mistress of the House told me the most dismal tales of the atrocities of the Cossacs: The furniture of the house was almost in ruins; and she Showed me the Graves of six of the most beautiful young girls of the place, who had fallen victims to the murderous horrors of savage war, with all its detestable concomitants— They were laid side by side, and to judge from my landlady, their relics were embalmed by the sacred tears of undying affection, and the purest sympathies of unadulterated compassion—

I was again on my way to Paris, pondering on the cruel evils to which the fiend like passions of men expose the world; when I observed a man on Horse back, who appeared to be making prodigious efforts to overtake us— With a mind already in some measure prepared for some catastrophy, and in the Foret de Bondy so long celebrated for Banditti exploits, it was natural that I should be ready for some disagreeable adventure— My courage was fast oosing out, when by some accident the Postillions slackened their pace, and my imaginary highway man, came up very politely, and informed me, that for the last half hour he had been apprehensive that the wheel of my Carriage would come off, and that he had been fearful I should meet with a bad overset— We thanked him for his timely notice, and he rode off— Dupin examined the thing, and the only resourse was to fasten it as well as they could, and to turn back to the place where we had dined to get it repaired— The necessary repairs were atchieved; and notwithstanding it was late in the evening, we again penetrated the wilds of Bondy, once so famed, and arrived in perfect safety and without molestation at the gates of Paris; and descended at eleven o clock at the Hotel du Nord Rue de Richelieu—Mr. Adams not returned from the Theatre; but he soon came in, and I was once more happy to find myself under the protection of a husband, who was perfectly astonished at my adventures; as every thing in Paris was quiet, and it had never occurred to him, that it could have been otherwise in any other part of the Country— My Poor Maid Servant went to her friends the next morning— The fright she had undergone was too much for her; and she was siezed with a brain fever, from which she had not recovered when I left Paris two Months after—

I was carried through my trials by the mercy of a protecting Providence; and by the conviction that weakness of either body, or mind, would only render my difficulties greater and make matters worse— My security and faith, was in my husband: who I was sure would have taken every precaution for our safety, had there been any danger. And thus I was lured on to accomplish an undertaking in itself simple, but by extraordinary circumstances rendered peculiarly interesting— A moral is contained in this Lesson— If my Sex act with persevering discretion, they may from their very *weakness* be secured from danger, and find friends and protectors: and that under all circumstances, we must never desert ourselves— I was fortunately neither young nor beautiful; a fact in itself calculated to prove my safegaurd; and I had others under my protection to whom the example of fortitude was essential; and above all the object which drew me on, was the re-union with my beloved husband, and alas, with my now departed Children— Years have rolled on: but memory recurs with delight to the past! that past, with all its associations pleasing and painful, which is left to glad the heavy march of time, and to rob it of its tedium— The rosy hours of youth have fled, and the Cypress and the Willow cast their deep and shadowy tinge oer the coming years, whose last remnant is at least blessed in the consciousness of innocence of guilt, however tainted by slander, and almost unremitting misfortune— Under this pressure may it please my Almighty Father to strengthen me in the faith—to teach me to subdue the erring passions of my nature; and while I abhor guilt, and wickedness; to be merciful to the Sinner, that I may be enabled to turn him from the evil of his ways, and lead him into the paths of Repentance; and when it is his will that I lay me down to sleep; that sleep, from which we wake no more, in this world; may I die in my Saviour Jesus Christ; in the full hope of those divine promises, which lead the purified Soul to heaven for evermore—

CHAPTER SIX

"The Wife of a Man of Superior Talents"

Washington, D.C., 1819–1820

Louisa, John Quincy, and Charles Francis spent two months in Paris in the spring of 1815 before moving on to John Quincy's next assignment, Great Britain. They traveled to London in May and were reunited with their two elder sons—the first time the whole family had been together in almost six years. Unfortunately, Louisa neither kept diaries nor wrote any memoirs of the period when John Quincy was U.S. minister plenipotentiary to Britain. Based on her letters, however, it was a happy time, with a quiet but fulfilling social life, a not too busy pace, and the children at school nearby. As Louisa wrote to Abigail in July 1816, "I cannot conceive how it happens, but this mode of life seems to agree perfectly well with me; for I never enjoyed such health, particularly since my marriage, and I am only afraid of growing too fat." Still, despite being generally content in England, both Louisa and John Quincy missed the United States and their families. In April 1817, when John Quincy received the news that he had been named secretary of state under President James Monroe, he promptly accepted the position. The Adamses returned to America in the summer and settled in Washington, D.C., in Brent House at the corner of C and 4½ Streets.

Louisa resumed her diaries in 1819 in a new form, so-called journal letters—letters written in diary form but directed to and intended for a specific recipient. In Louisa's case, initially, this recipient was her father-in-law, John Adams. Now a widower, he looked to Louisa for news of events in the nation's capital, and she obliged, mixing society news and politics to amuse and inform him. She also kept him up to date on the family, especially John Quincy. While she left no record of her writing process, it seems likely that Louisa wrote out her diary on a day-to-day basis in journals, then sporadically copied it over, sometimes amending entries, into letters to be mailed. Some of her journal letters

survive in both journal and letter form, some in only one form or the other;
only those in her journals are included here.

 At this time, while Louisa, John Quincy, and Charles were in Washing-
ton, the other boys were in Massachusetts: George had begun at Harvard in
1817, and John was preparing to enroll there later in 1819. In the capital, the
major topic of the day was the proposed congressional censure of Gen. Andrew
Jackson for exceeding his authority during the First Seminole War in 1818.
After considerable debate, Congress voted not to reprimand the general, a
move John Quincy supported.

 Mentions of "Mr. A—" below refer to John Quincy.

12 February 1819

Arose very unwell with a violent cold attended with great soreness of the
breast and throat was engaged out but declined going. A heavy Snowstorm
all day— Had some chat with Mr. A— after dinner— He is continually
reproached for want of sociability and I for pride hauteur and foreign
manners— These are so absurd that I cannot listen to them without laughing and they really are too ridiculous to merit the most trifling attention and
I am always surprised at a man's being the least susceptible upon such subjects which may do very well to occupy the young Gentlemen of the age—
His habits of study have unquestionably given a sort of coldness to his
manners which to those who do not seek his acquaintance and only see
him in public make him appear severe and repellant but America is much
changed since we left it. A man's manners formed but a small portion of his
qualifications for Office formerly and it is only since cabal and intrigue have
become the despotic rulers of the Nation that the courteous bribery of affected affability and the plausable solicitude of deep interest in concerns to
which you must feel totally indifferent have become the first and leading
steps on the ladder of promotion—

 If things go on at the rapid rate in which they are now growing the systematic bribery and corruption of England will not have much to boast over
our own— Congress makes Presidents and unmakes them at pleasure and a
few leading members take the reigns in their hands and declare open hostil-
ity to every one who still has sufficient respect for the Government in its

purest form to resist *any* unconstitutionality and glaring impropriety—
When the highest Offices of the Government are made to hang upon the
smiles and frowns of every popular demagogue whose personal ambition
and gratification is his only study and who has neither principle or modesty
to scuple at any means to ensure his success it is not surprizing that the effect is felt by every person from the highest to the lowest in the actual service of the Government and the extent of such influence must be felt to the
extreme injury if not the total destruction of all the Institutions which have
hitherto been our honour and glory— It is an evil requiring the hand of many
able persons to correct but one too serious in its tendency to be neglected—
and I sincerely hope the time is at hand that will unveil some of the *mystiries*
so prejudicial to our Country— You will laugh my dear Sir at these observation's but though I am far removed from actually witnessing every thing
of the kind I see and hear too much not to be fully aware of its truth—

13 February 1819

A very bad cold. The day so stormy could not go out and remained at home.
Mr Bailey passed the evening with us— The Question on Genl. Jackson's
affair gives up altogether in the Senate— The sentiment of the people too
strongly expressed to admit of it—and the Gentleman from Georgia [*John
Forsyth*] who was to take the lead might perhaps have found it useful in
procuring the attention of the Spanish Ministry in the course of his possible negotiations though the mere report of his being at all concerned in it
has not operated favourably for him—

14 February 1819

My cold still continues as bad could not go to hear Dr. [*John Thornton*]
Kirkland. Mr A— went and was much delighted with his discourse. Passed
the day at home. Judge [*John*] Marshall and Judge [*Henry Brockholst*] Livingston called and were particular in their enquiries after you— Eveng at
home alone. Cards of invitation sent to 400.

15 February 1819

A company of 25 expected to dine only 11 of whom came Genl Brown Major Biddle Mr. Storrow Mr Sanford Mr. Garnett Mr. Barbour Mr. Morton Genl Smyth Col Trumbull Mr. Todd. Dinner very pleasant— Much conversation concerning the fatal practice of Dueling which unfortunately was continued until the Gentlemen quitted the Table— I was informed by Mr [*Nathan*] Sanford who sat next me that one of our guests had fought a Duel with a Gentleman of New York when they fired three rounds but fortunately without fatal consequences. I observed he sat silent and did not enter at all into the conversation— These are unpleasant circumstances to occur but are almost impossible to avoid— Went to a Ball at Mrs. [*Mary*] Bagots [*British minister's wife*] after dinner all my company being invited there. The Party not large the road, dreadful beyond any thing you can conceive and we saw two Carriages overturned nobody hurt fortunately; and I am surprized we got home safe as our horses were so frightened at seeing one of these Carriages laying in the road it was scarcely possible to make them pass it— Mrs. Bagot had a bad cold— She is so happy at the idea of returning home that she will have no peace till she is gone— We shall never find a couple who were so desirous of pleasing and who have conducted themselves so well as they have done. Passed a delightful eveng and never laughed so much in my life— Mr. Adams beat Genl [*Jacob Jennings*] Brown in a game of Chess— Had the happiness of seeing an American Military Dandy a being compounded of all the follies Europe and America can boast without possessing even the qualification of beauty peculiar to the Peacock which when it spreads its beautiful plumage makes you for a moment forget all its glaring defects— Genl. [*Alexander*] Smyth who dined with us made one of the best if not the very best speech on the late Debate—but he is unfortunately a heavy speaker and did not do himself justice— Mr Sanford is a very Gentlemanly man a Senator and said to be strongly in the interest of Governor Clinton of New York. He is mild and modest—

16 February 1819

Passed the morning in writing very busily, and in the eveng. went to a Ball at the Spanish Minister's [*Don Luis de Onís*]. A large company was assembled.

The room is large and handsome and the House perfectly convenient for receiving visitors. It is the only one in Washington suited to the purpose— The entertainment was elegant The company brilliant and I heard more wit and pleasantry than usual and was kept in a state of laughter and amusement during the whole eveng. We returned late the roads dreadful— Mr Harris was there just arrived— Major Biddle was also there in full uniform as were all the Military part of the company which adds much to the splendor of our parties more especially as their actions have contributed more than their dress to this effect—

17 February 1819

House all in confusion for the party of tomorrow. Went to the Presidents in the evening and had to sit three quarters of an hour in the Carriage literally at the risk of life— As we cannot have recourse to Constables the Hackney Coachmen are Masters of the field and the confusion bad language quarreling and noise exeed every thing I ever heard in any Country— The company was not so large as usual and the greater part strangers. Mrs. M[onroe] told me that notwithstanding she had continually two or three cards of invitations out she was always fifty a head—

18 February 1819

The evening brought my expected guests or rather a part of them and on the whole the party went off cheerfully. The night was fearfully cold and my company left me early on account of the complaints of the Hackney Coachmen who declared they would not wait for them— We are drawing near a conclusion and I certainly shall not regret it— We had some music and some dancing—

The Supreme Court case to which Louisa refers below was that of McCulloch v. Maryland, which debated whether Congress had the right to incorporate the Bank of the United States and whether states had the authority to tax or limit federal activities. Argued by Daniel Webster, William Pinkney, and William Wirt for James McCulloch and the federal government, and by Walter Jones,

Joseph Hopkinson, and Luther Martin for the state of Maryland, the case was settled in favor of the federal government's right to establish a national bank and denying states' rights to limit federal operations.

In a sign of improved relations between the United States and Britain, the citizens of Washington, D.C., hosted a ball for Charles Bagot, British minister to the United States, and his wife, Mary, on 26 February upon learning that they were to be recalled. Louisa and John Quincy of course attended, though John Quincy's status as secretary of state meant he could not help to finance the occasion (which was paid for by a subscription), lest the other foreign ministers feel slighted.

The treaty mentioned throughout this period of Louisa's diaries was the Transcontinental, or Adams-Onís, Treaty, negotiated by John Quincy and Don Luis de Onís, the Spanish minister to the United States. The treaty transferred Florida to the United States in exchange for portions of western Texas and confirmed Spanish acknowledgment of the boundaries of the Louisiana Purchase. The treaty was signed on 22 February and approved by the Senate on the 25th, though the exchange of ratifications took nearly two years longer and additional negotiations, due to unresolved private land grants in Florida.

23 February 1819

The Supreme Court is now quite the fashion and is thronged with Ladies every day. Mr Webster's speech is spoken of with delight by every body and Mr. Hopkinson who followed tho' he is said to have spoken admirably is not by any means equal. Tomorrow Mr. Wirt is to speak— The question upon the right of taxing the U.S. Banks and the Counsel employed are Mess Webster Pinckney & Wirt on one side and Messrs Jones Hopkinson & Martin on the other. The Cause will last some days and Mr Pinckney closes. The Gentlemen knowing the fondness our sex have for talking mean to do all in their power to gratify them— It is said that Mr. P— will probably speak two days— The Senate have taken up the Seminole question and the Report was read to day— As there are several exGovernors they think their dignity impeached by Jackson's Letters to Govr Raban [*William Rabun of Georgia*] and must support his letter for the sake of *good fellowship*— A Ball in the evening at Mr. T. Peters in honour of the birth day which Mr. A. and myself declined. Miss [*Mary*] Buchanan went with her Cousin Mr. Rogers—

24 February 1819

Went to the Supreme Court and heard Mr. Wirt who is a very fine speaker and I thought made a very able speech in favour of the Bank. Mr Jones followed on the side of Maryland but his manner is so heavy I grew tired and left the house. It is singular that the district Attorney should be employed in opposition on a question in which the government is concerned. Paid a number of visits afterwards and returned to dinner— Mr. Rogers dined with us and we Mr A— Mr. Rogers Mary Hellen [*Louisa's niece*] and myself went to hear Mr. [*Joseph Linna*] Artiguenave [*a French actor*] who performed very well— He will not meet with much encouragement here I believe— My health is becoming quite good again and every body says I am growing fat—

25 February 1819

A snow Storm all day— Company at 17 at Table instead of 22 The Party Mr B Vaughan Mr P Vaughan Mr. Harris Mr Worcester Mr Ingersoll Mr Parrott Mr Little Mr Law Mr. Silsbee Mr Hale Mr. Rogers Mr. Artiguenave, Mr. Bailey Mr Upham. An odd sort of mixed dinner. I sat between Mr. [*Thomas*] Law and Mr. Vaughan and never was more amused in my life— Mr. L— entreated me to read a work of his entitled instinctive impulses which he insists upon it is admirable. I told him if he would not insist upon my conversation I would but I a little doubted one of the principle points of his theory which is that all our natural impulses are pure and good— If in fact they are, naturally good our earliest impressions would be virtuous and we should take longer time than is usually required to become corrupt— But experience hourly teaches us that this is not the case and I fear that human nature is prone to vice from the earliest period of existence— He is as wild as possible and his doctrine as he explains it very mischievous. They left us shortly after dinner—much conversation concerning the author of Junius— Mr. V. does not think Sir Philip Francis the author—

26 February 1819

The day very unpleasant— In the evening at a Ball given to Mr. & Mrs. Bagot— We went as guest's it being impossible for us to be subscribers— Every thing was well conducted the decorations appropriate and Mr. Bagot made a handsome address on the occasion— Mrs. Bagot opened the Ball with Yankee Doodle and would only dance with American's. The Speaker [*Henry Clay*] would not attend on the plea that it set a bad precedent and a great many person's are of the same opinion— I will only say that the French Minister [*Baron Jean Guillaume Hyde de Neuville*] has rendered services so important that I hope they will do as much for him as he is a true and honest friend to the Country and has much influence with his Court— The Treaty has produced a wonderful sensation and is another proof that real unassuming ability will confound intrigue. Station is nothing when unsupported by talant and this is its only solid basis. A great Nation will never submit to be long cajoled by party factions and will learn how to appreciate unadulterated merit— My husband, now stands on the highest pinnacle of elevation for he can concsienciously say he has deserved well of his Country and I desire no other reward— May my Children walk in his steps and may their greatest ambition be to "go and do likewise"— Then indeed I shall have room to be proud with such a husband and such Son's. I may raise my head in thankfulness to my maker just for having been so greatly blessed.—

Tickets of invitation were issued to see the launch of the 74 [*U.S.S. Columbus*] lately built here at which such great offence has been taken that the Tickets of all been recalled and the public are at last appeased— I was informed tickets had been issued in consequence of the bolts having all been stolen at the last launch— I forgot to mention that the Table was decorated with small Frigates bearing The American & English Flag united which gave rise to many good observations and good wishes— Who could have anticipated such an event as this three years ago? It will probably produce a good effect in England and teach them to send us respectable people— What will be said at home is another thing!— Mr Bagot made a handsome speech on the occasion and immediately after the Band played God save the King and then Yankee Doodle which was clapped—

27 February 1819

Remained at home all the morning. Mr. Adams dined with Mr. [*William*] Lowndes. In the evening went to the French Ministers where Mr. Adams acompanied me it being their last public night— God save the King produced a great effect I understand last night and the papers are to ring with it tomorrow— The managers three of whom were Members of Congress had determined that it should not be played and Mrs. [*Martha Parke Custis*] Peter in direct contradiction to their wishes sent a private order from the supper Table to the Band and they supposing it the desire of the mangers played it immediately— The managers are outrageous and I should not be surprized if something disagreeable occurred in consequence of this foolish circumstance—but Mrs. Peter is so notorious for her follies that her name afferds sufficient excuse I mean only as it regards her politicks for her private character is every way amiable and unexceptionable. The Commissioners are much enraged at this affair of the Tickets as they declare they had nothing whatever to do with it and Com [*John*] R[*odgers*] seems inclined to take his revenge of one of the Editors of the papers here with that delightful weapon so much in vogue here a Cow-hide— We endeavoured to laugh him out of it but he says this is the best restriction of the Press—

Thus you see my dear Sir we have here a wonderful mixture of great & little events to keep us in agitation. But I assure you that Genl Jackson and The Spanish Treaty cannot compare in interest with the Bagot Ball and the unfortunate launch and you could scarcely believe the two former were of vital importance to the Country and Nation at large— Com R told us that he was one evening in company with a number of Ladies and Gentlemen when one of the former asked why a Ship was always called she. The Com said he did not know when Mr Madison immediately replied it was "because her hull was not worth more than her rigging"— You will laugh at this *bon mot*— Your Letter was brought me and I was quite disappointed at not receiving the copy mentioned— If I dare give you as much trouble I would ask your opinion upon those very subjects as also upon the Treaty— I much fear my journal which you are so good as to desire will become more and more insipid after Congress adjourns as we sink immediately into uniform dullness and neither see or hear anything to excite even a momentary interest. The party was very crowded and every body appeared inclined to show the greatest respect to Mr. & Madame de Neuville— He is a firm friend to the Country and I hope will be duly appreciated by it— Mr. A— says he is afraid that I am very indiscreet in my joural— I fear it is true but you will undertake my defence I am sure—

28 February 1819

Returned a number of visits went through the ordinary service of the day and in the evening received social visits from Mr. [*John Murray*] Forbes and Mr. Hopkinson who sat with us until 1/2 past ten o'clock— He is a man of lively wit shrewed and subtle I should say rather than solid and relying much more on sophistical ingenuity than on sound rational reason. He is quick and penetrating but incapable of the slow process of close and accurate investigation. This is the opinion I have formed of him but as my failings are precisely of the same stamp It is probably very incorrect— Mr A quizzed him a little about his Speech in Congress insisting that the mariners Compass ought to have formed part of the charge against the Genl. and stating that it should have been worded "the Mariners Compass and Genl J— &c &c." He took it very good humouredly.

1 March 1819

The morning was excessively clowdy and it began to rain hard just at nine o'clock the hour appointed for the launch. We however sat out and I got into one of the buildings affording a very pleasnt view of the Ship— The issueing of Tickets which had given such mortal offence had nearly produced a very disagreeable Scene— One of the members of Congress assured me that the Mechanic's had intended to march in Procession as to a funeral with the Cap of liberty hoisted on a Pole and bury it at the Gate of the Navy Yard— After patiently waiting about three hours she glided most majestically into the Stream and seemed proudly to announce that she was destined hereafter to confer honour and glory on the Nation for whose service she was built and whose safety she was to guard— Mr. Adams was launched in her and she was called the Columbus— I went from there to the Supreme Court but it was so crowded I could not get in— In the evening Mr. Adams miss Buchanan & myself went to a ball at Mr. Bagots. It was not very full but tolerably agreeable— There is a stiffness which pervades all their parties impossible to shake off which always appears to worry her and makes her *labor too much* in the exercise of her functions as entertainer— To entertain well you must forget that you are so engaged and your company will feel perfectly at their ease and forget they are visiting the very recollection of which creates uneasiness and géne— This like most other things is easier in theory than in practice and I experience its difficulty every hour.

William Steuben and Catherine Johnson Smith continued to depend heavily on the Adamses for financial support, even having to borrow money from Louisa for their return trip to the United States in 1814. William held a variety of minor governmental posts, but, as Louisa relates below, John Quincy refused to give his nephew preferential treatment, and William failed to obtain any more significant positions on his own. Similarly, George and Harriet Johnson Boyd sought help from John Quincy and Louisa in obtaining a government post. George Boyd, who had been a diplomatic courier at Ghent in 1814, was eventually named an Indian agent, first at Michilimackinac, Michigan, and later at Green Bay, Wisconsin.

5 March 1819

Rose with a sore throat and cold— Received visits all the morning and in the evening went to hear Mr. Artiguenave whose performance was very good. He had more company than I expected although his room was thin— We are left in sober sadness to reflect upon past events and trust that benifit will result from the labours of those occupied in the duties and for the welfare of the Nation— It is said as usual that half the work is left undone and much time has no doubt been wasted in deliberation's which were evidently not essential to the real welfare of the public but whose direct aim only time can unravel— Experience will enable you to unveil some of the mysteries which are to me unfathomable and you will better understand the game at a distance than I as a looker on— I have always thought weakness of character infinitely more dangerous in its consequence than actual vice— The one excites the crafty passions of all who surround it while the other is in some measure concentrated within itself and acts individually. The mischief can therefore never be so extensive or so dangerous in its results.— And here end all my political observation's for the Winter which I think must already have excited your laughter— Were I ever admitted behind les coullisses [*the scenes*] I should avoid writing my opinions on the subject at all—but as this is never the case I feel a right to take as much latitude as I please on this subject. Many odd question's are put to me every day and among the rest if I dont write Mr. A——s papers? This will shew the spirit in which such question's are asked but he has too much real sense to be affronted by it— Received a visit from Mr. [*Samuel Whittlesey*] Dana the Senator from Connecticut who arrived to take his seat the last day of the Session—which has occasioned some animadversion. He is as pleasant as ever but quite a Cripple— We had much conversation but mostly of the quizzing kind.

6 March 1819

Arose very ill and not able to speak above a whisper. Mr. A recommended to me to keep home which advice I followed. At about five o clock Mrs. Smith came and finding me so unwell determined to stay the evening with me— After dinner Mr. Forbes joined us and we had some pleasant chat— Poor William has been buoyed up with false hopes all the Winter as it regards his promotion and just as he had flattered himself success was certain he was informed by one of his patron's that he could do nothing for him as he was answered when he made the application that nothing could be done without appearing to act in direct contradiction to his *Uncles principle.* Is it fair or is it generous thus to pervert a good and proper principle—and can any one pretend to understand it as a total exclusion to those who were in the service of the Government before he arrived here? I can never admire or approve what appears to be a meaness in any Station however exalted— My two Sisters and their husbands have been the only two families who have been totally neglected this winter at the chateau— I feel *this* because it makes them unhappy—

16 March 1819

A large Dinner at the Presidents yesterday to the Diplomatique Corps as a parting interview— The four principal powers France, England, Russia, & Spain, are likely to change their Ministers. Mr Bagot we know goes home. Don Onis has a leave of absence. Mr. [*Andrei*] Dashkoff [*Dashkov, Russian minister*] is recalled and the change which has just taken place in France will probably remove Mr. de Neuville— This change is occasioned it is said by the Sister of De Cage who is the Mistress of Louis 18—and they were in the service of Buonaparte's Mother— Where will all this end— It is here said universally that the rigid ettiquette established which amounts almost to banishment will prevent any Ladies being sent in future— Mr. Bourquenay passed an hour here in the evening—

17 March 1819

Received a visit from Mrs. Graham who is soon to sail for Rio Janeiro. She seems very much averse to the situation but I dare say will find it very pleasant— I went to see Mrs. Frye and Mrs. Smith— William is very sore about his disappointment of promotion and I sincerely [*hope*] some of his *near friends* would write to the P. about him— He has behaved so well that he has gained the good opinion of every body. Had it been any body but R[*ufus*] King who had received such an answer to his application I should have hesitated to have believed the fact but this authority is indisputable and I cannot help feeling shocked that so base a use is made of so honorable a principle— Eveng at home alone—

18 March 1819

Mr. Scott called to take leave— He is about to return home and is much dissatisfied at Mr Nat Pope's having accepted the appointment of a Judges place. Spoke very highly of Govr Edwards and very indifferently of Mr. Thomas the two Senators— I do not know if his judgment is to be relied on as he is guided very much by party feeling in all he says and does— Dined at Mr. de Neuville's with a very large party all the Corps diplomatique The Heads of Department Mr. & Mrs Middleton, Mr. & Mrs. Forrest, Dr. Ewell, Genl & Mrs. Mason,

Mr. Van Ness, and several others— The dinner was dull and we all seemed to feel that it was only to precede a general parting— There is something painful in this idea and however indifferent we feel to people in general it is sufficient to imagine that you are never to see them again to be impressed with a sentiment of regret— This is one of the amiable impulses of our nature which is really flattering to humanity— Just received the news of Johnson Hellen's [*Louisa's nephew*] being dismissed from College for a very slight offence and Mr. Middleton told me he thought he had been very ill used— I am very much concerned about it and do not know how to proceed—

19 March 1819

Went to a Ball at Com [*Thomas*] Tingey's. The evening was very dark and it rained hard— Had much conversation with Mr. De Neuville concerning the change of Ministry in France— I fear he will be a sufferer by it— But though I like him very well I cannot admire his party or any of the Ultra system— He will return to France in two Months— The dance was small but animated and we did not get home till twelve o clock— The President leaves Town on Thursday and commences his Southern tour— The Secretary of War [*John C. Calhoun*] accompanies him to Charleston with his family—

At this time, the whole federal government largely shut down while Congress was in recess over the summer and resumed activity when Congress returned each fall. John Quincy kept to a similar schedule, even though he was now a member of the executive branch. Because Louisa and John Quincy spent their summer in Massachusetts, she naturally cut off writing her journal letters to John Adams. She did not begin them again until the family went back to Washington, D.C., in October 1819 for the new congressional session. This year, both George and John stayed in Massachusetts to attend Harvard, while Charles Francis continued his schooling in Washington. The older boys would come to visit their parents during their winter vacation.

A new member of the family was Louisa's niece Mary Catherine Hellen, the daughter of Walter and Ann (Nancy) Johnson Hellen. Born in 1806, she came to live with the Adamses in 1817 following the death of her father and ill health of her stepmother and aunt, Adelaide Johnson Hellen. At one time or another, all of the Adams brothers expressed some interest in her, but she ultimately married John in February 1828 in the White House.

During the recess, workers had completed renovations of the Capitol building to repair damages caused by the 1814 burning of the city by British forces. The Sixteenth Congress, meeting in December 1819, was the first to sit in the redesigned building. Unfortunately, the renovations failed to fix a long-standing problem of poor acoustics in the House chamber caused by the smooth, arched ceiling.

6 December 1819

Our City being reanimated by the return of Congress, I shall attempt to renew our correspondence in the old form, in the hope of enabling you in some measure to participate in our pleasures and troubles; which we must expect to have intimately blended. Your Letter is I fear too justly prophetic, and your ideas on the present prospect of affairs, accords but too well with those of our experienced people here— Yesterday my visitors began the winter routine, and this day has brought a number, in consequence I presume of my having sent cards out for an Evening party on Thursday— Major [*William*] Jackson arrived and came immediately to see us. His old claim calls him here, and I hope he will prove successfull. It concerns the old revolutionary Officers, and the P. is said to take much interest in it. But there are many fears as to its fate in Congress. Mary has the Influenza very badly— Mr. Clay was chosen speaker by a large majority— The Halls of Congress are magnificent but report says the Members cannot hear each other— This may have one good effect, as it may induce many to be silent, who would otherwise be very talkative.

7 December 1819

This morning made my debut at the [*Washington Female*] Orphan Assylum as one of the Trustee's. About fifteen Ladies met and much was said and somewhat done but our poor Institution has to struggle against two giant evils poverty and ridicule and the best and most laudable intentions of the Society are cramped by the difficulties of the times. Some good has however resulted from the persevering charity of the first Institutors and I hope it will still have sufficient claims to the attention of the public to enable us to support it— The donations are very small and not very plenty and to day the funds were so low as to be only sufficient to pay the outstanding debts— A number of the Members of Congress called to day among the rest Mr. Storrs of New York—5 of them were from that State one from Pensylvania and the remainder from Massachusetts—and two from Virginia— The Secretary of the Navy [*Smith Thompson*] also called—he is becoming very unpopular in consequence of non residence— The Vice President [*Daniel D. Tompkins*] has not arrived. Mr. Lowndes ran away I am told to avoid being made Chairman of one of the Committee's— Mr. Epps of Virginia is said to be dying of an Appoplexy— There is a vacancy in consequence in the Senate to be filled it is said by Mr. Pleasants and Mr Giles is, very desirous of taking his place in the House. Mary still very sick.

8 December 1819

Mary was still so ill that I sent for a Physician—she will probably be confined some time— Many visitors—and returned many among the number called on Mrs. [*Sally*] Otis [*wife of Harrison Gray Otis*] who has just received the melancholy news of the death of her daughter— I did not see her as she is in deep affliction— The Presidents message occasions much conversation and hitherto, I have heard it well spoken of— All is quiet as yet— It is said that there are a great number of Strangers in Town who are come to seek amusement— Who is to create it? Evening at home alone—

9 December 1819

Went into George Town and then called on my Sister Frye to engage her to come in the evening— Left Mrs. Smith at her house and returned home to dinner— At seven o clock my company began to Assemble and we passed a tolerably agreeable evening— Among the company Mr Parkman of Boston appeared much to my surprize as I was not aware of his being at Washington, also many new Members and all the Corps Diplomatique— The Russian Minister [*Pierre de Polética*] very bustling and very busy the French very consequential and stately looking as if the whole welfare of the Nation was in his hands: his Wife [*Anne Marguerite Hyde de Neuville*] charming as usual. The Prussian new married couple very interesting as Bride and Bridegroom [*Virginie Bridon and Frederick Greuhm*]. The Sweedish looking frightened out of his wits as if afraid his *place* was not secure; and the Minister from the Netherlands, elegant and courteous; his face dressed with diplomatic smiles with a heart envelloped in gloom; while the English Chargé ensconced in the brazen effrontery of public licentiousness appeared to find no shelter but in his impudence— The company quitted us at eleven. My Sisters both attended with their husbands. Mrs Hay excuse.

One topic dominated political life in the fall of 1819: debate over admission of Missouri to the Union. Because the state was the first to be organized out of the Louisiana Purchase, its situation raised the important question of whether slavery would be allowed to spread westward. Also, Missouri's admittance jeopardized the balance in Congress between slave and free states. Ultimately, Congress enacted the Missouri Compromise in March 1820: Missouri would be admitted as a slave state; Maine, which had long been part of Massachusetts, would be admitted as a new free state; and slavery's expansion would be limited elsewhere.

While congressmen fought over Missouri and slavery, Louisa was vexed by quite a different problem—the so-called etiquette question. Since the federal government had first been organized, people had debated what constituted appropriate etiquette in a republic. Unlike at European courts, where social mores and protocols had long been established, the United States needed to find its own way socially. Who could visit whom, and who must make the first visit? Who should be invited to which parties and "sociables"? What titles should be used? How should seating be arranged at formal dinners? While seemingly minor, these issues took on outsized importance during this period as politicians and their wives jockeyed for position.

Louisa—as the wife of the secretary of state and possible future first lady— frequently found herself at the center of these debates. Her behavior could set the tone, and her actions were closely monitored. She keenly felt the burden of responsibility even as she acknowledged the absurdity of it all. More than once she expressed to her father-in-law her exasperation at the myriad demands placed on her by those who expected her to seemingly single-handedly uphold an indeterminate etiquette as a model to others.

21 *December 1819*

Remained at home all the morning and prepared for my Evening party—
Mr. A dined at the Presidents which I was obliged to decline— My company
assembled at 1/2 past seven and the party was unusually social and pleasant—
Strange to say even these things are made party questions and this evening
was expected to shew whether I was to fall or to stand for the remainder of
the Winter— My Rooms were crowded and Mr A— had the satisfaction of
seeing every body tolerably pleased with their entertainment, which it is
my *desire* to render as social as possible— There is something so insupportable in the idea of being put as it were upon a trial; that I felt my spirits sink
and was much more ready to cry than to laugh when my company arrived:
being without pretension altogether, it is a very painful thing to me to be
dragged into public notice, and made an object of debate in every company—
but these are the penalties I must pay for being the Wife of a man of superior
talents; who by his real and extraordinary merits throws those who are more
ambitious than himself into the shade.

The ettiquette question has become of so much importance as to be an
object of State— This I know you will scarcely believe; but it is true nevertheless, and I am only a secondary object in this business— More of this
hereafter— It ought certainly to be very flattering to me as a plain individual having no claim to any station; but on the contrary being continually
told that I cannot by the Constitution have any share in the public honours
of my husband; it is certainly very flattering to me that people should insist
upon becoming acquainted with, and *force* me even against my will to visit
them—but my health and the common intercourse which I am under the
necessity of maintaining with society will not and cannot admit of it; and I
am now more resolved than ever to defend *myself,* and maintain my rights
and privileges as a common Citizen and private individual— And if any
Gentleman in the United States will prove to me that he insists upon his Wifes
visiting every stranger who may happen to visit the City where she dwells—
I will give up my argument, and if absolutely necessary change the rule of
my conduct and give up the point—

In this place it is more difficult than in any other— I have now on hand a
number of visits 1 of which is nine miles from here another 4 and ½ and
three or four of 2 and 3 lying in opposite directions—with parties almost

every evening and one pair of Horses— You may judge from this of the misery of morning visits and the intolerable waste of time it occasions— They will do very well for very fashionable and great folks in Europe who have large establishments plenty of Horses and equipages and Servants to leave their families with but do not at all accord with our republican simplicity one pr of old Hacks a carriage little better than a Bakers Cart and often only a little black Girl to take care of house and family during our absence or perhaps a set of Slaves who would delight to see the whole fabrick destroyed during our ceremonious excursion's— The Speaker a little too much elevated to be entirely agreeable.

22 December 1819

Went to visit a neighbour and walked as far as Mrs Smiths. In the evening at a small sociable party at Mrs. Forsythes where I heard some good music by Mr & Mrs Meigs the former of whom has a remarkably fine voice— Mr & Mrs Lowndes were there. She has visitted me in the most friendly manner all the Summer during the absence of her husband—but has now dropped my acquaintance on the score of ettiquette— Mr Lowndes as well as all the Members of Congress visit at the House very freely—but it is understood that a man who is ambitious to become President of the United States, must make his Wife visit the Ladies of the Members of Congress first; otherwise he is totally ineffecient to fill so high an Office— You would laugh could you see Mr. A. every morning preparing a set of cards with as much formality as if he was drawing up some very important article, to negotiate in a Commercial Treaty—but thus it is; and he has been brought to it by absolute necessity— You will at least have had the happiness of living to see the day when the prosperity of the Country has arrived at such a pitch of greatness; that Congress can find no better subjects to regulate than the common and social intercourse of general society— I dwell too much on this subject; which is certainly become much too high for my poor abilities, and which is to be decided by much higher powers— It will soon be before the people then we shall see and hear much— Rank or no Rank is the Question—

23 December 1819

Morning spent in seeking for two Ladies who have done me the honour to visit me and after travelling through this spacious City for two hours and stopping at nine or ten boarding houses was obliged to return home fretted and fatigued to death and almost unfitted by my anxiety to return the civilities shewn me and the ill success of my efforts for which I shall never have the least credit— To attend a very large party at Col Bomfords where I felt myself bound to go they having been at my home last Tuesday and made it a point— In the evening we stopped at Mr Sanfords to take Mr Adams who we met a few doors from it just returning home on foot— We took him up and proceeded with Mr & Mrs. Smith to Col Bomfords where we literally had a jam as it was scarcely possible to move when we had squeezed ourselves into the presence of the Lady of the House who however did the honours very handsomely. She is a pretty and pleasing Woman and much beloved— Was perfectly stupified by the heat and dullness of the party. Returned home at ten o clock— Our Dear John arrived this day in fine health— He left George in Philadelphia—

24 December 1819

Rode out again to day in search of the Ladies and proved successful. They were however not at home and I left cards and cards of invitation— Called on Madame de Neuville.

25 December 1819

Xmas day— Passed the day at Mrs. Frye's George having arrived time enough to go with me after being detained a day at Baltimore in consequence of the Steam Boat having run aground. A family party social and agreeable— Mr A dined at the Russian Ministers to celebrate the Emperors birth day— Returned home before ten o'clock.

26 December 1819

Went to Church at the Capitol and heard Mr Post the Chaplain of the Senate—very insipid— The echo is so distinct in the House it almost produces a ridiculous effect— Drank Tea Mrs. Smith's.

***

1 January 1820

Miserably sick but went to the Presidents to pay my respects on the return of the New Year— Not so crowded as usual in consequence of the extreme cold which exceeded by six degrees any thing before experienced in this place— Passed the Evening sociably with my Children who have hitherto been blessings of fair promise. God grant they may continue so—and glide gently through this World of passion and temptation— Mr Forbes passed the Eveng with us— He brought a copy of a Letter which Mr A. had written to the Vice President on the subject of ettiquette— To this he has been brought much against his Will in consequence of a formal complaint made to the President concerning his not paying first visits to the Senators—After having had a Cabinet meeting in which no agreement could be made as to the establishment of an ettiquette— This has necessitated the step he has taken and tho' it may make you smile it will shew you that we are not what we profess to be in this Country and that trifles may be magnified into things of serious import— And it is evidently understood by some persons high in station to be a step to the Chair of State— This is perfectly confidential at present although I have no doubt it will soon be public—

2 January 1820

The weather intensely Cold. Did not go to Church but was under the necessity of going to see one of my Sisters on business of importance and made a few calls on my way home— Nothing occurred during the day worth notice excepting the visit of one of the new Senators from Virginia—

3 January 1820

Left home at twelve o clock on my usual business and despatched nine visits in a circle of about six miles— A continuation of the American has appeared in the Richmond Enquirer in which there is a very splendid and bold defence of Slavery— These papers like the former which appeared in the National Intelligencer are written by George Hay the Presidents Son in Law. He is a man gifted with great talent but of principles so free that neither Religion or morality have any influence over his mind— His papers make a strong impression and dazzle by their brilliancy the minds of unreflecting youth who are naturally led away by their imaginations and I fear they are calculated to do much mischief.

4 January 1820

The weather still severely cold— My Sons are gone to the House of Representatives to hear the Debates— Your Letter has just been put into my hands and I observe all you say upon the subject of Missouri. She has unfortunately a very intemperate Delegate [*John Scott*] who is not calculated to soften the impending storm. Much alarm evidently exists as to the consequences of this Question and Congress are endeavouring to evade it by a variety of means and trying to produce something which shall by exciting the passions and prejudices of the people to draw off their attention from this difficult business which combines all the great interests of the Union and either way is dangerous to the Southern Dominion— It is said that if the Bill should pass with the restriction that the P[*resident*] would not sign it as he feels bound by the Louisianna Treaty— And the restriction is here declared altogether unconstitutional by the Southern interest— Some say the purchase of *Louisiana* was unconstitutional— How will matters stand in this case? In the Evening my company assembled as usual and we had a full (seemingly a very essential thing) and pleasant party—with very little music—

5 January 1820

Several morning visits among which Mrs. & Miss Dickinson very charming women from the State of New York. Dined at the Presidents—the dinner very stiff and the President unusually silent— In the Evening a large Ball at [*Sec-retary of the Treasury*] Mr. [*William H.*] Crawford's 450 invitations out— The party very pleasant and social— Some conversation with Mr Craw-ford— The night very cold—

6 January 1820

Morning visits as usual— At a party at Mr. Kerrs in the evening where I had some conversation with Mr Meigs of New York concerning the incorporation of our Orphan Assylum society which he is to manage for us in Congress. A new ettiquette I understand is established no gentlemen is to be allowed to talk longer than six minutes with any Lady— George and John were much amused— There never was so much beauty in Washington as this Winter—

7 January 1820

Went out to pay morning visits and [*see*] Mrs. & Miss Dickinson. The Vice President was very chatty and pleasant— Mr & Mrs. Smith came and passed the evening with us.— The most difficult thing I find to do is to be exact in regard to titles which has become a perfect torment.— My omission is immediately resented and I often feel very awkward and fool-ish for not being aware of the *rank* of my visitors— George is quite un-well—

17 January 1820

Very busy all day preparing for my Ball tomorrow, taking down beds, and furniture of every description, and oversetting all my poor husbands papers— I cannot therefore pretend that the day was passed quietly. How-ever we were all pleased at having accomplished this great labour, and went to bed full of expectation and anticipation, of what our exertions were to produce—some auguring nothing but delight, others more experienced and less sanguine, foreseeing nothing but toil and disappointment.

18 January 1820

We were so busy all the morning, as to be almost exhausted by the time our company arrived, which they began to do at about seven o clock: during the first hour there came only four ladies, and Mr. A. who is apt to take alarm, began to be uneasy and anxious— The rooms were nearly full of Gentlemen, most of them Members [*of Congress*] 80 of whom attended, besides 13 Senators; when the young Ladies began to assemble so fast I could scarcely have time to make my salutations and some even left the House without coming into the rooms at all— We had about three hundred perhaps more, and the evening was more than commonly animated— I could give them no supper but substituted as well as I could all sorts of refreshments, and all my guests were apparently satisfied, but what was best of all, Mr. A was so pleased with my success, that he joined in a Reel with the boys and myself, and you would have laughed heartily to see the surprize of our people, and the musicians, who were the only witnesses of the sport—

We retired to bed much fatigued, and I not much pleased at "the prospect before me" of the cleaning and scrubbing which must take place ere we could resume with any comfort our usual occupations— The uncomplaining good humour with which your Son submits to my follies, excites no small portion of my gratitude— My Boys all assisted but John did the honours of my Ball with a grace which won all hearts, and proved to be my sheet anchor— They all danced and acquitted themselves very well— Only the Secretary of the Navy honoured me with his company and that of his family— Mr Crawford after having received my invitation asked Mr. A— to dine with him on Tuesday, which I was under the neccessity of urging him to decline, as I could not entertain my company without him. John Boyd in full Uniform having entered the Navy—

19 January 1820

As usual I paid the price of a violent headache for my exertions and a pain in all my limbs in consequence of running so often up and down Stairs— I therefore staid quietly at home all day, and had the comfort of seeing every thing restored to its pristine order before dinner, and my husband once more in possession of his comfortable apartment surrounded by his papers, but freed from the accumulation of dust & dirt which had been gathering the whole winter— Went to bed early as every one was anxious for a good nights repose after their toils, the greater part of which fell upon poor John, who most amiably assisted in restoring every thing to its place— He has as usual won the affection of all the Servants— George's health is very delicate and I feel under considerable apprehension concerning him—

20 January 1820

Remained at home all day— George went to the Senate and heard the debate on the Missouri and Main question— He was much pleased by a Speech of Mr Burrill, of Rhode Island and one of Mr Macon of North Carolina— They became warm, and something was suggested concerning a division of the Union, which produced considerable alarm— Evening at home which Mr. Smith spent with us— Mr. A— dined at Com. [*Stephen*] Decaturs— We hear of nothing but Mr. Pinckney who has threatened to speak in the Senate for many days and has excited a *sensation* even greater than could possibly be imagined; The Senate Chamber in which they now admit Ladies on the floor, has been occupied quite early every day—and his fame has attracted the attention of a part of the fair [*sex*] who if the tongue of scandal speaks any thing like truth, out of gratitude must naturally be desirous of affording their admiration, and bestowing it in as public a manner as possible on one who is so ready to distinguish them— However as the grave fathers of the Senate are supposed to be *old enough* to set a good example to the lower house, it has been thought by the public rather indecorous and the Respectable Ladies of Washington can now only get admittance through the medium of a Senator— As however Ladies of a very public character did get in and take seats on either hand of the Vice President he has been subjected to some jests for having been thus supported—.

28 January 1820

Went in the morning to see Mrs. Smith from whom I had received a very urgent Note— I found her in great distress as William had again been ar-

rested on the old ground [*debts*], and had at last to free himself from difficulties which were constantly accumulating taken the benefit of the [*bank-
ruptcy*] act. His Uncle is rejoiced that he has at last brought himself to this
as in the circumstances in which he is without a prospect of promotion it
was utterly impossible for him to do any thing to extricate himself from the
pressure of his debts— Mr. Adams and George went to dine at Mr Crawfords and from thence to an Evening party at Col Freemans which I declined
as I did not feel in spirits for company of any kind— John and I staid at
home with Charles and Mary who took their drawing Lesson as usual.

29 January 1820

I felt in such wretched spirits all the morning I was absolutely good for
nothing— Sat at home and read [*Francis*] Halls Travels [*in Canada, and
the United States*]— Mr. A. at dinner time said I had better go to Mr. de Neuvilles. George John and myself accordingly attended and I should have
passed a very pleasant evening if I had not been teazed to death by mistakes
and explanations about missing notes of invitation and want of punctuality
in returning visits for which I am everlastingly reproached— I wish from
my heart people would not give me a consequence I do not in the least desire to possess and would suffer me to sink into my native and natural insignificance but as long as my parties are fashionable and the Secretary gives
good wine it is in vain to contend against this *torment of pleasure*— As a
young Woman I detested society and always looked upon it as a toil. As an
old one it is becoming an insupportable burthen upon the footing on which
it is set in this place.

Mr. [*John*] Holmes made a Speech in the House upon the Missouri
Question and occupied the floor of the House two days it is said to very
little purpose as he has produced no effect as it regards the question before
them of any consequence and expressed sentiments which neither party
approve— How difficult it is to steer a middle course in such circumstances— Poor Massachusetts was very roughly treated by him and his
threats to Virginia through her were tremendous— Where Passion is already so high would a prudent man endeavour to encrease jealousy and
natural hatred by exaggerating danger and inspiring terror? Surely this is

not wise and cannot be approved by the majority of his Constituents— He came to me several times in the course of the evening and complained of low spirits repeatedly saying how much he envied me for possessing a flow of spirits which was the chief support of my frail existence.

I received many flattering messages in the course of the evening, one from Senator Pinkney who sent me word he was gone to fetch his Wife who would make it a point to come and visit me as soon as she arrived and one from Mrs. [*Dolley Payne*] Madison inviting me to see her and saying she intended to visit Washington next winter and should take a corner at my parties— All this is very civil but what does it amount to. I fear I am growing cinical since I find the most trifling occurrences are turned into political machinery— Even my countenance was watched at the Senate during Mr. Pinkneys speech as I was afterwards informed by some of the gentlemen— If my husbands sentiments are to be tried and judged by such variations the gentlemen will have hard work to fix a standard to form their opinions upon—

30 January 1820

Read prayers at home the weather being very bad— The boys were to have dined with their Aunt Frye but found the weather too bad to walk so far— Staid at home all the evening—

31 January 1820

At home all day— In the evening the boys went to a party at Mrs. Pleasanton's with Mary— They expected to dance but in consequence of the Music disappointing them they had a dull party. They left me at Mrs. Smiths on their way and returned with considerable ill humour at least an hour earlier than I expected.

1 February 1820

The day severely cold. Went and paid several morning visits at one of which I was pretty closely questioned about my Tuesday Evenings [*weekly sociables*] especially to assertain if I was not liable to have *improper* persons at my house— As people come by invitation and no one without an introduction by one of our acquaintance I can scarcely understand what this means— There is such an attempt to introduce distinctions here and to class our society it is to me perfectly sickening— I am the reputed author of it which is the most laughable part of it—as my own family connections rank according to this new scale among the inadmissibles— This is too preposterous for common sense!— And it is absolutely disgusting to me to hear of the rabble and such stuff as we used to laugh at so much previous to the french Revolution under the appellation of the *Cannaille*— Returned home to dine with the Boys Mr. A— being engaged to dine with Mr. Calhoun— In the evening we had a small party on account of the severe cold and we made out tolerably with singing and dancing on the Carpet—

2 February 1820

The boys went to hear Mr. Randolph but were quite disappointed. He is said to have fallen off prodigiously since he was in Congress formerly— George went from thence to dine at his Aunt Fryes and in the evening Mary, John, and Charles went to a party at Mrs. Ramseys and I brought them hope after taking Tea at My Sisters— Every thing appears to go on more smoothly than was anticipated— The young folks were quite enchanted with their party—

3 February 1820

This day a party of 22 to dinner selected by Mr. A— that the boys might see the most striking members of Congress— Mr. Calhoun the Secretary Mr Pinkney Mr Burton Mr. Foote Mr Hemphill Col R M Johnson Genl Bloomfield Mr Mellen Genl Mercer Mr. Metcalf Joe Joe Monroe Mr Morrill, Mr. Parker, Mr. Roberts, Mr. Simkins, Mr Storrs Mr Taylor, Mr Vandyke & Mr Warfield— Mr Rufus King and Mr Livermore declined— I did not dine at Table there not being sufficient room for our company and wishing that my Sons might not lose the opportunity offered to them— The Gentlemen all went away *gay* to say no more.

4 February 1820

Went into George Town to make some purchases and to do some business for George and they left cards for the Heads of Departments to take leave— In the [*afternoon*] George and John and myself took Tea at Mrs. Smiths and bade her farewell—

5 February 1820

This morning was passed in confusion and very disagreeable anticipation, at the approaching separation which cost me all the fortitude I possess to meet it without shrinking— George has become a valuable companion for his father and I think is forming fast— He is subject to a depression of spirits and a nervous irritability which makes me very uneasy otherwise we have been much gratified by his general improvement— John is still quite the boy and would enjoy himself more if he did not persevere in a principle altogether foolish of never doing any thing during the vacation— This often occasions weariness and the time always hangs heavy on his hands— We passed the evening at Mr de Neuvilles at the request of them both and George appeared to be much pleased— John began to enjoy it just as the dancing ceased and we were obliged to return home.

6 February 1820

My Boys went off in the six o'clock Stage and Mr. A myself and Mary went to the Representatives chamber and heard a Mr [*Luther*] Rice one of the Indian Missionaries who has had a great reputation in the western States— I thought very little of him— There was a great attempt at eloquence which however to my idea proved entirely abortive. His language was mean and ill chosen and when he rose at all above the common standard it only served to make its general vulgarity more conspicuous— From thence I called on Mrs. Brent [*to*] pay a lying in visit and at Mrs. Anderson's who had not returned from Church. The evening at home alone—

27 *February 1820*

Went to the House of Representatives and heard Mr. Rice again for whom they are about to build a new Church here— His manner is pompous his language Vulgar and his ideas pretty generally poor with much of the affectation of [a] would be thought Orator— I fear I am very difficult and hard to please, but true religion appears to me to be in itself so simple so clear and so striking that the tawdry dress in which its precepts are sometimes taught to the publick by men who have mistaken their genius, almost always mortifies me as it casts a shade of ridicule on things in themselves the most sacred. Its simplicity is in my mind its greatest security and unquestionably its greatest beauty for in its simplicity consists its superior excellence— It was made for the sole advantage of the great Mass of mankind and the Mass of mankind cannot understand it if this simplicity is lost for to them it is no longer comprehensible— Plain truths will speak for themselves they require not the aids of art— And vulgar embellishment of things divine, is altogether so grossly inconsistent that it is religion in a Caricature—

Passed the evening at Mrs. [*Susan Wheeler*] Decaturs with a small party where I met Mrs. [*Eliza Kortright Monroe*] Hay with whom I had much conversation— There are some Women who seem to found their own excellence entirely upon the errors and failings of others and therefore take a sort of unnatural delight in ransacking the histories of private families with a view to spread their scandalous history—abroad with a desire to shine as it were by this borrowed but unholy light— Even from my earliest years I remember to have been too proud to think that the faults of others could excuse my own— So far from it that I have always considered them as examples set before me as a safeguard from committing what appeared to me odious in them, and human nature is so frail I think we ought when it is possible to be lenient to one another in all cases where it is possible— My Poor father used to tell me when I was a girl, that I should defeat my own happiness in this world in consequence of my anxiety to trace even the commonest actions to their motives— This I believe has injured me in some measure as it has taught me to measure men and things by a very circumscribed rule and sometimes to judge them unjustly— Such as I am my character is before the World and from it I expect no mercy— My only shield is a pure conscience and that shield is a brazen one.—

Poor Mrs. Bagot who was so popular here has left a reputation so tatered and torn to very shreds that it is wonderful what pains must have been taken to collect the morsels so as to form any thing out of them— Is it because she was beautiful and accomplished and that few equal her? Is it from that natural envy of unwillingly acknowledged superiority that this insatiable craving to destroy proceeds. I do not undertake to vindicate her because I am not acquainted sufficiently with her family to enable me so to do— But her conduct during her residence in the Country was such as to entitle her to the greatest respect and the breath of Slander dared not attack her added to which in England the supposed Scene of her follies where characters so prominent cannot escape the lash I never heard a whisper against her— If I cannot vindicate her I at any rate am not bound to believe all that I hear and I will hope that the whole is a fabrication and wish that I may still be allowed to admire what appeared so excellent—without seeking to know more— My burning Cheek must sometimes lead people to suspect me of guilt— For on these subjects I am alas too sensitive as they have been made to reach my heart which has suffered almost to bursting—but though it is vulnerable to the attacks of the cruelly unfeeling I can yet trust in heaven to support me through my trials and to give me strength and spirit to maintain myself in the path which I have yet to travel ere the hour arrives which will transplant me to a better World— These are bitter poisoned Shafts aimed by a pretended friendly hand but my Cup is full and I must drink it to the very dregs.

28 February 1820

Went out to return morning visits and set some time with Mrs. Frye and Mrs. Smith— Returned to dinner and remained at home the whole evening having sent an excuse to Mrs. Gales as I am absolutely weary of parties.

29 February 1820

Received my own company as usual and had quite a crowded party— Only one Member of Congress came in consequence of the House of Representatives sitting very late and the debate was excessively violent— Charles went to hear it being as tired as I am of parties—

1 March 1820

Another turbulent day in Congress but a very quiet one at home. As the opposing parties are determined to bring the thing to a conclusion they leave no method untried to put an end to the debate and as the Southern people have the most at stake they are in hopes of obtaining that from weariness which they cannot procure by fairer means—

2 March 1820

Company at Dinner consisting of Chief Justice Marshall, Justice Washington, Justice Todd, Justice Story, Justice Livingston, Mr. Story, Mr. Ingersoll, Mr. Hopkinson, Mr I Ogden, Col Taylor, General Brown, Col Morrison, Genl Winder, Mr. W. Jones— The dinner was pleasant and the Bottle did not circulate too freely— The House was in Session when the Gentlemen arrived— Nothing heard of but Mr. Randolph— The company left us early—

3 March 1820

The famous question [*of the Missouri Compromise*] was decided this morning— While we were looking at Sully's picture [*of* Washington's Passage of the Delaware] Mr. Nelson of Masstts. came in and told us that the business was over— They having passed the bill with a compromise— Mr. Randolph rose and moved to reconsider— The Speaker called him to order stating that they had not acted upon the order of the day which Mr. R. was obliged to submit to— The Speaker took advantage of the circumstance to send the Bills to the Senate and when the time came for Mr R— to make his motion the business was completed and every thing terminated— The honesty of our Congress has been displayed in such exalted colours this Session that the next generation will certainly have cause to be proud of their fathers— Indeed it is a pity that we have not a Homer to chant in the most elevated strains the glory of *such patriots*— At least we shall be allowed to have attained a high pitch of excellence when such knavish trickery can be practiced in the face of an enlightened nation and delight in the glory of *tricks atcheived* which would do honour to a gamester or a blacklegs. These are the rulers I am bound to admire— If this is the case, if this is the vaunted superiority of our Government, and the purity of our elective Institutions, I do not think we have much to be proud of, and morality and Religion are of little use if they cannot teach us to discern the difference between right and wrong—

If such is publick virtue, may my Sons have nothing to do with it— May they be far above polluting their name and fair fame in such a School; I had rather see them live in the most secluded state than thus sell their honour to favour the views of any man, or any party, even tho' that man were my husband— A place obtained in such a way would be an incessant scourge to conscience and I should be ashamed to fill it lest I read the contempt of the good in every speaking eye— It is all barter and he who can afford to bid the highest is the most sure of success— Enough however on this subject excepting that I understand the Clerk of the House was publickly reprimanded for doing the dirty work of his Masters— I think very little of Trumbull's picture [*the* Declaration of Independence]. There is nothing very striking, certainly nothing very novel in the design and some confusion in the colouring— Altogether it does not please me— I passed the evening quietly at home and Mr Connell from Philadelphia spent it with us—

4 March 1820

Remained at home until dinner time reading Ivanhoe the last new Novel of [*Sir Walter*] Scott in which I was so deeply immersed that I had scarcely time to dress for dinner at Mr. de Neuvilles; where however we arrived in good season, we found a large company assembled, and the dinner was served almost immediately— The party was pleasant but somehow or other I was not in very good spirits, and it appeared to me that there was an odd sort of crowing tone among some of the members of Congress which seemed to aim at my husband, and some queer questions were asked me concerning his opinion on the Missouri business which I could not understand; all this might be fancy however, as I am ridiculously sensitive— I have never pretended to understand the question in all its bearings as a political one; in a moral and religious point of view and even as a gross political inconsistency with all our boasted Institutions, liberty, and so forth, it is so palpable a stain that the veryest dunce can see it and understand it without the foreign aid of education or art—Returned home very weary tired of myself and all the World— I see too much, and was certainly never intended by nature to enjoy the Matchiavelism which is performing around me—

A major event of the social season was the marriage of Maria Hester Monroe, James Monroe's youngest daughter, to her cousin and his former private secretary, Samuel Lawrence Gouverneur, on 9 March 1820, the first wedding to take place in the reconstructed White House. The wedding presented a new social challenge for Louisa, who became in part responsible for determining the appropriate etiquette for the diplomatic corps on such an occasion.

10 March 1820

Went out to dine at Col Tayloe's where we found a small company consisting of Mr [*James*] & Mrs. [*Nancy Hart*] Brown Mr. & Mrs. Lowndes The Russian Minister and Secretaries The English Chargé d'Affair and the Consul with Mr. & Mrs. Pleasanton and the family made up the party— The dinner was rather formal but tolerably pleasant— We heard a great talk of the Wedding and as usual many ill natured remarks— A Person in a publick Office in this Country is very much in the situation of the man in the fable who endeavouring to please every body entirely failed— In all things which do not concern the publick I am very much inclined to do as I please and I think the P[*resident*] should do so too for his own comfort— I have heard nothing concerning the ceremony except that there were 7 Brides maid's and 4 Bridesmen and a very handsome supper at which 42 persons sat down— There are to be two drawing rooms on Monday and Tuesday next— Returned home very early— I mentioned that the Corps Diplomatique were not to be admitted on the occasion to the Ladies and they were all excessively shocked— Poor Mrs. Brown who has an eye to the french Mission seemed to feel her dignity terribly wounded through them and was quite solicitous that they might not be told of it at all but alas the thing was done and the éclat could no longer be prevented—

11 March 1820

Went to see Mrs. Hellen who is very dangerously sick. I found her very low and feeble with a violent cough and two blisters on. Made some calls as

I went—returned home and on my way called on Mrs. Smith to inform her of the situation of our Sister— Mrs. [*Floride Bonneau Colhoun*] Calhoun is in great distress in consequence of the illness of her Infant who is not expected to recover. Col Aspinwall promised to call and take a small parcell of shoes for Susan which have been waiting for an opportunity sometime— Mr. Sanford of the Senate called on me and chatted about half an hour— It has often struck me that he would have been a much more proper person for the Spanish Mission than that poor flighty Forsythe who is in great disgrace here— I must confess I think those that sent him ought to bear the blame; as it was very evident he had no one qualification suitable for such a Mission; unless it was to enlarge the breach which had been twenty years nearly closing— Mr Crawford his patron is the resposible person; and I cannot bear to hear Mr. A— charged with it who was averse to him, but who could have no influence even tho' it came within his own Department— The only Minister whose appointment he has had any thing to do with is [*Alexander Hill*] Everett— This fact speaks for itself— Came home to dinner and passed the evening at home alone—

12 *March 1820*

Being very unwell and the weather very bad Mary and myself could not go to Church— We read prayers and afterwards received visits— Mr. Warren brought me your Letter. I had been very uneasy about your indisposition but am very happy to learn that you are recovering. I shall certainly pay him every attention in my power but as Washington is likely to be very gay in consequence of this Wedding he will have little time to spare to us—

Mr & Mrs. Smith passed the evening with us: and among the numerous visitors I heard the rumours of the day one of which is that Mr. A— is to be Vice President if Mr. Tomkins should be elected Governor of the State of New York— I have long thought that it would be a pleasant circumstance to some people to put him out of the situation he now fills: as his talents are feared and his disinclination to every kind of intrigue dreaded and looked upon as a tacit and continual censure of those, whose ambition leads them to adopt and persevere in such practices— By curtailing his usefulness to the publick they propose to prevent his obtaining popularity, and thus make it impossible for him to look higher— As I only hear these things from the publick; I think myself authorized to write my sentiments very freely upon the subject— I have no personal interest. I can safely declare before heaven, I have seen too much of publick life not to value it for what it is worth— I think however I know my husbands character, and with the conviction that his habits and tastes are fixed beyond the possibility of change, I fear that he could not live long out of an active sphere of publick life and that it is absolutely essential to his existence—

I have since the first year of my marriage entered upon my *great honours* with tears; and I do not recollect ever having lost them with regret— Submission to circumstances has been my doctrine, and as I have had nothing to do with the disposal of affairs; and never but once been consulted—I am perfectly indifferent about it— I have never seen that situation in which the pleasures, and the pains, the advantages, and the disadvantages, were not pretty equally balanced— The severest trials I had to undergo are gone by, now fate may do its worst— If Mr. A— could bring his mind to it, I believe the best thing he could do would be to resign his place altogether; but I never should dare to give him such advice, or take upon myself the responsibility of its consequences— He certainly understands and knows best what is right, and I have often found and I know not from whence it arises, that my sentiments are too lofty for my Station— These are subjects which I never or very very rarely venture on with him, as he can have no better guide than his own judgment— The Collector of the Port of Alexandria died suddenly and before he was buried it is said that the P. had one hundred application's—

13 March 1820

The weather is so excessively disagreeable that it was impossible for me to go out as I intended in the morning— The Presidents Nephew called to say that the Corps Diplomatique would be allowed to pay their respects to the Bride and the she would condescend to return their visits with her husband; but that there would be *no further intercourse between them*— I informed Mr. A— of the message at dinner time when he came home, but it was too late to do any thing with it— In the evening went to the Drawing Room and paid my respects— The President shook hands with me— The Bride was attended by her Bride maids 7 in number all very pretty girls—but the Drawing room was very thin in consequence of the bad weather— The Speaker was in high spirits, and came and spoke very graciously to me, and offered his hand which I immediately accepted— We meet but to *War* and each of us are ready with a jest on all occasions— Mr. Smith accompanied us— I did not get a bit of cake and Mary had none to dream on— So much for this *little great affair* which has occasioned so much talk and so much ill nature—

Mrs. Hay asked me if I had received the message sent in the morning; I told her I had delivered it to Mr A— according to order; but the lateness of the hour at which he received it, prevented him from giving the information required— She said the message was to me, and not to Mr. Adams! I told her that I was desired to give it to Mr. Adams from the President; but that if it was to me I had already given her answer; and informed the Corps Diplomatique they were not to know that there was any thing uncommon in the P's family. She said if I had done so she believed the best way was to let it remain so, and make the best of it— I told her I agreed with her in opinion: as there had never been any thing official in the business which was very evident; *myself* having been the medium of communication instead of Mr. Adams: and that it was merely a civility customary between individuals in society, established among all classes of people; and acceptable as a mark of respect and friendship— Here the matter rests, and I know not what to do more on the subject—

What a dangerous thing it is to step out of the common routine of things! one little step taken without thought often most innocently; leads to troubles ad infinitum; and its results frequently produce great and unlooked for events— Yet my dear Sir, human nature would lose its greatest charm were all our ideas and our actions calculated by rule, and there would be no scope either for genius or character— There is something about Mr. Clay; that pleases me in spite of reason—and it is this: that if you watch his character; you almost immediately discover that his heart is generous and good, and that his first impulse is almost always benevolent and liberal— But a neglected education, vicious habits, and bad company, united to overweening ambition, have made him blush to act the better part, and covered with foul blots that which might have been made perfect— Heard of the death of the King of England [*George III*] and Duke of Kent.

Dueling—ritual combat to settle matters of honor—had a long tradition in American society. In the 1820s, most duels by residents of Washington, D.C., took place at nearby Bladensburg, Maryland. In the case Louisa relates below, Stephen Decatur and James Barron fought there on 22 March. Decatur was one of the most noted naval commanders of his era, having served with distinction during the wars with the Barbary pirates and the War of 1812, among other engagements. Barron too was a naval commander but had lost his position in 1807 over the Chesapeake *affair. Decatur's opposition to Barron's reinstatement led to the challenge. Barron was hit in the thigh but survived; Decatur's stomach wound proved fatal. John Quincy strongly objected to the practice of dueling; in 1839 he helped to have it made a criminal offense in the District of Columbia.*

22 March 1820

Remained at home in consequence of a head ache when Mr Smith and Mr Forbes came in with the shocking news of Com Decatur's being mortally wounded in a Duel with Com Baron— My blood ran cold as I heard it and Mr. A— immediately went off to see him and to offer every assistance in his power. I followed and when I got there was informed that there were faint hopes of his life— The whole Town was in a state of agitation and [a] great part of the day his door was crowded with people waiting the sad event— He expired at eight o'clock last evening to the grief of the whole Nation who will long mourn the loss of a favorite Hero whose amiable qualities as a private Citizen entitled him to the esteem of all whose esteem and friendship were worth possessing— His style of living has excited some envy in narrow minded people for such there are and such there ever will be. Incapable of such exertion as will promote their own interests and envious of all who rise to emminence they gratify their spleen by the basest calumnies—

Com. Baron is slightly wounded. He is a miserable man whose services it seems have been rejected by the Government as he supposes at the instigation of poor Decatur who did not deny the charge— What this man has gained by destroying a felow creature with a view to patch a broken reputation I cannot understand but this I am sure of, were I in his situation where my pillow had been strown with one thorn, I should now find a Million to aggravate my former sorrows— The shock to his poor Widow was dreadful beyond measure— She breakfasted with him in good health and spirits at eight o'clock, and at ten he was brought back mortally wounded only to languish a short space and then sink I trust to everlasting rest. Oh what an agonizing scene. What irreparable mischief in a few short hours— The very thought makes one shudder and we dare not look into futurity— The President was deeply interested and went to see him several times— He was wounded in the side and the Ball went through his body and was extracted just above the Hip. It was remarked that the wound did not bleed and it was hoped that extracting the Ball might produce good consequences— He was speechless many hours after the operation.

23 March 1820

Our City is more and more deeply envelloped in gloom and every moment seems to teem with new trouble— A hundred different stories are in circulation concerning this dreadful affair, and I am told that his Wife has not seen him Since the night before the duel took place, as instead of breakfasting at home he stopped at the Congress Hotel, and there ate an unusually hearty meal, which the Surgeons say was very much against his recovery— Mr. A— was anxious to have some law passed with a view to check this fatal practice, but the people of our Country still seem to possess a little of their aboriginal barbarism, and I fear he will have few supporters, more especially as our Chief Magistrate seems to approve the spirit— In the Army there is a regulation which it is said has been of actual service, as few chuse to risk the forfeiture of place— Surely the same rule might be prudently adopted in the Navy— At least it would be worth the trial— It was reported currently all day that two more were gone to fight yesterday, in consequence of some strong expressions used on the field when Decatur fell, and we are still in a state of anxiety on the subject, more especially as [*Como. William*] Bainbridge is said to be one of the parties concerned— We attended the funeral of Mrs. Calhoun child at four o'clock and I spent the evening at home Mr. & Mrs. Smith came in and spent two hours with us—

The Adamses purchased a new home in April 1820 on F Street in Washington, D.C. After considerable renovations to expand it and make it habitable, they moved into it in the fall of 1820 and remained there until they relocated to the White House in the spring of 1825. The family continued to own the building, however, renting it to tenants. They did not return to live in the house until 1838.

6 June 1820

Spent the Evening at Mrs. Frye's— The morning went with Mrs. Weightman to a meeting of the Orphan Assylum— The meeting was full and our finances in better order than common— It was laughingly proposed by one of the Ladies to encrease our buildings in consequence of the rappid encrease of our population, Congress having left many females in such difficulties as to make it probable they would beg our assistance— To this I made some question and asked on what ground they could make such a claim and was informed that as the Session had been very long the *fathers* of the Nation had left forty cases to be provided for by the publick and that our institution was the most likely to be called upon to maintain this illicit progeny— I recommended a petition to Congress next Session for that *great* and *moral* body to found or establish a foundling insti[*tu*]tion and should certainly move that the two additional dollars a day which they have given themselves as an increase of pay may be appropriated as a fund towards the support of the Instit[*tu*]ion— I mentioned this circumstance to Mr Adams when I returned home but he said that the Ladies had been so urgent to have their society *incorporated* they could not wonder at what had happen'd— Not a little wicked this joke!!

7 June 1820

Went on a fishing party over to the Virginia side and had a tolerably pleasant day— Returned to dine and afterwards rode out and went to the bath—

8 June 1820

Accompanied the Carpenter too look at our house and to give orders as to what alterations and repairs are to be made— Found it in a miserable condition and came and reported to Mr. A— Entered of course into no agreement— Mr. & Mrs. Smith passed the Eveng with us— Judge Cranch very unexpectedly came to dine with us and appeared to be in uncommon good spirits— He told me Mrs. J[*ohn*] Greenleaf [*Lucy Cranch Greenleaf*] was in town.

9 June 1820

Drank Tea at Mrs. Fryes with Mrs. Smith. Met Johnson Hellen. There heard nothing new excepting a marriage of one of Mary's schooll mates— My journal becomes miserably stupid neither worth writing or reading— Count [*Jules de*] Menou called a new french Secretary—

10 June 1820

Remained at home all the morning— In the Eveng accompanied Mrs. Smith to Tea at Mrs. Pleasantons. Was informed that Mr. & Mrs. Graham were coming home from Rio Janeiro Mr. G— being in very ill health on account of the Climate— Our Missions seem to be altogether unsuccessfull— Two little boys were drowned in Rock Creeks one a Son of Mr [*George Corbin*] Washington the other of Dr Clark— They were under ten years of age—

11 June 1820

Mr A— and Charles went to Church. It poured with Rain in consequence of which I presume there was no service and they returned home immediately— Mr. Baily called in the Eveng and I took a short walk with Mr. Adams—

12 June 1820

The weather continued very bad but as Mary was invited to a party at Miss Van Ness I took her there and then went to Mrs. Frye's— Mr. & Mrs. James Greenleaf called in the morning— I invited them to Tea on Wednesday but they declined— There is a profound silence on almost every political topic. It is therefore impossibl to write on any subject which can prove either amusing or interesting— All is at present calmly profound but I suppose the cold weather will bring us something both to warm and to rouse us.

The Adamses spent the summer in Washington, D.C. In the fall, John Adams was elected a member of the Massachusetts Constitutional Convention, called to amend or revise the constitution John himself had written almost single-handedly forty years earlier. It was a sentimental election, but, not surprisingly,

John took his responsibility quite seriously. He declined the post of president of the convention but sat in a place of honor to the right of the president, attending each day and actively participating in the debates.

John Adams's young namesake, the son of John Quincy, was engaged, unfortunately, in less auspicious events. He participated in a student riot at Harvard protesting the suspension of three other students and was himself suspended. He was allowed to return to the school but was permanently expelled after another riot in 1823.

13 November 1820

I do not know if I ought to congratulate you or not on your acceptance of the trouble and anxiety attending you as a Member of the Convention my dear Sir but I hope it will yield you amusement as well as occupation and rely on your taking it quite easily without making it laborious or oppressive.

Congress has convened again and as you will percieve by the ballots for speaker which occupied three days and discovered a temper rather inauspicious to the future harmony of the Session. Mr [*John W.*] Taylor [*of New York*] has proved the successful candidate altho' there was considerable opposition from his own State he being a very high toned Clintonian. The Southern interest is terribly galled at this unlooked for success of the North and can scarcely concieve what could produce it—but the fact is too evident; and the feud is likely to wax warm and renew all the blaze of the Missouri question; with a fire more keen and solid if not more destructive than it was last Winter, which has lain smothered so long only to *burn more fiercely.*

14 November 1820

Many visitors this day— An accident of a very terrible nature. One of the workmen fell off the roof of the adjoining building and was most dreadfully injured. Mr Adams accompanied him home and took a Surgeon with him. Every attention was shewn him and there are some hopes of his recovery. He is a man of property and much respected.

15 November 1820

Mrs. [*Caroline Langdon*] Eustis and Mrs. [*Isabella Ramsay Macomb*] Bloom-field called to day. The Doctor [*William Eustis*] with General Smith and General [*Joseph*] Bloomfield called early in the morning— We are very un-easy about College Matters having just heard of the Rebellion— My Chil-dren seem to have some very intemperate blood in them, and are certainly not very easy to govern— Mr. A— and myself are very uneasy about it. John is somewhat like his Mother a little hot headed, and want of timely reflection will I fear often lead him to error, as long as he suffers the first naturally strong impulse to guide him— Experience is scarcely sufficient as I too well know to counteract this all powerful feeling: and even age sometimes has to contend for the mastery of reason against passion— It is singular that the most generous natures are the most liable to this failing: and that quick sensibility a quality so amiable in itself, should often lead to the most pain-ful results, but alas! such is the lot of humanity! even our virtues become dangerous if not kept under due controul.— We rest our hopes on the mild-ness of the Government, and flatter ourselves that John will still be allowed to continue his studies—

16 November 1820

Went out yesterday to execute a piece of business for Mr A— and as usual did it wrong: however the fault is reparable so that it is of no great consequence— Again many visitors. Mrs. Bloomfield is very pretty— She is about thirty and is just married to General Bloomfield who I should think is near seventy— He settled thirty thousand dollars on her it is said the day before the Wedding— We are told that there are several Candidates for the Vice Presidency— You I suppose will vote for Mr Tompkins.

17 November 1820

My ramblings have begun and all my time is spent in visiting in the morn-ing and I return too weary to do any thing afterwards— The Town is full of Strangers but there are not many Ladies.— An invitation from the President for Mr Adams to dinner on Tuesday next and it is said that the Drawing Rooms are to begin on Wednesday. Sent out Cards of invitation for a dinner on Thursday— Thus the routine begins for the next four Months and evening and morning will be fully occupied. The roads are in such a state in consequence of what are calld repairs that I fear there will be plenty of work for the Surgeons. 28 visits yesterday.

Johnson Hellen, Louisa's nephew by her sister Ann, would spend much of the winter with the Adamses. Now twenty years old, he had been raised in Washington, D.C. He attended Princeton but was dismissed in March 1819 "for a very slight offence," as Louisa described it above. He would eventually become a lawyer, practicing first in Maryland and later in Washington.

Fanny Johnson, Louisa's cousin on her father's side, proved a far more troublesome house guest, as Louisa relates below. An "accomplished Coquette," Fanny proved a significant distraction to all of the young Adams men but most especially George, who would nearly become embroiled in an "affair of honor" regarding his relationship with the young woman. Fanny did eventually settle down, marrying Col. John McPherson of Frederick County, Maryland, in 1823. They would live to celebrate their golden wedding anniversary.

The presidential election of 1820 proved largely uneventful. With the Federalist Party essentially defunct, James Monroe, representing Democratic-Republicans, ran unopposed. Despite some discussion regarding a possible change, he kept his vice president, Daniel D. Tompkins, on the ticket. This would be the third and last uncontested presidential election in American history.

28 November 1820

The day very cold. Sent for Johnson Hellen who is to make me a long visit this Winter. He is an uncommonly fine young man and I think bids fair to be an honour to his family. In the evening I had about 200 Persons— The party was very pleasant and extraordinarily large for a first night— We had some good music and only wanted space to make it quite agreeable. Three of the young Ladies performed charmingly on the harp one sang and Mr. [*Gaetano*] Carusi's flute was most excellent. There were about two and twenty

Ladies. I was disappointed of a number in consequence of the funeral of Mrs. Mansfield.— Should my large Room be finished this Winter I shall be enabled to entertain much more agreeably and conveniently to myself then I now do— The poor Carpenter is recovering most surprizingly—

29 November 1820

Rode out in the morning and called to see my patient who is able to sit up and to raise his broken arm— In the Evening went to the Drawing Room. It was well attended though not crowded— I was teazed in the course of the Evening with questions concerning how I should behave in the same situation as it was likely I should be tried in four years from this time— I laughed and said I was so unruly I feared I should be censured for breaking through established customs, and defying all settled rules— It would be of little consequence as I believe it quite impossible to give general satisfaction— I met Mr Palfrey who told me he was going immediately to New Orleans— He complains bitterly of the cold of our Climate— He mentioned that one of Mr. Otis's Sons was to accompany him—

30 November 1820

Remained at home in the morning and in the Eveng went to a party at Mrs. Tayloe's. We had not the pleasure of hearing the bells [*that rang mysteriously*] and it is said they have not rung since the Col. returned. The party was small and pleasant the young Ladies danced. Mary accompanied me but did not dance not being very well— Mrs. Tayloe is much mortified at the punishment inflicted on Edward [*Tayloe, who was expelled from Harvard*] and seems inclined to take him from College—

1 December 1820

Having bad Colds we should have been glad to have staid at home but being engaged to accompany Mrs. Calhoun to see two famous dwarfs we went to Strothers at twelve o clock and were somewhat amused during our visit at what appeared to be the quaint pertness of the little Lady. You probably heard of them in Boston— My inclination never leads to such sights. I love the beauties of Nature not what must be termed her Defects— Every thing out of the immediate course to which we are accustomed seems to shock the understanding and tho' these two persons have nothing disagreeable in their formation or appearance still we are not willing to consider them as any thing but Children— They Sang. The girl had nothing remarkable in her voice but the Boys voice sounded like that of an old man and to me was painfully unpleasant— Mr. A— dined at the Presidents and during our dinner Anthony [*Giusta, Adams family servant*] told us that the P— had quarrelled with his Butler and in a passion had beat him— He is an Englishman but I believe a good for nothing fellow—And most likely the story is altogether without foundation— The dinner was to the Foreign Ministers the first given to [*British minister*] Mr [*Stratford*] Canning since his arrival. Passed the Evening at home.

2 December 1820

The weather is more severe than we ever remember it so early in the Season and we all remained at home to Nurse— Dr [*Jedidiah*] Morse dined with us— He gave us a great deal of information concerning the Indians and some much more welcome concerning the comfortable establishment of Col & Mrs. Boyd from whom we have not heard since May.— I received a Letter from Mr. Heard of New York presenting me with the famous Weathersfield Bonnet to my great astonishment— I shall certainly sport it very often in honour of my Country womans ingenuity and exertion— Answered the above Letter offering my thanks for his politeness— I endeavoured last year to obtain one of the Turkey Down Tippets [*a long scarf*] but was unsuccessful. Passed the Evening alone.

3 December 1820

As they were to have a Methodist Preacher at the Capitol again I did not go and there was no service at Mr. [*William*] Hawleys [*at St. John's Episcopal Church*]. Busily employed in writing all day—

4 December 1820

The day was stormy and disagreeable— In the Eveng went in to George Town to fetch Fanny Johnson who was expected in Town to stay some time with me. The Stage had not arrived when we got there and we drove to Mrs. Frye's where I heard of the sudden death of Columbia Peter who was on a visit to her Aunt and died before her Parents could get to her being only twenty miles distant— We returned to Crawfords Hotel but the Stage had not arrived although it was near ten o'clock— The shock I had received made me quite low spirited although I doubted the news and thought it probable they had blended the circumstances of Mrs. Lewis's having lost a daughter about five weeks since—

5 December 1820

Went to the Funeral of poor Columbia which unfortunately proved the information too correct which I had recently received the last Evening— Returned to the house and found Major Graham and Fanny Johnson who had just come from George Town— In the evening my company assembled about seven o'clock. The party was not very large in consequence of the funeral— Mrs. Frye & Mrs. Smith were both here though the latter did not arrive until the party broke up—

6 December 1820

Took Fanny to pay her "visits of ceremony" and in the Evening went to Mrs. James Thompson. We found a small company and had some good music by Miss Van Ness and Miss Thompson on the Harp now the most fashionable instrument— Nothing new in the Political World who are busily employed upon the Missouri Constitution. It is thought they will have a majority in the house against it as the dough faces [*northerners not opposed to slavery in Missouri*] appear to have shaken off their panic and are likely to stand firm on this occasion added to which the circumstances being considerably changed admits of many of the Gentlemen changing their ground without in fact appearing to change their principle of conduct—

Returned home at ten o'clock the Girls in high spirits— Mr A— did not accompany us.

---

20 December 1820

Remained at home all day teazed to death with chilblains and expecting hourly to see John and George— My anticipations are far from pleasant. When young people get together it is scarcely possible to keep order. Tastes characters and dispositions all combine to create differences jealousies and squabbles and among the females a natural tendency to coquetry which involuntarily produces unpleasant discussions and observations. My Sons are ardent admirers of the Sex and the charms of Fanny are too striking to escape their observation— My fears are only of momentary disquiet and can produce no consequences beyond the hour of trial—

21 December 1820

George and John arrived and prepared for a large dinner. We were disappointed of six persons and of course the party was very small— During dinner the conversation turned on the Queen of England [*Caroline of Brunswick*]— Mr. R King and Mr. [*Freeman*] Walker made many observations concerning her which displeased Mrs. Brush who appears to be a very warm partizan of her Majesty— In the Eveng we went to a party at Mrs. [*Elizabeth Washington Gamble*] Wirts and found them dancing— After some time they opened the new room which struck so direfully cold that it struck almost to my heart and I was apprehensive that the Girls would seriously suffer. We therefore returned home early and retired to bed directly considerably fatigued by the exertions the day—

22 December 1820

My Boys were so much fatigued I could scarcely judge how they looked— This morning I examined them well but found them very little changed— George appears to be as excentric as ever and John as wild— Mr A. and

Johnson dined at Mr. Calhoun's and we went to a dance at Mrs. Thompson's where we passed a very pleasant evening— I had some conversation with Mr [*John Williams*] Walker of Alabama a very agreeable man who appears to be in the last stage of a decline— Mrs. T. is a most singular character who has for the last two years been devoted to all the begotry of religion even to its utmost excess— From this she has suddenly relaxed and set out anew in defiance of all the Washington Saints with a Ball— This of course has afforded diversion on one side and scandal on the other— Every thing was handsome and the party was gay— Mrs. Hay overpowered me with civility and we are better friends than ever.

23 December 1820

Remained at home this morning while the young folks took a lesson of dancing.— In the Evening went to Mrs. Smiths to Tea. Mr. A dined at the Russian Ministers to celebrate the Emperors birth day. Nothing material occurred— The season is more than dull—and the present organization of my family is not calculated to make my journal an easy occupation. I am only sensible how old I grow and how little its realities equal its anticipations— Morning visitors as usual— Mr [*Benjamin*] O[*gle*] Tayloe appears to be much enamoured of my beautiful Cousin— I wish it may be a match—

·[CHAPTER SEVEN]·

"I Am a Very Good Diplomate"

Washington, D.C., 1821–1824

Continuing on directly from her previous diary, Louisa and John Quincy remained in Washington, D.C., through the winter of 1821. It was an eventful time—James Monroe's second inauguration took place in March, and Missouri once again became a source of controversy in Congress. The situation between son George and Fanny Johnson came to a head as George narrowly avoided being dragged into a duel with another of Fanny's suitors, Robert Nicols Martin. And the Adamses finally completed renovating the F Street house and began to entertain there regularly.

At some point, Louisa's journal letters ceased to be directed to her father-in-law and began to go to her brother, Thomas Baker Johnson, who was living in New Orleans at the time. No corresponding letters have been located to confirm when this change took place, but certainly by January 1821 she was directing her letters to Thomas.

7 January 1821

Went to the Capitol and heard Mr. Macklavain a very promising young man who is extremely popular here. I do not think him to compare with either Mr. [*Edward*] Everett or Mr. [*Sylvester*] Larned though he is far superior to the common run of Preachers in this place and according to our standard would shine out as a star of the first magnitude— (He is handsome a necessary qualification in a young preacher now a day's) and naturally eloquent and if not spoilt has all the requisites to form a good preacher. Read part of the first Vol. of Charles the fifth which is admirably written. I find the lazy lounging system does not agree with my nerves. As I came out of Church Mrs. Bloomfield stopped me to apologize for her husband having written to say she accepted of an invitation to dine with me which she had never received. This placed her in a very awkward situation and made me very uncomfortable— The poor old man behaves just like a fool, and she earns her thirty thousand dollars most dearly— This was altogether a very disagreeable circumstance as it was a tacit reproach for my not having invited her. I adopted the plan of not inviting ladies to dinner because my rooms were small and it was impossible to entertain all the Ladies who came to Washington without an expence which would be utterly insupportable. All the Secretaries' Ladies thought proper to follow this example as they found it convenient and the President's family have this Winter condescended to adopt my practice surely forgetting the difference between a Salary of 25000 and six thousand dollars a year.

All the odium of this business falls upon me but as I have long known that nature seems to have marked me out to excite no feelings but hatred I am as indifferent to this as I endeavour to be to most other things— Since God in his Wisdom took my daughtre on whom I madly doated I have never found a thing which could fill the void made in my heart and tho' I fondly love my Sons I have always considered them more as subjects born to gratify my pride or ambition than as beings calculated in any shape to meet my feelings of affection or sympathy— Oh how ardently and humbly I thank my God for having removed this stumbling block so early from my path. Had any thing happened to her madness or suicide must have been the result to me.

8 January 1821

Rose with a head ache and suffered so much with cold I confined myself to my chamber— Indeed my gloom seems to infect my family so much the moment I appear all seem to be silenced and the laugh and smile which have echoed through the house are suddenly stopped— This has determined me to remain as much as possible in my own chamber as long as my Sons remain here that they may enjoy themselves without controul— How often I have wondered at my Mother when she practiced the same thing and I dare say they wonder at me. But so it is I never could bear the idea of laying a restraint on any one and had rather punish myself than them— I feel that I have strange exaggerated ideas on most subjects which must be utterly incomprehensible but which it is as utterly impossible for me to eradicate—

9 January 1821

My head was so much worse to day that I concluded to remain in my chamber to day in the hope that I might be enabled to receive my company in the Evening. I dressed myself and went into the room but was entirely incapable of remaining and retired to bed without notice— The company was received and the young Ladies set them to dancing without even appearing to know that any thing was the matter with me and without condescending to make any enquiry concerning me altho' I lay in the next chamber. The noise the sense of neglect and unkindness which this conduct indicated proved too much for me and I believe I was thrown into a state of delirium almost amounting to madness and Mr Adams found me in this state when the company retired. For several days I continued very ill. By some unaccountable fatality my whole family had been determined not to observe my indisposition and the same idea of proving a restraint on their pleasures had kept me silent until suffering real true and unaffected illness forced itself upon their attention and obliged them to see and feel my situation. That my head ache was aggravated by the perpetual succession of noises— Mary took her lesson of Music at ten o clock accompanied by her Master on the violin. Charles then began his which lasted an hour and a half in the same manner after which the dancing master came and they danced three hours. George and Charles then played on the flute and violin for about an hour and then followed the party. I will leave you to judge how this would agree with such headaches as you have seen our mother suffer and to decide if it should have been set down to ill temper. My feelings were deeply deeply wounded for which I am told I am very whimsical and fanciful—

10 January 1821

Continued very ill all day. This was the most dreadful day I ever passed in my life. I must have been raving mad—

11 January 1821

Still confined to my bed entirely exhausted but in a state of extreme agitation. A large party at dinner consisting of Gentlemen which was very gay— The attentions of this day were excessive but extremes seldom produce a good effect— God forgive me I tried to be happy but I fear it was but hollow. The boys came into my room they were all too gay. The evening passed off very well— I see many things I dont like.

12 January 1821

The young ladies were invited to dine at Miss Thompson's and as usual there was considerable discussion about it. Mary seemed to decline it but having refused to dine there once before—I told her she had better go, but she said she was sure Mr. [*Robert*] Martin was to *be* there and she would feel very awkward as a third person. It has been reported for some time that Martin is engaged to Fanny Johnson against the wishes of her friends and he has followed her to Washington and behaves in such a manner as to make every one believe that there must be something between them— She has received him here and granted him many private interviews and in public she treats him with contempt and meets him at the house of Col Thompson who is a relation of his. Under these circumstances I told Mary she might do as She pleased as I would not interfere. While the matter was in debate a note came from Miss Thompson stating that if Miss Hellen did not come to dinner she hoped that she would come in the evening with the young gentlemen. This decided the business and upon such an invitation I would not permit to go at all. Fanny therefore went by herself to dine; and George and John went in the evening. When they returned they all said they had had a delightful party and appeared in high good humour. I was able to dine down stairs for the first time, but excessively weak and low. Mrs. Frye came to see me.

13 January 1821

I came down as usual tho' still very poorly and so reduced you could scarcely believe it— The boys went out to dine with Mr. Cook. Johnson Hellen was too unwell— I observed all day that Fanny was very dull and thought she was sick but she said that she was very well— She ate nothing at dinner and only appeared to rouze herself after the Boys returned who immediately proposed to play whist with her to which she agreed. Mr A read the news papers I was reading a novel and Johnson and Mary Hellen were sitting and looking on the game. A servant came into the room with a note saying that the Gentleman desired to see George directly— George started up after reading it and ran out of the room without speaking accompanied by Johnson Hellen who desired Mary to play Georges hand and in a few minutes Johnson returned saying the note was from Mr. Martin and that George had gone to meet him at Strothers Hotel— Knowing that G— had no acquaintance with him Mr. A— and myself were excessively uneasy but mutually endeavoured to conceal our anxiety.

In about twenty minutes G— returned very much agitated and apparently angry and I Rose as soon as I could without appearing particular and bade them good night. But hearing George going out to smoke his segar I called him as softly as I could to enquire the meaning of this note and message which I soon discovered to be a sort of challenge. When he went into the room at Strothers he found Mr Martin there with a Horsewhip on the Table who immediately Said to George that Miss Johnson having informed him that G— told her Mr. [*Harrison Gray*] Otis had stated to him that Mr M. had told Mr O. he was engaged to Miss Johnson he had called on him for an apology or satisfaction— George immediately, unarmed not even having a cane with him told him as to apology he would make none but he would declare that he had said to Miss Johnson that Mr. Otis asked him if she was engaged and that he had answered no and that he had asked her if she would permit him to deny this engagement hereafter as the question was frequently put to him, and that he was ready to declare this *before* Miss Johnson— On this Mr. M. pretended he was going out of Town and should probably not see Miss Johnson *again;* but pretended to be satisfied.

George returned home much agitated and distressed at the idea of appearing to have basely misrepresented a conversation with Mr. Otis; which this man informed him he had called on Mr Otis to ascertain— His situation was dreadful and I determined to inform his father directly of the whole circumstance, which I accordingly did; and he called George into his office that he might state to him all the particulars in a cool dispassionate manner— While Mr. A. was with George, Ellen my Cook came running to my chamber to say that Mary was very ill; and begging I would go to her directly which I did, and found her in deep fainting fits; which continued attended with occasional delirium about three hours— The distress of the family was at its height, and I really was almost distracted— Sleep under such circumstances was out of the question; and the night was passed in forming plans for the settlement of the affair— George's character was at stake, and *any* interference on the part of his father was totally out of the question. Mr. A— at last suggested that a simple statement of the words used by George should be drawn up, and Miss Johnson requested to assert, whether G had said *those words,* and *if not,* to write the words he had used; which we mutually thought the most advisable course to pursue—

14 January 1821

Rose early to learn how Mary was? She had had a bad night but was much better— I accordingly presented the paper to Miss Johnson; who had an interview with George; and "declared she had never said what Mr M. affirmed." After cautiously avoiding every thing like reproach or censure; and endeavouring to command my feelings with regard to her conduct— she kept us until one o clock without deciding what to do; and at last declined signing the paper, requesting Mr M. might be immediately sent for, as she would meet him and George to-gether. A Note was written and sent; but before it was delivered Mr M. came and she went down to him— declining the offer of George to accompany her— He remained here an hour and no offer was made to see G— when Mr A— came in, and not knowing that she had wished to see him forbid Mr. M. The House. Thus the matter rested for that day; the quarrel having become more violent instead of being decided. The day of course was passed in a manner altogether insupportable— John and Johnson exciting George to fight by every possible taunting speech and all so irritable; what with the coquetish airs of the young Lady who was alternately playing upon them all; and I believe very willing to foment the discord: my house was pretty much like a Bedlam broke loose—

15 January 1821

Matters still remaining much as they were; I again presented the paper to Fanny which she answered, and by this means one of the great difficulties was settled— Mr Otis called on Mr A— and left word that he was very desirous of seeing him. Mr. A— and George therefore went down to the Senate.— But

Mr Otis was so much engaged in the Debate, that he told Mr A. he would call on him at the Office; George took the opportunity of apologizing to Mr O— for the misrepresentation upon which Mr O. answered it was quite unnecessary as he had already told Mr Martin; that he knew G. too well to believe it.— At four he called on Mr. A— stated he was commissioned by Mr. M. to say, he thought himself very ill used in being so rudely dismissed from the house; and that he requested Mr A— to *readmit* him without any apology or expression of regret, at what had passed: insisting on it that the note he had written was a very polite one.— This gave Mr. A— occasion to state every circumstance to Mr. O. as it had occurred; which much surprized that Gentleman as it did not at all tally with the story he had heard. He therefore informed Mr A. that he would have nothing more to do with the business; since he found the young man had conducted himself so improperly— This decides the affair and I trust we shall hear nothing more concerning it— Mr M. is to leave town with William Otis tomorrow. As to Johnson Hellen there is another disappointment to my *expectations,* "a blank my Lord" he ever tells his love to all the world, and is a public joke! Mrs. Smith spent the day with me—

---

23 January 1821

Returned a number of visits— In the Eveng had a very large party and opened my new Room— It opens from the drawing room which you are acquainted with, and is twenty eight by 29 feet in size— It was found very convenient and tho' barely half finished answered the purpose amazingly well. The addition to my house contains two of these halls two back rooms and six chambers with kitchen &c. It is so planned as to make a separate house whenever we are inclined to Rent it— The company were so much amused they did not leave us till passed Eleven o clock— Mrs. Com Stewart [*Delia Tudor Stewart, wife of Charles*] was the prodigy of the night— She is a very fine and very excentric woman: in other words *too* accomplished for the Country in which she lives; a very serious *calamity* tho' not much understood—

24 January 1821

This was a Russian day the cold was intense— In the Evening we went to the Drawing Room which was very thin; and as usual in that house there was fire to Cook at but not to feel: and we had the delight of *waiting* half an hour for our Carriage. Fanny Johnson went off this morning and left our young men in the depths of the belle passion, but relieved me by her departure of a load of care and anxiety— She is a beautiful creature: but the most accomplished Coquette I ever saw—

29 January 1821

Went to the House of R. to hear Mr. Clay who made a very fine speech, but was said to be very inferior to his former reputation. I was disappointed in him—I confess!— The style of oratory of the present day does not please me— It is too much studied; too theatrical, and of course too cold— His feeling and sentiment I understand forms the great charm of his eloquence— But to hear a champion of defiance as he has hitherto been to the Administration; and the general Government, a man of such loose morals and lax habits; talk in high strains as a conciliating spirit; was a novelty calculated to astonish but not to excite confidence either in the man or his motives— His arguments were weak and his speech generally declamatory. John Randolph rose after him and spoke with all the fervour and real eloquence which he most certainly possesses: what he said as usual was calculated to set Congress in a flame but fortunately the great *State* knows its interest too well to suffer their passions any longer to decieve them— In the Eveng. you will be astonished to find that I went to a party at *Dame* Brown's; and I have the pleasure to assure you that the ettiquet question will either die or be revived on the occasion. At any rate we are now on visiting terms— and I expect her tomorrow Eveng. The party was large and admirably conducted— Mrs. B receives her company remarkably well and has that happy tact I will not say *esprit,* which enables her to meet her friends with something pleasant and easy, and enough of *bon ton* to feel at home every where.— My appearance excited much surprize; and you would have thought some great political event was likely to be the result of this insignificant visit—

For the first time, Charles Francis accompanied his brother John to Massachu-setts to prepare for his entrance examinations to Harvard in February 1821. He was accepted and began his college career the next fall. He would graduate in 1825.

George remained in Washington, D.C., to study law, not with William Wirt, as Louisa suggests below, but with John Quincy.

4 February 1821

We were alarmed by a cry of fire in the night and for some minutes sup-posed it to be the Department of State which was burning— Mr. A— with the boys and three Servants rushed out, and fortunately found that it was a large Tavern opposite to that building; and being no wind that the Depart-ment was in no danger— I was so ill as to be unable to go to Church and George was likewise very sick all day. I attempted to sit at dinner but was obliged to leave the table—

5 February 1821

Johnson Hellen is this day 21 and comes into the possession of his property which he does not appear to be very willing to manage— The worst trait of his character that I perceive, is a tendency to the most penicious indolence which he makes little or no effort to conquer. In the Eveng Johnson, John, and Charles, went to the Circus and Mr A, myself Mary and George played Bragg until they returned—

6 February 1821

Went to return several visits and in the Eveng had a party of two hun-dred persons. It was by far the most brilliant party we have had this win-ter and appeared to give general satisfaction— Mrs. Eustis told me every body was delighted with my entertainments but that they think it very singular that Mr A— can able do so much while the President with his large Salary can do so little? This staggers me a little and I believe I will have no more dancing this Winter and I have an excellent excuse now my boys are going— This was to celebrate Johnson's birth day and I spread the report far and wide.

7 February 1821

My Boys were allowed a reprieve and passed the day with me. George and his father went to the Drawing Room in the Eveng which was unusually crowded— There were a great many Strangers in consequence of the sitting of the Supreme Court and all the Judges were there except Judge Washington who is very ill and will probably not be here during the Winter. We played Pope Joan a very stupid game.—

8 February 1821

The Boys left us this morning— Poor Charles went off with a good deal of fortitude considering it was his first trial. I tremble for the consequences to him of so sudden a change and a too early independence— In consequence of Georges foolish entanglement his father has decided that he shall come here and Study Law with Mr. Wirt. I think this an excellent plan unless by removing from Scylla he should be flung on Charybdis— For there are many objections in my eyes to a connection with Mary and if they are thrown together it is natural to suppose that such an approximation at their time of life may produce such results— She may yet make a very fine showy woman but she will have a great deal to learn and it is nearly impossible to correct a number of vulgar habits which she has acquired— I do not wish by any means to refine her too much for the world in which she is to live: I wish to purify a little the natural tendency to grossness which she ever displays and which if suffered to grow will make her what I most thoroughly despise a woman of loose conversation of course of impure mind— Delicacy through every stage of life is the greatest charm a Woman can possess and where the mind is early vitiated I have very little faith in the chastity of the person—

We had a large party to dine consisting of Mr Crawford, Mr Clay, Gov Tichenor, Judge Smith, Col Trimble, Mr Sergeant, Mr. Silsbee, Mr. Mallory, Mr. Crowell, Mr. Reid, Mr Anderson, Mr D. P. Cook, Mr. Brent, Mr. Brown, of Louisianna, Mr. Archer, with us four made up the party. Mr. Clay was in one of his affectedly pleasant humours in which he snarls at every one and is perpetually touching on subjects which are most likely to produce disagreeable conversation or restless uneasiness betraying a fear of something painful to the feelings, from the habits required by leading a party he is always domineering and arrogant and usurps by his dictatorial manner the greater proportion of the discourse which he generally contrives to make offensive to some one or other— Altogether he is the oddest compound of vulgarity and courtesy I have ever met with and is another strong evidence of my assertion that man has nothing to boast of but his littleness when he can be governed [*in*] spite of his better reason by such a compound as this! A man made up of shreds and patches formed ~~in a Brothel~~ and polished in a gaming house and whose chief talent consists in working on the weaker or baser passion's of mankind. Nature seems to have intended him for something better but circumstance and opportunity with the general corruption of bad society have made him what he is. Among the reports of the day it is whispered that Congress having passed a Bill recently to lower the price of public Lands our patriotic Legislators are very busy in purchasing it in large quantities for the good of that public— Do you not admire such disinterested proceedings?— Mr. Brown is off to Louisianna in a Month his Lady remains here—

9 February 1821

Paid several visits in the morning and finding the House insupportably dull went to the Circus at which I laughed most heartily the performances being altogether absurd and as usual exaggerated. They however appear to fascinate our very wise Members of Congress who are evidently as much delighted with the wit of the Clown who by the by is the worst and most stupid I ever saw as any boy of six years old and almost shout with joy at his very common somersets; The music was too ridiculous and I assure you one of the greatest taxes I have to pay is that of concealing that I am a travelled Lady.

12 February 1821

This day I am 46— The Report on the [*admission of*] Missouri was lost in the house and occasioned a most turbulent debate. There is no means left untried by Mr. Clay and you would suppose his very existence depended on it. Cajolery and the most undignified appeals to the passions of his opponents with his natural overbearing and insolent personalities produce scenes unsuitable to a legislative body and ought to degrade us in our own eyes— The house of Representatives of such a Nation should not be a Bear Garden. His provocation has been greater [*than*] the common for he has been defeated in a project better than usually conceived by the melancholy Jaques John Randolph who remained uncommonly still and sober until his great Rival entered on the Scene of action. This brought him out in all his strength and though his hour is universally acknowledged to be he once more atchieved a victory which according to account restored him even from the arms of death and the famous compromise which was to have lulled Missouri to repose was once more defeated and I much fear will produce another debate as warm and perhaps as useless except in exciting unpleasant feelings as those which have preceded— We however begin better to understand the terrific threats so awfully pronounced against its fatal consequences and go on with our gaieties as if nothing was the matter— Conciliation is the order of the day and the great Western Hero has played his part to admiration having alternately begged and bullied until the last and still labouring in the good cause with all the sincerity of his nature— Went to a Ball at the Barracks or rather to Col [*Archibald*] Henderson who has just come into the Command [*of the Marine Corps*] and in possession of the House formerly occupied by Col [*Franklin*] Wharton. The party was brilliant and animated and he appeared to be delighted with the compliment paid by the attendance of so many of the fashionables of the City. We left the Ball at eleven.

13 *February 1821*

Returned some morning visits. I fear I am becoming too popular as I am honoured with visits from all *quarters*— This is one of the conveniences of public life but as I allow but few persons to be intimate with me it is of very little consequence— I have perceived that all familiarity is dangerous therefore I form *friendships* a thing by the by which appears to be incompatible with my nature which assimilating itself to yours is I believe a little inclined to Misanthropy— The gloss which a mere common indifferent intercourse throws over society does not oblige one to penetrate farther than we please into realities and this is all that I desire and will if possible maintain against my gossipping neighbours— In the Eveng. according to my plan I renounced regular dancing in consequence of which I expected a very small party but my new Room was crowded to overflowing and we had a great deal of good music. They however ended with a dance which kept us until eleven o clock. We were agreeably surprized by the arrival of Mr now Baron and Madame de Neuville who took possession of their old Mansion attended by the really joyful greetings of many friends. Ettiquette chained me to my house but Catherine and Mary immediately left cards which was thought more discreet than to call in person. I sent invitations. Mr de Neuville came to see me immediately. He is looking remarkably well. It is supposed they will stay but a short time but negotiation is a treacherous thing and who knows how it may be. He goes Ambassador to the Brezils— Poor fellow I wish him joy of his Bargain. They declined coming in the Eveng.

James Monroe's unopposed reelection in 1820 and his inauguration on 5 March 1821 were a celebration of American unity. Less united was the U.S. Congress. While party affiliations had (temporarily) ceased to have much meaning, regional loyalties were becoming increasingly important, with sharp divisions among northerners, southerners, and westerners. Furthermore, preparations had already begun for the presidential election of 1824. Supporters of the various candidates—at this point in time John Quincy, John C. Calhoun, Henry Clay, and William H. Crawford—created another set of factions, only partially following regional lines, that further served to undermine consensus in Congress.

The "Florida Treaty" mentioned on 3 March, below, was another name for the Adams-Onís, or Transcontinental, Treaty. While the treaty had been approved by the Senate two years earlier, the exchange of ratifications had taken place just a few weeks before.

2 March 1821

We had a party at dinner intended to be a large one but as Congress is about closing the Session we were disappointed of several Members who could not leave the house— They grow more and more turbulent and a universal disgust is expressed at their Conduct. It is difficult to know the cause of all this but it is chiefly owing to there being no decided party and still more to there being no man of sufficient nerve to take the command of these very raw troops. The consequence is that there is no combination as to any particular measures and our Legislators are guided only by the workings of their own individual passions or of those out of the house who by their cabals and intrigues to gratify their own personal ambition take pains to keep up the ferment against the best interests of the Country— The day is altogether past in which self devotion or rather real patriotism actuated the men who ruled this Nation and I am sorry to say that the encreasing extent of our territory appears to extend the patronage of certain Departments until we shall be governed altogether by the creatures appointed to suit the views of the existing head of it. So strange a state of things has not yet existed and it is very difficult to foresee how it will terminate. The factions of Crawford and [DeWitt] Clinton are very busy— The Executive is unpopular in Congress and the great pleasure of this honourable body appears to be as they cannot succeed for the different characters they support to do as much injury as possible to those who are likely to defeat them—

3 March 1821

Went into George Town and called at Mrs. Frye's who I found very well and her infant grow's finely— In the Eveng went to the House of Representatives to see the closing of the Session. I had the pleasure of hearing one or two speeches which betrayed strong indications of *spirit* perhaps not altogether properly applied but evincing much of that sleepy energy which is so peculiarly calculated to attract attention and to convince us of its happy effect if not on the hearers at least on those who have so joyously imbibed it— One of these disordered Gentlemen insisted upon being allowed to prove that he was in order but as the hour was altogether unsuitable it being then eleven o'clock the house manifested such signs of impatience as to oblige the Speaker to request him to take his Seat—which he did with some reluctance and fortunately was shortly after altogether incapacitated to discharge his great duties towards his Constituents— The house adjourned at about half past twelve more quietly than was expected and though it is universally acknowledged that they have done nothing but mischief they did not do all that was anticipated. Among the wonders of this wondrous Session I must inform you that Mr. Lowndes who is Chairman of the Committee on foreign relations has been confined to his chamber [a] great part of the time in consequence of which John Randolph became Chairman; of course when the Florida Treaty was presented to the house Mr Adams anticipated much trouble when to his utter astonishment he recieved [a] message from Mr: R informing him that he would do every thing he could to promote its success— And the business is happily terminated—

4 March 1821

It being Sunday in consequence of an opinion given by Chief Justice Marshall that Sunday was a day of rest the Inauguration was postponed until tomorrow; I went and heard a miserable Rhapsodist from whom I much fear I derived very little additional devotion. And these gentlemen only convinc alas that my hour is not come—to be born anew—as I am alas much too much alive to the ridiculous let me see it in what form I will— I flatter myself I shall have your good wishes to hasten the happy period which is to promote a durable and happy change in my nature— The Eveng quietly at home—

5 March 1821

If yesterday was not a day of labour I can certify that this fully deserves the name. We left our house at Eleven and took up Madame de Neuville who accompanied me to the Hall. She being the only Lady of the Corps diplomatique I offered to accompany her and introduce her to the Seats appropriated to the Ladies of the Heads of Department. It was fortunate we went so early as the crowd was immense and the President was near losing his Coat and his Hat on his way to the Chair— He arrived safe and sound however though looking frightened to death and considerably agitated—and went through the ceremony with a great deal of dignity— From this we went to the Drawing Room where I took the opportunity of offering my congratulations which were graciously accepted— In the Eveng at Mrs. Monroe's request I went to the Ball expressly to meet her— She looked more beautiful than I ever saw her and I thought acquitted herself remarkably well as far as I am a judge and I only wish should it be my fate to exhibit under the same circumstances that I may perform my part as well— To what is a poor unfortunate Woman exposed in such a situation to the envious observation malicious insinuation's and illnatured remarks of all who surround her who even without a motive excepting that of having something to say think they must censure to ensure their own consequence— It is a most awful trial and much, much more to be dreaded than to be desir'd.

The eye of the public is already on me and altho' I endeavour to give them as little opportunity of attacking me as possible and continue to be as simple in my habits as nature originally intended me to be yet I cannot escape and my very dear five hundred friends begin to think my manners too generally *courtly* the fashionable expression and that I am not choice enough in the selection of my company— Could I once ascertain what Republicanism is it would be possible to find some rules by which to regulate my future conduct but while the Nation itself appears to be wavering as to what the essence of this said Republicanism may really be it would be very difficult— Your description of our manners is correct and as it regards myself I feel the full force of your reasoning but you must recollect that since we saw you we have been thrown into more worldly and busy scenes than when you lived with us and that we are in every respect become different creatures—as for instance I am a very good diplomate— You may laugh but it is so— Egotism is the quintessence of journalizing so that I need make no apologies; and I am so silly as to believe that nothing is more agreeable to an affectionate correspondent than a full history of ourselves and all the little events of our lives— Unless in cases of business there would have been no use for Letters had they not been adopted as a medium of affectionate and friendly intercourse between separated friends—

10 March 1821

A great diplomatique dinner at the Baron de Neuvilles I was the only Lady present excepting Madame— The dinner was quite Ambassadorial and being seated between England and France I was so beset by fine things that my blushes bespoke my embarrassment and confusion for I really could not play them off— As the blushes of an old Woman are never very interesting I presume you will agree with me in opinion that I looked consciously silly and felt ridiculous— The Baron drank the health of the old President Adams and requested me to join him which I did very cordially. Mr. Canning asked to be of the party and immediately drank to the last and future President Adams which made such an alteration in the toast I did not know how to behave and felt like a fool— In the Eveng after the circle was enlarged by the usual party I conversed a long time with the lord and Lady of the Mansion who wished to make enquiries concerning the ettiquettes of the different Courts at which I had resided and the account I gave of the Splendour of the Ambassadors alarmed them very much as they appear to admire the grade without wishing to make the show generally expected from Ambassadors— Mary danced until very late and it is now almost impossible to get her from a party— This is very unpleasant to Mr: A— and myself who are always expected to make the first move—

11 March 1821

Went to St Johns Church where I heard a Mr. Robinson. There was nothing remarkable about him— The Service was very long and the most striking thing I observed was the very affected devotion of [*British diplomat*] Mr [*Gibbs Crawford*] Antrobus who appeared to think that the fervour with which he made the responses was to wash away all the guilt of the preceeding week— I could scarcely help smiling at his answers in the Litany to which he must have had some difficulty with his conscience tho' according to all account he needs much to pray to be delivered from the "sinful lusts of the flesh and all the deceits of the world the flesh and the devil"— I much fear that the spirit in which he prayed was tantamount to the general run of his character— This Gentleman is however so much the rage with some of our young Ladies that they even sacrifice reputation without regret to gratify his foolish vanity— He has thought it necessary I am told to intimate that he did not propose to marry any Lady in this Country as there was but one family in it with whom he could condescend to connect himself. He leaves this Country in a few days I presume to return no more— The Minister is a moral man it is said I believe from what I see of him he is a very vain and weak man who is not much in danger of pring the Potowmac— Mr & Mrs. Smith took Tea with us.

12 *March 1821*

Received morning visits from Mr G[*eorge*] A[*lexander*] Otis and Mr. Todd who came to beg my influence in procuring a place the one for himself the other for a friend— This is a new honour that people do me and I really could dispense with it without suffering any inconvenience from its loss— Having a very bad cold I walked out to cure it but without success. Passed the Eveng at home. Mrs. Gouvernour had a daughter on Saturday last. A Son was much desired— I have applied to the President for a place for William Smith which he gave me a very formal promise the night of the Inauguration to do as soon as he possibly could meet with an opportunity—

Walked out the weather being uncommonly fine and met W. S Smith with whom we continued our promenade. Being unsuccessfull in the purchases I intended to make we soon returned home and in the Eveng remained alone— The applications for Commissioners on the Florida Treaty are so numerous that there are above a hundred for those three places; of course the rest in proportion—

After spending the remainder of the spring in Washington, D.C., Louisa left the city on 12 July with Mary Catherine Hellen to head north to Quincy. John Quincy remained behind to conduct business, so the next series of diary entries, also journal letters, is directed to him. Unfortunately, this also meant that the couple was separated on 26 July, their anniversary, as Louisa ruefully notes below. Once John Quincy too arrived in Massachusetts, Louisa began writing to her brother again. Mentions throughout of "my father" refer to her father-in-law, John Adams.

The "bitterly attacked" oration, as Louisa comments in the entry for 28 July, was one John Quincy gave in honor of Independence Day in Washington. In the speech, he championed anti-imperialism and argued that Americans need not go abroad "in search of monsters to destroy. She is the well-wisher to the freedom and independence of all." Contrary to Louisa's assessment, it was generally well received.

25 July 1821

We arrived at Providence and went to Madame Chapoutins under the protection of Mr: Whipple who very kindly sent his Servant to assist poor Joseph who was in a terrible fit of the ague as we landed and almost incapacitated for attending to his particular charge— He however made out to come to the house and ere he would go to bed he gave his pretty creturs a complete dressing and washing and put them into a comfortable Stable— We were all very sea sick— Mary and Elizabeth [*Coombs Adams, Louisa's niece*] both declare they will never go to sea again and I dare say poor Dash [*Adamses' pet dog*] who was not the least sufferer on the occasion would have joined in the cry had he the gift of Speech— I was threatend with much such a fever as I had eighteen Years ago on such a journey and was obliged to doctor myself pretty severely— The House at Chapoutins is worse than ever and so noisy we were almost distracted— Hitherto we have not lost a horse Shoe or a nail from the Carriage and all but the Packet Voyage has been delightful— The Country never looked more lovely and the weather was enchanting neither too hot nor too cold—

26 July 1821

Left Providence at eight oclock and took the wrong Road on which we rode about three miles before we discovered our mistake the Coachman having Received his directions from a man who did not know his Right hand from his left— No incident occurred after this worthy of notice until we reached Fullers where I stopped to dine when George to whom I had written from New York accompanied by John opened the door and marched in much to my astonishment as I had given up all hope of seeing them— They are in fine health and spirits— We went on to Dedham where I was obliged to stop being very weak and exhausted to pass the night— We amused ourselves with playing Bagatelle a game which I think would suit the heads of our belles in Washington provided it were possible to steady their heels. This day we once celebrated in a different way but alas old age has come and all attraction is flown forever.

27 July 1821

We arrived safely this morning and found Your Father more feeble and changed than I had anticipated but in tolerable spirits— Your Brother has the jaundice all others well. John went into Boston to fetch his brother Charles and in the evening Mr. Quincy came with a number of Ladies and Gentlemen Mr Lawrence and daughter Mr & two Miss Le Roy's several frenchmen with Josiah Quincy and his Sisters— They did not stay long and we ended the evening very merrily.

28 July 1821

Mrs. [*Eliza Susan Morton*] Quincy and her daughters called to see me. She is looking remarkably well the young Ladies as usual— Your poor Oration has been bitterly attacked and nothing so strongly marks its merit. Were it not excellent it would have passed unnoticed. John has shown me his conventicle poem some lines of which *I* think beautiful. George has likewise shown me two Class Songs one of which it seems produced a great effect among his Classmates. One of them is very good written with much feeling and calculated to produce the same in his auditors— I am glad you concluded to dine with the Baron more especially as things now are it may operate as a paliative to the bitter dose which he is condemned to swallow. Your father is much better and only looks to your arrival to be quite well. Mr. F[*rancis Calley*] Gray here.

29 July 1821

Went to meeting with ~~your~~ my father and heard Mr. Gannet. Mr. Shaw came out last Eveng— We dined alone and I did not go out in the Evening. After Tea Mr. & Mrs. & Miss Apthorpe with Capt Beales Mrs. T[*homas*] Greenleaf and her daughters [*Elizabeth and Mary Ann*] and Mr [*John*] & the Miss Marston's called— Rode with John to Squantum.

30 July 1821

Went to Boston with George. We dined at Mrs. [*Abigail Kent*] Welches and the two Boys left me immediately after dinner to go to Cambridge—

Mr [*Joseph*] & Mrs. [*Sarah Gray*] Hall came to see me at the Drs [*Thomas Welsh*]. He was gone to the Castle [*Island*]. I was exceedingly unwell and hastened home.— Mary remained at Quincy and I found cards from the two Mrs. Millers Mrs. B Smith and Mrs. Otis when I return'd. Not a word of news.

1 August 1821

Went out to ride with my father who takes great pleasure in showing me all the fine prospects— They are in fact beautiful and the Country improves so much in cultivation that every day adds to its embellishment. The natural scenery is lovely possessing all the charms that hills, Valleys Rocks Woods Water and Forrest can bestow— But there is a mellowness in the Scenery of older Countries which this appears to me to want and I do not know how to explain it unless it is owing to the artificial arrangement of the Parks and Gardens of Europe which ever and anon break into the rougher views of nature unadorned and operate like the fine passages in Byrons poetry to dazzle and astonish the imagination if not to satisfy the understanding—

Among Louisa's activities while visiting Quincy were venturing to Cambridge along the new Boston road, known as Western Avenue, and entertaining a troop of West Point cadets at the Adams Old House. The corps from West Point, two hundred cadets in all, came through on 14 August to pay homage to John Adams during a broader tour of New England. They stayed for breakfast and a brief ceremony at which John spoke and then shook hands with each.

9 August 1821

Went to Cambridge accompanied by my father and paid John a visit at his Room. My father was much pleased with the new Avenue which if it does not say much for the taste of the people of Boston speaks loudly for their industry— It is really a stupendous work and makes a handsome Entrance into Boston— We left the old Gentleman at John's room and Mary and myself went to look at Charles's chamber which we found neat and comfortable. We then went to Town to dine at Mr [*James Hiller*] Fosters and returned to Tea at Quincy. In Town I called at the Sheriffs and settled my business with him— John entertained us quite handsomely with Cake and lemonade and we gave ham and Brandy and water to the old Gentleman.

10 August 1821

The day passed quietly enough. Last Eveng One of the Cadets came out to announce the visit of Major [*William J.*] Worth and the Corps and came from thence to Mr. Fosters where we were with the message. Tuesday Morning is appointed and orders were given to day for a breakfast to be prepared— The Corps itself amounts to 240 and all the Quincy people of any note are invited— In the Eveng. walked out with the Judge [*Thomas Boylston Adams*]. Mr Marston came to hear all the news concerning the proposed fête. John [*Quincy Adams*] Boyd [*Louisa's nephew*] left us to return to the Ship.

11 August 1821

Was quite ill all day and unable to leave my Room. Mr Shaw came out and brought me Miss [*Frances*] Wrights Book. It is light reading full of flummery and old stories—but it pleases universally—

12 August 1821

Did not go to meeting being too unwell— Mr [*Nathaniel Langdon*] Frothingham dined with us and in the Eveng. we had Mr. and the Miss Marstons Mr Quincy and Son Mr Miller Capt and Mr. Beale. George and Josiah Quincy went to visit Miss Whitney— Mr Shaw went to Town.

13 August 1821

Mr. Shaw returned from Town in my Green Carriage with Mrs. [*Elizabeth Smith*] Foster and her Son. The day has been devoted to preparations and every thing is ready for the Banquet. The old Gentleman say's little but this noise and bustle affects him very much. I keep myself quite cool and have nothing whatever to do with it—

14 August 1821

We were all up at six and the Tables were spread with refreshments— Three Tables were spread in the Paddock between the Stables and the House with Hams Tongues Beef Cheese, bread, Crackers, Coffee Chocolate, Lemonade, Punch, and Wine— In the long Room there were Tables for the Officers and company— An Awning was spread over the heads of the Cadets and the multitude were scattered in every direction forming the most picturesque view you can imagine—

The Corps marched up very handsomely and formed in lines within the Yard— When my father had recieved them with the usual compliments the Staff mounted on the Piazza and silence was ordered when he addressed them in a very good speech which he had written the day previous. He spoke in a manner which astonished and gratified all who heard— He was considerably agitated at the commencement but his voice became stronger every moment and he was distinctly heard by the greater part of the company— The exertion was too great for him to make and I confess I was under the greatest apprehension lest he should be overcome by the effort— After it was over I enjoyed myself very much and was enchanted by the band who made sweet and excellent music such as ears innured to melody could enjoy and admire. The breakfast seemed to be welcomed with glee by our young visitants round whose tables I strolled with my Son's to seek out my acquaintance two of whom I made a point of speaking to one a Son of Mr. Wirt the other of W[*illiam*] Lee and I was afterwards introduced to Major Worth and all the Officers. There are many fine young men among them and they all do honor to the Institution— It would indeed be a disgrace to our Congress to destroy a school so every way calculated to do honour to the Nation and to form Generals who may be enabled by real skill and Science to protect it in a case of need; and to shew the World that in peace we can remain quiet but that a War will call for the Lions of West Point to convince them that we fear nothing and can maintain our Rights whenever we find them invaded or insulted.

They paired off to take leave of the Reverend Page and passed him in military procession then formed in the field opposite the house and went through their different evolutions with considerable elegance and dextirity— The discipline is severe and the Major appears to have entire command of his men as well as their affections— The greetings and compliments of the company embarrassed me so much it was with difficulty I could restrain that sentiment of disgust which naturally arises in the mind of a well educated being accustomed to good society. Coldness of course must have been attributed to me and well I meerit the imputation— At a little after twelve they marched off to Milton to dine with Mr Barney Smith. Our Company all retired in the space of half an hour and the day was left on our hands a blank or rather worse for we felt a burthen to each other. Of beauty we could not boast. Quincy has never been so deficient in that Article since I have known it and of our *fashion* you in your day have been able to judge when you honoured this retreat with your presence. At Milton to which the Judge went there was a great concourse of people. The Table was sumptuously spread and there was some good singing by two of the Cadets. We were all very tired except the Old Gentleman who seemed to gain strength by the exertion— John & Charles came out and returned in the Eveng.

15 *August 1821*

The day was very warm and oppressive but I agreed to accompany my father to Mrs. Quincy's to see the two old Ladies above eighty who graced our yesterdays party— In the afternoon while we were preparing for our visit Mr Marston brought out four young Naval Officers— I left my room to pay my respects to them when I was informed by George that the Judge had been overset in the Chaise with his two Children and that he was seriously injured— When I went into the parlour I found Mrs. Adams sitting there perfectly unconscious of the accident and I really did not know what course to pursue when her little boy came and told the whole circumstance. I followed her out to send the Carriage and George to the Judge when he walked in the blood streaming from his head and looking the most piteous object I ever beheld. His head was dreadfully bruised and his breast hurt— The Children fortunately escaped. Our visit was of course postponed to a future opportunity. Went to ride with the old Gentleman The Girls at a party at Miss Marston's accompanied by Elizabeth Foster who remained here since Tuesday. Mr. Alden came to see George.

16 August 1821

The Judge very ill in consequence of his bruises almost unable to move. Mr. Blake a Classmate of Georges came and was invited to pass the day— Mr M[athew] Carey likewise who sat the whole morning with my father. At dinner we had a very unpleasant Scene between the two old Gentlemen and I wished myself at home most heartily more especially as Mr. C— thought proper to appeal to me and place me in a very awkward if not in a very ludicrous situation— My father made rather a forcible attack upon his book [entitled The New Olive Branch] which the energy of his manner rendered extremely pointed— These are little invasions of the laws of good breeding which are very unpleasant to the bystanders and always dangerous to the Actors for though the inflamation excited subsides the Sting always remains in the wound— Mr. Quincy called to see the Judge in the Eveng and informed as much mischief had been done at Milton to Mr Smiths Garden he having foolishly treated the multitude with that quickener of the spirit Brandy or Rum.

Mr Carey threatened on taking leave to write *me* a letter on the subject of the foregoing fracas but as I told him I was no politician I wuld be no judge of the matter. It is curious that the *Olive Branch* should have caused the rupture— We rode out in the Eveng. Had much conversation with my father on family matters—

George has been very unwel this two or three days— We have been much pleased with him— When John is away he is a different character. John's perpetual flashes of *Johnson wit* produces a bad effect upon the formers temper and makes him irritable to sickness. Poor fellow he is I fear doomed to much of that suffering which you so well understand and permit me to say which is so much owing to our own disposition. Easily distressed he equaly magnifies his joys and sorrows until the real world in which he moves vanishes from his sight like the baseless fabrick of the vision's which continually beat his imagination where all is Poetry fiction and Love.

John Quincy returned to Massachusetts in time to attend his son George's commencement from Harvard. This annual event was an important social occasion for the whole Boston area and frequently drew large crowds. Members of the graduating class gave orations, and families celebrated their sons' accomplishments with lavish parties afterward. When John Quincy himself graduated, his aunt hosted a party in which they "din'd above a hundred People & treated with cake & wine above four hundred." The celebration for George was far more modest, but Louisa's pride in her eldest son still shines through.

John Quincy Adams Boyd, the son of Louisa's sister Harriet, and John Quincy's godson and namesake, mentioned frequently below, had arrived for a visit with the Adamses on 7 August. Boyd had joined the U.S. Navy in 1819 and been serving on the Columbus *in the Mediterranean. He remained in the navy as a midshipman until his dismissal in 1827.*

With John Quincy's arrival, Louisa once again began to direct her journal letters to Thomas Baker Johnson. And as before, "Mr. A—" refers to John Quincy.

25 August 1821

Went to Dedham with John to meet Mr. Adams. We amused ourselves with playing Bagatelle and at five o'clock the Stage drove up and I had the pleasure of seeing Mr. A. jump out of it. We returned to Quincy soon after and the old Gentleman had the pleasure of once more embracing a Son whom he perfectly adores. It is not wonderful for in him all his highest hopes have been fulfilled, and his pride and his affection have been equally gratified. I never saw Mr A. look better and he is in very good spirits— Mr. Shaw came out from Boston—

26 August 1821

Mr & Mrs. Boylston dined with us and Mr Francis who gave a remarkably good Sermon. The text was "sufficient to the day is the evil thereof" and the explanation of the text was excellent the style nervous and the Language elegant. In the Eveng it rained and I did not go. Part of the family however attended and as usual we had our circle although it was very small in consequence of the bad weather. Mr A. brought an order from the Secretary of the Navy to transfer John Boyd to Com [*Charles*] Stewarts Ship the Franklin which is going out on a three years cruise to the Pacific. He is a very fine Boy and I wish to keep him out of his fathers reach until he is old enough to be out of danger— He stands very high for his age among the Officers— Mr. de grand here—

27 August 1821

George went into Town to make preparations for Commencement (at which I fear we shall fare shabbily) with one of his friends— In the Eveng we rode out and the Stage drove up with John Boyd who had been to Town to inform Com Bainbridge of his new orders. Just as we returned He gave Mr Adams a note stating that there were no lodgings to be had in Boston and we know not what to do. Mr. Quincy brought Mr Skinner the Post Master of Baltimore and Mr. [*Pomeroy*] to see the old Gentleman and he informed me also that it was scarcely possible to find a lodging in Town. We must however venture in and take our chance— My Father has declined going and I am glad of it as I fear the exertion would be much too much for him—

28 August 1821

John Mary and Mrs [*Susanna Boylston Adams*] Clark went into Town in the Stage and we told the former to search for lodgings and to let us know if we could obtain them. At four oclock he came out to inform us that he had procured very good ones and we immediately set out to take possession of them. We arrived in Town at six and I went directly to visit Mrs. Brown who had arrived a few days since and Mrs. [*Marianne Caton*] Paterson of Baltimore. After our return to the House a Gentleman came in whom I did not know and announced himself as Mr. Shaler our late Consul at Tripoli or Algiers. He staid but a short time and Sheriff Hall came in and insisted on my going to sup with his Wife who resids two doors from me— We had quite a pleasant time and returned home at half past ten o'clock—

29 August 1821

Rose early to prepare for Cambridge after a bad night occasioned I believe by the extreme anxiety I suffered for my boys. We left Town at eight o'clock and arrived in Cambridge about nine o'clock and went to Johns Room. From thence we repaired to the meeting house. The Performances were generally good but the anxiety which I could not subdue absolutely affected my nervous system to a great degree and for a time I was apprehensive I should faint. George spoke as I wished a Son of mine should speak and you who know what an ambitious thing your Sister is can readily understand he must have spoken well. His voice is fine his manner easy, at times even graceful, and his emphasis, modulation, and action perfectly natural— We had a small party at Georges chamber consisting chiefly of the friends of the family with the exception of Mr & Mrs Paterson Miss Campbell and Mr. [*Robert Goodloe*] Harper of Baltimore and Mr. & Mrs. R. Derby— They left us soon after dinner and I then received the visits of the Governor [*John Brooks*] Lieut Governor [*William Phillips Jr.*] and the Council with [*Harvard*] President [*John Thornton*] Kirkland &ce. We went to Tea [*at*] Dr. Kirklands and then returned to Town I feeling quite exhausted by the exertion and excitement of the day— Ball at Mrs. [*Sally Foster*] O[*ti*]s.

30 August 1821

Again went to Cambridge in company with Mr & Mrs. Boylston to hear the Declamation for the Boylston Prizes for which John was to speak. We arrived at nine o'clock and in consequence of the arrangements I was obliged to go directly to the meeting House and of course could not speak to John ere I went in. The performances began a few minutes after and I sat literally in an agony of anticipation until John's turn to speak when I was gratified beyond my best expectations by his performance which would have equalled his brothers in every respect had he spoken a little louder— For this defect he lost the prize though the Judges unanimously declared he was the best and most natural speaker of the whole. After this exhibition was terminated we had the Phi Beta Cappa Oration by Mr J C Gray which was good though tame and a Poem by Mr. [*William Cullen*] Bryant which was a little in the modern style of *prose gone mad* with some few flashes of genius or perhaps excentricity which frequently passes for the same thing. We returned to Town to dine in Town and in the Eveng went to a party at Mrs. J Gores. The company was small and select and they danced the whole Eveng. I omitted to say any thing about Mrs. Otis's Ball last Eveng which was much more brilliant and the company much larger— She as well as her husband are looking remarkably well. Old Mr. [*William*] Foster is dead and has made a Will which has produced a shism in the family. By some strange accident Mr. Otis's family have six thousand Dollars the Sons about five hundred Dollars a year a piece and Mr. Apthorpe who got the Will made has 30000 and Charlotte Foster 25000— This circumstance makes some talk and there are many shrugs and winks as to the cause of the partialety displayed in the distribution which was sufficiently novel to appear a little suspicious—

In mid-September the Adamses set off on a journey to visit John Adams's second cousin Ward Nicholas Boylston and his wife, Alicia, in Princeton, Massachusetts, some sixty miles west of Boston and north of Worcester. Born Ward Hallowell, Boylston took the name Ward Nicholas Boylston to honor his uncle Nicholas Boylston, who, in turn, left Ward his fortune. A loyalist, he left Massachusetts in the early 1770s and traveled through Asia before settling in London. His Massachusetts estate was confiscated in 1779, but he was able to recover it through a legal suit and returned to the United States in 1800. He moved in 1804 to Princeton after inheriting another substantial estate from an aunt and settled there permanently. John Quincy had visited Boylston at various times while in London in the 1790s, and made regular trips out to Princeton in the 1820s. When Boylston died in 1828, John Quincy became the executor of the estate.

10 September 1821

My father myself and George Left Quincy in the Carriage and Mr A— and John followed in a Chaise. We stopped at Mr. [*Henry*] Colemans according to promise but he had not arrived from Hingham where he had passed the night. We had the pleasure of seeing every part of his home which was recently built upon a very pretty plan combining every convenience with taste and elegance. We arrived at Framingham at about six o clock after a very Dusty and disagreeable ride— The Carriage being very uneasy I took Mr. A—'s seat in the Chaise notwithstanding I suffered considerably from the fatigue— We had comfortable lodgings at Framingham and most excellent Coffee and retired early to bed— The Country rather Dull after passing Brooklyn [*Brookline*] the roads very good being Turnpike all the way—

11 *September 1821*

Met at Breakfast at about seven. I observed Mr A reading a Letter and from his countenance was convinced there was bad news into which I immediately enquired and learnt that an Express had arrived from Quincy informing him that a fire had broken out on the Roof of the House and that much damage was done to the furniture in the endeavour to save it from total destruction. Mr. Quincy from whom the Letter was forwarded expressed a wish that my father might not be informed of the accident until after his journey was completed but Mr. A— thought it best to tell him immediately which he did and he bore it with the greatest composure stepping into the Carriage and ordering it to proceed to Mr. Boylstons— We arrived at Worcester to dinner and there met Mr. B— A number of Gentlemen flocked in to pay their respects to the old President and Mr A. and our dinner was considerably retarded. We were there informed that an Address was to be presented to the Secretary of State no one having expected my father would undertake the journey and that he was to be escorted to Princeton by a cavalcade of Horsemen all the most prominent Gentlemen of that Town— Mr. A— was excessively vexed and absolutely declined to make any answer to the Address whatever always disliking these publick marks of attention to which he seems to think no one is entitled but the Chief Magistrate of the Country and since I have known him he has ever taken infinitely more pains to avoid than to court them as most other persons in his situation would do— We arrived at Mr. Boylston's at about nine o'clock and we were all pretty well considering though much fatigued.

12 *September 1821*

My father rose quite well having derived the utmost benefit from his journey— We had a party at dinner consisting of Dr. Thayer Mr. & Mrs. Clarke and Mr. John Boylston— Mr. B. is so sociable and talkative it was impossible not to be amused— The Eveng rather dull— He gave us old Hock and some Madeira of 45 years old—

13 September 1821

Rode round the bottom of the famous Wachuset but did not attempt to mount it being too heavy and not sufficiently alert to walk up so steep a Mountain— Mr. B. has a very handsome property consisting of a number of Farms of considerable value and beauty— He has built a very handsome House here which is extremely ornamental and susceptible still of great improvement— He is very wealthy and does not appear to know what to do with his property— His eldest Son [*Nicholas*] is supposed to be of doubtful birth and excessively vicious and his youngest [*John*] a man of weak health and weaker intellect—

14 September 1821

The old Gentleman and Mr. A— Set out on their return home and John and Charles accompanied them as far as Lancaster to see some famous Cotton manufactories and returned to dinner with Mr. Boylston— Mrs. Boylston and I remained at home quietly all day— She told me many laughable anecdotes of some of my Boston friends—

15 September 1821

George went to Lancaster to fetch Mr Wood one of his Classmates who returned with him to stay until monday morning— The dinner was very pleasant to the young people as Mr. Boylston knows remarkably well how to adapt his conversation to his company and he encouraged the Collegians to argue which gave them the most exquisite delight it being the thing of all others that University Students are most proud of but which I confess is the most unpleasant and least amusing to me as they know little of sound reasoning and much of sophistry—

16 September 1821

Went to meeting and heard a tolerable discourse from Mr. Clarke— The meeting House is pretty and was well filled with neat looking people— We were to have had a great parade if the heads of the family had stayed. As it was we had only the best singers from two other parishes to do us honour. Dined alone the boys in remarkable high spirits and the house resounding with laughter all day. Mr. Boylston's little Grandson a lovely boy of about six years old came over. His Grandfather is very proud of him but he has been so unfortunate he appears to be afraid of indulging hope lest it should end in bitter disappointment— Mrs. B. is an amiable friendly woman to whom I feel most grateful for her constant kind attention during the whole of my visit— Mr. B. gave us some anecdotes of some of the members of the Suffolk bar not much to their credit and of some individuals who stand high with the publick almost too infamous to credit—

17 September 1821

It poured with rain so constantly, I was under the necessity of postponing my journey home until tomorrow— George is to drive me home in a Chaise and John and Charles will return in the Stage. Day dull rainy and stormy without and gloomy within in consequence of the approaching separation.

18 September 1821

George and I left Mr. Boylston's at about 9 o clock. The weather was beautiful and our ride was delightful— There is something in the perpetually varying Landscape of Mountainous and hilly Countrys that attunes the mind to cheerfulness. The mind is elevated to a higher strain of thought and raised to higher conceptions of power— In the smooth monotony of level plains simply enamalled with a gay coat of green there is a calm sweetness which lulls us into an equal state of easy serene constent inspiring nothing, desiring nothing—not exactly wearying but tame and sleepy— What a contrast in the sensations produced by such different views of natural Scenery— In the great and rugged paths of nature we are insensibly led to think of that great Omnipotent by whose power all was harmonized to order, and even the flinty barren Rock made an object of beauty, blending its arid points with the softer shades of Hills and dales to complete the vast and perfect whole— George's love of Poetry and his continued quotations from the lofty descriptions so ably coloured by Lord Byron's pen gave interest to each surrounding object and the neat little Towns with light frame Houses, and little Gardens, recalled our attention to the wants and whims of man, the greatest and the least of created beings— At five o clock in the Evening we arrived at Stow where I proposed to pass the night—

19 September 1821

Again started on our way to Boston where we arrived at about two o'clock. Mr. A— was gone to Salem with the Carriage and John had accompanied him— The lodgings which I had had where engaged and the accommodations altogether uncomfortable we therefore decided to go immediately to Quincy and arrived there to Tea— The family were all well and every thing was restored to its accustomed order excepting the Staircase which had been plaistered and was not quite dry— The old Gentleman received me with joy and I was almost inclined to feel proud at a reception which indicated so much affection and pleasure— A friend of Mrs. T. B. Adams and her Son drank Tea with us—

Louisa briefly resumed her journal letters upon her and John Quincy's return to Washington, D.C., in the winter of 1821. But ill health, including an unexpected pregnancy and yet another miscarriage, prevented her from participating in many of her regular activities, and she wrote no diary between 24 December 1821 and the beginning of December 1822. She spent the first half of 1822 in Washington but passed the entire summer in Philadelphia with her brother, Thomas, nursing him during his recovery from surgery for a "Paralisis of the Bowels." Louisa also sought treatment for her own health problems. She returned to Washington in mid-October.

As before, Louisa converted her diary into journal letters, which she once again sent to her father-in-law, John Adams.

1 December 1822

This day being in tolerable health I renew my journal with the intention to pursue it through the winter. This in consequence of the violence of party and the intriguing for the Presidency will be such an one as will furnish sufficient incident to make it interesting but as usual will be subject to the uncertainties and prevarications of the times in the perpetual fluctuations of public report and the tattle of every day rumour—

We attended at St John's Church to hear a funeral Sermon on the death of Mrs. [*Ann Elbertina Van Ness*] Middleton a young lovely and interesting woman whose sweetness of disposition had gained the affection of all her acquaintance. In a public eulogy of this kind however we require subjects of more importance and lives sufficiently active and enlarged to afford material and scope for panegyric and though her death was uncommon it was not of such a nature as to bear the touch of public record without the risk of infringing that delicacy which is the principal charm attached to her memory— Genl [*John Peter*] & Mrs. [*Marcia Burns*] Van Ness were present as well as Mr [*Arthur*] Middleton. This was no doubt a strong effort at fortitude but there is to me something so sacred in the grief of Parents and so near a connection as a husband in the first days of their loss it is a sort of sacrilege to display it to the cold unfeeling gaze of common spectators who feel a *minutes woe* then turn to gayer things and think of it no more— Was invited to spend the evening with Mrs. Smith but was not well enough to go— Alone all day reading [*Barry Edward*] O Meara [*author of* Napoleon in Exile].— The little mean tormenting tricks of Sir Hudson Lowe [*governor of St. Helena*] remind one of the fairy Grognon and all those malign imps which we read of in the Tales of the Genii. Napoleon seems to have felt at this sight as Jack the Giant killer did at the sight of his Ogre or more elegantly as Ulysses did at the Vast Brute that he calls Polyphemus. Oh the littleness of England. O tempora O Mores. It is a disgrace that no time can heal— Great intriguing and cabaling is going on for the Clerk's place in the House of Representatives— There are thirty candidates and North South and West in contact.—

2 December 1822

Com Rogers and his Lady and Sister called on me. I was however so unwell that I could not receve— Being however much better at about three o'clock I had a visit from a Member of Congress who I believe was Mr. Patterson. In consequence of my sickness last winter I am almost a stranger to many of them and find myself much at a loss to know them— We had a singular sort of conversation in which I gave my opinion very freely upon some of the measures of the last winter which I represented in as strong a light as I could as being cruel and unjust and bearing much too hard—that on undertaking to make such laws they ought to be mordified so as not to take the bread out of the mouths of hundreds of suffering families who are thus plunged into misery and want— It would be better far better to make character and conduct a requisite to appointment than to take needy and vicious individuals into office as pay for their powers at intrigue among their connections in different parts of the Union— This is indeed a base practice dishonourable to the Government who sanction it and disgraceful to the heads of Department who *offer* places to people with such views too palpably acknowledged and understood—

Mr Adams went to a party at Com Tingey's which I declined and did not return until near twelve o'clock— Mary got a Letter from Miss Meredith stating that Miss [*Elizabeth Borden*] Hopkinson and herself would come on in January and stay some time with us— No choice of Clerk in the House after six ballots. Many Members brought their Wives— Mexican Minister [*José Zozaya*] taken two of Strothers houses. Mr A— brought home a capital caricature. It is mexican and represents a Carriage full each of the Wheels being dragged by a pair of Horses and the Drivers whipping them up in opposite directions that is East, West, North and South— Over it is written this is a Republick. There is a Strong fortified Castle in the rear on the Battlements of which stands a man quietly examining the business through a Tellescope and calmly waiting the event. It is ridiculously applicable to our own times— Who that is near the helm and see's the petty workings of petty factions can avoid being struck with the wit of this production— God gave Nations Kings (the Bible xpressly tells us so) as serious evils but perhaps as the least of two— I am far however from acknowledging their divine rights according to the modern Legitimate system and know not but that DISTURBED is as good or good for nothing as any of them— The Vice President has arrived and as he is on a water Diet it is thought that the State of New York may make a President of him if Dr. Tillery spoke truth not one so suited to the *taste* of the State as when he took more generous liquors—

11 December 1822

Without a head ache— Mrs. [*Eliza Sibley*] Johnston of Louisianna came I suppose to return Mary's visit and left a Card. As it was not turned I do not know what to do as it is a sort of quibble which she may injure me by more especially as she is under the guidance of Mrs. [*Anna Payne*] Cutts— Mrs. Calhoun brought Mrs. [*Nancy Irwin*] Findlay and Mrs. [*Deborah Kay Hall*] Ingham with her. The husbands of these Ladies have not called on Mr. Adams and this reverses the order of things. N'importe. I shall invite the Husbands because the wives have called. In general I invite the Ladies because their husbands have visited mine— Judge Mc.Lean and Mrs. Way also called after which I went to see Mrs. Van Ness and Mrs. Rogers. Found Mrs Van Ness more composed than I could expect on seeing strangers— Mr A— dined at [*French consul general*] Mr. [*Jean Baptiste*] Petry's— We had received an invitation from the President but Mr A— thought himself obliged to decline it— They accuse him so constantly of Aristocracy that perhaps it was prudent particularly as the notice was only of three day's— The times are such we scarcely know what to do or how to behave— For my part I am very willing to show that I am the publick *Servant* but I will never be the *Publicks Slave*— I have too much of the Southern Dominion in me— Mrs. Smith came over to pass the Evening and while we were playing at Whist Mr Laborie [*secretary to the French legation*] came in as full of Espieglerie qui un Diable [*mischief as a devil*] and literally made me laugh until I cried—

12 December 1822

Mrs. Frye called to see me and I went with her to Mr [*Charles Bird*] Kings Picture Gallery and appointed Monday for her to sit to him— Her husband has one of the vilest things I ever saw which was taken of her by some miserable dauber it is not fit to adorn a sign post— Had 21 visits and went out to see Mrs. Calhoun Mrs. Findlay, and Mrs. Ingham; The former is a respectable looking elderly Lady the latter a Bride and a very pleasing intelligent woman— We had a large party to dine consisting of the Vice President Mr Crawford Mr. Thompson Mr Boardman Mr. Eaton Mr Brown Col Johnson Mr Taylor Mr Gilmer Mr. Tatnal Mr Rhea Mr Farrelly, Col Dwight; Judge Mc.Lean—Mr. Bates Mr. Garnet and Mr. Newton— It was a strange heterougeneous mixture and one or twice I feared would clash but we got through very well though I foresee an amazing difficulty during this winter for the buble must burst and produce both toil and trouble that will be very difficult to avoid. If Mr A— instead of keeping me back when I was a young woman had urged me forward in the world I should have better understood the maneouvring part of my situation— But instead of this I find myself almost a stranger to the little arts and intrigues of the world in which I move— Mr. [*James*] Pleasants a most excellent and worthy man is elected Governor of Virginia very much to the honour of the State— Mr John Randolph appears to be humanized by his journey for we hear nothing of him. Political sparring without any thing very much worth relating at Dinner— It is said that the V. P. cannot be brought forward for a higher station but that efforts will be made in favour of S[*ecretary of the*] N[*av*]y.

13 December 1822

Cm. [*David*] Porter has offered his services to exterminate the [*West Indies*] Pirates and Congress have voted a large Sum to carry on the War which must necessarily be of a dreadful nature— We have already lost one very valuable Officer and this loss appears to have roused a proper spirit— How dreadful it is that we can never be urged to proper measures until we have suffered some severe calamity— God I hope will preserve Porter. His loss would be a national one and our Navy has been severely despoiled this Summer from bad Climates— Went out and paid a number of visits and in the Eveng went to a Ball at Mrs. Brown's— Her house is elegantly fitted up and the party was very pleasant. The Members of Congress did me the honour to greet me with a flattering welcome and I was much congratulated upon the recovery of my *health* if such it can be called who are sick every two days— My Tuesday Evengs. appear to have some attractions at least they afford the probable certainty of giving opportunity for amusement throughout the Winter and in this consists the charm— As I do not mean to give dances my reputation is likely to crumble to the dust— We returned home at about eleven o clock—

The great novelty of the Evening were the Mexican Legation who made their first appearance. The Minister is a very small man with a true Spanish face and person— He does not speak a word of English or french and is likely to find his residence among us very ennuyant— The Secretary [*Don José Anastacio Torrens*] is a mean looking little man who speaks very bad french and who did not give any strong proofs of Diplomatic discretion as the first thing he said to me was that he was glad to be sent any where from his Country in its present state which was dreadful as no thing was organized and there was neither Government nor morals— The Minister was very much struck by the beauty's of the Ladies more especially with the elder ones as in Mexico he says that they become old immediately after having children— He showed me the miniature of his Wife which he wore round his neck— She would have accompanied him but the accomodations of the Vessel were not such as would admit of it. There is a priest with him said to be nearly related to the Emperor who is a bad looking man—very tall larged boned and only one eye and looking much like an inquisitor to our imagination's an odious and disgusting animal. There is likewise a fair handsome looking young man who is an interpreter. He has been educated in England and speaks English of course with facility— Mrs. Tomkins was of the party but I found her so cold when I spoke to her that I believe she did not recollect me— She is a very fine looking woman— He say's he did not bring his daughters because he could not *afford it*— His manners are remarkably pleasing and popular and he is in better training under his Wifes care—

---

22 *December 1822*

Went to the Capitol and heard Mr. [*John*] Breckenridge a pupil of Dr. Mason's and Chaplain of the H. R. His discourse was good and his manner impressive— The House was not crowded and I saw but few person's whom I knew— Mr Wilmot Mr. Baker Mr. Johnson and Dr. Huntt called to see us—and Mr A— Went to George Town and returned a number of visits— We passed the Eveng alone. Mary went to Church with Miss Forrest— Count de Menou came to see Mr Adams concerning an ettiquette question which has arisen among the foreign Ministers who are invited to dine at the Presidents on Tuesday with the Mexican Minister— It has always been customary for a Minister newly received to sit at the Presidents right hand— This Mr Canning objected to and refused to dine there unless that seat was assigned to him. The President would not give up the point and intimated to Mr C. that he should take no offence by his declining the invitation which Mr C accordingly did and made many efforts to induce the other branches of the Corps to do the same— In the first instance they were all so intimidated that they resolved not to go and came to consult Mr A— on the subject who told they might act as they thought most prudent themselves without any apprehension of offending as the P— wished to make it agreeable to them in any way— Upon which they all declined apparently yet without sending their excuses—

23 December 1822

At home all the morning excepting about an hour when I went and paid some visits— In the Eveng a great Ball at Mr. Cannings which was very brilliantly and well attended. Mr. A— after having given notice to the President that the Corps Diplomatique declined to dine with him was informed by them that they had decided to accept the invitation to which Mr A— assented though he knew that the P— had filled his Table. The pride of the Gentlemen was touched and they redeemed their National honour by daring to act for themselves and proved they had been subdued, not conquered— They are all to dine with us on Friday but Mr. C— has stipulated for my hand which was immediately agreed to as we can give no rank therefore they settle it among themselves— It is I suppose a trick to show his Mr C's dislike to the acknowledgment by our Government of the South Americans a thing which the British in good policy ought to have done long since— And these little ridiculous punctillios are only intended to display the power England possesses over the poor prostrated Nations of Europe. The Russians fortunately heard of the death of the Emperors Infant Nephew which put them out of their delemma— We returned at about eleven all well satisfied with our amusement—

24 December 1822

Mr A. went to the President and informed him that the foreigners would dine with him— The P. said he thought they had all declined and he had filled his places but he would Lengthen his Table and that would settle the difficulty— Mr A— dined there and in the Eveng we had a party of one

hundred and thirty odd persons all very sociable and good humoured—
The young Ladies danced played and sang and were very merry— Neither
of my Sisters attended— The famous belles Miss Ridgely & Miss Coleman
honoured me with their company and like all old women I was satisfied that
the beauties of my day were of a much higher order— Mr. Canning of course
was not here nor the Russians having declined the Presidents invitation—

25 December 1822

This day Charles arrived from Boston just as we were preparing for company
at dinner— He was very much fatigued and I found much grown and altered in face— The resemblance to his father is not so striking as it was and
he is now thought more like me. Mr & Mrs. Lloyd of Boston Dr Mease Col
Dwight Mr Cambreling Dr Cushman Mr Cook Mr & Mrs. Frye with their
Son Johnson Hellen and my own family made up the party with Mr. Tracey.
Mr & Mrs. Smith declined and Dr & Mrs. Eustis whom I had asked to meet
Mrs. Lloyd— The only striking circumstance of the day was the meeting
of Mr Adams with his two Classmates Mr. [*James*] Lloyd [*Jr.*] and Mr.
[*Joshua*] Cushman— The Eveng was spent in a round game for the amuse-
ment of the young people— This was the most social Christmas I have
passed for many years that is freer from family bickerings and nonsense—

26 December 1822

On Tuesday Count de Menou invited us to a Ball at his House into which
he had not moved. I therefore thought it might be a joke but this morning he
came again to ask us and we engaged to go. We therefore made our preparations and went leaving Charles at home who was too much fatigued for
dancing. Mr. Adams George and myself attended and I was really surprized
to see how comfortably they had arranged it considering they only moved
in in the morning— It was a very large party and more animated than common on account of the shortness of the invitation and the style of the mansion—
Mr Rocafeurte a Gentleman from Columbia was introduced to me. He is
one of the most sprightly animated beings I ever met— He gave me some
account of Lima particularly the habits and customs of the Lima Ladies.
He says it is a perpetual masquerade. The Costume of the females is cal-

culated to conceal and encourage intrigue. They always appear in black and their faces are so covered as to display only one eye thus they never can be known. Much severity is exercised towards single women but married Ladies have unbounded licence— Mrs. [*Maria Provoost*] Colden of New York informed me she was very intimate with Mrs. [*Abigail*] Adams who used to take much notice of her when a Girl. We returned home late Mr A— having engaged Mr Canning in a game of Chess in which my good husband was defeated—

27 December 1822

We had this day a great diplomatic dinner which passed over much better than I anticipated. Mr Canning led me to Table according to ettiquette and the Mexican sat on my left hand a most uncomfortable honor as I could not speak to him not knowing a word of his language— The poor man looked quite belwildered— Mr. Canning conversed very agreeably during dinner and repeated some lines which he had seen of Lord Byron's very little honour- able to his Lordships heart though they may indicate strong native genius— Such genius becomes a curse to the possessor and to mankind at large when it is used to bad purpose— Mr C. says he is engaged in a publication in England of a very bad character as Mr. C. say's of a most blasphemous nature which will prevent his Lordship from coming to this Country as is at present expected— After dinner Mr A— through the medium of the inter- preter asked the Mexican Minister if he had seen the City. He answered he had been round what would be a City when our Grandchildren were grown— The french were a little peevish in consequence of some quarrel among themselves and the Russians were almost as silent as the Mexican's though not from the same cause—

28 December 1822

Went to dine at Mrs. Decatur's although it snowed heavily and I was not well. In this Country I am conscious that people put themselves to great expence and frequently to great inconvenience to make such entertainments and I make it a point not to disappoint— The Secretary of War the Secretary of the Navy and Lady and Mr. Canning and suite were the only guests beside

our selves and the entertainment was very elegant displaying all the beautiful
Plate which was presented to her husband as tributes of National approba-
tion. I will not say gratitude—Republicks acknowledge not the sentiment—
Passed the day very pleasantly. Mr Calhoun gave us some pretty Indian
Romances which would cut a figure in the Hands of Chateau-Briant Mr
A— has become too phlegmatic to be caught by tinsel. John arrived in good
health as lively and animated as ever—

---

31 December 1822

Went with Mrs. Frye to Mr. Kings to whom she is sitting for her portrait
which promises to be very like— He is amusing in conversation but is apt to
introduce religious topics with so much levity and disrespect that I took the
liberty of telling him he had better confine himself to subjects which he
understood— This was no doubt impertinent but I made it a principle early
in life and I have adhered to it whenever I have been able to exert authority
never to suffer such levity in my presence— Philosophers may say that by
this means I shut my eyes to the truth— Be it so—on this subject I want nothing
better than my own conviction and would not change my opinion with the
wisest or greatest man dead or living— In the Evening we had a large party
upwards of a hundred and as it was the last day of the old year I had the
band of Musick— They kept it up merrily until near twelve o'clock— Mrs.
[*Sally Brooks*] Holmes the Senators Lady from Masstts. condescended to
come with her daughter— As Capt Partridge delivered a lecture on the Battle
of Waterloo we had but few Members of Congress— The subject is very
interesting and some Gentlemen who came from thence spoke highly of the
performance—

---

1 January 1823

If the weather of to day is ominous of the storms of the ensuing year we must
not expect much quiet— Let it come I will not flinch be the end what it may—
We went to the Presidents where we found a much larger party assembled
than could have been expected considering the difficulties attendant on a
sortie in such an inclement day— The Corps Diplomatique paid their usual

compliment and we had a company of twenty at dinner Mr King Genl Stokes Gov Brown Gov Jennings Gov Knight Mr Eddy Mr Fuller Dr Holcomb Dr Darlington Mr. Breckenridge Mr Helmes Misspi. Mr. Harris Mr. Ingham Mr. Mills— Genl Cocke did not come but we waited for him an hour— This was not so agreeable as the last dinner— Mr King is not in good spirits this Winter— He is labouring under the worst feelings of discontent and mortification which having once siezed on a man's mind render him fretful unsocial and unhappy— God grant that whatever is in store for me yet I may never embitter the remnant of my days by this sort of restless irritation which is calculated to prove a torment to ourselves without a shadow of benefit to any human being— Let me be satisfied with my own conduct and I defy slander and the foul fiend.— Eveng. alone—

---

21 January 1823

The day was lovely and I was induced to ride out and pay visits at the Capitol Hill to Mrs. Genl [*Margaret Spear*] Smith and Miss [*Nancy*] Spear and Mrs. Livingston— Mr. [*John*] Sergeant called but by some accident was denied admittance— Mr A— told us a good anecdote— A Gentleman called at the Department and was shown into his Room upon entering which he asked Mr A. if he was Mr Adams? Who said he was. Was he the Secretary of State?— Yes he had that honour.— He took a Chair with his hat on and said he had come from Virginia and that he was determined not to leave the City without having seen him— Mr. A— made many enquiries concerning his farm the State of Virginia Agriculture generally and they continued to converse very sociably above an hour when the Gentleman took leave observing that he was perfectly satisfied— This was a man who was not to be gulled by the stories propagated about Mr A—s manners &ce which it has been so much the fashion to decry and he was resolved to judge for himself—

In the Eveng we had upwards of a hundred but not more than twenty Ladies. The Corps Diplomatique excepting Mr. Canning and suite sent excuses it being the Anniversary of Louis XVI Decapitation which is always strictly celebrated by the French Legation by high Mass and all the funeral pomp which the Roman Catholick Church admits in this place— The other

Legations generally pay the compliment of attendance— But Mr C——g said he thought the morning Service quite sufficient and that there could be no impropriety in visiting so sober a person as the Secretary of State and if they were affronted he should shelter himself under that plea— Mr [*Isaac*] & Mrs. [*Ann Bowly*] Mc.Kim a New Member from Maryland and his Lady said to be immensely wealthy were here for the first time— She is handsome but not so beautiful as I had heard— A Mr. Maulsby and Mr. Emery two of the Governors Council from Anapolis were likewise here— They danced as usual— Mr Thompson and his daughter Louisa also came to my great astonishment as it is said their eldest daughter [*Catharine Livingston Thompson*] is to be married tomorrow— This is altogether a singular marriage more particularly as there is no french Minister here— She is to marry the Secretary of Legation [*Charles de Bresson*] and is to continue in her fathers house a thing altogether singular he being one of the Cabinet Council and Ministers of State— There is something awkward in the business which in any other Country might lead to disagreeables— The City is becoming crowded with Strangers even to excess and this Wedding will encrease our gaiety so as to make it almost oppressive—

22 January 1823

The day was very unpleasant and I remained at home until the Evening when we went to the Drawing Room notwithstanding it poured with rain— To our great surprize however we found a number of Ladies and Gentlemen and quite a sociable party— We remained there about an hour and were rejoiced to get safe home— The young men went to the Circus to see the wonderful rider who has just arrived. He is said to be inimitably graceful and performs the most wondrous feats without saddle or bridle— The boys could not withstand the temptation of seeing him in preference to the formality of our Court.

26 January 1823

Went to the Catholic Church expecting to hear the Bishop of New Orleans preach. In this I was disappointed and heard a ridiculous discourse from the Curé whose language is vulgar beyond description and whose manner is altogether unsuited to the solemnity of their ceremonies— There is something very imposing in their worship well calculated to attach the ignorant and I am not at all surprized that Nations should endeavour to cultivate a Religion so well adapted to insure political Institutions more particularly those of a Despotic or Monarchical Government— It is said that the Emperor of Russia already repents the little he has done towards enlightening his half civilized subjects and the Religion of that Country even worse than the Catholic whose Clergy are mostly educated men whereas in Russia a fine voice is all that is requisite to make a Pope [*priest*] and it is very rare to see one who knows how to read or write— And he is priviledged to get drunk by way of celebrating the Church ceremonies and thus gains unbounded influence over the Community who find in him a jolly boon companion— Can any thing in nature be more preposterous than such Institutions to common sense— One of the privileges of the people always struck me as being odious and most horribly immoral— This is the great part of Lent when the people abstain from food of every description excepting Cakes made with bad oil and dried Mushrooms. This fast is of seven weeks and they drink nothing but water. On Easter Sunday they feast and during the Week they may be dead drunk in the Streets without fear of punishment as the Laws sanction any degree of intoxication for that period— Thus the Government itself permits that at one moment which it stigmatizes with disgrace at another for the mere convenience of keeping the people quiet— Passed the Eveng at Mrs. Thornton's which was rather stiff and dull—

27 January 1823

Had a small party at dinner Mr. Sergeant Mr. Barstow Mr. R. Amory Mr. Lewis and Mr. Pinkney— We had a delightful dinner being all intimately acquainted and having a mutual esteem for each other— They remained with us until nine o clock when Mr. Petry came in and we sat chattering about an two hours of old times and old friends to his utter astonishment he found when he got home that it was midnight— Mr Sergeant is in poor health but tolerable spirits—considering the loss of his Son which he has never entirely recovered—

28 January 1823

Went out and paid a number of visits and in the Eveng had as usual a very pleasant party of about one hundred and twenty. Thus my Evengs. keep up their reputation without any effort on my part— The great news which excited so much interest in Congress has sunk into nothing and [*newspaper publishers*] Gales and Seaton if not their patron is likely to escape without blemish— Asbury Dickins will most likely prove the scape-goat for the benefit of his Master who will reward him probably in some way or other should he rise to the situation to which he aspires— The party was the most agreeable we have had this winter— We kept it up until near twelve— Mrs. Johnston a Lady from New Orleans valsed very beautifully— If I live to get through the Winter I shall find it very difficult to keep them up with the same spirit—

29 January 1823

We passed the morning in preparations for a Ball at Mr. Cannings— As I generally cut out and fix my own Clothes—This occasion brought out a gown which I have had seven years and which I have never made up and taking some trimmings from one nearly worn out I put the Materials together and produced a dress so splendid that it created great admiration. The truth is that Mr A furnished my wardrobe very handsomely in Paris and I have nursed it so as to make it answer my wants for seven years— This is however such a trying winter that I am a little afraid it will be entirely demolished and I shall never have the means to afford a fresh supply— It is singular what an affect a showy appearance makes and I have long thought that person's who are thrust into prominent and elevated stations must set themselves above the vulgar prejudices of mankind and dare uncommon things— If we trace the course of nature we shall find that even minds of superior order are caught by the tinsel trappings of outward splendour— even when reflection does its utmost to conquer the impression and external advantages give point to what is called affability and makes it more grateful to the multitude— The only art requisite is to adapt splendour to occasion— and to know how to be simple and unostentatious according to circumstances. In Philadelphia I was a Nurse and only known there as such; in

Boston as a traveller, in Washington as the Lady of the Secretary of State a situation admitting of every thing but extreme familiarity— Mr Adams and the Boys dined at Mrs. Decaturs and met us at Mr Cannings— They found Mrs. Decatur was very affable and agreeable and they were much delighted with their entertainment— The Balls at this house are always elegant but there is still something flat and stiff resulting from the knowledge of the Masters rigid love of ettiquette and ceremony— Beauty always appears to advantage here—

As Louisa notes on 11 February, below, John and Charles Francis were preparing to return to Harvard at the end of their winter vacation; George remained in Washington, D.C. John stayed in school for only a few more months. He was expelled, for participating in yet another student uprising, on 2 May. After that, he went to live with his grandfather in Quincy for the remainder of the summer, then came down to Washington in October to begin studying law with his father.

7 February 1823

We remained at home all the morning. Mr Adams dined at the Capitol with Mr. Hill and walked part of the way home. This encreased his Cold and he was quite unwell when he got to Mrs. Brown's where we all went to a Ball which was very splendid and elegant— I had a great deal of conversation with many persons and one with Mr. Archer of Virginia upon second marriages which was quite interesting. Mr [*Henry Unwin*] Addington [*British chargé d'affaires*] and myself frequently have long conversations— He is a pleasing man who has travelled and although he does not appear to me very deep or very striking his mind is sufficiently cultivated to make him a very pleasant companion— He is Nephew to Lord Sidmouth who was formerly Speaker of the House of Commons. Mr. Clay is playing a new game— I always mistrust these sudden changes and though I do not interfere in Politic's It is difficult for me to avoid knowing transactions which are talked of by every one and which places a man in the light of a decided enemy to my husband— How much discretion and discernment it requires to be the Wife of a great man, and how very difficult to avoid irritating enmity without an appearance of fawning and intrigue which is despicable to the soul of a proud and virtuous woman to endeavour to conciliate those whose good opinion it is worth while to secure— It has ever been my desire to obtain the esteem and good will of men whose respectable characters, shining qualities, or superior merit make them objects of public praise or of publick notoriety—I care not of what party.

8 February 1823

The Girls went and paid visits notwithstanding the day was so cold it was hardly supportable— In the Eveng we remained at home, and Mrs. Smith came over as Mr Laborie had engaged to come and read a french Comedy to us. He however disappointed us, and we had a visit from Mr. Petry at near ten o clock, who sat with us more than an hour— My House is now very attractive, and I every hour deplore the necessity I am under of wasting time which I could enjoy so greatly, in empty show and flighty conversation in crouded parties— To be an object of attention to the busy censorious multitude, whose praise is tinctured by envy, and whose approval is embittered by irony— To persons so situated, there is only one course open and that is to rush on impetuously, without enquiring why or wherefore, lest reflection should make me shrink from a life altogether so wearisome, so toilsome, and in a religious point of view so unprofitable— The addition of Miss Hopkinson to our society is delightful, for mind scintilates in every glance of her eye, and that mind though enthusiastic, and brilliant, is corrected by a stern judgment, and right principles— This is a Girl after my own heart, and when I look at her, I grieve again the loss of the lovely creature which God for wise reason's thought fit to take from me, least I should have been tempted to worship the creature instead of the Creator—

9 February 1823

I slept so late that I could not go to Church— Mr. Adams went to Bakers Church and heard Mr Breckenridge who gave them a curious Sermon describing Voltaire, Hume, Tom Paine and Mahomet, with all their disciples forming a conclave in Hell.— And although the picture was aweful, it unfortunately proved that Madame de Staels observation is correct, that there is not much more than a hair's breadth "between the sublime and the ridiculous"— It were perhaps more prudent not to force the errors of transcendent genius into light, which by exciting curiosity spreads the deadly and dangerous doctrines of infidelity— We passed the Eveng sociably at Mrs. Brown's—Where we met a small party among whom was Miss Spear whose tongue is a glaive which inspires terror, and cuts into the very soul— She is an old maiden Belle, whose hoard of acrimony is ever venting itself against the stupid generation, that had not either possessed the wit or the discernment to grasp such preeminet merit and hand down transcripts to posterity for the benefit of the future race— I am but little acquainted with her but at all events cry her mercy as I should sink under her lash— She is a Hebe of sixty alway's crowned with roses; *not with myrtle.*

10 February 1823

The weather is dull and gloomy and the Boys are about leaving us which makes our hearts more sad than the weather— In the Eveng we all went to Col Tayloe's and being already out of spirits passed the most unpleasant Evening— Col and Mrs. Tayloe have always lived upon the most friendly terms with us— The family is of the highest respectability but in the whole though so numerous there is nothing that indicates more than mediocrity— Their wealth And high standing in Virginia gives them great influence and they are ever tendering to us proffers of service and friendship— Mr Clay last Eveng took an opportunity of assuring me that it was his wish to be on terms of friendship with me and my family and expressed a hope that if he should not be able to come to all my Tuesday's that I should not believe it was intended as a mark of enmity—

11 February 1823

My boys were to have left Town this morning but the Stage omitted to call for them— Charles and the Girls rode into George Town to secure a place for them for tomorrow— I am so worn out that I seldom attempt to go out of a morning— In the Eveng. notwithstanding the weather was very bad I had a very large party and the most part of them were Strangers— It was very gay and the Bride and Bridegroom [*Catharine and Charles de Bresson*] attended— My boys were not in spirits and Charles would not come down— Mr Laborie a youth of nineteen who has got into some little difficulty owing to some childish folly sent word he was sick— He had requested me to intercede for him and I spoke to Mr Petry on the subject and I believe with success. This Youth was recommended to the protection of Mr Adams by Talleyrend and the notice I have taken of him excites jealousy— What a farce— He is wild and imprudent but has the most promising talents which are utterly neglected in consequence of the French Legation having at present no respectable head— It was near twelve ere my company separated— Mr & Mrs. Gilmour took leave of me on their return to Baltimore—

Louisa again took a break from her diary and journal letters over the summer months. During the spring, she nursed George, who had broken his arm in a fall, and visited Bladensburg, Maryland, to "take the waters." She visited Quincy from August to October, then returned to Washington, D.C. Her journal letters for late 1823 and early 1824 are primarily directed to George—who had moved to Boston to continue his legal training with Daniel Webster— though Louisa wrote them with the intention that George would also read them to his grandfather, John Adams.

By the time Louisa returned to the capital in the fall of 1823, discussion of the presidential election of 1824 was already in full swing, and maneuverings in Congress reflected political divisions. John Quincy remained a leading candidate. Still competing for the post were John C. Calhoun, Henry Clay, and William H. Crawford. Over the coming months, Calhoun would remove himself from contention as a presidential candidate and become essentially the sole vice presidential candidate. Crawford received support from the congressional caucus, traditionally the mechanism used to select a candidate. But opposition was growing to the caucus system, which made its support a double-edged sword for Crawford. Furthermore, he suffered a stroke that raised important questions about his ability to serve. Most significantly, in the spring of 1824, Andrew Jackson chose to enter the race, greatly complicating the geography and electoral math of the process. In the end, no single candidate received a majority of the electoral votes, so the contest was thrown into the House of Representatives, which selected John Quincy. But this decision was marred by charges of corruption, especially between John Quincy and Clay, and these accusations undermined John Quincy's entire presidency.

30 November 1823

In a righteous cause I dare both good and ill—

This Session begins with me pretty much as I suppose it will pass in Congress that is to say with chills and fevers alternately low and high and at all times very unequal to labour in my fatiguing vocation—with the additional aggravation of being thought to suffer in consequence of hopes and fears during this tremendous struggle for the Presidential election for which in fact I care very little, more especially since I have acquired the certainty of our perfect independence in point of fortune to ensure our future *comfort*— My ideas upon this subject are these— In the eight years of Mr Adams's service as Secretary of State independent of all his former public services he has done more to establish his fame and to deserve the gratitude of the Nation than any man in the Country. In this respect he has little in fact nothing to gain and should he lose the election which is most likely from present appearances the disgrace will not fall on him but heavily on that *very enlightened* Country and people who could not discriminate between sterling worth and base intrigue— For him therefore I consider a private station as glorious as the Chief Magistrates Chair and as far as I am personally concerned Tis in comparison perfect freedom to the prison house of state—

As usual a stormy winter is foreboded and it is whispered that a caucus is to be called immediately to counteract the effect produced by the election's in New York or rather with a view to intimidate the Legislature of that state and force them to support the caucus Candidate. The War party will be very active to maintain its independence from all others and the weight of the battle in the beginning will probably be between these two. The City will be crowded and the Ladies are hailed with pleasure as the medium which is to soothe and calm the turbulent spirit which is likely to be roused by party feeling— Mrs. Monroe is dangerously ill and the House of the President will probably be closed at least for sometime— There are no Foreign Ministers Mr Crawford quite out health The Secretary of the Navy in Lodgings and Judge Thompson's family sick. You can judge of the brilliant prospect of gaiéty for the winter in addition to which Mr Brown is going to France— I have determined to have my parties once a fortnight as I am not able to undertake it oftener & what all these strangers are to do for amusement I dont know.

1 December 1823

This day Congress meets and it is expected that the Session will be one of the most important that have passed for many years— It was ushered in by a melancholy event. Mr. [*Frederick*] Greuhm the Minister from Prussia expired at five o'clock in the morning and the official communication was made in great form by the Baron's Tuylle & Stackelberg— In the afternoon Mr. Adams went to announce it to the President of the Senate & Speaker of the House and in the Eveng Baron Stackelberg called to make arrangements with Mr. A. about the funeral— Tis' singular that one of the Representatives of the holy Alliance should have died the very day of the first meeting of a Congress which is likely to be called upon to resist the encroachments of these rapacious Sovereings and I hope it is ominous of their defeat— He was a good and amiable man and the situation of his poor wife is really pitiable—added to which it is rumoured that he has not left her in good circumstances— The Speaker Mr Clay was elected by a majority of 139 votes Mr Taylor having declined— Mr Barbour was put forward as a trial of Mr Crawfords strength and the issue has not been favorable— Poor man he is in dreadful health and at this moment confined to his house by a dreadful inflamation in his eyes brought on by the quantity of digitalis which he took during his illness— Mr Clay it is said is in very bad health likewise but much better than report led us to expect— Genl Jackson is sick at Staunton in Virginia but expected in a few days. The struggle is terrific when it oversets the great the small & the brave— Numerous visits—

2 December 1823

Received a number of visits after which I went to visit the poor widow but did not see her— She is at Mr Lee's and the young Ladies are very kind to her— Saw Mrs. Frye whose children have the Measles but are getting well over it. Mr Adams dined with Mr. Petry— The Presidents message went in to day but I have heard nothing about it. Received a present from my Sister Boyd at Mc. Kinaw of an Indian Pipe for Mr. Adams with a petition to procure the situation of Collector for her husband. Mr Steward also wants to change his situation and wishes to be made Pay Master— Mr Adams went again to the President of the Senate and to the Speaker of the H. R. expressly at the request of the Members of the Corps Diplomatique to announce that the funeral of Mr Greuhm would take place tomorrow at eleven o'clock— This is a very disagreeable business as it will probably give rise to many unpleasant remarks and give opportunity to renew the question which has for some time lain dormant upon ettiquette— It is however unavoidable as this is the first instance of the kind in the Country and will probably do away future difficulties. He has merely been the medium of communication and Congress must suggest what they think proper— He stayed out until eleven o'clock— We passed the eveng alone—

3 December 1823

My whole morning was occupied with visits and writing Cards of invitation— We have had forty or more Members of Congress already here and all who call I invite to my Evengs. If I can help it I will invite only those who call lest it should be said I am courting them to further any particular purpose— We dined alone and Mary being sick I denied myself company— Mr Petry called and several Gentlemen have been passing the Evening with Mr Adams. Mrs. Talbot the Wife of the Senator who has just arrived from the West Indies called this morning— Mrs. Mc Kim & Mrs. Bailey likewise made me a visit. I went to Mrs. Crawfords. The family are still quite sick. Gave Mr Wyer a lecture which he did not like upon discretion a virtue the poor man is not much troubled with— The P[ost] M[aster] G[eneral] seems as if he wanted to shake off responsibility by transfering appointments to the Senate. He is said to be a great man. I fear he is a dealer in little things—

4 December 1823

The morning was stormy and it rained most heavily so that some of the orders for the funeral were countermanded and there were but few person's attended excepting some of the heads of Department and one Senator— The funeral was handsome but nothing extraordinary— We had some Gentlemen to dine with us— Mr Salazar Mr Pallacio Mr Gomez Mr Vilanella

Mr Poinsett Mr Newton Mr Garnet Mr Trimble Genl Swartout Mr Larned Mr John Mason and Col Dwight— Four or five Gentlemen disappointed us— among them Mr [*John*] Forsyth who neither came nor sent an excuse— I mark this as he is lately returned from a foreign Mission— The dinner was pleasant— After dinner was over Mr Trimble told Mr. A— he supposed he knew that as it regarded the Presidency he should support Mr. Clay or rather that Mr A— must know for whom he would vote— Just as if he supposed that we expected that the dinner we gave him was to bespeak his good word— It is a strange ignoble state of things and I cannot comprehend such littleness— Mr. Petry came in the Eveng and we played Boston [*card game*] until twelve oclock— Mr Adams finds so much amusement in it I encourage his visits as much as possible by way of relaxation and to keep him from thinking of the passing events— I have twice to day been given to understand that the game is nearly up for him— The caucusing is eternal out of doors— Mr Poinsett say's he is worn out with it already. He has taken a house to himself that he may not be in the way of hearing so much concerning politicks out of the house of representatives— Mr Durand de St André the french Consul has arrived to take the place of Mr Petry who goes to Madrid very much against his will having been forty years employed in this Country—

---

9 December 1823

Mr. Wyer called to inform me that Genl [*Winfield*] Scott was very desirous to get an invitation from me which I immediately sent— He is anxious to be reconciled to Genl. Jackson and the Genl is willing to meet him half way. Supposing that Jackson would be here he wished to adjust the difference at our house in which however he was disappointed the weather proving so bad that numbers who intended coming failed— Our party was however very brilliant notwithstanding the Snow and the young folks enjoyed themselves as much as if there was no such thing as Snow in the world— Theirs is the happy time of life when all is sunshine and the hours are winged with joy however evanescent— Col Dwight acted as my aid de Camp and fortunately only one Member arrived previous to Mr. A—s return— That was Mr Hogeboom of New York with whom I had much conversation— He insisted on it that the pillars of the House of Representatives were of rough stone and covered with some sort of stuff which *they call marble* and I could not pursuade him that they were solid blocks. He said the building was a fine one and that we were fortunate in having fine *Architectors* in this Country— They staid until eleven o'clock. Mr & Mrs. Brown our new Plenipo[*tentiary*]'s to the Court of France appeared for the first time in their new character and like most others affected not to be pleased with that for which their hearts have panted for upwards of two years and for which half the Washington world envy them and among these I may perhaps place myself for I confess my ambition has always tended that way in preference to the highest office in the gift of the Nation— This is a fact not to be whispered abroad—For the *American* world would indeed wonder how I could like what they would deem *carrion* better than ortolan; but so it is and temppis pour moi [*so much the worse for me*]— Again I say tell it not in Gath—

10 December 1823

To my great astonishment I got up without a head ache and was able to go about the business of the day without inconvenience— Baron Stackelberg called on me and sat sometime— There is a rumour going about that the body of Mr Greuhm was not buried and that all the parade which was made was to follow the Coat &c—&c— I taxed the Baron upon the subject and I thought he wished to evade it. I therfore put the question very direct but he spoke low although I think he said the body was buried. He said he was very sorry he ever had any thing to do with the funeral but regretted still more that the ceremonies of his own particular Church had not been properly attended to— When the Minister a rigid and inflexible Presbyterian came to that part of the ceremony in which according to our ritual the earth is thrown upon the coffin as an emblem of the destiny to which it is doomed the omission struck him with such horror he could scarcely refrain from siezing the shovel and performing that part of the ceremony himself— How strange and unacountable it is that men openly professing to scoff at religion and viewing it only in the light of a mere political institution to bind society together should by the simple ommission of a form be affected even to grief and receive a shock capable of assailing all those feelings which I firmly believe every human being has even by intuition struggle as much as they may and will against the conviction. On consigning the body of his poor friend to the earth he felt the truth flash upon his soul and knew that the soul that once inhabited that clay cold corpse was to be judged and he hoped received by an Almighty father and any want of that respect which we are all taught to manifest toward the dead roused a sense which probably had lain dormant for years. We passed the Eveng alone— Mr [*Nicholas*] Biddle arrived from Philadelphia—

In the winter of 1823, Andrew Jackson had not yet declared himself a candidate for the presidency. Hoping to win his endorsement for John Quincy (and, not incidentally, to keep Jackson out of the race), Louisa agreed to throw a major ball in Jackson's honor on the ninth anniversary of his victory at the Battle of New Orleans. The event became the social occasion of the season and secured Louisa's position as the preeminent hostess in Washington, D.C. Five hundred invitations were issued, and somewhere between seven hundred and a thousand people attended the event, causing traffic jams around the district as carriages fought to get close to the house. The whole family spent the weeks leading up to it preparing, including making wreaths; chalking the floors with decorations of eagles and flowers; and organizing a "sumptuous cold collation" of pies, pastries, sweetmeats, game, candied fruits, fresh Florida oranges, and "a variety of generous wines." Jackson only stayed through supper, but others remained to dance most of the night. From a political standpoint, the ball failed in its mission: Jackson entered the presidential race and became John Quincy's implacable enemy. But from a social standpoint, the night was a huge success, talked about for years to come and setting a new standard for Washington entertainments.

20 December 1823

It was agreed this day that we should give a Ball to General Jackson on the eighth— I objected much to the plan but was overpowered by John's arguments and the thing was settled— A Note was drawn up to be printed and an order sent to have five hundred struck off immediately and we prepared a list Alphabetically to make it more easy— In the Eveng Mr Petry came and played Boston— Genl Browns ball was given to Genl Gaines who has just exchanged his Station with Genl. Scott— The Genl and his Lady and Niece were there but I was not introduced to her and although her husband entertained me with a long string of her perfections I was stupid enough not to be able to discover them— He however told me that during his actual service she had written the accounts of his campaigns with infinitely more accuracy in all their details than he or his aids could do— Genl Brown is not so fortunate as his Lady is a very domestic pleasing woman who does not appear capable of tracing or following the maneuvers of an army particularly on the field of Battle— America is doubly blessed in being possesed of Genl. in petticoats as well as Genls in breeches— Went to bed very late—

21 December 1823

Went to Church at Mr. Baker's and heard one of the best Sermon's I ever heard in my life and remarkably well delivered— In the Eveng went to Mrs. Thornton's to meet Mrs. Brown a farewell party previous to her departure for France— Met there Mr C Manigault the Columbian Legation a Mr. Cox of New Jersey— Mr Manigault sang two Songs which he accompanied with his Guitar with great sweetness and sprightliness— Returned home very early as I was really quite overpowered by the parade of wealth and ostention displayed by the good Lady who is so soon to figure in a Parisian circle— The superabundance of Cashmeres &c &c &c which are to adorn the Thuilleries in which by her own account she could not walk last time she went to France without seeing the people jog one another and exclaim *superbe magnifique delicieux*— Found the young men busy writing Notes which task they had nearly accomplished and soon after we retired— Mr. Hellen arrived this morning—

22 December 1823

Was out all the morning returning visits and distributed Cards of invitations for the Ball— Have a beautiful plan in my head which I shall endeavour to have executed— In the Eveng began to make Flowers. Mr. [*Joseph*] Blunt came in and sat an hour. He is a very intelligent little man of very agreeable conversation—

23 December 1823

A very rainy disagreeable day— Had a very large and brilliant party notwithstanding which was as gay as usual— A great many Members of Congress— Dancing & Cards all the Eveng. Madame Durand came Dressed in black Velvet with a Bonnet and Shawl— She apologized and said she was not aware of there being dancing and appeared to regret the indecorum she had committed. She is very handsome and quite a Dasher— The party staid late and my Tuesdays are as popular as ever—

27 December 1823

You must observe that I never speak of the great question for I am really so tired of it that I endeavour to forget that it is stirring— I could not help smiling at Mrs. Brown's Ball. Mrs. Calhoun was complaining so bitterly of being so small and declaring she never would dress herself in dark colours again as nobody could distinguish her—but she thanked God her husband was so tall he could not *be* overlooked— There was I believe nothing intended by the speech but I could not help laughing at the idea and thinking it was after all but a poor distinction— This day like many others was passed in running about the Town to carry invitations. The number of person's who come to be invited on this occasion exceeds belief and we have been obliged to order Pillars to be placed in our rooms to support the Ceilings to conceal which I must make some sort of ornament and this of itself will occasion more talk than I like— For this however I must take my chance and brave it as well as I can—

1 January 1824

This day we commenced a new year which will probably be fraught to us with both good and evil— The weather was abominable and I hope not ominous of what is to be expected in the course of the impending question— The Crowd at the Presidents was immense and more gay than I ever saw it although the weather was intolerable. We had a large party at Dinner—Mr

R King Dr Holcomb Mr Williams of Misspi Mr Letcher Judge Isaacks Mr I S Barbour Mr Mangum Mr Talbot Mr Marvin Mr. Hobart Mr Jennings Mr Wood Mr. Sharp and Mr. Cuthbert— The dinner was pleasant enough they staid quite late and I was very glad to retire to bed as soon as they were gone—

2 January 1824

This was a very busy day as we found that we must make all the Laurel wreaths ourselves. I worked very hard as well as Anthony in preparing them besides receiving visits which crowd in in such a manner that I really fear for the house— In the Evening we went to Mrs Wirts. It was a great Ball and one of the most agreeable I have been at. I was introduced to Madame De-Larue and find her a charming woman— Mrs. Durand dances most elegantly and it is quite the fashion to admire her— I had considerable conversation with some Gentleman whom I did not know. Our topics of conversation were not very interesting but he appeared to be very anxious to know if John Randolph was coming to my Ball to which I answered that he had been invited as a Member of the House but had *politely* declined on account of his health— We returned at the usual time—

3 January 1824

Mrs. Fry came and assisted me all day and we had quite a pleasant time while busy at our work— Poor Johnson is so deeply engrossed in the Presidential Question that it really affects his health and spirits. According to the fluctuations of public rumour so are his fears and his hopes excited and at moments he suffers it to make him unhappy. In the Eveng we had Mr Petry.

4 January 1824

Went to Church and heard Mr. Baker— Mr Blount came in the Eveng— Much talk about the Ball and a great deal of nonsense in the Newspapers—

5 January 1824

It rained hard all day— We remained at home engaged in flower making— Mr Sullivan sat here in the Eveng. He is much displeased with Mr King of Maine who he say's is carrying on intrigues with Mr. Crawford through the medium of the Claims.

6 January 1824

Mary & Charles went to George Town with notes of invitations as the people flock here so continually it keeps us constantly employed. Small party in Evening— Many came to see what arrangements were made and were much disappointed to find the house looking much as usual—

7 January 1824

Mrs. Frye spent the day with me and assisted in completing my preparations— Mrs Fuller called to know why I had not invited some ladies that had called and to request that I would send them invitations. I sent them accordingly and continued to send out all day— Towards Eveng Mr Frye came in and we had some jokes about the Crowd expected on this occasion—

8 January 1824

Busy all the morning in fixing the Laurel wreaths which John under my direction hung around the Walls of the apartments. These wreaths were intermixed with Roses and arranged in festoons in the centre of which was placed a small variegated Lamp. Chandeliers to match were suspended from the Ceiling in the centre of the Rooms and garlands were hung from the pillars within so as to fasten them up which had altogether a beatiful effect. The four lower rooms were ornamented alike and all the doors removed which afforded as much space as we could make and looked very showy. At half past seven every thing was ready and the guests began to arrive in one continued Stream so that in one hour even the Stair case up to Mary's chamber began to be thronged— Mr Adams and I took our stations near the door that we might be seen by our guests and be at the same time ready to receive the General to whom the fete was given— He arrived at nine o'clock and I took him round the Rooms and introduced him to the Ladies and Gentlemen whom we passed and then left him to amuse himself until supper was announced— I then took his Arm and led to the top of the Table Mr A. leading a Lady to the other. Our company appeared to enjoy themselves very much more especially as there was no pretence of ettiquette as I was afraid of giving offence by making distinctions— The General drank my health and professed to be much gratified by the compliment and went to Carusi's Room's where he expected to be greeted by the *people* with great joy but I believe he was disappointed and found very few person's there— While sitting in the dancing Room one of the lamps fell upon my head and ran all down my back and shoulders— This gave rise to a good joke and it was said that I was already anointed with the sacred oil and that it was certainly ominous— I observed that the only certain thing I knew was that my gown was spoilt— I changed my dress in a few minutes and returned to the Ball Room and my Company dispersed at about half past one all in good humour and more contented than common with their entertainment. To have got so well through this business was matter of gratulation to us all—

CHAPTER EIGHT

"This Apparent Fate"

Retirement

Louisa's life, as well as much in America, changed dramatically between January 1824, when she wrote the last of her extant journal letters, and November 1835, when she resumed keeping a diary. John Quincy was elected president in the fall of 1824, and the family moved into the White House the next spring. The nature of his election—selection by the House of Representatives after losing the popular and electoral votes to Andrew Jackson—gave John Quincy's presidency an air of illegitimacy from which he could never recover. He had little support in Congress and was unable to move forward any part of his political agenda. For Louisa the years were equally difficult. Challenged as a foreigner and a Tory of aristocratic birth, she had to defend herself as "the daughter of an American Republican Merchant." Still, much as she had done as the wife of the secretary of state, she made the most of her place as first hostess, but the success of her parties could not overcome political intransigence. Louisa was offended by John Quincy's loss in his reelection bid in 1828 but also almost grateful that she could finally leave public life.

Her reprieve, however, was short-lived. In 1830 John Quincy accepted election to Congress, representing the Plymouth district of Massachusetts. He would continue in that position until his death in 1848, becoming known as "Old Man Eloquent" for his impassioned and principled opposition to slavery. While Louisa understood her husband's need to continue to serve and be involved politically—she commented to her son John, "Family is and must ever be a secondary consideration to a zealous Patriot"—she was less than happy to have to return to political life. She initially refused to move back to Washington, D.C., from Quincy but was eventually persuaded, and she and John Quincy resumed their routine of wintering in Washington and summering in New England.

Family life was equally trying. Following flirtations with each of the three Adams sons, Mary Catherine Hellen finally settled on John, and the couple married at the White House in early 1828. But John had already begun to show the effects of alcoholism, and lived only until 1834. The couple had two children, Mary Louisa and Georgeanna Frances (Fanny); they and their mother would continue to live with the Adamses in Washington after John's death, although Fanny herself survived only to 1839. George too began to suffer from alcoholism, failed to develop any real career, and died after falling off a steamboat in 1829. To this day, it remains unclear if this was an accident or suicide, but George was en route to Washington to confess to his parents that he had fathered an illegitimate child with a chambermaid. Only Charles Francis had begun to develop a somewhat successful career as a lawyer and writer, and in 1829 had married Abigail Brown Brooks, the daughter of the very wealthy Peter Chardon Brooks of Boston. The beloved "Old Gentleman," John Adams, had passed away in 1826, leaving Louisa with no remaining parental figures.

All of the entries in this chapter come from Louisa's diary—her first true diary, written solely for herself, since 1812—which she kept extremely sporadically from 1835 until 1849, when a stroke prevented her writing anything more. She titled the volume "Mélanges d'une Délassée" (Miscellaneous Writings of One Who Is Forsaken), which aptly represents this particular journal. Interspersed between entries Louisa included poetry (her own and that by others), essays on topics of interest, and other random notes. She added new entries only irregularly and may have gone back to add material, as the entries do not always appear in chronological order. This diary, much like that which she kept following her daughter's death in 1812, reflects Louisa's profound grief over the loss of her sons. It also traces her thoughts as she slowly faces her own mortality and that of her cherished husband.

6 November 1835

Is it not singular that I can scarcely ever make an observation upon any subject without clashing with the opinions or the prejudices of some one or other?— I know not how to account for this. It is my wish and desire to think right; and I commune often with my own heart and meditate upon my actions, with a perpetual anxiety to act up to those principles of moral rectitude, which were early and abundantly inculcated by ever watchful and tender parents— Speaking of participation in the holy communion to day; I said that I felt afraid to present myself at the Lords table; as there was still a livid spot in my heart, which made it impossible for me to kneel down at the Altar of the Almighty with a man; Genl [. . .] who had so deeply injured me with the fear that there was no real cordiality in my forgiveness.— What was there in this fact which so violently shocked Mary and Mrs: Frye. If it was the acknowledgment, that with all my pains, I had not conquered this rebellious feeling, the sentiment was proper and just— But would it be proper for me, feeling that this passion or sentiment (give it any name) still lurks in my breast; for me to appear at the sanctuary of the Lord, "and to him who can read all hearts and from whom no secrets are hid;" affirm that I was at peace with all men; and had eradicated from my mind this bitter feeling of insulted innocense; at the very moment that this thorn rankled in my breast. Surely it would be mockery, and while such is my thought it would be wickedness—

The spirit of forgiveness is angelic; and I would fain feel as my loved Son did, when four or five months before he died he said, in that tender tone of melancholy enthusiasm. "Mother I am at peace with all mankind; I know not the living being that I would harm"— Such I hope and trust is the sentiment of my heart— I would help and assist my bitterest enemy in the hour of his need and do him all the good in my power. But as long as the sight of him flutters my heart with pain and disgust, it is too clear that I have not cast off the weakness of my nature: and while this spirit last's I dare not meet the frown of my Creator; and I can only pray that this lurking evil may be removed from me and that by the divine inspiration of Christ I may in time conquer the weakness of an untoward nature—

7 December 1835

A gloom is cast over the City by the death of Nathan Smith Senator from Connecticut— It was sudden and altogether unexpected—An enlargement of the heart— It was fortunate it did not occur in the [*railroad*] Car— All the passions appear to be afloat and stormy times must necessarily be expected— *Old combustion* threatens War and the publick mind is in a state of anxious suspence— Intrigue of every description is busy and faction threatens to grow turbulent and all this will probably end in—nothing.

—————

14 December 1835

I should say conscience dictates—Reason regulates—and impulse is the action of human instinct—always true to human nature but often in contradiction to conscience and reason combined—

How bitterly sick I am of all the nefarious details of political life! Condemnation would be passed upon me generally for my opinions—but when the grave yawns before us we see with different eyes and the tinsel glitter of the world palls upon the mind and betrays in all its raggedness the empty nothingness of its aims— The most insignificant minds, the basest characters; most disgusting means; the basest intrigues; the most unblushing lies; the most malignant misrepresentations; backbiting, slander, and all the fabrications of the lowest and most venal minds; perpetually goaded by the worst passions form its basis; and in an elective government where the flame is never allowed to expire: but like the vestal fire is forever renewed and kept alive by the most combustible materials: even the hearts of the most honest must at last be kindled into rage; by the constant unshrinking malevolence of party spirit; and the judgment obscured by the rankling and ever accumulating thorns, that like the venemous bites of paltry musketoes wound by the perpetual itteration of the sting, until the whole mass of the blood is enflamed and corrupted—

In this unmittigated war of petty spite; of degrading littleness; the morals of the best people are perverted: and the everlasting stimulous to the passions; excites equally by its constant repitition to rash but often noble impulses; as well as to the Iago like attacks of smooth'd face hypocrites; who wear the mask of friendship, to stab more securely the victims whom they assail— It is a dark view of human Nature!—but the close examination and the personal knowledge of the history of two generation's; has *too* thouroughly imbued *me* with these opinions, to induce me to hesitate in the expression of them; and every coming day stamps deeper the ineffaceable truth—That Government is unquestionably the most moral and the best, which keeps the evil passions of mankind in abeyance—

16 December 1835

Surely sorrow comes upon me in every direction! My God! my God! have mercy upon me and teach me to bear up against my trials; for they are too much for me without thy help—

In thee I put my trust! Forsake me not in the hour of my distress, and if this is religion teach me not to despise it, but fill my heart with the dictates of truth that I may bear that persecution which a humble christian servant ought to suffer, with humility and resignation— If my husband and my departed Children have 'erred in thy sight forgive them O Lord; in thy mercy forgive them, and turn the hearts of those who are left: but O spare me Lord, and fill not my heart with the bitterness of the pharrisee; that I may still believe in the spirit of Jesus Christ; whose religion is mercy and who condemns none who wish and desire to do well according to the best of their understanding—

Louisa's writings suggest that her thoughts frequently swung from the deeply spiritual to the heavily political. As the wife of a congressman, she found herself engaged in some of the most divisive issues of the day, especially that of slavery.

John Quincy focused much of his energy as a representative on opposing slavery. He was especially active in challenging the notorious "gag rule" in the House, which initially prevented citizens from submitting antislavery petitions to Congress and later automatically tabled them when submitted to prevent any debate on the topic. John Quincy used his parliamentary acumen to circumvent the rule as much as possible and was instrumental in organizing the coalition that eventually overturned it in 1844. Although Louisa also disapproved of slavery, she struggled with the divisions it caused within both the nation as a whole and her immediate family. At least two of her brothers-in-law were slave owners, and presumably other relations of hers from Maryland were equally supportive of the institution.

24 December 1835

The awful question of Slavery is before the publick and the question is of so fearfully exciting a nature it keeps me in a state of perpetual alarm— God has said blessed are the peace makers! Then why should we to promote the ends of a few factious politicians endanger the lives of thousands? or occasion panics and alarms almost worse than death?

If I suffer apprehension continually from the unruly bursts of feeling excited by the artful on an ardent and impetuous nature what must be the terrors of those who tremble for all their near kindred horrors, even worse than death.— If in the wondrous wisdom of the Almighty Power the decree has gone forth may he mercifully grant that my husband may be spared from becoming the scourge through which this great event is to be atchieved, and may heaven inspire my lips with persuasion to prevent mischiefs so threatening and awful— My reason tells me that much is to be said on both sides of the question— It is a great struggle for power and dominion equally subjecting the rights and privileges of both parties— And when the master passions of men are concentrated upon the vital interests of wealth and power reason loses her hold of the minds of men and the overweening stimulous of jealousy adds fuel to the fire— By the encrease and magnitude of the Slave States the Northern confederacies must in the end be over powered in so far as the influence of the Government is concerned and from thence already arise the mortal enmities so rapidly encreasing throughout the northern territories of this vast continent— Wealthy, powerful, educated and religious they feel and disdain the manacled population of the South, and the good and respectable part of the community, suffer the religious feeling of misguided sympathy, to hurry them on to measures, without observing the terrible results to which they really expose their haughty, but really afflicted bretheren— And these in their turn arrogantly assume the imperial and dictatorial tone appertaining to the very nature of their jurisdiction; operating perpetually to exasperate the deadly feuds which irrisistably grow from the radical influences of their joint positions— God in his judgment alone can prevent the calamity which sooner or later must end the strife; and let us heartily pray that he who rules the hearts of men will so dispose them, that some wise and temperate course may be pursued which shall prevent the direful evils so fearfully anticipated—

25 December 1835

Christmas day was spent delightfully at Mrs: Fryes with real family sociability and we did not return until ten o'clock at night. Notwithstanding this the pleasure derived from our visit as usual produced a painful reaction yesterday and the shortlived enjoyment seemed to render the reality of our loss more bitter in the home of my darling Son— Poor Mary! these trials awaken all her sorrows and produce a degree of nervous irritability truly distressing— Utterly incompetent to conquer my own feelings I can offer no consolation and our mutual misery is encreased by the contact and the different manner in which the nature of our affections operate.

O memory with thy magic ~~spell~~ hue
Let fancy ~~picture~~ gay ~~delight~~ my mind imbue
On thy bright tablet ever ~~dwell~~ shine
The vivid joys of ~~heavens pure~~ light divine
Where Angels in their robes of fleece
Exalting shout the song of ~~grace~~ peace
Expand their glitt'ring wings above
And come as messengers of love
To heal the bleeding broken heart
The dews of heavenly grace impart
To cheer the drooping sinking mind
And blessings shed among mankind

29 December 1835

A fearful sickness assailed my darling Grandchild [*Mary Louisa*] and for some hours my mind was subdued by the pangs of agonizing apprehension— Humbly I beseech pardon for my unholy terrors. They had nearly reduced me to the grave, and the gratitude of my soul is raised in thankfulness and praise to my maker for sparing one yet unfit to die— O may I rejoice in thy mercy and to be thankful for thy manifold blessings and let "my Soul praise the Lord, and speak good of his name"—

The Year has expired and once more the family met the busy world with *seeming* joy. The future again opens before us! and what is the future! to what does it reach! where does it end! Like the ineffable rays of the Sun, it may tint all with gladness and beauty; or it may cast into shadow, the prospects of hope, and peace— Alone for those who are left me can I have a care: for if I read my heart aright, no selfish thought o'er shadows its views

or its desires—for the grave yawns too widely; to give up its yielding victims—
For others I would fain exert myself whose age and circumstance makes
life desireable; and to whom the allurements of society naturally possess a
charm however evanescent— Tis Nature— The Rainbow spreads its beauties
to the eyes but for a moment; When lo 'tis gone, and leaves no trace behind—
The glowing meteor darting from the sky becomes extinct ere yet it is beheld;
its course to all unknown— The winds arise and fall with quickly changing
skill, in dreadful force arrayed; and man in pride of might, must succumb
to its will! The thunder's sullen roar, the lightnings vivid flash in union
great combine, to teach mankind their Power! In what does it consist? Man,
feeble man can GUESS; but whence it comes, or goes, a problem yet remains.
The Soul aspiring aims at high knowledge far beyond mans means; and
proudly rattles the chains he so unwilling wears, to cope with the majesty
of Deity itself: and prates with Pea cock vanity of *possibility!* Yet can no
satisfactory reason *give,* why such and such things are? Atoms of Clay! To
play their little part; their pompous pride would lead their little wits to play
with vast infinity! And why? Because the vital spark that lights them on to
heaven, will brightly shine when earth is seen no more; to seek those themes
unknown which only scintillate with gleams of partial light, upon the human
mind, in worlds of space more pure;—where unmixt love commingling with
the Skies, shall ope the heavens to our view—

I have written a few lines with which I am not satisfied— What could I
find worthy to deck an Angels grave? Maternal love and Poetry, have nought
within their scope to satisfy the mind, when excellence worn down by misfortune is the theme, and the out pourings of the warmest heart seem cold,
when they attempt a panegyric—

Johns Grave

Softly tread! for herein lies
The young, the beautiful, the wise;
Sorrow untimely nipped the flower
He sunk beneath her blasting power
But left a loved and hallow'd name
~~That Orphan's, Widows, and the poor proclaim~~
Tears of the poor! His living fame!
Lay him where the violets creep

Where roses clust'ring wanton sweep,
To woo the Zephyrs as they fly
And blushing sweetly, fade to die—
Where the pale Seringa's nod
And shed their fragrance o'er the sod;
Where heartsease rich in beauty glow
And fair white Lilies trembling blow;
There let the mourning glory shine
To court the heavenly light divine—
The Willow waiving o'er his head
To weep the relicks of the dead—
The Cypress evergreen bestow
A Mothers tears unceasing flow—

1 March 1836

Six long weeks have elapsed since sickness of a violent character prostrated me to deaths door— Mercy! great mercy has been shown to me by my Almighty Father: and I bow in patient resignation to his decrees; he knows best what befits his creatures— I have suffered much of pain both of mind and body; and I have prayed, and do constantly and incessantly pray, for strength from above to guide me through the labrynth, through which my path is doomed to stray— Nursed with great care and kindness, my whole heart is filled with gratitude to Mary, and to all who have assisted; and I heartily wish it was in my power to prove it, in a more effective manner: but poverty stricken in spirit, and in purse, the wish only betrays imbecile weakness. May the Almighty restore my poor shaken mind to its usual soundness, and forgive its dark wanderings.

The Second Seminole War, sometimes called the Florida War, a response to the Indian removal policies of Presidents Andrew Jackson and Martin Van Buren, began in 1835 and continued until 1842. Seminoles joined forces with fugitive slaves to oppose the U.S. Army and resist relocation out of Florida. A lengthy series of battles over seven years led to a stalemate and eventual resolution in which Seminoles accepted a reservation within the state of Florida.

At around the same time, Americans became increasingly interested in acquiring territory controlled by Mexico. In April 1836 in Texas, Gen. Sam Houston successfully fought for independence. John Quincy believed Jackson was encouraging Houston and his followers in the hopes of eventually annexing Texas as a slave state, once again creating an imbalance between slave and free states.

Louisa makes clear in these passages her disdain for Jackson, no doubt a holdover from the bitter political campaign fought between him and John Quincy.

April 1836

The extreme uneasiness I feel at the state of Mr Adams health is beyond language to express! Why will he waste all the energies of his fine mind upon a people who do not either understand or appreciate his talents— Surely his family have some claims on him as well as the Nation and it is cruel to deprive them of his aid and strength for exertions ruinous to his fortune his peace of mind and the domestic comfort of his family— They tell me I am too anxious and fret unnecessarily! Have I not already seen my darling Son wither away before my eyes! And was not the same cry set up! Did any one note the direful change until it was too too late to do any good— O my racked conscience night and day I reproach myself for my passiveness and never shall I cease to regret the past for I was a—*Mother—*

26 April 1836

The anxiety I suffer on Mr. Adams's account, is beyond expression; but the same fate which has followed me through life, presses upon me still, and the fears which beset my mind are as usual attributed to an exaggerated fancy, and a too vivid imagination— It is most remarkable how this *apparent* fate pursues me— Yet have I no faith in predestination or fatalism; for more and more am I convinced as I journey on through life, that God is good and gracious to his creatures, and that half the troubles which assail mankind, originate in their own waywardness, their mistakes and their indomitable pride; which leads them perpetually from their obedience to the laws of their great Creator, and through the influence of their baneful passions, to defy even those safe-guards, which their own reason present— In the great chain of events; man is necessarily linked with man for evil and for good: and no single individual effort can insure his success, however virtuous, however good, however excellent; and this undeniable fact destroys all the theoretical pretence of unlimited freedom—

The experience of Ages teaches mankind for ever its inadequacy to promote the ends desired; for in every forlorn instance, however successful for a period, it ends in licentiousness; and from the very seeds of its own intemperance, produces excess, and in its ripeness; tears down all the judicious barriers of restraint, necessarily overthrowing those fundamental bulwarks of religious controul; emanating from God himself; and founded and adapted to the nature, and the necessities of his creatures, those creatures of his hands, whose Natures he must best have understood— Rebellion whatever may be said to the contrary is defiance of Law— Law is essential to man's benefit, as he cannot live in a social or a civilized State without— Law is in its best forms liable to corruption, or to what is equally evil, to fall into laxity; and impunity has the natural and ever encroaching tendency, to encrease of *liberty,* or that advance to wickedness and crime, which deadens conscience, and Destroys the fear of punishment: while familiarity with guilt, gives vigour to the mind; and man strides with rapid and gigantic pace, into misery and bloodshed; boasting of those deeds which should sink him with eternal shame— The history of Man from the Creation to the present time is the same—disobedience to laws virtually good, improperly administered, and the proud disgust of beneficial controul; and such must be the course of man; for he lives in extremes but I am fully convinced cannot live "unwhipt of justice."

How mysterious are events— The splendour of this Country originated in the persecution and extermination of a large portion of the aboriginal owners of this Country: and now see them rising in their strength, and struggling to maintain themselves upon the last remnants of their mighty possessions still unjustly coveted; and pouring with a fierceness of energy hitherto unknown; upon the abodes of their oppressors—and sustaining with more than civilized skill, a regular warfare with a disciplined Army— Hordes of barbarians are rising in every direction and indescribable horrors are committed in a christian land— And we look on amazed and bewildered while such scenes are performing by the choice friends of our highly favoured Chief Magistrate, who steal into the bosom of a neighbouring Country, and there in ridicule and to the disgrace of our Country: Declare themselves *independent!* and collecting the refuse vice of our people; pretend to form themselves into a Government, with our Institutions; and elect their Officers from the most wicked and debased among them, to give dignity to our *glorious Republic*— What a Lesson!!! Have we not set them the example? Are not the very scum of the Community now the Rulers of our Land!!! Is it not the fashion to say that a man cannot *flourish* if he is not a rogue? And is not a *just man* sunk, ruined, condemned, and persecuted!!! America thy glory has passed away! and thy honour is in the Graves of thy once illustrious dead! They were thy Towers of strength; and in their names was thy honour and thy freedom!— To be of them, to belong to them was glory; and will be glory in time to come,

> Sweet! sweet be thy sleep in the tombs of the brave
> Where honour contentedly lies
> My children embalmed in the peace of the Grave
> To honours eternal arise—

My pen as usual has run wild— To return to the subject of Mr. Adams's situation; my fears are as usual founded on the positive assertions of the Physician; who makes no mystery of his opinion, and that opinion is anxious and unfavorable! Yet I am laughed at for my apprehensions. O God mercifully save me from this calamity; and spare me in thy goodness— I cannot look forward to such an evil—its magnitude is too awful— Gracious God preserve me and grant me strength; thou only can'st help me.—

7 May 1836

The May Ball has passed and our two lovely little Girls performed their little dance with great success— They looked sweetly in their scotch dress and danced Cotillons with ease and spirit— But into what a new world I seemed to be plunged— My spirits sank as I gazed around me when I found myself almost desolate in the midst of a Crowd and my little Grand daughters kneeling at the feet of Miss [*Ellen*] Woodberry— Time is granted us to heal the sore wounds of bitter feeling and I thank God that repeated lessons are breaking down and humbling the overweening pride of my corrupt Nature or more properly passions— If the sainted spirit of my injured Son could see his lovely ones may he view it as the offspring of Peace descending through his sainted means as blessings on his little darlings to blot out the remembrance of past strife and obliterate the faults and the errors of those who in the very outset of his life brought disgrace on *him* for a noble deed— O let the waters of oblivion steep away in their depths profound all these recollections that my latter days may not continue pierced by the thornes of past troubles which are gone by I trust to return no more.

The Ball was very pretty—but I doubt if such balls are suitable to our manners— They are calculated to create false notions of life bordering on reality in forms without casting such a shade of absurdity over the performance as to destroy the early taste for distinction and flattery— The Adams's at the feet of a *Woodberry* [*a Jackson supporter*] even in playful parties kneeling and presenting a crown was a picture to teach America to blush! O tempora O Mores!— I could indeed cry out with the Psalmist "Lord! now let thy Servant depart in peace." Am I not yet humbled enough?

June 1836

Genl Jackson it is widely rumoured intends to take the command of the Army, and go against the Indians— Time must prove the truth of this rumour; but if it is true, and he should prove successful, he will not stop his career until he is in possession of Mexico! Who then can foresee what is to follow! If as it is stated there are already twenty thousand Americans there, ready to play into his hands, and probably subservient to his views; what changes may we not expect? For whatever is in store for us let us patiently abide the will of heaven— Whatever is to happen amid the perils of War and threatened famine, the arm of the Almighty can save us, and give us strength to support the inflictions— At present gloom is around us and thick coming terrors stare us in the face; but light may arise when the darkness appears to be the deepest—

28 August 1836

Much time has elapsed since I last opened this book—and the revolving months have rolled on in rapid succession, full of great events; mighty in their consequences to the future; yet little noted by a Nation, swelled into arrogance by uninterrupted prosperity; and into cruelty and injustice by the grasping covetousness of unruly passion; love of our neighbours treasures, which has already prostrated and levelled as of old the greatest Nations of antiquity— Among the most striking events which have occurred, is the death of Mr. Madison; the last of that list of able men, who shed a steady and unwavering lustre upon this Country; and whose undying fame will long outlive the Government, and institutions which he so eminently assisted to build; but which like all the works of man can last but for a time— The career of this man was neither brilliant, nor calculated to dazzle the senses, by the gulling claptraps of warlike action, which in their nature address themselves to the senses; and fetter the minds of the unreasoning multitude; ready always to admire the deeds which licence their evil passions; and which yield example for the gratification of all those wicked and alluring tastes which corrupt mankind; and defy the moral laws of civilized society— That Mr Madison could not stand "blood and carnage with composure" is most true; but that he could bend all the energies of a great and powerful mind, to heal the wounds inflicted by a long and merciless civil war; has been seen and substantially established, by a system of practical facts, on which in a great degree in combination with the greatest men of the past age; the present wonderful prosperity of this Nation is founded; and has laid the basis of a solid reputation—

The men of that age are now laid low; and like the Stars who formed a rich galaxy of light, to lure the world from darkness among the Ancients, by the radiancy of mental power; they though laid low in their earthly graves; form a Nebuly of clustering light, which although indistinct, lend a cheering ray to guide succeeding generations in the paths of wisdom and science— Man like the beasts of the field is I fear naturally ferocious: and for this reason, did the Almighty issue his commandments; to show that this boasted superiority of man over all other creatures; consisted in his capacity to curb the besetting sins of his earthly nature, prone to fail by excess of temptation; and only preserved by the wholesome discipline of mental energy, essential to the government of conduct; and adapted to soften the asperities of human character, and the vicious impulses conducive to crime— Let the blood-stained Hero then beware of his latter day; lest he there find perdition, instead of the fallacious glory acquired by the praises of unthinking man: and remember that every leaf of the Laurel crown *he* wears, sheds the dew of human blood upon his brow; which cries to heaven for revenge: and never forget, that though war is a necessary evil, from which apparently the world cannot be exempted; that even success is, and must be attended, by the curses of mutilated thousands; and the groans and tears of widows, and Orphans; whose cries are heard at the throne of grace, with pity and compassion—

The long and almost even tenure of life granted to Mr. Madison; the calm and delightful influences surrounding his latter days; and the benignant acts of his dying hours; cast a glow of heavenly peace around his death bed when ripe in the fullness of years; blessing and blessed he closed his eyes in that sleep, which leads to eternity, and which is embalmed by the tears of love— In him was found the *simplicity of mental greatness;* yielding a rich harvest of excellent fruit, for the benefit of the Country to which he did honour; and to the friends and family who surrounded him with respect, affection, and veneration. A far nobler reward, than the meretricious glare of public parade, got up for party purposes; and rarely bestowed where eminently due; but often neglected to the shame of the Nation; which it stamps with everlasting and shameless ingratitude—

> Mourn o'er thy Country and her rifled Laws
> Thy spirit guard, and still protect her cause
> With golden thoughts posthumous, wake the mind
> The words of wisdom yet shall save mankind
> While on the page the ling'ring eye shall rest
> Thy ecchoed voice resounds from mansions bles't,
> A happy medium 'tween thy race and God
> To save thy Nation from th' avenging rod—

In the early 1830s, Charles Francis embraced the task of organizing—what he called "methodizing"—the family papers. From that work emerged a lifelong effort to publish the writings of his ancestors, especially his grandparents, John and Abigail. At this time, as Louisa relates below, Charles had begun what became Letters of Mrs. Adams, Wife of John Adams, *published in 1840 to considerable acclaim. He would go on to publish three further editions of Abigail's letters and a similar collection for John, along with the ten-volume* Works of John Adams, *reprinting primarily John's public correspondence. Louisa appreciated this labor but also particularly enjoyed the opportunity it provided to recollect John and especially Abigail through their writings.*

1 September 1836

On perusing the Letters of Mrs. Abigail Adams we are struck by the vast and varied powers of her mind; the full benevolence of an excellent heart and the strength of her reasoning capacity— Full of energy, buoyant and elastic; although often depressed by affliction and tried severely by the unfavorable influences which surrounded her—we see her ever as the guiding Planet around which all revolved, performing their separate duties only by the impulse of her magnetic power, which diffused a mild and glowing radiance over all who moved within the sphere of her fascinating attraction. She possessed the art of softening the asperities of grosser natures; and in some measure of moulding them to her will, by the effect of example; and attained a sway over the mind, by the rich and highly cultivated superiority of her own, where lay garnered in rich abundance, the stores of wisdom, and experience, gathered from books; and collected from long and varied practical observation; dispensed in the most agreeable form, and adorned by the pure principles of genuine christianity— Her Letters are treasures richer than the Mines of Golconda, which will shed a lustre upon her race, from which a harvest may be gleaned, calculated to promote their happiness in this world, and the next if properly applied—

Under the sway of accute and disappointed feelings, I have sometimes been led to miscontrue acts intended to be kind, which I now sincerely repent— We did not understand one-another; and half of the enjoyment I might have possessed in the early part of my career, was lost to me by the paltry rival jealousies of those, whose interest it was to deceive her— After my return from Russia these impressions were happily removed; and she herself told me, she was sorry she had not better understood my character, and proved herself on every occasion a kind and affectionate Mother— And here I will add that from the hour that I entered into his family, The

Ex-President John Adams never said an unkind word to me; but ever to the hour of his death, treated me with the utmost tenderness, and distinction the most flattering— I loved him living, and I venerate his Memory Ardent and impetuous in his passions, with a mind

> Of depth a vast profound; from whence
> Rich ever living sources spread
> Their Streams of radiant light; flowing
> Impetuos as the rainbow Falls,
> From great Niágàra
> Its splendid hues in brighter wisdom found,
> Expansive knowledge gleaned,
> Thro' tracks of varied lore; imparted
> With delight amid the listning throng—

Would that my feeble pen could do justice to this exalted pair whose worth

> Was all too high for praise so paltry—

May they live as bright examples in the memory and the hearts of their descendants; and to quote Popes line with a trifling change I will only say

> If to their share some mortal errors fall
> Think of their worth and y'ill forget them all—

10 September 1836

On perusing the Letters of Mrs. Adams I cannot refrain from wishing that they were published and that talents so superior should be allowed to shine as bright lights among the luminaries of the past and to gladden the hearts of many a timid female whose rays too feebly shine, not for want of merit but for want of confidence in the powers, and encouragement in the exercise of those capacities, with which the Almighty has gifted them— Many of the Sex might thus redeem the reputation to which it is entitled and by proving themselves equal as Mrs Adams to practice all the most virtuous and feminine duties convince mankind that the native mind clear, full, and vigorous in its perceptions; is as capable of solid attainment, and enlarged improvement; as that of man; though unadorned by that extrinsic ornament attained by classical acquirement; which however it may embellish, more frequently gives a vicious taint to the tastes; in its too exciting effect upon ardent imaginations; and perhaps by weakening that faith in the doctrines of christianity, which is the only certain basis of moral rectitude—

Louisa's son John died in debt. In 1827 he had taken over responsibility for managing the Columbian Mills, a flour mill on Rock Creek in Washington, D.C., that John Quincy had purchased in 1823. Son John continued to manage the mills, with some success, even occasionally helping to work the mill itself, until his health became too compromised to allow him to continue. But he had no other real source of income and had "extravagant tastes," according to his brother Charles Francis. Little money was left for John's widow and children, who depended on the Adamses for financial support.

24 April 1839

This day Mary found the Deeds of John Adams's little Estate adjoining her own Land. In the settlement of his concerns I am under the strong impression that there has been mistakes in point of understanding; in the original terms of agreement between him and his Father— He repeatedly told me, that there was a debt due to him of 3000 dollars, prior to his death; and as we never paid rent for his house, in which we lived, and which Rent would have contributed much towards his Board if so charged; it should stand as an offset to the charges brought so heavily against him; and which charges were the expences of the two families, and not incurred especially for his own—

Of the Mill Affairs I cannot speak—but his memory is too dear to my heart, to make it possible to endure that any unnecessary stigma should attach to his name; and I do not think that among the numerous publick avocations which occupy Mr Adams, that he has time to examine minutely into the affairs of the family— I mean to cast no reproach fault or blame to any one; but justice is duty, and duty I will perform—

2 June 1839

This morning I have been reading some pages of President John Adams's Journal— In these pages I was much struck by his power of reasoning his impartial self examination; the systematic deliberation with which he studied his subjects and the judgments, with which he formed his decisions. With a mind thus accustomed to self scourging is it wonderful that the sophistical flummery resorted to by half the race of what are called the *great* of mankind whose minds deluded by vanity and unchastized by cool deliberation and studied judgment is it surprizing I repeat that he should often have turned disgusted from the mere subtlety of argumentative genius and been provoked by the mere wordy colloquy of the half learned pedant who often visited him in his old age more to gratify their own vanity than to glean from his lips the words of Wisdom? The very ardour of his nature led him to seek that source from which the fountain of wisdom alone yields its treasures, books; action:, the result of energy and indefatigable exertion in the interests of his Country; enforced that knowledge of mankind, which experience and constant association in their multifarious pursuits alone can teach; Here he learnt the hidden workings of the passions of mankind; how fearful, yet how almost impossible judiciously to controul—

Among all the great characters that it has been my lot to meet in the devious paths of a long and mingled life, I have never met with a mind of such varied powers, such accute discrimination, and which if I may use the expression, was so intrinsically *sound;* with a memory so fertile, so clear, and so perspicuous— Every thing in his mind was rich, racy, and true; and his conversation was one continued stream of glowing reminiscences; gleaned from books, from his intercourse with mankind, from travel, and from reflection and experience. The young listened to him with delight; the old with veneration. No ambition of praise; no insidious and puerile vanity; lurked beneath an effort to please, to catch the momentary applause of a gaping multitude. His conversation was the bare echo of that mine of thoughts, which his rich intellect yielded in language the most easy and familiar to his hearers; and most impressive to their understandings. But sometimes, like the streams of the bold Niagara rushing with impetuous force, they would intimidate, the common place beings, who live only to pander to the appetites of the many; and who only

"Softly speak in Lydian measures"

lest perchance they should awaken the ears of men to *truth's* which many think, not good for man to know—

Thus I knew him and thus I describe him— He always appeared to me to despise your mere political Demagogues, and perhaps to make too light of their pretentions: and thus laid the foundation of a bitter enmity among the factions, who were very inferior to himself; but who found their level in the generality of men less gifted and less worthy—

Why is it that *duty* is rarely pleasing or rather why is it that its performance is almost always irksome and consequently never agreeable— Is it not because it interferes with the gratification of our *self Will,* and that we dislike to be tied down by the moral obligations which bind society, more by custom than by law; and which we fancy check the freedom of what we vulgarly term our independence?

It has been the fashion to say that as Children were not born to please themselves, no real ties bind them to their parents; and that blood relationship, should exact neither affection or gratitude— To my mind there is no truth whatever in such an assertion; unless man like the animal should cast off its young as soon as it can walk, and eat; and thus man leave his Child in the helplessness of its infancy, to find its way through life without the aids of a steady, unflinching, warm parental affection— From the moment of the birth, we incur a vast debt of gratitude which a life cannot pay, even if we acquire nothing more than the common cares of paternal tenderness which rears us to maturity— How much more then do we owe to those who with unsparing means, with anxious watching, with incessant love, have poured out upon us all the advantages of education, of accomplishment, of morals, and of virtue; which are to fit us for a sphere of useful action in those stations of life, high or low, which we may by circumstances be called upon to assume; and the duties of which we should never have been competent to fulfil; had we not reaped those beneficial influences; on which our capacity and fitness was solely founded— There must be a direliction in that mind which could for a moment shrink from the acknowledgment of so vast a debt: founded in the weakest of all vanities, self idolatry! of all the delusions the most deceptive; and the most conducive to the formation of erronious opinions; and false deductions of the opinions of others— Those who have received ten talents must be faithful Stewards; and repay the Master who loaned them, with large interest; or they prove themselves unworthy of the treasure.

―――――――――

17 June 1839

I have sometimes regreted that I have left off my journal— Diary's are amusing while you are drawn into the focus of active society, where events follow each other in rapid succession, and create a thirst for fresh intelligence as the hours fly round— But when time speeds his course in a monotonous circle of given things; a Diary becomes a memeto of puerilities; better forgotten than remember'd as they are considered rather as *test's* of the failure of the human faculties; than as the nice characteristics of a discriminating mind—

Ca. 17 June 1839

When I lived in the stir and bustle of political life I thought it my duty to avoid all marks of distaste to persons whom I did *not like*— When I retired to a private station, I resumed the privileges of an individual in the right to choose my associates— Was I right. I fear not! For I have narrowed my circle of acquaintance to nothing; and what is infinitely worse it has led to an indulgence of feelings of dislike, and often antipathy; unsuited to christian charity— For my Children, for myself, where have I found friends! Could the Butterfly life of a Politician, procure them, or fix them! Has it not rather turned to gall the few drops of honey that was mixed in my portion? Has it not embitered the whole of my domestic life— Fame! what a shadow!!

21 June 1839

What is the meaning of transcendentalism? I do not understand it— If the Soul which animates the human body is an emanation of the Deity granted to us as the guardian ruler of our course while in the flesh thro' the knowledge of good and ill and the capacity of improvement does it follow that we are to believe it endued with the attributes of the Creator? And that intoxicated by the possession of a little more *ability* to shine than our neighbours we are to adore the light that burns within such an unhalowed shrine and glorify it? Every flower bears its vital escence in billions of multiplied divisions; and man is but a flower like the grass that withereth away—

22 June 1839

In the observations which I carelessly make in this silly Book; I mean not to point at any especial objects, or to censure any individuals:— I mean only to fortify my own mind, in its convictions of the truth; although I am conscious of my utter incapacity to act up to the doctrines which I deem so super excellent— One of the greatest difficulties which we have to contend against in the course of a long life; *is,* what we term Amour propre! which is so exquisitely sensitive, that it is barely possible to praise one person without wounding his neighbour—for that still sly monitor conscience; however it may appear to slumber; always wakes to feeling when aroused by the flattering eulogy of qualities in others, which we know we do not possess ourselves; and the snarling propensity which wrestles within us on such occasions; acts pretty much as matrimonial squabblers do at the interference of another person; on whom the ire of both the belligerents falls with equal impetuosity, and they make up *their* difference, at the expence of the Peace maker— Thus the flatterer is seldom punished for his adulation; but the flattered is never forgiven for being *supposed* to possess superior merit—

It is often said that we should never seek into the motives of action!!! If this is true by what scale is action or conduct to be tried? It appears to me if we are to hurry along without some knowledge of the actuating principle which propels us we may commit much mischief and much harm and both to the community and to ourselves— Actions to be beneficial must be weighed and considered and it is only the habits acquired by a sound moral education and a pure religious one that will produce spontaneous acts of benevolence from one creature to another— Men often err in their systematised schemes of charitable beneficence because being vast the mind of man can only grasp the superficial and they must necessarily overlook the multitude of ramifications in which this extended scale may place the interests of mankind and in their general schedule they are too apt to forget that in the effort to produce partial good they elicit and bring into operation all the bad and oppressive passions of the wicked— The motives of action in such schemes we must suppose originate, in the purest philanthropy; and the good of mankind must be their basis— To rush into such schemes without a motive is nonsense for without such motives to positive and continued action their could be no result to reward for their exertion— The impulses of man are I believe naturally good: but toil and suffering and contact with his own species in the different interests of life soon rubs down the keen edge of his natural sensibilities and alas he too soon learns that he must live on the defensive with his race or be crushed in his struggle for life property and subsistence—

25 June 1839

Every day brings its thorns and every day I find my temper growing worse and my reason less powerful to controul it— I feel sensible that I am outliving the strong affections of my nature and that I can no longer combat against the little everlasting jarring of what is termed social life— My soul turns with absolute disgust from the mean fluctuations of political strife and in the common associations of life I feel that I cannot think like others— My opinions I know are altogether unsuited to my situation and I have the conviction hourly that they do more harm than good— Yet at sixty can I become another creature?

The First Church of Quincy, established in 1639, celebrated its bicentennial on 29 September 1839. As one of the leading families of the town, the Adamses were expected to participate in and support the event, which was overseen by Rev. William Parsons Lunt. But Louisa, educated by Roman Catholic nuns and reared in the Church of England, had never accepted the Unitarianism of New England—yet another issue that kept her feeling like an outsider in church-oriented Quincy—and was uncomfortable marking the anniversary. Furthermore, she could not reconcile the rigid Puritanism of the original church with the loose theology of its current Unitarian iteration. Still, as she discusses below, she did her duty and aided the "Ladies of Quincy" in drafting a letter presenting gifts to Lunt for the occasion.

Louisa was also concerned about the Panic of 1837, a severe economic depression that would last until 1843. The financial situation was aggravated by inadequate amounts of specie (gold and silver coin, as opposed to paper money) in the system. Banks began to suspend payments in specie in an attempt to protect their falling reserves, but inadequate controls led to numerous bank failures.

Ca. 29 September 1839

Next Sunday there is to be a Centenial Celebration of the first settlement of the Church in this town or township— Mr Lunt will, I have no doubt make a great deal of the occasion— But I confess I am very much puzzled to understand how this matter is to be worked— The original settlers were a bigoted sect, whose religious opinions and enthusiastic *faith,* enabled them to accomplish difficulties of a stupendous character, which could only have been sustained by the vigourous minds of persons, supporting a cause, productive in every age, of the highest atchievements Religion; and *that* the Religion of Christ, the only Religion the basis of which is meek forbearance, and patience under long and accumulated suffering; in the promotion, and furtherance of a great purpose— Unswerving faith, severe morality; were the practical effects of a rigid Creed, which bound them together, if not in the spirit of carnal love; by the strong ties of devotion to a cause, in which their safety or their destruction depended— This bond of union was sustained merely by their enthusiastic *zeal;* and that *zeal* led to an abundance of reward, and to a rich harvest for futurity— Now unless this celebration is to show the changes produced by "the march of intellect" so much boasted of by mankind; and to show that *apostacy* from all these *holy* opinions, is a proof of the folly of all *those* maintained by their forefathers; by their most enlightened successors; I cannot see the use or the propriety of this celebration, in a Church, diametrically opposed to the *creed* on which the Church was founded; and whose opinions are so very, very latitudinarian, that even their morality, is next akin to nothing—if I may judge from the general instability of their code, as expressed in their conversation—

19 October 1839

What a curious state the world appears to be in! It would seem to a fanciful imagination as if some great convulsion was about to shake the Nations as in times of old; to call them back from their wickedness and to convince them of the Omniscience of the Almighty Power who alone can ordain "thus far shalt thou go and no farther" and who alone can check mankind in its mad career and its most adventurous daring—

Within a few short months have we not been tried by Flood, by Fires, by Shipwreck, by deseare [*disease*]; as if the apportioned suffering was exactly suited to the different passions and interests of the community in which they fall? as if adapted to their individual lusts, and the idols of their peculiar worship—

One might almost believe that the Rod of Aaron was again wielded to reprove them, as it did the Egyptians; and to impress upon the minds of the Jews, ere they were led from captivity; the miraculous Power of the Deity, under whose superintending guidance, they were to become a *great people:* and through their obedience; to be cherished and protected, from generation to generation— We are now threatened with a suspension of the Banks; and the pockets of our good Yankee's are quivering with an ague; that threatens to terminate in a Specie Fever: which probably will occasion the mercantile death of many of the great pretended Capitalists— The luxurious extravagance of this race, has not been sufficiently admonished by a persecuting Government: and their last painful lesson's, and this renewal of their perplexities; may prove beneficial, though I suspect there is more of political, than *dire neccessity* in this state of thing's— Thus does a bad and corrupt government engender vice, in the defence of persecution—

The double Centenial anniversary of an exploded creed; has given so much satisfaction, that Mr. Lunt has obtained quite a renown, which I hope will obtain preferment for him in his Church— I do not agree altogether with his opinions—but they are rendered less harsh by his mildness; and more interesting by the sencerity and modest language in which he conveys his belief, and the moral discipline preached in his discourses— He has received the most flattering proof of the approbation of his Parishioners, in a General subcription, to procure him a suitable present; which must have been very gratifying to himself, and to his family— Dr [*Ebenezer*] Woodward censured the thing and stood nearly "alone in his glory." So much for a parvenue!!!

Yesterday I was called upon to perform a task not altogether suitable to my sense of right— It was not proper to refuse lest that refusal should appear personal; yet, I had a conscientious scruple founded upon a somewhat rational principle— It struck me that the offering presented by the Ladies of Mr. Lunts Church, should have been made by a *Member* of his Church: for although the Note is drawn up in the name of the Ladies of Quincy, it will be perfectly well known, that it was written by one, who does not approve of the doctrines which form the basis of his Creed— Such as the Note is, I wished only to testify my personal regard for himself, and his family: and to express my conviction in the sincerity of his zeal, and approbation of his moral rectitude— He is a man of talent, modest, unassuming, and even timid in the exertion of his powers; and I am really glad that in these days when the arrogance of conceit, and self assurance are productive of so much trashy, though amusing matter from the Press; that this amiable man should meet the encouragement which he eminently deserves.

26 October 1839

In the events which necessarily occur in a long and protracted life we are almost led to believe, I fear wickedly that there are human beings who are so constituted, that no effort can succeed; no affection satisfy; no endeavours please no duty gratify; no prayers mitigate the asperities, the wants, the desires, the caprices, or the cravings of those who surround them— Rectitude of purpose; unceasing wishes to make others happy; the watchfulness of care; the anxities of fear; the perplexities of a household, and the subdued but not altogether hushed pangs of greif; and the afflictions of family bereavement, have an undue influence upon the character, and render us unamiable, and perhaps tincture our *manners,* with severity when our hearts are full of all the benevolent feelings which naturally stimulate to kind actions— I cannot in any other way possibly imagine how it is that I am always wrong; and always wounding the feelings that I most wish to spare! The impossibility to extinguish early habits of thought, engendered among a different people— the difference of practical principles, all tending to the one end, though unlike in action; the perpetual misconception of language originating in the same causes, must have produced this effect: for the very qualities for which I have been loved and valued elsewhere have from the moment that I arrived in this Country to this hour, been those which have rendered me odious here— I am now nearly sixty five years old— No one understands me one bit better than they did the day I arrived; and I feel a desolate loneliness in the very midst of a family, that I have too much idolized; when I think and feel that through these causes they have suffered.— Ill health, circumstances over which I have no controul, and a succession of painful calamities which have been brought upon me by others; may in some measure excuse the irritation of a deseased mind, which cannot regulate itself— Our poor Fanny is apparently better, and may God Almighty grant that she may recover; and be a blessing to her poor widowed Mother—

10 December 1839

Our Lovely and beautiful Fanny was removed to her native Sphere, at ten minutes before six o'clock on Wednesday Eveng. the 20th of Novbr. the Eveng on which the Planet Venus irradiated the heavens with a light that shone with an unusually resplendent glory— Its brilliant rays darted into the chamber directly on her Mother as she lay in bed; shedding a soothing light oer the chamber of the suffering Child, who was so soon to be transplanted to her native heaven. May God sanctify her death to us all—

O gracious God who has thought fit again to manifest thy displeasure with thy erring creatures, and hast taken from us the blessing which thou hadst granted to us, in mitigation of the many sorrows which have befallen us— Pardon us merciful God, and accept the humble repentance of thy creatures, for whose Sins there is no help; and teach us O Lord God to humble ourselves with submission to thee, who knowest best what is good for us, and how much we can bear— Save us, graciously save us from the vices of our own hearts; and deliver us from the evil of our ways, through the mercy of Jesus Christ our Lord and Saviour, Amen!

Not surprisingly, Louisa became increasingly preoccupied with death and the afterlife as she reached her own later years. Thomas Baker Johnson died in 1843, as did numerous other friends and family members over the following

years. By the mid-1840s, John Quincy's health was beginning to fail. He suf-
fered a cerebral hemorrhage while in Boston in November 1846, from which he
recovered sufficiently to return to Washington, D.C., by February 1847. But he
remained quite weak—his convalescence was "slow—scarcely perceptible . . .
without any substantial restoration of health"—and Louisa's concern did not
abate, especially since John Quincy was clearly preoccupied with making
preparations for his death. Louisa turned to prayer, particularly asking her
deceased children to intercede on her behalf.

Louisa was also making preparations for death. From 1843 to 1844, she
drafted the outline of a will—a final version has never been found—leaving
most of her property to her granddaughter Mary Louisa Adams, with Charles
Francis as executor. As the entries below show, however, she continued to revise
her plans and leave additional instructions for various bequests and funeral
arrangements.

Still, John Quincy and Louisa lived to celebrate their fiftieth wedding an-
niversary in July 1847, a joyous occasion with a large party organized by
Charles and his wife, Abigail.

September 1845

On the 3d of Sept Nancy Adams the Widow of T B. Adams departed this
life after a long and dreadfully suffering illness of five Months, accelerated
by the death of her Daughter Abby S Angier, who died on the 4th. of February in the same year 1845—

They died in the full hope of that blessed future, which our merciful
Saviour has promised to believing christians; in the full forgiveness of
Sin— May his blessing abide with them for ever— Amen—

14 March 1847

When sorrows bitterly assail us, griefs rend our hearts; wilt thou merciful
Lord and Father allow us to turn to thee in humble penitence, and submission; to implore for strength in our need, and patience to endure the trials that
it is thy Will to inflict? With deep humiliation and a breaking heart, I implore thy help in this my great necessity; and O graciously hear my prayer for
the restoration of thy Servant, my Dear Husband; imbue him with thy grace,

and ease his heart of the heavy burthen which oppressessies his spirit, under the affliction which it has pleased thee Almighty Father in thy wisdom to inflict— And we petition thee merifully to support and sustain him by thy grace; that he patiently submit to thy will; and through the redeeming love of our Saviour, he may be enlightened in thy Gospel truths through his holy Spirit!— Amen!

This Morning March the 14th Mr. Adams made me look for his Will which was found Sealed with Seals; enclosed in a brown Paper; and Addressed "My Will" in Charles hand writing— With a desire that *I* should *remember* where it was deposited, with the deeds of his Estates; in the Drawer next to the Window, by his Bed Side in the lower tier of the large Book Shelves, between the Window and the door leading to the Stair case— I here solemnly declare that I have never *seen the Will;* but that I firmly and faithfully believe that my beloved husband has remembered with kindness and perfect justice all his Family; measuring by his love! not their deserts or *mine*—So help me God!!— Should I be able to fulfil this duty?

Louisa Catherine Adams
Sunday 14 March 1847.

O tempora! O Mores!!—

Gaze not on my sorrow. And thou my Darling George if it is permitted smile on thy poor Mother and comfort her drooping spirits—

7 April 1847

O God! from whom alone we thy Creatures can hope for mercy or grace; restore thy afflicted creature through the great and compassionating mercies of our Savior, and graciously hear the cry of deep sorry which gushes from our agonized hearts for his sad and helpless condition— Spare O Lord that great mind thy bounteous gift; and enable him to endure with patience and submission the trial which in thy wisdom thou hast imposed on him to wean him to thy will— Strengthen him to obedience; fortify his spirit in the faith, and graciously encourage him to struggle against the worldly passions, which war with his Soul; that he may be purified by humility, to bow down to thy will in holiness and grace, through the redeeming pity of Him who died for our Sins, and to bless and save us through repentance from despair— Hear us O Lord! mercifully hear us! and help us O Lord our God!— Amen—

In great distress of mind pardon; pardon—

L. C. Adams

12 April 1847

*The Birth day of my
First born Son.
George Washington Adams*

O God! who didst hearken to the prayer of my deep distress; and didst mercyfully grant me the blessing I so ardently craved:— Pardon! pardon! the Sin of thy Servant for deserting the Children of my tenderest love, thy gifts, for mere worldly purposes; at that tender age when they most required a Mothers watchful cares— Forty seven years this day have elapsed since I first pressed this treasured blessing to my breast with joy almost ecstatic! It was thy Will to take both my Cherished Sons from *me,* who knew not how to value thy blessed mercies, and left to others to perform those lovely duties, which thy goodness had called me to fulfil— My heart bleeds in sad repentance; and I would humbly beseech thee to pardon my sad and manyfold offences— And spare me, and strengthen me gracious God, to better perform the duties that are yet left to me, that I may die in the full hope of the forgiveness of my Saviour and redeemer Jesus Christ—Amen. This day 47 years since I gave birth to my poor lost Son!!!

7 May 1847

In the expression of an earnest wish I feel assured that Mr Adams will gratify me should I be called hence e're he departs; that Mary C Adams Widow of my Poor and beloved John may have given to her especially; the Service of Angouleme China in use in my Family as also the Dessert Servine of Prussian China with Cornflower Pattern— As this request in no way interferes with the interest of *any one;* I feel assured it will be granted to me—

L C Adams.

4 Silver Bottle stands Mr Adams gave to Mary C Adams when He gave the like 4 to C F Adams.

L C A.

The Plated Tea Urn Teapot Sugar Bowl and Milk Pot are also gifts made to her some years since—

L C Adams

Ca. 1 June 1847

Dr [*Thomas*] Miller [*of Washington*] about a fortnight since made a demand of Mr. Adams of 14 inches of Land which by a new Survey he says belongs to him and required him (Mr A) to pull down the Wall of our Stable which he said encroached on his *property*— Mr. Adams was very much surprized and offered him such terms as he thought would cover the value with the right to the use of our Wall as a partition— This was rejected, and then Mr Adams and Mr Frye offered Arbitration— This also was rudely rejected with a message that Dr. Miller would send and have [*the*] Wall pulled down— Mr Borland brought this answer who had been employed to make the proposition on Wednesday the 29th of May. And this morning Albert came in at breakfast time and inform Mr. Adams that his Carriges were turned out of the Stables and that the Bricklayers employed by Dr Miller had begun to pull down the *Wall*— It is now flat to the ground, our Carriages in the Street for want of room and Horses Harnesses and all the property belonging to the Stables left open to publick depredation—

Such is the state of things while I am writing—

1 July 1847

How wayward are our Spirits: and how incompetent is reason to controul the feelings of our hearts! Why should I suffer myself to be hurt, and galled by the indelicacy of persons who seldom evince a moments interest in any one circumstance that affects me.

4 July 1847

Johns birth day 4 July
1847.

Again the day returns that gave Thee birth
Thy cherish'd image still fond mem'ry hails;
Affection weeps thy loss, inestimable worth
With sorrowing tears the moaning heart bewails.
God in his mercy took thee hence away
To breathe in purer worlds the light of day—

L C Adams

Is it possible that the time has come when reason bids me rejoice in his death? Alas! alas!— No!! it never will come!!!

11 July 1847

This dreadful fluttering at my heart encreases so fearfully it seems continually to threaten my life. If it please God to release me suddenly; May he bless all I leave behind me whom I have ever tenderly loved and with whom I die in perfect peace; and in the hope that they may enjoy as much happiness as falls to the lot of Man in this World—

On this day Mr. Adams is eighty years of age—

O God in thy great mercy raise him up from the sickness which now so heavily oppresses him; and grant him strength to enable him to resist the encroachments of desease, that he may yet exert himself for the benefit of mankind and be the protector of his helpless family—

30 July 1847

Has half a Century passed since I was wedded to the Man of my choice? If I reckon by the time that has elapsed, it has sped its flight in its measured course so imperceptibly; it is difficult to realize its flight of so many many years; even in the natural decay of my faculties, or my loss of strength, or the changes in my person— In the course of that natural decay which is ordained for humanity; we lose that quick perception of things which we possess in early youth—

This loss is a gift of Providence which by thus sparing us from the painfull convictions of our woeful failures, which once begun continue ever in a downward scale; we are enabled to meet them with fortitude, through the means of this unconsciousness without pain; or what is worse the mortifications of neglect, or the weariness of exertion to those whom it oppresses. If I calculate the time by the bright or sad memorials of a truly eventful life blended with large portions of good, and evil, the time is long indeed; and I shudder to think what is yet in store for me when I watch the sad change in my loved companion— O Life! how wondrous art thou. Spare me good Lord!!!

On Monday the 26 of July 1847 the fiftiesth Anniversary of our marriage occurred and passed most quietly according to our own desire— Mr Adams presented me with an elegant Bracelet as a memento of the occasion— I have had the Words refering to the Subject marked on the back of the Medallion; and the Hair of Charles F and Abby B. Adams with that of Arthur [*Charles Francis's son*] placed within it— With the Initials of the three names shewing to whom the Hair belongs. I record this on 30 of July 1847.

In my 73d Year.

31 July 1847

On Tuesday 31st inst Charles and Abby celebrated the fiftiesh anniversary of our marriage; and the pleasure of meeting all our Quincy friends on the occasion and passed a very pleasant evening— God Bless our Children one and all—

28 August 1847

It is seldom that I attempt now, to write down the thoughts that are perpetually called forth in my mind by the change of feeling so every way perceptible in my particular family since it has pleased the Almighty to lay his hand on my poor husband with the heavy calamity which he has sustained in the loss of his health— The constant desire expressed to separate from us by one of its members; is to me a harrassing evil which destroys all the comfort of my existence, in addition to the coroding anxiety which oppresses my spirit and for which I meet with no sympathy to alleviate its suffering— As the remedy for this evil rests alone with those who have the power to remove which to *me* is impossible; as it must result alone from the party desirous of the change to determine to atchieve it;— I must remain the recipient of all the reproaches and complaints without the ability to produce a change which I believe would be conducive to the happiness of all—

My most fervent wish is that every one should seek those means to promote their happiness to their own taste— With the independence possessed by those whose dissatisfaction is so grievous to themselves, and so wearing to me; it would be more generous to make the change with all friendly means, than to persevere in a course so destructive to all peace and enjoyment; and mischievous in its future tendencies—

Long reflection on this matter convinces me that things cannot remain as they now are; whatever may be the consequence—

13 November 1847

"Murmer at Nothing! If our ills are reparable it is ungrateful; if remediless, it is vain!— But a Christian builds his fortitude on a better foundation than Stoicism.— He is pleased with every thing that happens, because he knows that it could not happen unless it had first pleased God (at least to permit it to happen) and that which pleases him, must be the best.— He is assured that no new thing can befall him; and that he is in the hands of a Father who will prove him with no afflictions that resignation cannot conquer, or that faith cannot cure.—"

Does not this doctrine give man too great a latitude for the commital of Sin? Man sinned in the sight of God! And Sin itself was doomed to be his punishment.—

O God purify my heart; for from thee alone cometh all good!!!

18 December 1847

Again have I suffered even more severely from the fluttering uneasiness of my heart which is so encreased by the least excitement or agitation; that I must expect that sooner or later an attack may prove fatal ere I can have the power to express my last wishes as it regards the little property which my beloved Brother so kindly gave to me— In consequence of this feeling which hangs upon my mind I earestly pray God to forgive my manyfold Sins and earnestly solicit that my body may be laid by my ~~Children~~ Husband in the Vault at Quincy and there be at *Rest*— That the Funeral Service may be read over me by an Episcopal Clergyman, as I can never deny my Crucified Saviour. And that the funeral obsequies may be as little expensive as possible and quite private.— This favour I entreat as a last dying favour from my only Son whom I pray God Almighty to Bless and protect and to watch and guard his Wife and Family that they may ever abide in the way of God and righteousness—

I have already made some disposition of my little property but my Children I have heard will be so amply provided for by their respective Fathers although I again assert that I have never known any thing of Mr Adams's property or a single item of his Will; he never in the 50 Years that I have lived with him having ever spoken to me on the subject—either publickly or privately— But his Landed Estates in Quincy and Boston testify to his means of providing for his Children and I trust of making some small Legacy to the Town in which he was born—

To the two Children of Joshua Johnson Boyd I give to each £100 to assist in their Schooling—

To Mrs. Goods or Eleanor Goods; I bequeathe in addition to the £50 already mentioned in my Will £50 more; the first Sum at my Death; the second at the end of the Year—

To Margaret Dulany should she be with me when I depart £25 With the hope that she will be a good Girl will deserve the blessing which I leave her—

Wearied with life; unsupported by health or strength to sustain my trials to Thee O my God alone do I offer up my prayers for help in my bitter affliction to save me from despair; and to guard my Husband and my Son my poor deserving Son from the evils which so heavily threaten— Hear me O Lord God! and grant help through the mercy of a blessed Saviour to thy weak and suffering Servant or I perish in mind and Body—

John Quincy died on 23 February 1848, two days after he collapsed on the floor of the House of Representatives. Louisa was too devastated to attend the funeral.

One year later, on 11 April 1849, Louisa herself suffered a stroke that largely incapacitated her for the rest of her life. Cared for by Mary Catherine Hellen Adams, Louisa lived another three years but wrote no further diaries, though she continued to write poetry and correspond with family members. After her death, she and John Quincy were interred together in the Adams family crypt in Quincy.

24 June 1848

T'was in a heavenly sign of grace—that Charles and Abby Adams's 7th Child [*Brooks Adams*] a fine large Boy was born this morning, at half past seven o clock this 24 June St Johns day 1848.

The blessing of God thus freely showered on us be on this Child, and its Parents; and may this Babe be blessed and prove a blessing to them—

18 March 1849

Thy fiat has gone forth O Lord my God: and I am left a helpless Widow to morn his loss which nothing on this dreary earth can supply—

Les Soupirs étouffe le Chagrin! Les larmes soulage le Coeur!!!
[*Sighs smother grief! Tears soothe the heart!*]

Epilogue

Henry Adams on Louisa

Louisa's literary legacy extends beyond her own writings. She was also the grandmother of one of the greatest authors of the late nineteenth and early twentieth centuries, Henry Adams. In The Education of Henry Adams, *Henry paid tribute to his formidable grandmother, whom he called "the Madam," noting particularly their shared status as outsiders in the sometimes parochial world of Boston society.*

The Madam was a little more remote than the President, but more decorative. She stayed much in her own room with the Dutch tiles, looking out on her garden with the box walks, and seemed a fragile creature to a boy who sometimes brought her a note or a message, and took distinct pleasure in looking at her delicate face under what seemed to him very becoming caps. He liked her refined figure; her gentle voice and manner; her vague effect of not belonging there, but to Washington or to Europe, like her furniture, and writing-desk with little glass doors above and little eighteenth-century volumes in old binding, labelled *Peregrine Pickle* or *Tom Jones* or *Hannah More.* Try as she might, the Madam could never be Bostonian, and it was her cross in life, but to the boy it was her charm. Even at that age, he felt drawn to it. The Madam's life had been in truth far from Boston. She was born in London in 1775, daughter of Joshua Johnson, an American merchant, brother of Governor Thomas Johnson of Maryland; and Catherine Nuth, of an English family in London. Driven from England by the Revolutionary War, Joshua Johnson took his family to Nantes, where they remained till the peace. The girl Louisa Catherine was nearly ten years old when brought back to London, and her sense of nationality must have been confused; but the influence of the Johnsons and the services of Joshua obtained for him from President Washington the appointment of Consul in London on the organization of the Government in 1790. In 1794 President Washington appointed John Quincy Adams Minister to the Hague. He was twenty-seven years old when he returned to London, and found the Consul's house a very agreeable haunt. Louisa was then twenty.

At that time, and long afterwards, the Consul's house, far more than the Minister's, was the centre of contact for travelling Americans, either official or other. The Legation was a shifting point, between 1785 and 1815; but the Consulate, far down in the City, near the Tower, was convenient and inviting; so inviting that it proved fatal to young Adams. Louisa was charming, like a Romney portrait, but among her many charms that of being a New England woman was not one. The defect was serious. Her future mother-in-law, Abigail, a famous New England woman whose authority over her turbulent husband, the second President, was hardly so great as that which she exercised over her son, the sixth to be, was troubled by the fear that Louisa might not be made of stuff stern enough, or brought up in conditions severe enough, to suit a New England climate, or to make an efficient wife for her paragon son, and Abigail was right on that point, as on most others where sound judgment was involved; but sound judgment is sometimes a source of weakness rather than of force, and John Quincy already had reason to think that his mother held sound judgments on the subject of daughters-in-law which human nature, since the fall of Eve, made Adams helpless to realise. Being three thousand miles away from his mother, and equally far in love, he married Louisa in London, July 26, 1797, and took her to Berlin to be the head of the United States Legation. During three or four exciting years, the young bride lived in Berlin; whether she was happy or not, whether she was content or not, whether she was socially successful or not, her descendants did not surely know; but in any case she could by no chance have become educated there for a life in Quincy or Boston. In 1801 the overthrow of the Federalist Party drove her and her husband to America, and she became at last a member of the Quincy household, but by that time her children needed all her attention, and she remained there with occasional winters in Boston and Washington, till 1809. Her husband was made Senator in 1803, and in 1809 was appointed Minister to Russia. She went with him to St. Petersburg, taking her baby, Charles Francis, born in

1807; but broken-hearted at having to leave her two older boys behind. The life at St. Petersburg was hardly gay for her; they were far too poor to shine in that extravagant society; but she survived it, though her little girl baby did not, and in the winter of 1814–15, alone with the boy of seven years old, crossed Europe from St. Petersburg to Paris, in her travelling-carriage, passing through the armies, and reaching Paris in the *Cent Jours* after Napoleon's return from Elba. Her husband next went to England as Minister, and she was for two years at the Court of the Regent. In 1817 her husband came home to be Secretary of State, and she lived for eight years in F Street, doing her work of entertainer for President Monroe's administration. Next she lived four miserable years in the White House. When that chapter was closed in 1829, she had earned the right to be tired and delicate, but she still had fifteen years to serve as wife of a Member of the House, after her husband went back to Congress in 1833. Then it was that the little Henry, her grandson, first remembered her, from 1843 to 1848, sitting in her panelled room, at breakfast, with her heavy silver tea-pot and sugar-bowl and cream-jug, which came afterwards to him and still exist somewhere as an heirloom of the modern safety-vault. By that time she was seventy years old or more, and thoroughly weary of being beaten about a stormy world. To the boy she seemed singularly peaceful, a vision of silver gray, presiding over her old President and her Queen Anne mahogany; an exotic, like her Sèvres china; an object of deference to everyone, and of great affection to her son Charles; but hardly more Bostonian than she had been fifty years before, on her wedding-day, in the shadow of the Tower of London.

Such a figure was even less fitted than that of her old husband, the President, to impress on a boy's mind the standards of the coming century. She was Louis Seize, like the furniture. The boy knew nothing of her interior life, which had been, as the venerable Abigail, long since at peace, foresaw, one of severe stress and little pure satisfaction. He never dreamed that from her might come some of those doubts and self-questionings, those hesitations, those rebellions against law and discipline, which marked more than one of her descendants; but he might even then have felt some vague instinctive suspicion that he was to inherit from her the seeds of the primal sin, the fall from grace, the curse of Abel, that he was not of pure New England stock, but half exotic. As a child of Quincy he was not a true

Bostonian, but even as a child of Quincy he inherited a quarter taint of Maryland blood.

Henry understood, first as a young boy and later as a seasoned writer, that Louisa did not entirely fit into the world of Quincy and the Adamses. Yet she lived a life fully worthy of that renowned family. As a diplomat in her own right, a social hostess of the highest order, and the tireless champion of her brilliant but difficult husband, she made possible his extraordinary accomplishments while herself living a life of considerable adventure. And when she died in 1852, after a lengthy illness following a stroke in 1849, both houses of Congress adjourned to attend her funeral—the first time they ever accorded anyone such an honor. While not born in the United States and never entirely comfortable with its society, Louisa, by the end of her life, had earned this singular distinction from the highest political body in the country. She may have seen herself as a traveled lady, with no single place to call home; Americans saw her as something rather different, the quintessential American citizen.

Chronology

1775

12 Feb.   Louisa Catherine Johnson (LCA) is born in London.

1778

Winter   Upon the outbreak of war between England and France, the
or early   Johnson family leaves London for Paris. They settle in Nantes.
spring   LCA attends a convent school.

1783

Apr.   The Johnson family leaves Nantes and returns to Cooper's Row,
            Great Tower Hill, London.

1785

22 Aug.   Joshua Johnson and Catherine Nuth are legally married at
            St. Anne's Church, Soho, in London.

1794

29 May   George Washington appoints John Quincy Adams (JQA) min-
            ister resident to the Netherlands. JQA and his brother Thomas
            Boylston Adams (TBA) depart for Europe in September, arriv-
            ing at The Hague on 31 October.

1795

11 Nov.   JQA arrives in London to exchange ratifications of the Jay
            Treaty. He and LCA meet at her parents' home.

1796

5 May   LCA and JQA become engaged.

28 May   George Washington nominates JQA to become minister pleni-
            potentiary to Portugal. JQA never serves.

31 May   JQA returns to The Hague.

1797

4 Mar.	John Adams (JA) is inaugurated second president of the United States.
20 May	JA nominates JQA to become minister plenipotentiary to Prussia.
26 July	LCA and JQA are married at the Church of All Hallows Barking in London.
9 Sept.	Joshua Johnson's finances having collapsed, he and Catherine Nuth Johnson leave England for the United States.
18 Oct.	LCA, JQA, and TBA leave London en route to Berlin, which they reach on 7 November.
19 Nov.	LCA suffers a miscarriage.

1798

18 Jan.	LCA is presented at the Prussian court.
18 July	LCA suffers a miscarriage.

1799

23–25 Apr.	LCA suffers a miscarriage.
17 July– 12 Oct.	LCA and JQA tour Dresden and environs.

1800

8 Jan.	LCA suffers a miscarriage.
17 July– 25 Oct.	LCA and JQA tour Silesia.

1801

3 Feb.	JQA is recalled.
12 Apr.	George Washington Adams (GWA), LCA and JQA's first son, is born in Berlin.
8 July	LCA, JQA, and GWA depart from Hamburg for Philadelphia. They arrive on 4 September; LCA and GWA visit Washington while JQA goes immediately on to Quincy.

1 Oct.   JQA purchases a house at 39 Hanover Street, Boston.

21 Oct.   JQA meets LCA and GWA in Washington.

25 Nov.   LCA and GWA, escorted by JQA, arrive in Quincy.

1802

5 Apr.   JQA is elected to the Massachusetts senate; he serves from 26 May to 11 May 1803.

17 Apr.   Joshua Johnson dies.

1803

8 Feb.   JQA is appointed U.S. senator by the Massachusetts General Court.

4 July   John Adams 2d (JA2), LCA and JQA's second son, is born in Boston.

16 Aug.   JA conveys to JQA the Adamses' original Penn's Hill farm (now known as the John Adams Birthplace and the John Quincy Adams Birthplace). JQA sells the Boston house in late September.

20 Oct.   LCA, JQA, GWA, and JA2 arrive in Washington and take up residence at the home of Ann (Nancy) Johnson and Walter Hellen. The Adamses will reside there while in Washington until 1808, usually returning to Massachusetts in the summers.

1806

22 June   LCA gives birth to a son who dies shortly thereafter.

10 Aug.   LCA arrives in Quincy. She and the boys will spend the winter in Boston, while JQA returns to Washington for the congressional session.

1807

18 Aug.   Charles Francis Adams (CFA), LCA and JQA's third son, is born in Boston.

1808

8 June   JQA resigns as senator.

1809

26 June   James Madison nominates JQA to become minister plenipotentiary to Russia.

5 Aug.   LCA, JQA, and CFA sail from Boston for St. Petersburg, arriving on 23 October. GWA and JA2 remain in Quincy.

12 Nov.   LCA is presented at the Russian court.

1811

12 Aug.   Louisa Catherine Adams 2d, LCA and JQA's daughter, is born in St. Petersburg.

29 Sept.   Catherine Nuth Johnson dies.

1812

15 Sept.   Louisa Catherine Adams 2d dies.

1814

28 Apr.   JQA departs St. Petersburg for Ghent to negotiate a peace treaty between the United States and Great Britain. The Treaty of Ghent is signed on 24 December, ending the War of 1812.

1815

12 Feb.   LCA and CFA begin their overland journey from St. Petersburg to Paris to join JQA.

28 Feb.   James Madison nominates JQA to become minister plenipotentiary to Great Britain.

23 Mar.   LCA and CFA arrive in Paris and are reunited with JQA.

16 May   LCA, JQA, and CFA depart Paris for London, arriving on 25 May. GWA and JA2 join them, reuniting the family for the first time in nearly six years.

1816

21 Mar.   LCA is presented at the British court.

1817

5 Mar.   James Madison nominates JQA to become secretary of state.

10 June   LCA, JQA, and their family depart London for Quincy, arriving on 18 August.

28 Aug.   GWA enters Harvard.

9 Sept.   LCA and JQA leave Quincy for Washington.

2 Nov.   LCA brings her niece Mary Catherine Hellen (MCHA) to live with the Adamses.

1818

26 Aug.   LCA leaves Washington; JQA joins her in Baltimore on 28 August, and together they arrive in Quincy on 4 September. They stay with JA and Abigail Adams (AA) at the Old House (now the Adams National Historical Park) in Quincy. LCA and JQA use the Old House as their Quincy home for the remainder of their lives, spending most winters in Washington and most summers in Massachusetts.

28 Oct.   AA dies.

1819

27 Aug.   JA2 enters Harvard.

14 Dec.   LCA begins hosting her weekly Tuesday evening "sociables" in Washington.

1820

21 Jan.   LCA attends the debates in the U.S. Senate for the first time.

18 Apr.   LCA and JQA purchase a house on F Street in Washington.

1821

29 Aug.   GWA graduates from Harvard. In October he begins the study of law with JQA.

28 Sept.   CFA enters Harvard.

1823

2 May   JA2 is expelled from Harvard. The following fall he begins the study of law with JQA.

1824

8 Jan.   LCA and JQA host a ball for Andrew Jackson on the ninth anniversary of the Battle of New Orleans.

1 Dec.   The electoral votes are counted for the 1824 presidential election, contested among JQA, Andrew Jackson, Henry Clay, and William H. Crawford. Jackson receives the most popular and electoral votes but fails to obtain the necessary majority, so the election is sent to the U.S. House of Representatives.

1825

9 Feb.   JQA is elected president by the House of Representatives on the first ballot.

4 Mar.   JQA is inaugurated. LCA is ill at the time and does not attend.

5 Apr.   LCA and other members of the Adams family sleep in the White House for the first time.

23 July   LCA begins her autobiographical work "Record of a Life."

31 Aug.   CFA graduates from Harvard. He had already begun the study of law with JQA and receives his degree in absentia.

1826

4 July   JA dies. JQA inherits the Old House.

1828

25 Feb.   JA2 marries his cousin MCHA in the White House.

2 Dec.   Mary Louisa Adams, daughter of JA2 and MCHA, is born.

3 Dec.   The electoral votes are counted for the 1828 presidential election; Andrew Jackson defeats JQA.

1829

26 Feb.   LCA moves out of the White House to the Commodore Porter House in Washington. JQA, along with JA2 and his family, join

her in March. LCA and JQA do not return to their F Street house until 1838.

30 Apr. GWA dies by either jumping or falling from a steamship in Long Island Sound. On 13 May the family learns of GWA's illegitimate child by Eliza Dolph, a chambermaid.

1 Aug. LCA and her extended family move to a house owned by JA2 on Sixteenth Street in Washington.

3 Sept. CFA marries Abigail Brown Brooks (ABA) in Medford, Massachusetts. LCA is too ill to attend the ceremony and remains in Washington.

1830

10 Sept. Georgeanna Frances (Fanny) Adams, daughter of JA2 and MCHA, is born.

1 Nov. JQA is elected to the U.S. House of Representatives from the Plymouth district. He continues to serve until his death.

1831

13 Aug. Louisa Catherine Adams, daughter of CFA and ABA, is born.

1832

13 Mar. TBA dies.

1833

22 Sept. John Quincy Adams, son of CFA and ABA, is born.

1834

23 Oct. JA2 dies in Washington from alcoholism. MCHA and her two daughters live with the Adamses in Washington and Quincy.

1835

27 June Charles Francis Adams 2d, son of CFA and ABA, is born.

1836

27 June LCA begins her memoir "Narrative of a Journey."

1838

16 Feb. Henry Adams, son of CFA and ABA, is born.

Nov. Upon their return to Washington from Quincy the Adamses rent out the Sixteenth Street house and move again to their F Street home.

1839

20 Nov. Georgeanna Frances (Fanny) Adams dies.

1840

1 July LCA begins her autobiographical work "Adventures of a Nobody."

1841

23 July Arthur Adams, son of CFA and ABA, is born. He dies on 9 February 1846.

1845

19 Feb. Mary Adams, daughter of CFA and ABA, is born.

1848

21 Feb. JQA collapses on the floor of the House of Representatives and dies at the Capitol on 23 February. His funeral is held at the Capitol on 26 February; LCA is too bereaved to attend.

11 Mar. JQA is buried in Quincy. LCA remains in Washington.

24 June Brooks Adams, son of CFA and ABA, is born.

1849

11 Apr. LCA suffers a stroke. Over the next three years, she is attended by MCHA.

1852

15 May LCA dies at her F Street home in Washington.

18 May Congress adjourns for LCA's funeral. She is buried in the Congressional Cemetery in Washington.

16 Dec. LCA and JQA are reinterred in the crypt of the First Church in Quincy beside JA and AA.

Acknowledgments

This work would not have been possible without the tremendous efforts of our coeditors on the complete *Diary and Autobiographical Writings of Louisa Catherine Adams,* Judith S. Graham and Beth Luey. Judy and Beth paved the way for so much future research into the life and times of Louisa Adams, and we are honored to have had the chance to work with them on that project.

The talent, patience, and good humor of all of the staff of the Adams Papers editorial project likewise gave us the opportunity to complete this book. We especially thank Sara Sikes for the keen eye and thoughtful research she brought to our illustrations, and Neal Millikan for her thorough fact-checking of the headnotes and chronology. The Adams Papers Administrative Committee has supported this project from the beginning and allowed us to make it a reality. The Massachusetts Historical Society provided us the use of its unrivaled collections and the assistance of its learned staff. Generous funding for the work came from Levin H. and Eleanor L. Campbell and L. Dennis and Susan R. Shapiro.

Jennifer Snodgrass and John Walsh, both formerly of Harvard University Press, had the original vision for this book and helped to lay its foundation. Kathleen McDermott and Andrew Kinney of Harvard University Press, John Donohue of Westchester Publishing Services, and Barbara Goodhouse, our copyeditor, saw it through to completion with skill and grace.

Index

Note: Since the present volume is not intended as a research tool, the reader is referred for more detailed entries to the index in volume 2 of the *Diary and Autobiographical Writings of Louisa Catherine Adams,* in the Belknap Press edition of *The Adams Papers.* The editors have tried (not always successfully) to supply forenames for persons who appear in the text with only surnames, and to identify by residence or occupation as many individuals as possible. People with identical names are further distinguished by birth and death dates.

Adams, Abigail, 2d (1765–1813, sister of JQA, wife of William Stephens Smith): Johnson family and, 16, 19, 56, 99, 132; described, 19, 20, 107–108; returns to U.S., 21; relationship with LCA, 91, 107, 125, 134; visits LCA, 130; health of, 180

Adams, Abigail Brown Brooks (1808–1889, wife of Charles Francis), 40, 327, 353, 358, 361

Adams, Abigail Smith (1744–1818, mother of JQA, wife of John): Johnson family and, 56, 100, 132; relationship with GWA, 92; relationship with LCA, 92, 93, 94, 107, 183, 341; character of, 95, 305; finances of, 101; health of, 106, 108; JA2 stays with, 123, 126; letters by and to, 185, 188, 216, 340–341, 342

Adams, Abigail Smith (1806–1845). *See* Angier, Abigail Smith Adams (1806–1845)

Adams, Ann Harrod (1774–1845, wife of Thomas Boylston), 58, 122, 123, 125, 126, 131, 132, 288, 353

Adams, Charles (1770–1800, brother of JQA), 80, 135

Adams, Charles Francis (1807–1886, son of JQA and LCA, designated as CFA): LCA writes for, 1, 40; correspondence with LCA, 41; birth of, 132, 134; baptism of, 135; health of, 135, 137, 141, 171, 179; naming of, 135; in Russia, 144, 156, 159, 163, 167–168; social activities of, 177,

293–296; education of, 182, 229, 241, 267, 273, 274, 285; on St. Petersburg-to-Paris journey, 187, 188, 192, 195, 197, 203, 208, 209, 210, 211, 212; attends congressional debates, 237, 243, 246; assists LCA, 239, 324; described, 304; goes to and returns from college, 304, 311, 313; marriage of, 327; family papers and, 340–341; as executor, 353, 354; parents' anniversary and, 353, 358; gifts to, 356; children of, 358, 361; prayers for, 360

Adams, Elizabeth Coombs (1808–1903, niece of JQA), 283

Adams, Georgeanna Frances (Fanny, 1830–1839, granddaughter of JQA and LCA), 327, 337–338, 352

Adams, George Washington (1801–1829, son of JQA and LCA, designated as GWA): LCA writes for, 1; owns portrait of LCA, 17; birth of, 76, 82, 83, 198; baptism of, 83–84; health of, 84, 87, 88, 89, 90, 122, 132–133, 134, 240, 314; meets grandparents, 88, 92; education of, 95, 123, 135, 141, 142, 217, 229, 289–290, 292; naming of, 97; expectations for, 104, 105; character of, 110–111, 117, 133; alcoholism of, 132, 327; horoscope of, 134; reunited with LCA, 139–140; social activities of, 142, 293–296; as correspondent, 175, 184, 314; goes to and returns from college, 235, 244, 263; attends congressional debates, 237, 240, 243; on etiquette, 238;

Adams, George Washington *(continued)*
assists LCA, 239, 283; described, 244,
263, 289; Fanny Johnson affair and, 259,
265, 269–271, 274; music and, 267, 284;
studies law, 273, 274, 314; Mary Hellen
and, 274; poetry and, 296; child of, 327;
death of, 327; birthday remembered, 355
Adams, Henry (1838–1918, grandson of JQA
and LCA), 362–365
Adams, John (1735–1826, father of JQA):
political career of, 21, 82, 256–257; JQA's
career and, 29, 82; Johnson family and, 56,
95, 100; health of, 80, 250, 284; relationship with GWA, 92, 133; relationship with
LCA, 92, 93, 107, 143, 282, 341–342;
finances of, 101, 104; JA2 stays with, 123,
126; social activities of, 132, 139, 285–286,
293–295; as correspondent, 216, 229, 230,
232, 237, 250, 297; honors for, 281;
speeches of, 287; argues with Mathew
Carey, 289; relationship with JQA, 290;
death of, 327; papers of, 340–341, 344;
poem to, 342; described, 344–345
Adams, John, 2d (1803–1834, son of JQA and
LCA, designated as JA2): LCA writes for,
1; birth of, 96, 100, 106; naming of, 100,
106, 108; appearance of, 108; health of,
115, 117, 122, 126, 128, 129, 130; stays with
grandparents, 123, 126; alcoholism of,
132, 327; relationship with CFA, 134–135;
education of, 135, 217, 229, 257, 258, 285,
292, 311; reunited with LCA, 138; social
activities of, 142, 293–296; as correspondent, 175, 184; marriage of, 230, 327; goes
to and returns from college, 235, 244,
263, 273, 274, 306, 311, 313; attends
congressional debates, 237, 243; on
etiquette, 238; assists LCA, 239, 240,
283, 320, 324; described, 244, 263;
compared to LCA, 258; relationship with
GWA, 270, 289; poetry and, 284,
333–334; death of, 327, 328, 335;
daughters of, 338; business activities of,
343; finances of, 343; birthday remembered, 357
Adams, John Quincy (1767–1848, husband of
LCA, designated as JQA): presidency of,
1, 314, 326; family of, 5, 16; as minister to
Netherlands, 20, 23; travels of, 20, 21, 84,
86; nicknames for, 21; courtship and
marriage, 23–30, 31, 56; character of, 24,
26–27, 41, 53, 56, 167, 217, 233, 294, 300;
poetry of, 24; relationship with Johnsons,
24, 28–29, 30, 32, 34, 35, 120; writes song
for LCA, 26; disputes with LCA, 27, 63,
64, 76, 78, 143, 182–183; correspondence
with LCA, 28, 30; as minister to Portugal,
29, 30, 54, 55; as minister to Prussia, 29,
33, 34, 54, 55, 82, 84; LCA's health and,
36, 37–38, 54–55, 66, 73, 75, 76, 90; in
House of Representatives, 40–41, 326,
330; diaries of, 41, 144; public service
and, 42, 130, 251; popularity of, 45, 180;
finances of, 51, 52, 54, 56, 94, 145, 152,
155, 162, 178, 266, 343, 360; Washington's
death and, 75; health of, 76, 119, 159, 160,
185, 335, 337, 353; as secretary of state, 82,
216, 221; in Massachusetts legislature, 86,
96, 97; in Senate, 86, 96, 103, 112, 119,
120, 135, 138, 140; romances of, 86–87, 94;
relationship with LCA, 94, 95, 106–107,
141, 214, 227; speeches by, 97, 282, 284;
patronage and, 100, 226, 227; assists
parents, 101, 104; religious views of, 103,
182; domestic life of, 105; summers in
Quincy, 116–117; birth of, 123; as Harvard
professor, 126, 138, 142; as gardener, 129;
at CFA's birth, 134; Federalist Party and,
135, 136; in St. Petersburg as youth, 135,
140; legal career of, 138, 140; as minister
to Russia, 140, 141, 143, 144, 150, 152, 153;
political views of, 156, 158, 168; Alexander
I and, 167, 179; reputation of, 169, 223,
315; negotiates Treaty of Ghent, 187; as
minister to Britain, 216; etiquette in
Washington and, 234, 236; as presidential
candidate, 234, 277, 314; dances, 239; on
William Steuben Smith's debt, 241;
rumored as vice president, 250; dueling
and, 253, 254; assists GWA, 269–271;
GWA studies with, 273; toast to, 281;
graduation of, 290; social activities of,
293–295; consulted on protocol, 302;
anecdote by, 307; Jackson ball and,

324–325; on Texas, 335; prepares for death, 353; prayers for, 353–355, 357, 360; will of, 354, 360; boundary dispute and, 356; wedding anniversary of, 357–358; death of, 360, 361

Adams, Louisa Catherine (1811–1812, daughter of JQA and LCA): birth of, 169, 177; baptism of, 177–178; health of, 179, 180, 181, 183; death of, 181, 182, 202, 266, 312, 327

Adams, Louisa Catherine Johnson (1775–1852, designated as LCA): as first lady, 1, 326; writings of, 1, 2, 5, 20–21, 40, 41, 144, 181, 187–188, 207, 216–217, 256, 280, 327, 346, 347; education of, 3, 5–6, 7, 9–11, 18, 20, 27–28, 55–56, 82; Roman Catholic influence, 3, 6–7, 72, 348; religious views of, 4, 103–104, 245, 279, 306, 308–309, 335, 348, 349, 351, 358, 359, 360; health of, 5, 8–9, 18, 54–55, 76, 111, 174–175, 222, 266–268, 334; relationship with Johnsons, 5, 24–25, 26, 27, 32, 49, 53; character of, 6, 9, 10–11, 13, 14–15, 26, 29, 41–42, 48–49, 91, 99–100, 115, 182–183, 185–186, 217, 291–292, 327–328; nicknames for, 6, 12, 21, 99; friends of, 9–10, 12, 16, 36–37, 76–77, 78, 276, 346; household management and, 12, 60–61, 93–94, 95, 99, 123, 128–129, 131; suitors of, 12, 16, 17, 19, 21, 22; books and reading of, 13, 241, 248, 265, 269, 286, 298; introduced into society, 13, 18; singing, 15; portraits of, 16, 17, 59; injuries to, 17–18, 129, 131, 141; appearance of, 18, 19, 25, 48–49, 77–78, 87, 88, 213; expected dowry, 22, 53; courtship and marriage, 23–30, 31, 56; on JQA's clothing, 24, 26–27, 151; letter writing of, 28, 29, 30; Johnson business failures and, 30, 31–32, 35; miscarriages, 36, 58, 66, 73, 75, 141, 159, 297; pregnancy, 36, 37, 58, 64, 76, 77, 80, 100, 104, 105, 123, 130, 141, 159, 169, 171–172, 174, 176, 297; presentation at Prussian court, 37, 38, 39–40, 46; JQA's career and, 42, 140, 141, 143, 232, 251; humor of, 43, 50–51, 119, 149, 255; clothing of, 46, 47; reputation of, 49–50; disputes with JQA, 63, 64, 76,

78, 182–183; gives birth, 82, 83, 134, 169, 177; health of after childbirth, 83–84, 85, 87, 134, 179, 180; travels of, 84, 86, 144; first impressions of U.S., 86, 92, 93; child-rearing and, 95, 345–346; guilt over leaving children, 104–105, 132, 143, 145, 174, 355; relationship with Adamses, 107; on republicanism, 116; children's deaths and, 123, 134, 181–184, 185, 266; presentation at Russian court, 149, 152, 153–155; as godmother, 172–173; gold stolen from, 203; on men, 206; on entertaining, 226; attitudes toward, 233, 241, 351–352; hosts balls, 238–239, 271, 273, 320, 321, 322, 323, 324–325; Tuesday sociables, 242–243, 246, 277, 301, 303–304, 306, 307–308, 310, 313, 314, 315–316, 317, 318, 322, 324; on politics, 247–248, 250–251, 262, 277–278, 315, 318, 328–329; public scrutiny of, 280, 300, 312; poetry of, 327, 332, 333–334, 337, 340, 342, 357, 361; religious reflections, 328, 330, 332, 334, 346–347, 352, 353–354, 355; on human nature, 329, 335–336, 339–340, 347–348; on slavery, 330–331; prepares for death, 352–353, 357, 359–360; estate of, 355–356; wedding anniversary of, 357–358; death of, 361, 365; Henry Adams on, 362–365

Adams, Mary Catherine Hellen (1806–1870, wife of John Adams 2d): social activities of, 222, 244, 268, 285–286, 324; described, 229–230, 274; health of, 230, 231, 269, 270; marriage of, 230, 327; lessons for, 241, 267; travels to Quincy, 282, 283–284; as widow, 332; cares for LCA, 334, 361; death of daughter, 352; as LCA's beneficiary, 355–356

Adams, Mary Louisa (1828–1859, granddaughter of JQA and LCA), 327, 332, 337–338, 353

Adams, Sarah Smith (Sally, 1769–1828, wife of Charles), 111

Adams, Thomas Boylston (1772–1832, brother of JQA): travels of, 20, 21, 58; Johnson family and, 21, 100; nicknames for, 21; relationship with LCA, 31, 33, 34,

Adams, Thomas Boylston *(continued)*
38, 47, 60, 87, 143; social activities of, 51,
132; career of, 58; marriage of, 122, 123;
Harvard oration, 127; visits LCA, 131;
health of, 284, 288, 289
Addington, Henry Unwin (Brit. diplomat), 311
Alexander I, Emperor of Russia: presentation to, 149, 152, 154; African guard of,
154, 166; birthday celebrations, 157, 235,
264; reviews troops, 158; intercepts
Adams mail, 159–160, 169, 170; Catherine
Smith and, 161, 162, 163, 165, 167, 169,
170, 172; relationship with LCA, 164–165,
169, 170, 171; relationship with JQA, 167,
179; purchases Adamses' residence,
175–176
American Revolution, 2, 3, 4, 15–16
Angier, Abigail Smith Adams (1806–1845,
niece of JQA), 125, 127, 353
Antrobus, Gibbs Crawford (Brit. diplomat),
281
Apraxin, Ekaterina Vladimirovna, Countess
(of Russia), 199, 203
Arnold, Benedict, 22
Art. *See* Paintings
August Ferdinand, Prince of Prussia, 47, 66
Augustus Frederick, Duke of Sussex
(brother of George IV), 60, 62, 63

Babet, Madame (Adams family servant), 187,
188, 197, 203, 209, 210, 212, 214
Bagot, Charles (Brit. diplomat), 221, 223,
224, 226, 228
Bagot, Mary (wife of Charles), 219, 221, 223,
224, 226, 246
Baptiste (Adams family servant), 187, 188,
189, 191, 192–193, 196–197, 203, 204–205
Barron, Como. James (U.S.), 253–254
Berlin, Prussia, 36, 37, 38, 52, 54, 198,
200, 202
Bezerra, Madame (of Portugal), 175, 176–177,
178
Biddle, Nicholas (of Phila.), 320
Bird, Savage & Bird (London banking
house), 101, 104
Bloomfield, Isabella Ramsay Macomb (wife
of Joseph), 258, 265–266

Bloomfield, Gen. Joseph (N.J. politician),
258, 265–266
Bonaparte, Napoleon. *See* Napoleon I,
Emperor of France
Boston, Mass.: residence in, 86, 92, 102, 108,
130, 138; travel to, 89–92; concert hall, 95,
125; society in, 128; development of, 130
Boyd, George (1781–1846, husband of
Harriet), 4, 119, 120, 226, 227, 261
Boyd, Harriet Johnson (1781–1850, sister of
LCA), 4, 5, 8, 16, 117, 119, 120, 226, 227,
261, 316–317
Boyd, John Quincy Adams (son of Harriet),
239, 286, 290–291
Boylston, Alicia Darrow (wife of Ward), 290,
292, 293, 295, 296
Boylston, Ward Nicholas, Sr. (of Princeton,
Mass.), 290, 292, 293, 294–296
Bray, François Gabriel, Chevalier de
(Bavarian diplomat), 166, 189
Bray, Madame de (wife of François), 152, 153,
157, 159, 162, 165, 166
Bresson, Catharine Livingston Thompson
de (wife of Charles), 308, 313
Bresson, Charles de (French diplomat),
308, 313
Brighton, England, 20
Brown, Dr. Charles (in Berlin), 37, 40, 42,
43, 52, 64, 66, 75, 84, 85, 319
Brown, Mrs. (wife of Charles), 37, 39, 43, 52,
61, 74, 83
Brown, Fanny (daughter of Charles), 37,
39, 44
Brown, Isabella (daughter of Charles), 37,
39, 44, 83
Brown, Gen. Jacob Jennings (U.S.), 219,
320–321
Brown, James (La. senator), 249, 275
Brown, Margaret (daughter of Charles), 37,
39, 43–44
Brown, Nancy Hart (wife of James), 249,
272, 275, 301, 311, 313, 319, 321, 322
Brown, Pamelia Williams (wife of Jacob),
320–321
Brown, William (son of Charles), 44
Brühl, Karl, Count von (of Saxony), 52, 69, 70
Bryant, William Cullen (U.S. poet), 292

Buchanan, Andrew (1766–1811, 1st husband of Carolina Frye), 4, 22, 131–132, 180

Buchanan, Carolina Virginia Marylanda Johnson. *See* Frye, Carolina Virginia Marylanda Johnson Buchanan

Burr, Aaron (N.Y. politician), 82, 120, 121–122

Byron, George Gordon Noel, Baron (Brit. poet), 285, 296, 305

Calhoun, Floride Bonneau Colhoun (wife of John), 250, 254, 260, 322

Calhoun, John C. (S.C. politician), 229, 243, 277, 306, 314, 322

Canning, Stratford (Brit. diplomat), 261, 281, 302, 305, 307–308, 311

Capitol, U.S., 230, 236, 318–319, 360. *See also* Congress, U.S.

Caraman, Victor Louis Charles de Riquet, Duc de (French diplomat), 65, 202, 207, 208

Carey, Mathew (Phila. publisher), 289

Caroline of Brunswick, Queen of England, 61, 263

Carter, Elizabeth (Brit. schoolmistress), 5–6

Carysfort, Elizabeth Granville Proby, Lady (wife of John), 76–77, 78–79, 80, 81, 82, 83, 84–85

Carysfort, John Joshua Proby, 1st Earl of (Brit. diplomat), 77, 81, 83

CFA. *See* Adams, Charles Francis (1807–1886)

Church of England, 348

Clay, Henry (Ky. politician): presidential election and, 1, 277, 314; social activities of, 223, 234; as speaker of the House, 230, 316; Missouri and, 247, 275–276; described, 251–252, 272, 274–275; speeches of, 272; relationship with JQA, 311, 313; support for, 318

Clothing: at court, 46, 150, 153, 157, 159; mourning, 47, 61, 80, 176; for wedding, 55; for pregnancy, 62, 63, 79; for dancing, 63, 322; appropriateness of, 65, 128, 150, 310; baby's, 73, 151; for servants, 73–74, 166; pockets, 81; for travel, 90, 91; humorous, 149; Wethersfield bonnet, 261; Peruvian, 304–305

Columbian Mills, 343

Columbus, U.S.S., 223, 224, 225, 290

Congress, U.S.: 1824 presidential election and, 1, 314, 326; diplomatic appointments and, 54, 140, 141; adjourns, 120, 229; debates Jackson censure, 217; powers of, 217–218; treaties and, 221, 277; Missouri and, 232, 275–276; sectional divisions in, 237, 240, 241, 247, 257, 262, 277, 298, 299; critiques of, 247–248, 255, 278–279, 299, 310; elects speaker, 257; closing session of, 278–279; West Point and, 287; gag rule and, 330; adjourns for LCA's funeral, 365. *See also* Capitol, U.S.

Court, Mrs. (of London), 32–33

Cranch, Mary Smith (1741–1811, aunt of JQA), 92, 123, 135, 180, 290

Cranch, Richard (1726–1811, husband of Mary), 123, 135, 180

Cranch, William (1769–1855, cousin of JQA), 100, 255

Crawford, William Harris (U.S. politician), 238, 239, 241, 250, 277, 278, 314, 315, 316

Cushing, Hannah Phillips (wife of William), 115, 121

Cushing, William (U.S. Supreme Court justice), 115, 121

Dana, Samuel Whittlesey (Conn. politician), 227

Dancing: at Johnsons, 12; at Prussian court, 51, 63–64, 65; in Töplitz, 68; in Boston, 128; lessons, 142, 267; at Russian court, 156, 160, 162, 164–165, 167; at Adamses, 239, 243, 277, 322; in Washington, 244, 260, 310; skill at, 323

Dearborn, Dorcas Marble (wife of Henry), 119

Dearborn, Henry (U.S. secretary of war), 119

Decatur, Como. Stephen (U.S.), 240, 253–254

Decatur, Susan Wheeler (wife of Stephen), 245, 253–254, 306, 311

Democratic-Republican Party, 138, 259

Denmark, 147–148

De Windt, Caroline Smith. *See* Smith, Caroline Amelia

Dorville, Miss (of Prussia), 36, 38, 39, 45

Dresden, Saxony, 66–73, 75

Duels and dueling, 120, 121, 142, 219, 252–254, 265, 269

Duer, William Alexander (N.Y. judge), 124, 125

Dupin (Adams family servant), 208, 209, 210, 213, 214

Durant (Durand) de St. André, Mrs. (of France), 322, 323

Education: in France, 3; in England, 5–6, 7, 9–11; governesses, 6, 11, 18, 20; tutors, 18; in U.S., 20; for diplomatic service, 55; housekeeping skills, 99; expulsion from college, 229, 257, 259, 260, 311. *See also* Harvard College

Eichstadt, Madame (in Berlin), 59

Elections: 1800 presidential, 80, 82; 1820 presidential, 259, 277; 1824 presidential, 1, 277, 297–298, 314, 315, 318, 320, 323, 326; 1828 presidential, 169, 326; Senate, 103, 104

Elgin, Thomas Bruce, 7th Earl of (Brit. diplomat), 45, 46

Elizabeth Alexeievna, Empress of Russia, 149, 152, 153, 154, 206

Elliot, Hugh (Brit. diplomat), 71, 72

Elliot, Isabella (daughter of Hugh), 71, 72

Embargo Act (1807), 135, 137, 138

Emerson, Rev. William (of Boston), 132, 135, 139

Engeström, Rozalia, Baroness von (of Sweden), 77, 81–82

English language, 6, 172, 301, 302

Episcopal Church, 103, 117, 360

Epps, Elizabeth (Adams family servant), 54, 70–71, 87, 88, 92, 93, 94, 95

Errington, Elizabeth Sophia (wife of George), 62, 66, 67, 71, 72

Errington, George Henry (of England), 62, 71, 72

Erskine, David Montagu Erskine, 2d Baron (Brit. diplomat), 136, 137

Erskine, Fanny Cadwallader Erskine, Baroness (wife of David), 137

Etiquette and protocol: at European courts, 39–40, 281; at Prussian court, 46, 62, 64–65, 66, 81, 82; in Quincy, 93; U.S.

versus European, 114, 115–116, 232; calling cards, 116, 234, 235, 244, 277, 285, 300; in Boston, 128; at Russian court, 150, 152, 153–154, 155, 159, 160–162, 164–165, 171; in Washington, 232, 233–234, 236, 238, 241, 242–243, 249, 252, 265–266, 272, 300, 302–303, 317; visits and, 233–234

Everett, Alexander Hill (of Boston), 135, 144, 250

Federalist Party, 96, 135, 136, 140, 259

Ferdinand, Prince. *See* August Ferdinand, Prince of Prussia

Ferdinand, Louise of Brandenburg-Schwedt, Princess, 37, 39, 47–48, 59, 62, 77, 199

Forsyth, John (U.S. statesman), 218, 250, 318

France, 2, 3–4, 113, 228, 229

Franklin, Benjamin, 15

Frazier, Mary. *See* Sargent, Mary Frazier

Frederica Louise of Hesse-Darmstadt, Dowager Queen of Prussia, 37, 39, 47, 61–62, 65, 75

Frederick II (the Great), King of Prussia, 42, 71

Frederick William II, King of Prussia, 38, 45, 57–58, 61–62

Frederick William III, King of Prussia, 36, 38, 45, 46, 50, 57, 61, 62, 63–64, 79, 84

French language, 3, 60, 119, 141, 172, 190, 200, 204, 207, 211, 301, 302

French Revolution, 18

Frye, Carolina Virginia Marylanda Johnson Buchanan (1777–1862, sister of LCA): marriages of, 4, 131, 132; compared to LCA, 14, 99; naming of, 15–16; portraits of, 16, 300, 306; described, 16–17; suitors of, 17, 21, 22, 102; relationship with Abigail Adams Smith, 20; relationship with LCA, 25, 26, 131–132; assists LCA, 89, 99, 106, 123; social activities of, 98, 100, 125, 228, 323, 324, 331; health of, 129; children of, 278

Frye, Nathaniel, Jr. (1778–1855, 2d husband of Carolina), 4, 324

Fulling, John (Adams family servant), 187, 188, 192, 193, 196, 203, 204–205

Gallatin, Albert (U.S. secretary of the treasury), 119

Galloway, Dr. (of Scotland), 159, 171, 173, 181

Games and pastimes: cards, 50, 51, 58, 66, 268–269, 274, 300, 318, 320; blindman's bluff, 62; reversi (othello), 78; role-playing, 142; fishing, 177, 255; chess, 219, 305; bragg, 273; circuses, 273, 275, 308; bagatelle, 283, 290

Gardens and gardening, 10, 68, 69, 129, 285, 297, 362

Garlike, Benjamin (Brit. diplomat), 57, 60

George IV, King of England, 61

German language, 43, 190, 193, 209

Geyersberg Mountain, Saxony, 67, 69, 70

Gibbes, Henry (of S.C.), 17

Giusta, Michael Anthony (Adams family servant), 261

Godfrey, Martha (Adams family servant), 159–160, 169, 170, 172–173

Gouverneur, Maria Hester Monroe (wife of Samuel), 249, 251, 282

Gouverneur, Samuel Lawrence (of N.Y.), 249

Granville, Granville Leveson Gower, 1st Earl of (Brit. diplomat), 50–51, 59

Graves, Thomas North (of Britain), 62, 64, 65

Gray, Francis Calley (of Mass.), 144, 172–173, 178, 284

Greuhm, Frederick (Prussian diplomat), 232, 316, 317, 319–320

Greuhm, Virginie Bridon (wife of Frederick), 232, 316

GWA. *See* Adams, George Washington (1801–1829)

Hall, Joseph (of Boston), 132, 138, 285, 291

Hamburg, Germany, 35–36

Harlberg, Mrs. d' (of Vienna), 64, 65

Harper, Catherine Carroll (wife of Robert), 128, 129

Harper, Robert Goodloe (Baltimore lawyer), 128, 292

Harris, Levett (U.S. diplomat), 148–149, 150, 153, 155, 160–161, 175, 177, 178, 185

Hartley, David (Brit. diplomat), 13

Harvard College, 126, 127, 138, 142, 217, 257, 258, 260, 273, 285, 289–290, 291–292, 311

Hay, Eliza Kortright Monroe (wife of George), 245, 252, 264

Hay, George (Va. lawyer), 237

Health and illnesses: pleurisy, 5, 141; typhus, 8; tooth extraction, 9; blindness, 19; seasickness, 37, 109, 110, 145, 283; consumption, 65, 85, 130; convulsions, 73, 181; broken bones, 74–75, 133, 260, 314; fainting, 75, 174, 212, 269; after childbirth, 83; congestion, 83; smallpox, 84, 127; dysentery, 87; stomach ailments, 89; yellow fever, 109, 111; chicken pox, 122; whooping cough, 122; worms, 128; dislocated shoulder, 133; ague (malaria), 137, 283; hemorrhage, 139, 353; eruptions, 141; erysipelas, 160; croup, 171; fever, 179, 202; climate effects, 184, 185; headaches, 212, 266; brain fever, 214; influenza, 230; apoplexy, 231; chilblains, 263; jaundice, 284; measles, 316; enlargement of heart, 328; strokes, 361, 365; poultices, 106; emetics, 130

Remedies: blisters, 8–9, 249; spa baths, 66, 67–68, 70; medicines, 73, 174, 316; nursing, 83, 85; vaccination, 84, 127, 135; weaning, 88

Hellen, Adelaide Johnson (1789–1877, sister of LCA), 5, 16, 229, 249, 250

Hellen, Ann (Nancy) Johnson (1773–1810, sister of LCA): birth of, 3; marriage of, 4; death of, 5, 174; education of, 10; introduced into society, 13; compared to LCA, 14; portraits of, 16; suitors of, 21, 22, 23, 24, 26; relationship with LCA, 25, 26, 27; character of, 49; home of, 89, 100, 112; children of, 111; health of, 111

Hellen, Johnson (1800–1867, nephew of LCA), 88, 229, 259, 270, 271, 273, 274, 323

Hellen, Mary Catherine. *See* Adams, Mary Catherine Hellen (1806–1870)

Hellen, Walter (1766–1815, husband 1st of Ann, 2d of Adelaide), 4, 5, 23, 100, 112, 229

Henning, Miss (governess of LCA), 26, 28

Henry, Wilhelmina of Hesse-Cassel, Princess, 37, 39, 50, 58, 66

Hesse-Cassel, Philippine Auguste Amalie of Brandenburg-Schwedt, Landgravine of, 47, 48, 59, 62

Hewlett, Elizabeth (wife of John), 6, 8–9

Hewlett, John (Brit. scholar), 6, 9, 13, 17

Hoare, Mr. (of England), 109, 110

Holidays: New Year's Day, 13, 62, 115, 136, 236, 322; Carnival, 78, 79; Thanksgiving, 92; Christmas, 136, 304, 331; Twelfth Night, 157; Easter, 162, 309; May Day, 164; Fourth of July, 282

Holmes, John (Maine politician), 241–242

Hopkinson, Elizabeth Borden (daughter of Joseph), 299, 312

Hopkinson, Emily Mifflin (wife of Joseph), 122

Hopkinson, Joseph (Penn. politician), 122, 221, 225

Horry, Daniel (of S.C.), 19

Hunter, Elizabeth Orby (of Britain), 80

Hyde de Neuville, Anne Marguerite (wife of Jean), 225, 231–232, 277, 279

Hyde de Neuville, Jean Guillaume, Baron (French diplomat), 223, 225, 228, 229, 241, 244, 248, 277, 280–281

JA2. See Adams, John, 2d (1803–1834)

Jackson, Andrew: presidential election and, 1, 314, 320, 326; relationship with JQA, 169; censure of, 217, 218, 221; health of, 316; Winfield Scott and, 318; social activities of, 320, 325; Native Americans and, 334, 338; Texas and, 335, 337; Mexico and, 338

Jay, John (U.S. statesman), 5, 15, 20, 21

Jay, Sarah Livingston (wife of John), 5

Jefferson, Thomas, 80, 82, 89, 95, 113–114, 115, 118, 135, 136

Jenings, Edmund (of Md.), 13

John Adams Birthplace, 101, 123, 125

John Quincy Adams Birthplace, 101, 123, 125

Johnson, Adelaide. See Hellen, Adelaide Johnson

Johnson, Ann (Nancy). See Hellen, Ann (Nancy) Johnson

Johnson, Carolina Virginia Marylanda. See Frye, Carolina Virginia Marylanda Johnson Buchanan

Johnson, Catherine Maria Frances. See Smith, Catherine Maria Frances Johnson

Johnson, Catherine Nuth (1757–1811, mother of LCA): marriage of, 1–2; family of, 2–3; friendships of, 4; described, 7, 14; assists LCA, 8; health of, 11–12, 17–18, 20; relationship with family, 15, 23; portraits of, 16; relationship with Adamses, 24, 100; treatment of LCA, 25; travels to U.S., 29, 30, 31, 32, 56–57; makes and receives visits, 98; resides with Hellens, 100; life of in U.S., 101; death of, 180; LCA compared to, 266

Johnson, Eliza Jennet Dorcas. See Pope, Eliza Jennet Dorcas Johnson

Johnson, Fanny Russell (b. 1799, cousin of LCA), 259, 262, 263, 264, 265, 268, 269–270, 272

Johnson, Harriet. See Boyd, Harriet Johnson

Johnson, Joshua (1742–1802, father of LCA): marriage of, 1–2; family history of, 2; as merchant, 2, 23; described, 7, 14, 22–23; religious beliefs of, 7–8; household of, 11–12, 13–14; as U.S. consul, 12, 16, 22; political attitudes of, 15–16, 18, 24; portraits of, 16; rents house, 20; promises dowries, 22; relationship with LCA, 25, 49, 245; returns to U.S., 28, 29, 30, 31, 32, 56–57; correspondence with JQA, 28–29; business failure of, 30, 31–32, 33, 34, 35, 53, 56, 95–96, 99; character defended, 35, 95; LCA visits, 88; death of, 89, 95; health of, 89; estate of, 95, 97, 120; relationship with Adamses, 100; as superintendent of stamp office, 100; relationship with Catherine N. Johnson, 101

Johnson, Louisa Catherine. See Adams, Louisa Catherine Johnson (1775–1852)

Johnson, Mary Ann (Mariane, b./d. 1778, sister of LCA), 4, 5

Johnson, Thomas (1702–1777, grandfather of LCA), 2

Johnson, Thomas (1732–1819, uncle of LCA), 15, 16, 89

Johnson, Thomas Baker (1779–1843, brother of LCA), 4, 5, 17, 20, 126, 265, 290, 297, 352, 360

Jones, Capt. John Paul (U.S. naval officer), 4, 15

Jones, Walter (Washington lawyer), 220–221, 222

JQA. *See* Adams, John Quincy (1767–1848)

King, Charles Bird (U.S. artist), 300, 306

King, Rufus (Mass. politician), 32, 33, 228, 263, 307

Kirkland, John Thornton (Harvard president), 218, 292

Kloster Osegg (Cistercian monastery), 68–69

Krehmer, Anna Dorothea Smith (Annette, wife of Sebastian), 151, 157, 158, 159, 170, 177, 178

Krehmer, Sebastian (St. Petersburg merchant), 151, 158, 178

Laborie, Mr. (French diplomat), 300, 312, 314

Lafayette, Marie Joseph Paul Yves Roch Gilbert du Motier, Marquis de, 18–19

Laurens, Henry (U.S. diplomat), 15

Law, Thomas (Washington author), 222

LCA. *See* Adams, Louisa Catherine (1775–1852)

Lettsom, Dr. John Coakley (of Britain), 8, 9

Litta, Ekaterina Vassilievna, Countess de (grand mistress of the Russian court), 152, 153–154, 155, 171, 176–177

London, England, 26–27, 216

Louis XVI, King of France, 18, 307

Louis, Frederica Sophia Carolina of Mecklenburg-Strelitz, Princess, 37, 39, 62–63, 79

Louise Auguste Wilhelmine of Mecklenburg-Strelitz, Queen of Prussia: relationship with LCA, 36–37, 64; LCA's presentation to, 38–39, 40; dinner with, 46; appearance of, 61, 62, 63; pregnancy of, 79; retreat from Berlin, 198; character of, 200; mausoleum of, 201

Louisiana Purchase, 221, 232, 237

Lowndes, William (S.C. politician), 224, 231, 234, 279

Lunt, Rev. William Parsons (of Quincy), 348, 349, 350–351

McIlvaine, Rev. Charles Pettit (of Georgetown), 265

McLean, John (U.S. postmaster general), 317

Madison, Dolley Payne (wife of James), 113–114, 117, 118, 242

Madison, James, 89, 113, 140, 187, 224, 339, 340

Maine, 232, 240

Maisonneuve, Commandeur Joseph de (master of ceremonies to Alexander I), 152, 153, 171–172

Maria Feodorovna, Empress Mother of Russia, 149, 153, 154–155, 157, 168, 171

Marie Antoinette, Queen of France, 18

Marshall, John (U.S. Supreme Court chief justice), 218, 279

Martin, Luther (Md. attorney general), 221

Martin, Robert Nicols (suitor of Fanny Johnson), 265, 268, 269–271

Maryland, 2

Massachusetts General Court, 86, 96, 97, 138

Menou, Jules, Comte de (French diplomat), 302, 304

Merry, Elizabeth Death Leathes (of Britain), 117, 119–120, 124

Mexico, 335, 336–337, 338

Middleton, Ann Elbertina Van Ness (of N.Y.), 298

Miller, Dr. Thomas (of Washington), 356

Milnor, Patty. *See* Walin (Milnor), Patty

Missouri, 232, 237, 240, 241, 262, 265, 275–276

Missouri Compromise, 232, 247, 248

Monroe, Elizabeth Kortright (wife of James), 220, 279–280, 315

Monroe, James: appoints JQA secretary of state, 216; southern tour of, 229; annual messages of, 231, 316; New Year's open houses, 236, 306, 322; dinner with, 237–238; daughter's marriage and, 249, 251; patronage and, 251, 282; visits Decatur, 254; presidential election and, 259; drawing room receptions, 260, 272, 274, 279, 308; rumor concerning, 261;

Monroe, James (*continued*)
　　inauguration of, 265, 277, 279; protocol
　　　and, 302–303
Moore, Thomas (Irish musician), 124
Morel, Jean Louis (Mitau innkeeper),
　　190–192
Mount Vernon (Va. estate), 88–89
Muir, John (Md. merchant), 23
Music: singing, 15, 24, 124, 166, 243, 261,
　　321; opera, 64, 75, 80; in churches, 72;
　　piano, 166; patriotic songs, 223, 224;
　　poor, 242; flute, 259, 267; harp, 259, 262;
　　lessons, 267; violin, 267; class songs,
　　284; West Point cadets' visit and, 287;
　　guitar, 321

Nantes, France, 3, 5
Napoleon I, Emperor of France: rumors
　　about, 74, 206; Europe and, 140, 144;
　　marriage of, 164; exile of, 188, 202, 203,
　　298; popularity of, 197, 204; return of, 199,
　　202, 203, 208; military support for, 210–211
Napoleonic Wars, 184, 188, 195–196,
　　197–198, 201, 203–204, 213
Native Americans, 334, 336, 338. *See also*
　　Seminole Wars
Néale, Pauline (of Prussia), 36, 38, 39, 40,
　　44–45, 48, 52, 84, 199
Nelson (Adams family servant), 149, 150, 166
Neva River, 158, 163
Norton, Elizabeth Cranch (1763–1811, cousin
　　of JQA), 174
Norway, 146–147

O'Farrill y Herrera, Madame (of Spain),
　　74–75
Old House (Peacefield, now Adams National
　　Historical Park), 86, 122–123, 125, 126,
　　285, 286, 287–288, 294, 297
Ompteda, Ludwig Konrad Georg, Baron von
　　(Hanoverian diplomat), 60
Onís, Don Luis de (Spanish diplomat), 219,
　　221, 228
Otis, Harrison Gray (Mass. politician),
　　269–271
Otis, Sally Foster (wife of Harrison), 231,
　　292

Paine, Thomas, 13
Paintings: portraits, 16, 17, 300, 306;
　　sketches, 59; galleries, 67, 71, 72, 76;
　　drawing lessons, 241
Panic of 1837, 349, 350
Panin, Nikita Petrovich, Count (Russian
　　diplomat), 46, 62, 65, 70
Panin, Sophia Vladimirovna, Countess (wife
　　of Nikita), 46, 62, 70
Pardo de Figueroa, Benito (Spanish
　　diplomat), 158–159, 164
Parella, Marquise Provana de (of Sardinia),
　　39, 40, 46, 47
Paris, France, 5, 214, 216
Parish, David (in Hamburg), 35
Passports, 189, 195, 202, 207, 208, 210
Peabody, Elizabeth Smith Shaw (1750–1815,
　　aunt of JQA), 135
Peter, Columbia Washington (daughter of
　　Martha), 262
Peter, Martha Parke Custis (of Georgetown),
　　224
Petry, Jean Baptiste (French diplomat), 300,
　　309, 312, 314, 316, 317, 318, 320, 323
Pinckney, Elizabeth Motte (wife of Thomas), 19
Pinckney, Thomas (U.S. diplomat), 19
Pinkney, William (U.S. politician), 220, 221,
　　240, 242
Pitt, Rev. London King (of St. Petersburg), 178
Pleasants, James (Va. politician), 301
Polética, Pierre de (Russian diplomat), 231,
　　235, 264
Pope, Eliza Jennet Dorcas Johnson (d. 1818,
　　sister of LCA), 5, 16, 121, 123, 167
Pope, John (husband of Eliza), 5, 167
Porter, Como. David (U.S.), 301
Portraits. *See* Paintings
Preble, Como. Edward (U.S.), 121
Protocol. *See* Etiquette and protocol
Prussia, 37, 42, 64–65, 66–73, 81, 82, 194–207

Quincy, Eliza Susan Morton (wife of Josiah
　　III), 87, 284
Quincy, Josiah, III (Mass. politician), 284,
　　286, 289, 294
Quincy, Mass.: residence in, 86, 122–123,
　　125; travel to, 86, 89–92; society in, 93;

described, 288; First Church, 348, 349, 350–351; burial at, 360, 361

Radziwill, Anton, Prince of Poland, 47–48, 51, 59–60, 62, 77, 200
Radziwill, Frederica Dorothea Louise Philippine, Princess, 37, 39, 59–60, 77, 199, 200, 201
Randolph, John (Va. representative), 113, 114, 120, 136, 243, 247, 272, 276, 279, 301, 323
Religion: LCA and, 3, 6–7, 72, 103; Johnson family and, 7–8; baptism, 83–84, 106, 172–173, 177–178; in Quincy, 93; Orthodox Christian, 172–173; missionaries, 244; memorial services, 307–308; funeral services, 319–320
Rice, Rev. Luther (Baptist missionary), 244, 245
Rocafuerte, Mr. (of Colombia), 304–305
Rodgers, Como. John (U.S.), 224
Rumiantsev, Nikolai Petrovich, Count (Russian statesman), 150–151, 159
Rush, Dr. Benjamin (of Phila.), 87, 90, 122
Russia, 140, 143, 157, 162, 309

St. Petersburg, Russia: Nevsky Prospect, 148, 162; residences in, 148–149, 151, 153, 166, 167, 175–176, 178; water in, 151; Twelfth Night celebration, 158; Hermitage, 167, 168, 169; weather in, 180; departure from, 188–189; described, 202
Sanford, Mr. (in Prussia), 64
Sanford, Mrs. (in Prussia), 64, 65, 66
Sargent, Daniel, Jr. (Boston merchant), 98, 104
Sargent, Mary Frazier (wife of Daniel), 86–87, 94, 98, 104
Savage, Edward (U.S. artist), 16
Sayre, Stephen (N.Y. merchant), 15
Schlossberg Mountain (near Töplitz), 69, 70
Scotland, 2
Scott, Gen. Winfield (U.S.), 318
Seminole Wars, 217, 221, 334, 338
Servants: marriage of, 3; LCA and, 9, 32, 36; importance of, 12; health of, 37; for Adamses, 54, 205, 208–209, 212, 234; behavior of, 60–61, 136–137; clothing for, 73–74, 166; character of, 108; selection of,

108; lack of, 123; former slaves, 126; mistreatment of, 261; bequests to, 360
Sharpe, Granville (Brit. abolitionist), 13
Shaw, William Smith (1778–1826, cousin of JQA), 92, 96–97, 98, 132, 139–140, 284, 286
Silesia, Prussia, 76
Slavery, 126, 232, 326, 330–331, 335
Smith, Abigail Adams. See Adams, Abigail, 2d (1765–1813)
Smith, Caroline Amelia (1795–1852, daughter of Abigail, later wife of Peter de Windt), 130, 132
Smith, Catherine Maria Frances Johnson (Kitty, 1786–1869, sister of LCA): marriage of, 4–5, 16, 161; portraits of, 16; finances of, 49, 240–241; relationship with Adamses, 138, 226; health of, 141, 184; in Russia, 143, 144–145, 155, 171, 172; Alexander I and, 161, 162–163, 165, 167, 169, 170, 172; popularity of, 162–163; assists LCA, 177; visits with LCA, 227, 228
Smith, Hannah Carter (of Boston), 92, 94
Smith, John Adams (1788–1854, nephew of JQA), 130, 132
Smith, Louisa Catharine (1773–1857, cousin of JQA), 93, 96, 97, 103
Smith, Margaret Stephens (mother of William Stephens), 90, 111
Smith, William Stephens (1755–1816, husband of Abigail Adams 2d), 16, 17, 19, 20, 21, 24, 91, 107–108
Smith, William Steuben (1787–1850, husband of Catherine), 5, 16, 144, 161, 226, 227, 228, 240–241, 282
Spear, Nancy (of Washington), 307, 313
Stackelberg, Berndt Robert Gustaf, Baron (Swedish diplomat), 316, 319–320
Sterrett, David (of London), 12
Stewart, Delia Tudor (of Washington), 271
Sully, Thomas (U.S. artist), 247
Superstitions, 57–58, 67, 134, 180, 195, 198–199, 203
Supreme Court, U.S., 220–221, 222, 225

Tayloe, Ann Ogle (wife of John), 118, 260, 313
Tayloe, Col. John, III (Va. politician), 118, 249, 260, 313

Taylor, John (of Mass.), 17
Taylor, John W. (N.Y. representative), 257, 316
Texas, 335, 337
Theater: in London, 12, 14; in Prussia, 38, 64, 65, 68, 70, 75, 76; in Philadelphia, 90; Shakespeare, 142; in Russia, 156, 161, 167, 168, 182; in Paris, 214
Thompson, Sara Burrows (of Washington), 262, 264
Thompson, Smith (U.S. secretary of the navy), 231, 239, 301, 308
Tompkins, Daniel D. (U.S. vice president), 231, 236, 238, 240, 250, 258, 259, 299, 301, 302
Tompkins, Hannah Minthorne (wife of Daniel), 302
Töplitz, Bohemia, 66–68, 69, 70
Transcendentalism, 346–347
Travel: across English Channel, 5; London to Berlin, 34–36; within Prussia, 66–73; Berlin to U.S., 82–83, 86, 87; Washington to Massachusetts, 89–92, 121–122, 123–125, 138, 282, 283–284; Massachusetts to Washington, 109–112; difficulties with, 114, 190–191, 192, 194, 196, 219, 220, 259; Massachusetts to St. Petersburg, 144–150; St. Petersburg to Paris, 187–214; within Massachusetts, 293–297
Treaties: Jay Treaty, 20, 23; Treaty of Ghent, 187; Adams-Onís Treaty, 221, 223, 224, 277, 279, 282
Trumbull, John (U.S. artist), 15, 21, 24, 248
Tufts, Dr. Cotton (of Weymouth), 129
Turreau de Garambouville, Louis Marie (French diplomat), 114

Unitarianism, 348

Vicence, Armand Augustine Louis de Caulaincourt, Duc de (French diplomat), 155, 156, 158, 164–165, 179
Vlodek, Alexandra Dmitrievna (mistress of Duc de Vicence), 155, 156, 168
Voss, Sophie Marie, Countess von (of Prussia), 39, 63, 65

Walin (Milnor), Patty (Adams family servant), 108, 110, 116–117
Wallace, Johnson & Muir (Brit. mercantile firm), 2, 23, 99
War of 1812, 187
Washington, George, 12, 15, 18, 20, 29, 30, 75
Washington, Martha Dandridge Custis (wife of George), 73, 88
Washington, D.C.: winters in, 100; infrastructure of, 112, 113, 114, 219, 220, 259; residences in, 112, 216, 254, 255, 257, 260, 271, 326, 327, 356; society in, 112–113, 116, 118–119, 123, 308; Navy Yard, 225
Washington Female Orphan Asylum Society, 230–231, 238, 255
Waterhouse, Dr. Benjamin (Harvard professor), 127
Webster, Daniel (Mass. politician), 220, 221, 314
Welsh, Charlotte (daughter of Dr. Thomas), 98, 106, 132
Welsh, Dr. Thomas (1752?–1831, of Boston), 105, 106, 130, 132, 133, 138, 139, 285
Welsh, Thomas, Jr. (1779–1831, son of Dr. Thomas), 58, 60, 83
West, Benjamin (U.S. artist), 16
West, Mr. (of Baltimore), 17–18
West Point cadets, 285, 286, 287–288
Whitcomb, Tilly (Adams family servant), 32, 54, 71, 76, 83, 88, 93, 95, 125
White House (Executive Mansion), 1, 230, 249, 326, 327
Wirt, William (U.S. attorney general), 220, 221, 222, 273, 274, 287
Women, 42, 64, 105, 114, 162, 188, 201, 214, 221, 240, 342–343
Woodbury, Ellen C. de Quincy (of N.H.), 337–338
Wyer, Edward (U.S. diplomat), 317, 318

Young, Miss (teacher of LCA), 10

Zinzendorf und Pottendorf, Friedrich August, Count von (Saxon diplomat), 46, 65–66
Zozaya, José Manuel de (Mexican diplomat), 299, 301–302, 305